KW-034-689

COMMITTED RELATIONSHIPS AND THE LAW

COMMITTED RELATIONSHIPS AND THE LAW

ORAN DOYLE

AND

WILLIAM BINCHY

EDITORS

FOUR COURTS PRESS

Typeset in 10.5pt on 12.5pt EhrhardtMt by
Carrigboy Typesetting Services for
FOUR COURTS PRESS LTD
7 Malpas Street, Dublin 8, Ireland
e-mail: info@fourcourtspress.ie
and in North America for
FOUR COURTS PRESS
c/o ISBS, 920 N.E. 58th Avenue, Suite 300, Portland, OR 97213.

© the various contributors and Four Courts Press 2007

A catalogue record for this title is available
from the British Library.

ISBN 978–1–84682–087–8

All rights reserved.
Without limiting the rights under copyright
reserved alone, no part of this publication may be
reproduced, stored in or introduced into a retrieval system,
or transmitted, in any form or by any means (electronic, mechanical,
photocopying, recording or otherwise), without the prior
written permission of both the copyright owner and
publisher of this book.

Printed in England by MPG Books, Bodmin, Cornwall.

Contents

Contributors

Professor WILLIAM BINCHY is Regius Professor of Laws in Trinity College, Dublin. He lectures and has written widely in the areas of family and constitutional law. A former Research Counsellor to the Law Reform, he is currently a member of the Irish Human Rights Commission.

Ms EIMEAR BROWN is a lecturer in law in Trinity College, Dublin. She is completing her PhD on the incorporation of the European Convention on Human Rights into Irish law. She has written and lectured widely in the area of European Convention on Human Rights law.

Dr EOIN CAROLAN is a member of the Law School in Trinity College, Dublin, where he lectures on administrative law. He has authored a number of law journal articles in the areas of constitutional law and administrative law and has recently completed his PhD on the separation of powers and the administrative state.

Dr NEVILLE COX is a member of the Law School in Trinity College, Dublin. He has written widely in the areas of comparative law and civil liberties and is currently completing a book on libel law.

Dr ORAN DOYLE is a member of the Law School in Trinity College, Dublin, where he lectures in jurisprudence and constitutional law. He has written widely on issues of constitutional law and jurisprudence, particularly as they concern equality.

Dr URSULA KILKELLY is a member of the Law Faculty in University College Cork. She has lectured and published widely on children's rights, the European Convention on Human Rights and juvenile justice. She is a member of the Board of the Irish Penal Reform Trust and a founder member of the Irish Youth Justice Alliance.

Professor JOHN MEE is a member of the Law Faculty in University College Cork. He has published widely on the rights afforded to those in non-marital relationships, writing *The property rights of cohabitees* as well as articles in Irish and international journals. He is a trustee director of the British and Irish Legal Information Institute.

Dr FERGUS RYAN is a member of the School of Social Science and Legal Studies at the Dublin Institute of Technology. He has taught and written in a wide variety of areas including family law and constitutional law. A Vice-Chair of One Family, Dr Ryan is a regular speaker at national and international conferences.

Professor LYNN D. WARDLE is a member of the Law Faculty of Brigham Young University in Utah. He is President of the International Society of Family Law and a member of the American Law Institute. He has written widely in the area of family law, particularly in relation to the issues posed by the recognition of same-sex partnerships.

Professor ROBERT WINTEMUTE is a member of the Law Faculty in King's College, London. He has published widely in the area of sexual orientation and the law, writing *Sexual orientation and human rights* as well as numerous law journal contributions and co-editing *Legal recognition of same-sex partnerships: a study of national, European and international law*.

Introduction

RECENT YEARS HAVE seen a coming together of two previously discrete social phenomena. On the one hand, there has been a growing questioning of traditional family forms. In Ireland, this has focused on the rights to be afforded to those in non-marital families (mothers, fathers and children) and also on the structure of the marital family itself, most obviously in the amendment to the constitution allowing for divorce. On the other hand, there has been a gay rights movement. In Ireland, this movement focused initially on the attainment of individual rights. Decriminalisation of homosexual activity between men was achieved in 1993. Discrimination on the grounds of sexual orientation in employment and with regard to the provision of certain services was prohibited by the Employment Equality Act 1998 and the Equal Status Act 2000 respectively. This movement has now largely shifted its focus to the family rights of gay people, i.e. the asserted right of same-sex partners to have their relationship recognized and protected by law. The gay rights movement has thus added a new dimension to the ongoing questioning of traditional family forms.

The debate on these issues has been both extensive and heated. The morality of homosexual conduct and the morality of discrimination have both been to the fore. People have discussed which family units are better suited to rearing children – although it is probably fair to say that empirical evidence on this issue is in somewhat short supply. Others have taken a pragmatic approach: while maintaining the heterosexual married family as an ideal, they have argued that something must be done to improve the practical situation of those who are excluded from that institution. The issues raised have often had a legal character. In several jurisdictions, such as Canada, South Africa and Massachusetts, court actions have been to the fore in securing family rights for gay couples. In Ireland, the legality of the debate is particularly acute for not only may it be the case that gay couples have rights under the constitution, it may also be the case that the constitution precludes the Legislature from granting family rights to gay couples.

Recognizing the significance of these issues, as well as the legal terms in which much of the debate has been framed, the Law School in Trinity College organized a conference in 2005. Many – but not all – of the chapters in this book are based on papers delivered at that conference. Fergus Ryan provides a comprehensive overview of the gay rights movement in Ireland, as well as addressing the issues that currently arise. Dr Ryan argues that the dichotomy between liberal and conservative perspectives can be overstated: the gay rights movement's claims for family rights represent a move away from radical individualism and an affirmation of traditional values. Lynn Wardle, in contrast, argues that the traditional marital family is the unit best suited to the task of raising children. Although Professor Wardle suggests that some legal recognition of committed relationships (including same-sex unions) is appropriate, these unions do not make overall contributions to the social purposes of marriage that are comparable to the contributions of heterosexual marriage. Accordingly, the status and legal benefits of marriage itself ought not be extended to non-marital heterosexual and same-sex unions. This view is emphatically rejected by Robert Wintemute, who undertakes a comprehensive survey of the moves towards equality for same-sex couples around the world. Professor Wintemute argues strongly that Ireland should reject the 'separate but equal' model of civil partnership adopted by the United Kingdom and instead opt for the fully equal model of gay marriage provided for in Spain and Belgium.

Neville Cox argues that much of the debate on gay marriage has asked the wrong question. The question, he suggests, is not whether people should be obliged to change their own definitions of marriage but rather which definitions of marriage the state should accommodate. Dr Cox then argues that the institution of marriage should be open to gay people, precisely because it is such an important social and personal statement. Oran Doyle addresses some natural law arguments underpinning the condemnation of homosexuality and (by extension) the recognition of same-sex partnerships, concluding that the arguments are inconsistent and do not support the conclusion reached. He then argues that equality provides the most convincing basis for arguments in support of state recognition for same-sex partnerships and sketches an egalitarian scheme of what such recognition could look like. William Binchy addresses a different issue that requires an evaluation of the institution of marriage being discussed by other contributors. He argues, on the basis of personal autonomy, that people should be allowed to commit themselves to a lifelong marriage, precluding in advance the option of divorce. He does not argue that this should be the only form of marriage recognized by the state but rather that it should be a legally recognized and supported option for people.

The remaining chapters address some of the more practical implications of the recognition of non-marital relationships. John Mee undertakes a detailed examination of the proposals suggested by the Oireachtas Committee on the constitution and by the Working Group on Domestic Partnership, chaired by Anne Colley. Professor Mee assesses the constitutionality of such proposals, arguing that an extensive civil partnership scheme could and should be legislatively introduced for same-sex couples, but that a more measured approach is required in relation to opposite sex couples. Ursula Kilkelly's contribution examines some of the issues that arise when children are born into or become part of the committed relationships of their parents, in particular those relating to the child's identity. Dr Kilkelly addresses what protection children's rights enjoy under Irish law, and details the guidance available from relevant international law notably under the European Convention on Human Rights and the United Nations Convention on the Rights of the Child.

Eoin Carolan assesses the constitutional implications for this debate. He addresses the forms of partnership recognition that the Legislature can provide, coming to a somewhat different conclusion from John Mee, but also considers whether the constitution may grant some form of family rights to same-sex couples. In this regard, he has provided a postscript to his paper analyzing the recent high court decision of Ms Justice Dunne in *Gilligan and Zappone v. Revenue Commissioners*. Eimear Brown undertakes a similar exercise with regard to the European Convention on Human Rights, assessing whether the convention may protect a right to partnership recognition for same-sex couples. She notes that the European Court on Human Rights has been slow to conclude that same-sex couples can rely on the family life guarantee in Article 8, but suggests that – in line with the court's approach to other issues – this position may evolve in the not too distant future.

The debate on all these issues is ongoing, both in Ireland and around the world. In Ireland, the Supreme Court will have to address the issues raised in the *Gilligan and Zappone* case. The new government will have to address the issue of legislative recognition for non-marital families, including same-sex couples. With all political parties committed to some action on this front, the choice and constitutionality of particular options remain a pressing concern. Recent years have seen a flourishing of discussion and debate on this issue. Law journals are replete with articles addressing the different aspects of the debate. The Irish Human Rights Commission has produced a report on the rights of *de facto* couples, co-authored by Judy Walsh and Fergus Ryan. The Law Reform Commission, the Oireachtas Committee on the Constitution and the Colley Working Group have all outlined possible schemes for the provision of rights to non-marital cohabitees. Conferences have been organized by, among others, the Law Society and the Equality Authority. This book is intended as a contribution to that rapidly evolving debate. Although the views expressed in the different chapters radically disagree, the book (as well as the conference from which many of the papers derive) has been based on the conviction that reasoned debate between conflicting views may help to point some way forward.

We are grateful to Four Courts Press for their agreement to publish this collection of essays, for their patience with the editors and for their skilful shepherding of this project.

ORAN DOYLE
WILLIAM BINCHY

From stonewall(s) to picket fences: the mainstreaming of same-sex couples in contemporary legal discourses

IRELAND IS IN THE THROES OF A debate about marriage and the family. The debate centres on two apparently distinct though inter-related discourses, both of which impinge on the extent to which the law should recognize and support patterns of family life that do not involve heterosexual marriage. The first discourse concerns the appropriateness of laws that confine a myriad of rights, privileges and immunities (as a well as duties) to married couples, thus denying the application of these laws to persons who cohabit outside marriage, including same-sex and opposite sex couples. The second, ostensibly more radical, discourse interrogates the application of the 'identity of sex' rule in marriage law,[2] the rule that confines civil marriage to two persons who are, respectively, of opposite gender.

This paper is based in part on a presentation originally prepared for the 2001 Annual Conference of the Academy of Legal Studies in Business, Albuquerque, New Mexico, August 2001. Some of the themes have also been rehearsed at the Annual Conference of the Association for Legal and Social Philosophy, University College, Dublin, June 2006. I am very grateful to Professor Robert King, Lisa Glennon, Bruce Carolan, Dr Oran Doyle and Judy Walsh for many invaluable comments and suggestions. Notwithstanding such invaluable assistance, the author assumes sole responsibility for any errors and opinions herein. The views expressed herein are the personal views of the author and should not to be attributed to any organisation with which the author is associated. This paper seeks to set out the law and the state of current developments as of 1 March 2007.   2 The proscription on same-sex marriage is well-established at common law – see *Talbot v. Talbot* 111 Sol. J. 213 (1967) and *Corbett v. Corbett* [1971] P. 83. See also *B. v. R.* [1995] 1 ILRM 491, where Costello P suggested that marriage in Irish law presupposed 'the voluntary and permanent union of one man and one woman to the exclusion of all others for life' (ibid., 495). McKechnie J concurred in *Foy v. An tArd Chláraitheoir* [2002] IEHC 116 (9 July 2002). See also *Murray v. Ireland,* [1985] IR 532, pp 535–6, *T.F. v. Ireland* [1995] 1 IR 321 at p. 373 and *T. v. T.* [2003] ILRM 321. Most recently, the ban on same-sex marriage received legislative affirmation under the Civil Registration Act, 2004, s. 2(2)(e) of which precludes the solemnization of a marriage between two persons of the same sex. The High Court has recently concluded, moreover, that such a proscription does not infringe the constitutional right to marry, and that 'marriage' as understood in the Irish Constitution, is confined to opposite sex couples. See *Zappone and Gilligan v. Revenue Commissioners,* unreported, High Court, Dunne J, 14 December 2006. On this topic generally

In this regard, of course, Ireland is not unique. Throughout Europe and North America, in particular, the shape of marriage and the legal status of alternative family forms has, in the past ten years or so, been hotly debated, litigated and legislated. Indeed, the debate in Ireland, though motivated to some extent by domestic concerns, is prompted in large part by international developments. Set in the context of developments in other parts of Europe (most notably in the neighbouring United Kingdom)[3] the pressure for reform mounted rather rapidly. The publication of several reports and discussion papers, some of which are discussed below, has served as a further rallying call to reform, despite, or maybe because of, the sometimes rather conservative content of these reports.

Although the debate affects opposite sex and same sex partners alike, the discursive focus in this essay is on same-sex couples, for a variety of reasons. While functionally such couples share much in common,[4] in practice significant differences arise. Not the least of these differences lies in the general ability of opposite-sex couples to resolve their legal difficulties through marriage, an option not currently open to their same-sex counterparts. Of deeper import, however, are issues involving the socio-cultural context in which same-sex couples are situated. While the essential difficulty facing opposite sex couples is that they are unmarried, same-sex couples face a double stigma in this regard in that they present both as unmarried *and* gay. Indeed, it is arguable that the non-recognition of same-sex couples arises not merely because of the privilege accorded to marriage under Irish law, but fundamentally because of society's equivocation around issues of sexuality. In short, the 'problem' with opposite sex couples is that they are not married; the 'problem' with same-sex couples, by contrast, is that the parties are not 'straight'.

Thus, the debate insofar as it affects same-sex couples involves more than simply the absence of legal protection. The non-recognition of same-sex couples is arguably not the core issue at stake: this non-recognition is indicative and symptomatic of the general social exclusion and invisibility experienced by people with alternative sexualities.[5] As such, there is some merit in

see further Ryan, 'The fundamentals of marriage' in Shannon (ed.), *Family law practitioner* (Dublin, 2000–6) at A164–8.   **3** The United Kingdom's Civil Partnership Act, 2004 came into force in December 2005. It permits couples of the same sex to register their relationship, thus accessing a variety of rights and responsibilities that largely equate with those applicable to married couples. For further discussion, see Department of Trade and Industry, *Civil partnership: a framework for the recognition of same sex couples* (London, 2003).   **4** On the functionalist approach to family law see further Glennon, '*Fitzpatrick v. Sterling Housing Association* – An endorsement of the functional family?' (2000) 14 *Intl. J. of Law, Policy and the Family* 226–255 and Bala, 'The evolving Canadian definition of family: towards a pluralistic and functional approach' (1994) 8 *Intl. J. of Law and the Family* 293–318 See also the approach of Ward LJ in *Fitzpatrick v. Sterling Housing Association* [1998] Ch. 304 at 339.   **5** On which see generally the Equality Authority Report, *Implementing equality for lesbians, gays and bisexuals* examining the phenomenon of non-recognition from a particularized perspective that focuses on same-sex couples.[6]

The combatants in this debate, in a pattern replicating that of older socio-sexual controversies (around divorce[7] and abortion,[8] for instance), have tended to divide along expected lines. On the one hand, liberals agitate for change, arguing the merits of inclusive reforms that embrace alternatives to the so-called 'traditional' nuclear family based on heterosexual marriage. On the other hand, conservatives extol the virtues of the *status quo* and rally against changes that will upset long-established patterns of family life.[9]

On closer reflection, however, the dimensions of the current debate are in fact more multi-faceted and complex than might first appear. The purpose of this essay is to challenge the dichomotimization between liberal and conservative viewpoints, arguing instead that the current debate around marriage and the family fundamentally serves to reaffirm certain values, which might be described as 'traditional', albeit in a reformulated manner. The reality, it is argued, is that supposedly liberal reformulations of the concept of family at root replicate, albeit in modified form, the norms promoted by traditional marriage – that is, stability, security, mutual trust and commitment – as well as some of the problems associated therewith.

(Dublin: Equality Authority, 2001).   **6** A point that the government appears to have accepted. In a speech to at the opening of the Conference on the Legal Status of Cohabitants and Same Sex Couples, Royal College of Physicians of Ireland, 26 May 2006, see http://www.glen.ie/press/docs/Address%20by%20Minister%20McDowell%20260506.doc (consulted 27 June 2006) the Minister for Justice Equality and Law Reform observed that '[t]he situation, of course, is different for same sex couples, for whom marriage is prohibited.'   **7** Up until Independence in 1922, spouses could petition Parliament for a private bill permitting divorce. This facility was withdrawn in 1922. Article 41.3.2 of the Constitution of Ireland, 1937, as originally enacted, expressly banned the granting of divorce by the state, or the introduction of legislation permitting a dissolution of a civil marriage. The removal of the ban has been hotly debated over several decades. A referendum to remove this ban failed in 1986, though a subsequent referendum proposing a restrictive divorce regime for the state narrowly passed in 1995. To gain a sense of the divergent perspectives on these changes, see William Binchy, *Is divorce the answer?* (Dublin, 1984) and William Duncan, *The case for divorce in Ireland* (Dublin, 1979).   **8** This issue has been the subject of perhaps the most heated debates on social morality in modern Ireland. Abortion is constitutionally and statutorily precluded by Article 40.3.3 of the Constitution of Ireland, 1937 (as amended by the Eighth Amendment, 1983) and by the Offences against the Person Act, 1861 respectively. A limited exception applies where there is a real and substantial risk to the life of the mother, including a risk of self-destruction. See *Attorney General v. X.* [1992] 1 IR 1. Though see *M.R. v. T.R.*, unreported, High Court, McGovern J, November 15, 2006, confirming that the provisions of Article 40.3.3 extend to unborn children from the point of implantation in the womb only, and not to fertilised embryos not yet implanted. **9** Some quite illuminating examples of each perspective can be seen in the submissions made to the All-Party Oireachtas Committee on the Constitution, as part of its consultations on the provisions of the Constitution that concern the Family. These are published in full in Appendix 3 of the All-Party Committee's *Tenth progress report: the family* (Dublin, 2006) pp A13–286.

In this sense, it is suggested that the current movement for family law reform is in fact not so radical or threatening as it might seem. In particular, it is argued that the debate on same-sex marriage and non-marital unions represents a softening not only of conservative discourses but also of liberal discourses, and in particular a definitive trend away from radical individualism. As a result, a quintessentially postmodern concept of family is emerging – one that, despite the reformist veneer, in fact seeks to reaffirm 'traditional' values not to replace them.

In particular, in tandem with the advancement of the legal rights of sexual minorities – namely lesbians, gays, bisexuals and the trans-gendered (henceforth 'LGBT') – the 'gay rights' discourse has experienced a pronounced 'familialization'. There is, in other words, a greater tendency to discuss gay rights using the language of 'family'. Gay activists and commentators once spoke of free love and subverting the norms of straight society, (particularly marriage). Today, by contrast, the dominant concerns of the gay rights agenda – same-sex marriage and equality in matters of child-rearing – involve decidedly conventional mainstream issues.

Although some commentators have criticized this apparent conservatization of the gay rights issue,[10] the present author argues that in its own paradoxical way this shift in discourses represents a radical and positive departure for both the discourse of family and the discourse of gay rights. Nonetheless some caution is necessary. In particular, a risk arises that in seeking to extend family rights and duties to alternative family types, some of the often dysfunctional features of family law will also – unintentionally – be replicated. It is arguable, in particular, that the discourse in favour of family diversity generally ignores the pitfalls of current family law measures as they apply to married couples. It is also propounded that the trend towards equal recognition of same-sex relationships – while welcome – may unintentionally prove to sideline queer discourses that seek to critique traditional norms and attitudes and to question and challenge social structures that subordinate marginalized persons and groups. In conclusion, however, it is argued that, provided that the pitfalls of such an approach are not ignored, the current debate offers an opportunity for same-sex couples to embrace and re-affirm, with modifications, the positive features of the traditional family model.

---

10 See for instance, Ettelbrick, 'Since when is marriage a path to liberation', *OUT/LOOK National Gay and Lesbian Quarterly*, 6, (Fall 1989) and Browning, 'Why marry?', *New York Times*, 17 April 1986. See also Harris, *The rise and fall of gay culture* (New York, 1997).

SHIFTING DISCOURSES: THE CHANGING
LANGUAGE OF GAY RIGHTS

Popular gay mythology[11] asserts that the Stonewall riots of 1969 marked the inception of the modern US gay rights movement, in turn inspiring gays and lesbians in other jurisdictions to challenge heteronormative expectations.[12] On the night of 27 June 1969,[13] New York police raided the Stonewall Inn, a Greenwich Village bar frequented mostly by gay men, some lesbians and drag queens.[14] Such raids were commonplace enough. The difference *this* time, however, was that some of the clientele struck back, precipitating a violent street riot that continued into the small hours of the morning. The primary catalyst, the purported starting point of the modern US gay rights movement was, in short, 'a wonderful moment of explosive rage'.[15] Protesters, for instance, physically ripped up a parking meter to force open the door to the Stonewall Inn, behind which the police were hiding.[16] It was not, in the words of one Irish commentator, 'the queens' tea-party'.[17]

Of course, there was plenty of less well-publicized activism taking place, on *both* sides of the Atlantic,[18] prior to this event. The Stonewall riots, however, clearly proved a catalyst for the development of a robust and radical gay rights movement in 1970s North America. The movement took its cue partly from the African-American Civil Rights and Women's liberation movements that had come to the fore in the 1950s and 1960s. There were however, even more radical underpinnings, emphasized by the sometimes-confrontational tactics as well as the strident language used and the names adopted by the movement. Rose[19] points out the special significance of the moniker 'Gay Liberation Front' for one of the major gay-rights groups that

11 In fact there was plenty of (admittedly more sedate) activism before 1969, for instance, from Harry Hay's brave Mattachine Society. See Mondimore, *A natural history of homosexuality* (Baltimore, 1996) at pp 234–8. On the gay movement generally in the US, see Hogan and Hudson (eds.), *Completely queer* (New York, 1998) at 230–40.   12 Kamikaze suggests that the Stonewall riots were 'hypocritically mythologized' suggesting that while the gay rights movement sentimentalizes the event, it would nowadays reject outright the violent, radical and flamboyant actions that accompanied the riots. Kamikaze, 'I used to be an activist, but I'm alright now' in O'Carroll and Collins (eds.), *Lesbian and gay visions of Ireland in the twenty-first century* (London, 1995) at p. 120.   13 It was co-incidentally, the day on which the film star Judy Garland had died. Garland was (and indeed remains) something of a gay icon. This may have contributed to the outburst at the Stonewall Inn.   14 For further commentary see D'Emilio, *Making trouble: essays on gay history, politics and the university* (London, 1992), and Mondimore, op. cit. at pp 238–9.   15 D'Emilio, op. cit.   16 Mondimore, op. cit., at p. 238. 17 Kamikaze, op. cit. at p. 120.   18 One complaint that could be (and indeed has been) made about the mythologization of Stonewall is that it wrongly suggests that the gay-rights movement was started in the United States, a perspective that ignores earlier European endeavours such as those of Magnus Hirschfield in Germany. See Mondimore, op. cit., at pp 232–3. 19 Rose, *Diverse communities: the evolution of gay and lesbian politics in Ireland* (Cork, 1994).

sprung up in the wake of Stonewall. This name, he points out, 'echoed that of the National Liberation Front in Vietnam,[20] a signal,' Rose continues, 'that the GLF saw itself as part of a revolutionary process'.[21] Indeed in its manifesto (cited by Rose) the GLF speaks of a universal sexual liberation 'for all people', a phenomenon that would be impossible 'unless existing social institutions are abolished'.

The language used is defiantly revolutionary. It suggests not an assimilation of sexual minorities into respectable society but rather, a radical overhaul of society itself. The focus of the movement was not simply on internal liberation of the gay and lesbian subject but also on the liberation of society as a whole. Hetero-normativity,[22] it suggests, was merely a symptom of society's wider pathology. Nor was the liberation that was envisaged by the movement intended simply for sexual minorities. The gay rights movement of the time tapped into the language of free love for *all*, regardless of sexuality.

The GLF's Statement of Purpose (adopted in December 1969) suggests, indeed, that the agenda of early gay radicals went well beyond the confines of sexual revolution. The Statement boasts a commitment not only to 'total self-liberation' for lesbians and gays but also a

> total opposition to America's white racism, to poverty, hunger, the systematic destruction of our patrimony; we oppose the rich getting richer, the poor getting poorer, and are in total opposition to wars of aggression and imperialism, whoever pursues them.[23]

Solidarity with other minorities is also affirmed, (albeit in now dated language) promising

> support [for] the demands of Blacks, Chicanos, Orientals, Women, Youth, Senior Citizens and others demanding their full rights as human beings. We join in their struggle, and shall actively seek coalition to pursue these goals.[24]

Notably, same-sex marriage was quite definitively not on the agenda. Marriage, in fact, was (in some quarters at least) seen as a sexist and patriarchal

20 Mondimore notes how the movement drew 'inspiration from the black civil rights movement and the movement protesting the Viet Nam War': Mondimore, op. cit., at p. 239. 21 Rose, op. cit., at p. 5. Mondimore, op. cit., notes how protests were at times 'aggressive and confrontational' (at p. 239). 22 That is, the social forces and conditions that position heterosexuality as the expected social norm, to the exclusion of alternative sexualities. 23 Gay Liberation Front, *Statement of purpose* (Los Angeles, December 1969), extracted from Hay, with Roscoe (ed.), *Radically gay: gay liberation in the words of its founder* (Boston, 1996) pp 176–7. See also Power, Lisa, *No bath but plenty of bubbles: an oral history of the GLF, 1970–1973* (Cassell, 1996) and Power, Lisa, 'Campaign', *Gay Times*, November 1995, p. 138. 24 Ibid.

institution that confined and oppressed the human spirit, an institution not to be embraced but to be abolished.[25] As Stiers notes:

> Until recently many lesbians and gay men considered the terms 'family' and 'marriage' to be the antithesis of gay identity.[26]

In fact, the tenor of the GLF's statement of purpose appeared to militate strongly in favour of the outright *abolition* of marriage and its replacement with looser models favouring sexual liberation:

> We are a revolutionary group of men and women formed with the realization that complete sexual liberation for all people cannot come about unless existing social institutions are abolished.[27]

The radicalism of this discourse is perhaps most vividly evidenced in Martha Shelley's essay 'Gay Is Good', first published in 1971, in which the author makes a provocative call to arms:

> Look out straights! Here comes the Gay Liberation Front, springing up like warts all over the bland face of Amerika, causing shudders of indigestion in the delicately balanced bowels of the Movement. Here come the gays … we are the extrusions of your unconscious mind – your worst fears made flesh … we are the sort of people everyone was taught to despise – and now we are shaking off the chains of self-hatred and marching on your citadels of repression.[28]

In Shelley's worldview, conciliation and assimilation are clearly not on the cards, a point stressed in the following rather chilling refrain:

> 'Are your uneasy?' she continues, '… we want you to be uneasy, to be a little less comfortable in your straight roles.'[29]

In this respect the discursive shift in the intervening years could not have been more dramatic. Today the twin themes dominating gay rights discourses are marriage and children. The language of free love and liberation has given way to the language of 'commitment', and 'partnership'. Gay and

---

25 See for instance Altman, *Coming out in the seventies* (Boston, 1979) pp 43–4, Hocquenghem, *Homosexual desire* (London, 1978) and Hunter, 'Marriage, law and gender: a feminist inquiry', *Law and Sexuality* 1 (Summer 1991) 9–30. 26 Stiers, *From this day forward: commitment, marriage and family in lesbian and gay relationships* (New York, 1999) at p. 18. 27 See also Shelley, M., 'Gay is good' in *Gay flames* (New York, 1972) at pp 3–6: 'We are women and men who, from the time of our earliest memories, have been in revolt against the sex-role structure and nuclear family structure.' 28 Shelley, M., 'Gay is good' at pp 3–6. 29 Ibid.

lesbian relationships are typically described in homely terms: as 'domestic partnerships', for instance, or as 'life commitments'. This trend is exemplified in the increasingly popular phenomenon of gay commitment ceremonies. Lewin's *Recognizing Ourselves*[30] notes the significance of these ceremonies in symbolically affirming the values of tradition, community and family:

> Just as heterosexual weddings convey to couples their place in the history of their families and remind them of the contribution they will make to the continuation of their line, so lesbian/gay weddings symbolically claim that lesbian and gay couples are not estranged from the values of the wider communities to which they consider themselves affiliated ... each of these weddings makes the claim that the marrying couple are members of the wider community, both the communities in which the couples have their origins and the implied community of the married ...[31]

Weeks[32] also highlights the growing appropriation by gay and lesbian partners of traditional familial norms, identifying amongst such partners

> a strong perceived need to appropriate the sort of values and comforts that the family is supposed to embody, even if its fails to do so; continuity over time, emotional and material support, ongoing commitment and intense engagement.[33]

Thus, it seems that the liberal-individualism initially espoused by the modern gay rights movement has given way to a decidedly more familial discourse, an 'alternative family values' of sorts. Indeed, in a legal context, one sees generally that in tandem with the gradual advancement of laws enhancing the legal position of gays and lesbians, the legal discourse correspondingly shifts from a highly individualized to a more relational stance. The debate, in other words, shifts from one focussed on the member of a sexual minority as a 'liberated individual' to the inter-relationships that that individual enjoys or wishes to enjoy with other persons.

THE IRISH EXPERIENCE – 'INDIVIDUALISED' LAW REFORM

A similar discursive shift is evident in the Irish context. Indeed, it is suggested that Irish legal and political discourses have witnessed, in just over

---

30 Lewin, E., *Recognizing ourselves: ceremonies of lesbian and gay commitment* (New York, 1998). 31 Ibid., at 86.   32 Weeks, 'Elective families: lesbian and gay life experiments' in Carling, Duncan and Edwards (eds.), *Analysing families: morality and rationality in policy and practice* (London and New York, 2000).   33 Ibid., at p. 218.

a decade, a remarkably rapid shift of focus from legal issues that concern the rights of the individual, to concerns of a more familial, collective nature. Regrettably, to date the contours of the law *per se* have lagged behind this discursive shift, though there is some considerable evidence of support for legal reform in this context.

Up until 1993, the discourse of gay law reform in Ireland was over-whelmingly focused on the criminal law, and in particular on matters pertaining to sexual activity. Ireland and Northern Ireland alike had inherited from their inception the same Victorian British laws[34] proscribing virtually all forms of male[35] homosexual sexual activity.[36] The Offences against the State Act, 1861 sections 61 and 62 penalized what was called the 'abominable' act of buggery, anal intercourse between men or between a man and a woman. Neither consent nor privacy was a defence to such charges and both parties, the active and the passive, could be prosecuted as 'principals' to the offence. While this Act applied to both heterosexual and (male) homosexual anal intercourse, the later Criminal Law (Amendment) Act, 1885 section 11[37] applied only to acts between men.[38] This provision criminalized any act of

[34] Northern Ireland continued to be part of the United Kingdom and thus remained subject to the laws of the UK Parliament, though the *Wolfenden Report* reforms forged by the English and Welsh Sexual Offences Act 1967 were not applied in Northern Ireland until 1982. In the South, by virtue of Article 73 of the 1922 Constitution, and Article 50 of the 1937 Constitution, all laws in force immediately before the creation of each Constitution were carried over into the law of the new jurisdictions created by those Constitutions, to the extent that they were not inconsistent with the respective Constitutions.   [35] Notably there is not and never has been any legislation specifically penalizing *female* homosexual acts. Elsewhere, this author suggests that this stance reflects a general ignorance of female sexuality. The absence of anti-lesbian legislation, I note, 'cannot be put down to any greater tolerance of lesbians than of gay men; in fact it is the clearest indication of an attitude that sees the female as the sexual subject of the male. Thus women, although being spared the stigma of criminality, were denied recognition in law of a sexuality independent of that of the male': Ryan, '"Queering" the criminal law: some thoughts on the aftermath of homosexual decriminalisation' (1997) 2 *Irish Criminal Law Journal* 38 at p. 39, footnote 4. In the words of Norris, '[i]t simply did not occur to the legislators that women might possess a sexuality independent of the male': Norris, 'Homosexual law reform in Ireland – a progress report' (1977) 1 *Dublin University Law Journal* 27 at p. 32. Lesbians were thus legally invisible, a point underlined by a peculiar lacuna in the law enacted by the Irish Free State in 1935. The Criminal Law Amendment Act, 1935 created a defense of consent to indecent assault where either party was 15 or over. This defence only applied, however, to sexual acts falling short of intercourse. As such, it effectively created a lesbian age of consent of 15, although this was probably an inadvertent consequence of the legislation. [36] On homosexual sexual offences generally prior to the enactment of the Criminal Law (Sexual Offences) Act, 2006, see O'Malley, *Sexual offences: law, policy and punishment* (Dublin, 1996), Chapter 7, 'Homosexual offences', pp 135–58.   [37] This, incidentally, was the provision under which the Irish author, Oscar Wilde, was successfully prosecuted in 1895, a crime for which he spent two years in prison with hard labour. See generally Ellmann, *Oscar Wilde* (London, 1987). [38] Section 11, indeed, was a rather peculiar provision in this regard, appearing as it did in a statute the primary purpose of which was the protection of young *women*.

'gross indecency' between men. Again consent provided no defence – in fact it was an essential element of this offence that the parties act 'in concert', that is, that they were both willing participants.[39] What was 'grossly indecent' was perhaps a matter of judicial taste,[40] but it appeared that no actual physical contact was required. A sexually explicit display directed to another (consenting) male, for instance, would constitute gross indecency, even if the parties never touched.[41]

The curious feature of the legislation directed against gay men was the rareness with which it was invoked in Ireland. Indeed, a review of police reports from 1971 onwards reveals that 'for some two decades prior to decriminalisation the incidence of prosecution of the so-called 'unnatural offences'[42] was comparatively low, less than 70 cases per annum.'[43] That said, the presence of such draconian legislation on the statute books was strongly perceived to be symbolic and symptomatic of Ireland's attitude to its gay community. In fact, the legislation was often invoked indirectly with a view to justifying, for instance, the censorship of gay-related media commentaries, and to excuse the refusal to fund the supply of condoms to the gay community.[44] The gay community North and South thus put decriminalization at the heart of their campaign for equality.[45]

In two decisions of the European Court of Human Rights, these criminal law measures were declared an infringement of the right to privacy guaranteed by Article 8 of the European Convention on Human Rights. In

---

39 *R. v. Hornby and People* [1946] 2 All E.R. 487 and *R. v. Preece and Howells* [1976] *Crim. LR* 392. If either party was an unwilling participant the act in question would constitute indecent assault, or what is now termed a 'sexual assault' (or if accompanied by violence, an 'aggravated sexual assault'). See Criminal Law (Rape) (Amendment) Act, 1990, ss 2 & 3. **40** In *Norris v. Attorney General* [1984] IR 36 at p. 48, McWilliam J 'assume[d] that it was intended that it should be left to the courts to decide what is, or what is not, an act of gross indecency in private', noting further that 'changing attitudes must affect such decisions'. The Wolfenden Report, *Report of the Committee on Homosexual Offences and Prostitution*, Cmnd. 247 (London, 1968) para. 105 suggests, however, that the offence of gross indecency usually comprised mutual masturbation or oral-genital contact. **41** *R. v. Hunt* [1950] 2 All E.R. 291, *R. v. Preece and Howells,* [1977] QB 50. **42** Which term included a variety of sexual offences, including homosexual offences, but also bestiality. **43** Ryan, '"Queering" the criminal law: some thoughts on the aftermath of homosexual decriminalisation' (1997) 2 *Irish Criminal Law Journal* 38 at p. 46. See also the comments of Norris, op. cit., at p. 27. Although see McCafferty's eye-opening account of a prosecution involving two consenting male adults: 'Consenting males bound over', *Irish Times*, 12 September 1975. **44** See Ryan, ibid., at p. 47. **45** Decriminalization strongly dominates both Rose and Robson's commentaries in Rose, *Diverse communities* and Robson, 'Anatomy of a campaign', in O'Carroll and Collins (eds.), *Lesbian and gay visions of Ireland* (1995). See also the pioneering essays of Norris, 'Homosexuality and law: the Irish situation' (1976) 1 *Dublin University Law Review* 18–19, and 'Homosexual law reform in Ireland – a progress report' (1977) 1 *Dublin University Law Journal* 27 which focus almost exclusively on the need for criminal law reform.

Dudgeon v. United Kingdom,[46] and *Norris v. Ireland*,[47] respectively, the European Court ruled that the 1861 and 1885 statutes offended Article 8. In both judgments, however, the Court reserved its conclusions to arguments based on the right to a *private* life and not their right to a *family* life (also protected under Article 8).

Legislative reform followed in both jurisdictions, although the Republic was considerably slower than the North[48] in this regard. Indeed, despite these judgments, in 1988 the Republic of Ireland continued to harbour what Robson describes as

> on paper at least, the worst legal regime in Western Europe for lesbians and gay men. There was no recognition or protection of any sort, and gay men faced a total ban on any type of sexual activity.[49]

The Convention, however, could not be ignored indefinitely. Under the Sexual Offences Act, 1993 the offences of gross indecency and buggery were finally removed from the statute books[50] in all cases save where at least one of the parties was 'mentally impaired',[51] or under the age of 17.[52] Notably, the Legislature avoided a discriminatory approach, opting instead for a (roughly) equal age of consent for heterosexual and homosexual sexual intercourse.[53] Nonetheless some disparity initially arose in relation to acts falling short of sexual intercourse – while the new laws created an age of consent of 17 for all but the mildest forms of male homosexual sexual activity, an age of consent of 15 applied to all activity between heterosexuals (with the exception of sexual intercourse) and all sexual acts between two females.

This has since been altered by the Criminal Law (Sexual Offences) Act, 2006,[54] marking a significant shift towards greater equality of treatment as

---

46 (1981) 4 EHRR 149, (1983) 5 EHRR 573. The rather odd aspect of this case was that the law had been relaxed in respect of other parts of the United Kingdom some years earlier, in England and Wales in 1967 (Sexual Offence Act 1967) and in Scotland in 1980 (Criminal Justice (Scotland) Act 1980, s. 80). Thus, one part of the prosecutor's argument was that he was being treated less favorably than other homosexual men also living in the United Kingdom. 47 (1991) 13 EHRR 186. 48 Northern Ireland was brought into line with the other jurisdictions of the United Kingdom by the Homosexual Offences (Northern Ireland) Order 1982 (S.I. 1982/1536, N.I. No. 19) which permitted homosexual conduct between consenting males over the age of 21. This was reduced to 18 by the Criminal Justice and Public Order Act 1994, Part XI, ss 142–8. 49 Robson, 'Anatomy of a campaign', p. 47. 50 Sexual Offences Act, 1993, s. 2, s. 14 and the Schedule to the Act. See generally Wilkinson, 'Moving towards equality: homosexual law reform in Ireland' (1994) 45:3 *N.I.L.Q.* 252. 51 Ibid., s. 5. 52 Ibid., ss 3–4. 53 See Robson, 'Anatomy of a campaign', p. 47. One of the further notable features of the legislation is that it does not provide any exception for the military or armed forces, the army or the marines (unlike similar UK reforms in 1967, which did exempt the armed forces). There was, in other words, no attempt to allow the armed forces to opt out of these reforms. 54 The 2006 Act constituted a relatively hasty response to the striking down

between homosexual and heterosexual sex. The Act replaces the provisions of the 1993 Act with an all-encompassing offence entitled 'defilement of a minor' criminalizing any person (regardless of gender) 'who engages in a sexual act with a child' under the age of 17.[55] The Act appears, *prima facie* at least, not to discriminate between heterosexual and homosexual sex, though some quirks remain. 'Sexual act' is defined widely,[56] and includes both vaginal and anal intercourse, as well as oral sex performed on a male, though it appears, curiously, not to include oral sex *per vaginam*.[57] Additionally, the Act appears (perhaps unwittingly) to have decriminalized a number of homosexual acts involving minors that would otherwise have constituted 'gross indecency'.[58]

Yet even before the initial 1993 criminal law reforms, the state had already embarked on an equality agenda – of sorts. In 1989 the Oireachtas enacted a Prohibition against Incitement to Hatred Act, which banned the utterance or publication in public of comments that stirred up hatred on the grounds, *inter alia*, of sexual orientation. Similar restrictions were placed on publicly distributed video recordings.[59] In the previous year, 1988, a decree from the Department of Finance had outlawed sexual orientation discrimination in the public service.[60] 1993, furthermore, saw the extension of unfair dismissals legislation to prohibit dismissals from employment (in the public and private sectors alike) on grounds of sexual orientation.[61] This was followed in 1998 by legislation banning (amongst other things) sexual orientation discrimination in the employment context generally, that is in relation to recruitment, training, pay, the conditions of employment and

of age of consent laws by the Supreme Court, on the ground that they failed to provide a defence of genuine mistake in respect of the victim's age. See *C.C. v. Ireland and Ors.* [2006] IESC 33, Supreme Court, 23 May 2006.   **55** Stricter penalties apply where the child is aged 14 or under (s. 2), or where the child is aged 15 or 16 and one of the parties is a 'person in authority' (s. 3).   **56** Criminal Law (Sexual Offences) Act, 2006, s. 1.   **57** An exemption also arises in respect of underage women who engage in sexual intercourse – if full intercourse occurs, the woman is exempt from criminal liability, though she will be liable, curiously, for attempted intercourse or other 'sexual acts' falling short of intercourse. Ibid., s. 5. The Act also appears to protect women from penetration *per vaginam* using an inanimate object, though similar protection is not afforded to males.   **58** The definition of 'sexual act' appears to exclude, for instance, acts involving hand to genital contact. In the course of the Dáil debates preceding the enactment of the Criminal Law (Sexual Offences) Act 2006, 621 *Dáil Debates* 32 (2 June, 2006), Deputy Brendan Howlin T.D. observed that if enacted, the 2006 Act would decriminalise acts previously banned under s. 4 of the Criminal Law (Sexual Offences) Act, 1993, involving gross indecency between two males, one of whom was under the age of 17 but aged 15 or over. These included acts of mutual masturbation and other acts involving intimate but non-penetrative physical contact. See also Joint Oireachtas Committee on Child Protection, *Report on Child Protection* (Dublin: Houses of the Oireachtas, 2006) at 4.6.7–4.6.12   **59** Video Recordings Act, 1989.   **60** Department of Finance Circular 21/88, 22 June 1988.   **61** Unfair Dismissals (Amendment) Act, 1993 amending the Unfair Dismissals Act, 1977.

promotion within employment.[62] Legislation enacted in the year 2000 banned such discrimination where goods and services are being sold or supplied.[63]

The Health Insurance Act, 1994, moreover, expressly precludes the setting of higher health insurance *premia* by reference to sexual orientation or HIV status,[64] though an exemption in the Equal Status Act may still permit discrimination in the context of life assurance contracts.[65] The Refugee Act, 1996 marked further progress in extending the state's protection to those who had a 'well-founded fear of persecution' on the grounds of their sexual orientation,[66] signaling, to all intents and purposes, that the state considered itself a safe and welcoming place for people regardless of sexual orientation.

COHABITING COUPLES AND THE LAW

On closer examination, however, the legislation noted above, however laudable, presents a distinctly atomized image of the gay subject. As individuals, divorced from the familial-relational aspects of the law, gays and lesbians fare relatively well. As members of (alternative) families, however, virtually no legal protection is made available. This position is, indeed, highly ironic. By definition, the state of being homosexual, bisexual or heterosexual fundamentally involves one's emotional and sexual relations with other individuals. Sexual orientation, in other words, is a phenomenon directed *outwards* from the individual towards other persons, whether of the same or of the opposite sex, or of both sexes. Yet in defiance of this fact, the law in

---

62 Employment Equality Acts, 1998–2004. On which, see generally, Ryan, 'Sexual orientation discrimination,' in Moffatt and Cotter (eds.), *Discrimination law* (London and Dublin, 2005). 63 Equal Status Acts, 2000–04.   64 Health Insurance Act, 1994, s. 7(2).   65 The Equal Status Act, 2000, s. 5(2)(d) permits differential treatment in relation to annuities, pensions and insurance policies on the nine grounds set out in the Act, provided such discrimination is justified by reference to legitimate considerations of risk based on reliable actuarial or statistical data. It might be argued that if a statistically higher risk of contracting certain sexually transmitted diseases can be established, discrimination on grounds of sexual orientation in relation to life assurance contracts (*e.g.* in requiring HIV tests, in the setting of higher *premia* or the denial of cover to gay and bisexual men) might be legally justified. (Though it would not excuse insurance companies and brokers in relation to insensitive or offensive behaviour towards members of sexual minorities.) On the other hand, it may equally be asserted that treating all persons of the same sexual orientation equally, without having regard to the actual sexual experience and behaviour of each individual person, is in itself discriminatory. A strong argument might be made that the correct criterion for assessment should not be sexual orientation but sexual behaviour. Arguably, and with all due respect to the personal sexual freedom of the individuals involved, a monogamous same-sex couple will likely pose a lower risk for STDs than a promiscuous heterosexual man.   66 Refugee Act, 1996, s. 2 (cf. interpretation section, s. 1).

Ireland largely ignores the relational aspects of sexuality in favour of a perspective that views the subject as an atomized individual in a relational vacuum – as a person divorced from the emotional and sexual relationships he or she has with other persons.[67] Most ironically, the Refugee Act, 1996, which expressly confers a right of asylum on persons persecuted on account of their sexual orientation, excludes from its family reunification provisions the same-sex partners of persons granted asylum.[68] The Employment Equality Acts, 1998–2004, while precluding discrimination on the basis of sexual orientation, similarly appear not to recognize same-sex relationships, a point addressed further below.

The landscape of non-recognition

Thus, while the law to date has afforded strong protection to gay and lesbian individuals, Ireland nonetheless lags considerably behind other states in its treatment of same-sex relationships. Ironically, this feature of Irish law is most starkly exemplified by equality legislation itself. Although the Employment Equality Acts, 1998–2004 and Equal Status Acts, 2000–2004 alike prohibit sexual orientation discrimination, the Acts do not, at least *prima facie*, afford specific protection to gay *couples* as opposed to individuals. In particular, the 'marital status' ground, that prohibits discrimination on the grounds that a person is or is not married, is worded in a manner that excludes the status of 'cohabitation'.[69] Marital status under the Acts is defined as 'single, married, separated, divorced or widowed' thereby excluding cohabiting persons[70]. The 1998 Act likewise defines a 'member of the family' of any person for the purposes of the Act as including only:

(a) that person's spouse, or
(b) a brother, sister, uncle, aunt, nephew, niece, lineal ancestor or lineal descendant of that person or that person's spouse.[71]

[handwritten margin note: deleted by 2010 Act]

---

67 On the relevance of relational concerns to law, see generally Ryan, 'Law at the margins: the displacement of law as a framework of governance' (2001) 19 (no. 3) *Dickinson J. of International Law (Penn State Uni.)* 407.   68 The Refugee Act, s. 18 facilitates family reunification for recognised refugees but only in respect of a limited category of persons, including spouses and minor children, but excluding non-marital partners.   69 See generally Carolan, 'Rights of sexual minorities in Ireland and Europe: rhetoric versus reality' 19 *Dickinson Journal of International Law* 387. See also Walsh and Ryan, *The rights of de facto couples* (Dublin, 2006) at pp 118–19. This interpretation appears to be borne out by comments made by the then Minister for Justice during Seanad debates on the Employment Equality Bill: 'this legislation seeks to ensure equality in employment and to eliminate prejudice and discrimination. It does not seek to change the marital status of individuals or provide for different types of marital status:' Minister John O'Donoghue, 154 *Seanad Debates* col. 379 (18 February 1998).   70 Employment Equality Act, 1998, s. 2(1). Equal Status Act, 2000 s. 2(1). A similar fate met homosexual cohabitants relying on the 'familial status' ground in Canada in *Canada (Attorney General) v. Mossop* (1993) 100 DLR (4th) 658.   71 Ibid. This definition is

The term 'spouse' is generally understood in Irish law as a person to whom one is married.[72] The 2000 Act, moreover, defines a 'near relative' as a 'spouse, lineal descendant, ancestor, brother or sister', again excluding cohabiting partners. The Acts thus ring-fence the concept of 'family member', with the result that same-sex partners are excluded from its remit.

Indeed, in general, the current legal position of non-marital partners – both opposite-sex and same-sex – is unenviable to say the least. Irish law reserves an expansive range of rights and obligations to married couples, confining these entitlements and duties to persons who are legally recognized as married. Of particular note are laws concerning maintenance, the family home, property rights on relationship breakdown, inheritance, immigration, taxation and pensions, the predominant legal trend being to confine legal recognition to married couples, at the expense of their non-marital counterparts. Thus, outside of marriage, cohabiting couples enjoy very few rights – and correspondingly very few duties. In short, the legal position of a cohabiting couple differs only marginally from that of flatmates.

In the main, these legal disadvantages generally matter little during the currency of a relationship,[73] though very significant hardship may be suffered in times of crisis, where, for instance, there is a relationship breakdown, or where one or other party dies. While it is not possible to provide, in this paper, a comprehensive review of the legislation in this area,[74] a few examples are offered of the differential treatment of marital and non-marital couples:

Financial support on relationship breakdown
A husband or wife may seek maintenance from his or her spouse, at any time either during the currency of the relationship[75] or after it has broken down.[76] Maintenance may even be sought for an indefinite period after a divorce is granted,[77] thereby creating a right (and obligation) to maintain even a divorced spouse for so long as both divorcees remain alive.[78] By contrast, a

relevant given that s. 34 of the Employment Equality Acts permit employers to provide certain benefits to, or in respect of, members of an employee's family.　72 A view confirmed by the decision of the High Court in *Zappone and Gilligan v. Revenue Commissioners*, unreported, High Court, Dunne J., December 14, 2006, ruling that a couple of the same sex could not be treated as spouses for the purposes of the tax code, notwithstanding their Canadian civil marriage. 73 The main exception being in relation to taxation, discussed below.　74 For which see Walsh and Ryan, *The rights of de facto couples* (Dublin: IHRC, 2006), Chapter 4.　75 Family Law (Maintenance of Spouses and Children) Act, 1976, s. 5. The term 'spouse' is not explicitly defined though s. 8 necessarily implies, in making reference to 'the parties to a marriage', that the term means a married person.　76 See Family Law Act, 1995, s. 8; Family Law (Divorce) Act, 1996, s. 13.　77 Provided the maintenance recipient has remained unmarried after the divorce.　78 In principle, under Irish law, a clean break is not available on divorce. The Family Law (Divorce) Act, 1996, s. 13, permits a divorced person to seek maintenance at the time of divorce 'or ay any time thereafter' provided that the maintenance recipient remains unmarried and the maintenance debtor remains alive. See Byrne, 'Foreword' (p. vii) and Shannon,

person may not seek maintenance in her own right from a former non-marital partner (though maintenance may always be sought in respect of the partners' minor children, regardless of the circumstances of their birth).[79] It is not possible, moreover, to enforce an agreement making provision for the payment of maintenance to a partner, if the parties are unmarried, such agreements being contrary to the public policy favouring marriage.[80]

The absence of maintenance may work a particular injustice where one partner has sacrificed his or her career to care for the partners' children or to work in their common household, there being no facility for providing relief or compensation to the partner in question. The injustice may be particularly acute where the partner has devoted a particularly long time to homemaking, at the expense of an out-of-home career. Unlike spouses, unmarried partners cannot seek a pension adjustment order requiring the allocation of a portion of one spouse's pension entitlement to the other spouse.

Property

Likewise, a variety of protections afforded to spouses in respect of property are not extended to unmarried partners. The various proprietary orders available on judicial separation[81] and divorce[82] (which permit a court quite liberally to readjust property interests on marital breakdown) are unavailable in cases of non-marital relationship breakdown. The Family Home Protection Act, 1976 – which precludes the unilateral disposal of any interest in the family home without the consent of the non-disposing spouse – applies only to married persons.[83] Any person may of course acquire an equitable interest in a partner's property through the making of financial contributions towards its purchase[84] (or indirectly by making financial contributions to the general family pool, for instance, by paying the electricity or gas bill, or purchasing groceries).[85] This facility however, applies only to contributions of a financial nature, and not to the performance of unpaid work within the home[86] – nor

'Preface' (p. xi) in Shannon, *The Divorce Act in practice* (Dublin, 1999), and Power [1998] 1 *Irish J. of Fam L.* 15. See also *K. v. K.* [2001] 3 IR 371 and *J.D. v. D.D.* [1997] 3 IR 64. There is evidence, however, of a trend, particularly in 'big money' cases, favouring finality: see *F. v. F.* [1995] 2 IR 354, *W. v. W.*, (*ex tempore*), High Court, McKechnie J, 17 December 2001 and *T. v. T.* unreported, Supreme Court, 14 October 2002. See also Hardiman J in *W.A. v. M.A.* [2004] IEHC 387. **79** Family Law (Maintenance of Spouses and Children) Act 1976, ss 5 and 5A. **80** *Ennis v. Butterly* [1996] 1 IR 426. See also Mee, 'Public policy for a new millennium' (1997) 19 *Dublin University Law Journal* 149. **81** Family Law Act, 1995, ss 9 and 15. **82** Family Law (Divorce) Act, 1996, ss 14 and 15. **83** Family Home Protection Act, 1976, s. 2 defines a 'family home' as the dwelling in which a married couple ordinarily resides, or in which a spouse whose protection is at issue resided before departure. **84** *Conway v. Conway* [1976] IR 254. Examples relating to non-marital partners include *Power v. Conroy*, unreported, High Court, McWilliam J, 22 February 1980 and *Maher v. Donaghy*, unreported, Circuit Court, McMahon J, 22 February 2000. **85** See *F.C. v. P.G.* [1982] ILRM 155. **86** See *B.L. v. M.L.* [1992] 2 IR 77. By contrast, on divorce, non-financial contributions to the wellbeing of a family,

does an equitable interest arise in cases where financial contributions are made after a property has been purchased, or towards its improvement (as opposed to its acquisition).[87]

Taxation

Married couples enjoy certain exclusive tax advantages including the right to transfer, *inter se*, unused tax credits[88] and to share tax bands, as well as the right to transfer property *inter se* without capital gains taxation implications.[89] Gifts and inheritances passing from one spouse to another, moreover, are free from Capital Acquisitions Tax.[90] Although some relief has recently been provided to unmarried cohabitants in respect of shared private residences,[91] the tax reliefs noted above are otherwise confined to married couples. Thus, effectively, an unmarried couple stands to pay more tax over a lifetime than a married couple, particularly where there is a significant income disparity between the parties.[92] Although this point is less pertinent where there is parity of income power in a relationship, the irony arises that persons may end up paying more tax in exchange for lesser protections than others enjoy. This point is particularly relevant in the case of same-sex couples, who may fairly complain that they are being asked to subsidize heterosexuality.[93]

Inheritance

Although it is always open to a person to effect a will in favour of a non-marital partner, in circumstances where this does not happen, the surviving partner is effectively entitled to nothing from the estate. While the Succession Act, 1965 makes provision for the spouse,[94] children and other relatives of a deceased person dying intestate, the non-marital partner of a deceased person has no avenue of redress unless a will has been made. Nor is

such as homemaking and caring for children, may be taken into account in making ancillary orders: see Family Law (Divorce) Act, 1996, s. 20(2)(f) and (g).   87 See *W. v. W.* [1981] ILRM 202.   88 Taxes Consolidation Act, 1997, ss 461 and 1015–27.   89 Ibid., s. 562.   90 Finance Act, 1985, s. 59 and Finance Act, 1990, s. 127.   91 Finance Act, 2000, s. 151.   92 For an interesting exposition on this point, see Mark Lacey's calculations of the potential differences in tax liability for married and unmarried partners respectively, at http://www.glue.ie/GCNArticalJan05.doc.   93 This issue was at the heart of the decision in *Zappone and Gilligan v. Revenue Commissioners*, unreported, High Court, Dunne J, December 14, 2006. Dr Zappone and Dr Gilligan, a lesbian couple of 23 years' standing, who went through a ceremony of marriage in Canada, claimed the right to be treated as a married couple in Ireland for tax purposes. The High Court concluded that the couple had no right, under the Constitution, the European Convention on Human Rights or at common law to be treated as a married couple, the constitutional definition of marriage, in particular, being confined to couples of the opposite sex. See Holland, 'Legal action by lesbian couple to have their marriage recognised', *Irish Times*, 2 October 2006 and Ní Aoláin, 'An historic opportunity to achieve a marriage of equals', *Irish Times*, 2 October 2006. At the time of writing, the case was under appeal to the Supreme Court.   94 Succession Act, 1965, s. 67.

there anything to stop a testator from excluding a surviving partner under his
or her will. Indeed, while every widow and widower enjoys an automatic legal
right to inherit a portion of a deceased partner's estate (even where the latter
has made a will disinheriting the partner)[95], no such facility exists in the case
of non-marital partners.

Children

Although all children, at law, are deemed equal in terms of their entitlements,[96] the rights and duties of the parents of children differ significantly
depending on whether the parents are married to each other. Fathers fare
particularly poorly in this regard.[97] While a marital father automatically
assumes joint guardianship on the birth of his child,[98] an unmarried father
may only acquire guardianship responsibilities by agreement with the
mother,[99] or by order of a court.[1]

The unmarried partner of a parent is also at a significant disadvantage in
that the law does not permit the partner any means of attaining joint guardianship with the parent. Similar complications arise where children are conceived through artificial insemination (the sperm donor being deemed in law
the father of the child) or are born as a result of a surrogacy arrangement.

Although non-marital couples may foster children, and unmarried
persons may in theory adopt a child,[2] Irish law does not permit the joint
adoption of a child by two unmarried persons.[3]

To summarise, while the state has proved remarkably progressive in its
treatment of individuals who are lesbian, gay or bisexual, it has compre-
hensively failed to recognize same-sex relationships. Same-sex couples thus
effectively reside in legal limbo, unable to marry and thus precluded also
from accessing the many rights – and responsibilities – that apply to the
married state. The state, in short, appears to be making a rather fine
distinction between the sexual orientation of a person, and the relationships
which that person may form, despite the reality that the latter almost
inevitably follow on from the former.

---

95 Ibid., s. 112.   **96** Status of Children Act, 1987.   **97** See generally 'The child as legal
object', chapter 6 in O'Donovan, *Family law matters* (London, 1993), O'Driscoll, 'The rights
of the unmarried father' (1999) 2 *Irish Journal of Family Law* 18 and Walshe, 'The legal rights
of unmarried biological fathers' (2003) 2 *Irish Journal of Family Law* 2.   **98** Guardianship of
Infants Act, 1964, s. 6.   **99** Ibid., s. 2(4) as amended by the Status of Children Act, 1987.
1 Ibid., s. 6A as inserted by the Status of Children Act, 1987.   **2** Adoption Act, 1991, s. 10(2).
3 Ibid., s. 10(3). See the discussion in *Implementing equality for lesbians, gays and bisexuals*,
(Dublin, 2001) at pp 24–5 and 30.

Policy concerns

From 'rights discourses' to 'discourses of duty'

The immediately preceding paragraphs set out a selection of the most prominent examples of what is typically regarded as 'disadvantage', as an absence of rights for persons living together outside of marriage. It is nonetheless equally fair to say that these examples also exhibit an absence of substantial *duties and liabilities*, on the part both of the partners *inter se* and on the part of the state.[4] In this regard, it is worth drawing on the theories of Hohfeld,[5] who propounded a useful taxonomy eschewing the notion that various entitlements – namely rights, liberties, powers and immunities – exist in a vacuum. Each entitlement, he argued, necessarily implies a corollary or 'corelative' residing in a corresponding social actor – respectively a duty (correlating to a right), the absence of a right (correlating to a privilege), a liability (correlating to a power) or a disability (correlating to an immunity). Every right thus implies a corresponding duty. Every privilege (or 'freedom') similarly presupposes that someone is precluded from acting in a particular way in respect of the particular person. For instance, if A has a contractual right to buy B's car, B has a duty to sell the car to A and *vice versa*.[6] Likewise, if C enjoys the privilege of free expression, the state is precluded from penalizing C for speaking her mind.

Applying Hohfeld's taxonomy to marriage, one might usefully distinguish between two overlapping sets of relationships, the first being between the spouses as a unit and the state, and the second between the husband and wife *inter se*. Married couples together enjoy certain privileges and rights that may be invoked against the state. A married couple, for instance, have a legal right to share tax credits; the state has a duty to facilitate this, if certain conditions are met. The State, moreover, may not interfere in the family planning decisions of a married couple; the couple thus is privileged from state intervention in this arena.[7] Each spouse, however, also enjoys certain rights (and bears certain duties) in respect of the other spouse. Maintenance

---

4 A point regularly emphasised by the former Minister for Justice, Equality and Law Reform, Michael McDowell TD. See for instance his speech to at the opening of the Conference on the Legal Status of Cohabitants and Same-Sex Couples, Royal College of Physicians of Ireland, 26 May 2006, see http://www.glen.ie/press/docs/Address%20by%20Minister%20McDowell %20260506.doc (consulted 27 June 2006).   5 Hohfeld, W.N., *Fundamental legal conceptions, as applied in judicial reasoning and other legal essays* (New Haven, CT, 1966).   6 Even in this private law context, there is a public dimension, involving the state. Each of the parties has a right under law to seek damages for breach of contract, should it occur. This right necessarily and correspondingly requires the state, through its courts, to consider claims for breach of contract, thus placing a duty on the state to assist in the resolution of private disputes. Provided certain conditions are met, the state has a duty (under contract law) to enforce the private bargain, though usually through the award of damages.   7 *McGee v. Attorney General* [1974] IR 284.

(financial support) is a good example: each spouse is required to maintain the other, even on divorce, provided certain conditions are met, though an added public dimension arises: the state likewise has a responsibility to enforce maintenance rights, where appropriate,[8] and in particular, a constitutional duty on divorce to ensure that proper provision is made for each spouse and any dependent children.[9]

Correspondingly, the absence of rights in the context of non-marital relationships also implies an absence of duties. While in many respects it is the state that is relieved of substantive duties and liabilities towards the citizen, it is equally true that the partners to a non-marital relationship are, while denied several rights, also freed from legal liability in respect of several important duties. To put it another way, under Irish law, a non-marital partner, regardless of the length of his or her relationship, regardless of the contribution or sacrifice of his partner, may dissolve the relationship at any time, without substantial legal consequences. He will owe no maintenance to his partner. He may legally remove the partner from his home (if it is his alone). He may disinherit the partner without legal consequence. As the law currently stands, moreover, if his partner is of the same sex, he may intimidate and abuse his partner without fear of being barred from the family home (though other remedies may arise in such cases).

There are certain other examples where the law effectively relieves same-sex partners from obligations that apply to spouses. One intriguing example flows from the Ethics in Public Office Act, 1996. A public official to whom that Act applies is required to make certain declarations regarding the assets and interests of a spouse, but not those of a non-marital partner. This is despite the fact that, in practice, the public official may stand to profit indirectly from a benefit that accrues to a partner.

The discourse of rights – particularly the discourse of gay rights – often clouds this important, perhaps rather more conservative feature of the debate regarding non-marital partners. The debate around the recognition of same-sex relationships nonetheless is as much about giving legal effect to the moral duties that partners owe each other as it is about effecting rights. This is not to suggest, of course, that activists and advocates are not interested in enforcing these duties – simply that the language of advocacy may be enhanced considerably through a paradigmatic shift from a rights-based to a duty-based discourse.

Incremental reform – compounding discrimination?
To the general trend of non-recognition discussed above there are some significant – though, admittedly, comparatively rare – exceptions. In recent years,

---

8 Through the Family Law (Maintenance of Spouses and Children) Act, 1976.   9 Under Article 41.3.2 of the Constitution of Ireland, 1937, as amended by the Fifteenth Amendment, 1995.

the Legislature has introduced limited reforms extending to non-marital families entitlements that previously were confined to persons in marital families. The most significant example of such reforms arose with the enactment of the Status of Children Act, 1987, an Act that removed most of the legal disadvantages previously applying to children born outside of wedlock. As a result of the Act, all children were deemed equal in the eyes of the law, regardless of the marital status of their parents. Thus, a child born outside of wedlock is entitled to seek maintenance from both parents and would enjoy inheritance rights on the same footing as a child born within marriage. Yet laudable as these reforms were, the Status of Children Act suffered from a fundamental infirmity: while guaranteeing equal rights for children, regardless of the circumstances of their origin, the Act failed to address the unequal treatment of their parents.[10] Thus, notwithstanding the egalitarian sentiments of the 1987 Act, children in non-marital families effectively continue to be treated differently from their marital counterparts, in that the families from which they hail remain legally disadvantaged. Their parents, after all, are denied significant rights and responsibilities in relation to maintenance, shared property and succession that automatically apply between married couples. The law thus essentially fails to protect the families in which those children reside, by failing to accord substantial legal protection to their parents, particularly in cases of relationship breakdown and the death of a partner.

Other reforming measures more emphatically ameliorate the situation of non-marital couples, though again difficulties have arisen. The Domestic Violence Act, 1996, for instance, expanded the remit of the civil remedy of a 'barring order' (legally excluding a spouse from the family home) to include some (though notably, not all) unmarried partners living together in a marriage-like relationship. The Act specifically permits a barring order to be granted to a person who though 'not the spouse of the respondent ... has lived with the respondent as husband or wife ...' for at least six of the previous nine months.[11] The reach of other measures, including safety and protection orders, was similarly expanded to include partners and family members.[12] Likewise, the Civil Liability (Amendment) Act[13] of the same year extended the right to

---

10 Most notably, the Act continues to deny non-marital fathers an automatic right to guardianship, which right is, by contrast, enjoyed by marital fathers (see Guardianship of Infants Act, 1964, s. 6). The Act did however, allow non-marital fathers to apply to court seeking joint guardianship rights (under s. 6A of the 1964 Act as amended by the Status of Children Act, 1987), though an award of guardianship is subject to the best interests of the relevant child and thus not guaranteed. A provision of the Children Act, 1997 permits a father to acquire guardianship rights by virtue of a statutory declaration, but such declaration requires the express consent of both parents. (See s. 2(4) of the 1964 Act, as amended by the Children Act, 1997.)   11 Domestic Violence Act, 1996, s. 3(2). 12 Ibid., ss 2 and 5, which also cover cohabiting persons living together in a relationship not based on a contract or commercial arrangement, a formula that appears (however obliquely) to include same-sex partners.   13 Civil Liability (Amendment) Act, 1996, s. 1 amending s. 47 of the Civil

sue for wrongful death to the opposite sex surviving non-marital partners of deceased persons killed due to the negligence of others. Similarly expansive trends can be seen in the Parental Leave Acts, 1998–2006[14] and the Residential Tenancies Act, 2004,[15] each of which extend protection to partners (though, in the latter case, only those of the opposite sex) who though unmarried, cohabit in a marriage-like relationship.

Perhaps the most expansive reform arose from the enactment of section 151 of the Finance Act, 2000. This measure introduced the 'Principal Private Residence Relief' exempting from Capital Acquisitions Tax any person who inherits a property (or a portion of a property) which was, for at least three years before the donor's death, the principal private residence[16] of the donor and donee. Although certain restrictions apply,[17] this provision provides significant tax relief in particular for (amongst others) the surviving partner in a same-sex relationship. Indeed, section 151 applies regardless of the relationship of the parties, the main condition being that the parties have cohabited for at least three years before the death of the donor.

Additionally, the European Communities (Free Movement of Persons) (No. 2) Regulations 2006,[18] offer some limited recognition to both the opposite-sex and same-sex non-marital partners of EU nationals (other than Irish citizens) for the purposes of immigration law. These provisions extend certain rights of residence to partners of 'Union citizens' traveling to Ireland from other EU states, where there is, between the parties, 'a durable relationship, duly attested.' Notably, however, the Regulations expressly define a 'Union citizen' for this purpose as a citizen of a member state of the EU *other than Ireland.*[19] In short, the Regulations do not apply where one of the parties is an Irish citizen,[20] even where the partners have lawfully resided in another EU State, thus putting Irish citizens in the ironic position of being less favourably treated in their own state than similarly placed citizens of other EU states coming to live in Ireland. These measures, moreover, apply only to the partners of EU nationals who are lawfully resident in a Member State other than Ireland prior to their arrival in the state. Thus, if the partner travels directly to Ireland from outside the EU, he or she is not covered by the

Liability Act 1961.   **14** See for instance s. 13, which permits an employee to obtain *force majeure* leave in respect of a cohabiting partner.   **15** See s. 39 extending to non-marital partners of the opposite sex the right to succeed to a protected tenancy on the death of a partner.   **16** The Act precludes relief where the partners have more than one residence at their disposal.   **17** Notably, the surviving partner must continue to live in the residence for a period of six years after the death of the donor, though rollover provisions apply allowing the survivor to sell the property if purchasing a new principal private residence in its stead.   **18** S.I. No. 656 of 2006 – these replace earlier regulations on the same topic – S.I. No. 226 of 2006.   **19** Notably the earlier regulations on this point – S.I. No. 226 of 2006 – did not exclude Irish citizens.   **20** Though the position is unclear where the citizen holds dual nationality.

Regulations. Non-marital relationships otherwise remain wholly outside the scope of current immigration law, a point of acute concern for many gay and lesbian couples.[21]

Indeed, in respect of same-sex couples at least, significant limitations arise in relation to many of these otherwise notable reforms. In particular, the formula generally used to embrace non-marital partners in the Domestic Violence Act, 1996, the Civil Liability Act, 1996, the Residential Tenancies Act, 2004 and (prior to a recent amendment) in the Parental Leave Act, 1998[22] – that the parties 'lived together (or 'cohabited') as husband and wife' – arguably serves to deny protection to same-sex partners.[23] While this point is debatable, it is suggested that the formulaic juxtaposition of the terms 'husband' and 'wife' serves to require an opposition of gender – that is, the partners necessarily have to be of opposite sex. As Lord Hutton observed in *Fitzpatrick v. Sterling Housing Association*,[24] '[a] person can only live with a man as his wife when that person is a woman'.[25] While the decision of the House of Lords in *Ghaidan v. Godin-Mendoza*[26] suggests that a more expansive, inclusive interpretation may be open to the Irish courts, the point is at least unclear, thus placing same-sex couples in a particularly unfortunate position when compared with their married heterosexual counterparts.

The exclusion of same-sex couples appears, indeed, to have been the express intention of the Oireachtas in employing such terminology, at least in relation to some of the legislation in which this formula was used. For instance, in the course of debates in the Seanad in relation to the Residential Tenancies Bill (enacted as an Act in 2004) some Senators and Deputies queried the use of a provision granting rights to succeed to a statutory tenancy to persons described as having 'cohabited with the tenant as husband and wife', arguing that this phrase unfairly precluded same-sex couples.[27]

---

21 See generally www.glue.ie. These concerns may ultimately be addressed as part of a policy statement under Section 9 of the proposed Immigration, Residence and Protection Bill, 2007, scheduled for enactment in 2007. 22 Though this has recently been remedied by the Parental Leave (Amendment) Act, 2006, which extends the right to *force majeure* leave (originally confined to parents, spouses and non-marital couples of the opposite sex), to same-sex couples. 23 A conclusion supported by *Harrogate Borough Council v. Simpson* [1986] 2 FLR 1 and *Fitzpatrick v. Sterling Housing Association* [1999] 3 WLR 1113, espec. at p. 1140. Mee and Ronayne, *The partnership rights of same sex couples* (Dublin, 2000) at pp 16–17, agree that same-sex couples are excluded by the use of this formula. See further Ryan, 'Sexuality ideology and the legal construction of family: *Fitzpatrick v. Sterling Housing Association*' [2000] 1 *Irish Journal of Family Law* 2. 24 [1999] 3 WLR 1113, at p. 1140. 25 Though see the comments of Ward LJ in the same case, [1998] Ch. 304 at 339. Adopting a functional approach to the phrase 'living as husband and wife', Ward LJ favoured an interpretation that included same-sex couples. A familial nexus, he argued, cannot be defined solely in terms of its structures or components: 'I would rather focus on familial functions. The question is more what a family does than what a family is.' Taking this functional approach, he concluded that functionally a same-sex couple could be embraced by the phrase in question. 26 [2004] UKHL 30. See the casenote by Ryan, (2005) 27:3 *Journal of Social Welfare and Family Law* 355. 27 See 177

The government minister responsible for the Bill, Deputy Noel Ahern TD, while agreeing that same-sex couples would be excluded by the use of this phrase, nonetheless refused to countenance any change to this formula.[28] Remarkably, the minister denied any discriminatory intent, but nonetheless indicated that the impugned phrase, as used in the legislation, did not, in his view, embrace same-sex couples. It appears thus, that the exclusion of same-sex couples from this Act – and perhaps like provisions of legislation – was not inadvertent but rather entirely deliberate and intentional, though the reasoning behind such exclusion is unclear.[29] Although the minister admitted that the measure excluded same-sex couples, the government nonetheless refused to remedy this defect.

In taking this stance, the state flies resolutely in the face of its international obligations. The European Court of Human Rights, most notably in *Karner v. Austria*,[30] has ruled, in relation to the application of the European Convention on Human Rights, that it is impermissible to treat non-marital couples of the same-sex differently from similarly placed couples (*i.e.* unmarried) of the opposite sex. In particular, the court ruled that differentiation between non-marital same-sex and opposite-sex couples in legislation on the rights of tenants infringed the terms of Article 14 of the European Convention, in that it discriminated on the basis of sexual orientation in relation to the Article 8 rights (specifically the right to respect for one's home

Seanad Debates cols.793ff and cols. 1119ff.   **28** Ibid., cols. 796 ff. and cols. 1119ff. I am grateful to Dr Oran Doyle for bringing the Minister's comments to my attention.   **29** One line of reasoning put forward by Minister Ahern in the context of the Residential Tenancies Bill debates appears to suggest that an extension to include same-sex partners might inadvertently take in other non-marital relationships of a non-sexual nature. The Minister argued, in particular, that replacing the phrase 'cohabited with the tenant as husband and wife' with the alternative 'cohabited with the tenant as his or her partner' would render the legislation too vague and would potentially expand the remit of protection well beyond the context of sexually-based, non-marital, intimate relationships. See vol. 177 *Seanad Debates* 1120 Noel Ahern: 'I am not in a position to accept the amendment [changing "husband and wife" to "partner"]. The amendment as worded is incompatible with the remainder of subsection 39(3), as the deletion of the words husband and wife would widen the provision to cover any non-tenant living in the accommodation at the time of the death of the tenant. It would render the other subparagraphs redundant. The extension of the provision to include same-sex partners in sexual relationships would require specific reference to the category of occupant rather than the mere deletion of the words husband and wife.' See also ibid., col. 793: 'The broader extension of the provision, to include partners other than those living together as husband and wife, is not possible. The expression is too vague and capable of a number of interpretations. It would not be appropriate to formulate a statutory provision using such a vague expression. It would be likely to include any person who had been living in the accommodation. Any extension of the provision to include same-sex partners in sexual relationships would require specific reference to that category of occupant.'   **30** Application no. 40016/98, 24 July 2003. See also the recommendation of the Human Rights Committee attached to the International Convention International Convention on Civil and Political Rights in *Young v. Australia*, Communication No. 941/20000, 6 August 2003. *Young* suggested that extending pension rights

life) of same-sex couples. Thus in *Ghaidan*[31] the English and Welsh House of Lords re-interpreted the phrase 'living with the tenant as husband or wife' in rent control legislation to include same-sex as well as opposite-sex couples, arguing that to rule otherwise would involve discrimination on the basis of sexual orientation contrary to the European Convention on Human Rights.[32] Nonetheless, and notwithstanding express reference to *Karner* in the Seanad Debates, the minister remained resolute (though admittedly he agreed that the legal position of same-sex couples generally required legislative attention.) Given that the Convention is now, by virtue of the European Convention on Human Rights Act, 2003, part of Irish domestic law, the Legislature's stance seems particularly peculiar.

Yet, the most ironic exclusion of same-sex couples arises in a most unlikely place, namely the Employment Equality Act, 1998, an Act that purports to eliminate discrimination on, amongst other grounds, the ground of sexual orientation. Section 34 of the Act contains two specific exemptions in respect of benefits accorded to the family members of employees. Though these exemptions apply across all nine grounds of discrimination, arguably they impact most significantly in the context of non-marital and particularly same-sex couples. Under section 34, employers are entitled to grant the family members of employees certain benefits on account of their family relationship to the employee. Benefits may also be bestowed in respect of an event related to members of the employee's family or any description of those members. This might include for instance marriage (from which same-sex couples are excluded) or the birth of a child. Ironically (given that this is a measure seeking to promote equality), the Act of 1998 defines 'member of the family' for this purpose as a person related to the employee by blood, marriage or adoption, thus excluding non-marital partners. Given that partners of the same sex cannot marry, this then means that it is legally possible to confine these benefits in a manner that indirectly favours heterosexual employees.

to non-marital partners of the opposite sex, while simultaneously excluding same-sex partners, infringes the anti-discrimination provisions in Article 26 of the Convention.   **31** op. cit. **32** Given that the Oireachtas expressly intended to exclude same-sex partners from the Residential Tenancies Act, it is an open question whether a *Ghaidan*-like conclusion could arise in Ireland. It is arguable that an interpretation that flew in the face of the express intention of legislators would be impermissible, though the court in *Ghaidan* did not appear to be concerned with the contemporary views of legislators enacting the legislation under review. The present author has argued elsewhere that the conclusion in *Ghaidan* most likely contradicts the express intentions of the majority of parliamentarians in enacting the impuged provision: Ryan, (2005) 27:3 *Journal of Social Welfare and Family Law* 355. The question thus arises whether it is appropriate to interpet the Act in a manner that contradicts the intentions of the legislators, in other words, whether the courts should consider the real intentions of the legislators, or whether they may ascribe *ex post facto* to legislation a purpose that may not have been in the minds of the parliamentarians enacting the relevant legislation. This question, though worthy of consideration, is beyond the scope of this current paper.

In rare instances, however, the failure to recognize same-sex couples ironically serves to privilege such couples. The current definition of 'cohabitation' for the purposes of social welfare, while including unmarried partners, nonetheless excludes same-sex cohabitants.[33] While this may lead to the disadvantage of the latter in relation to the allocation of dependent allowances and family income supplements, the non-recognition of cohabitation serves to permit parents in same-sex relationships to continue sourcing the One Parent Family Payment, despite the presence of a cohabiting partner (which is not currently possible where opposite-sex partners cohabit). Likewise, entitlement to unemployment assistance is unaffected where the recipient is in a dependent relationship with a partner of the same sex. Ironically, thus, same-sex couples of more limited means in fact stand to lose out if legal recognition is generally extended to such couples. Indeed, as Colker has observed[34] in the context of the discussion around same-sex marriage, arguments for the legal recognition of non-marital couples tend disproportionately to favour wealthier couples, who stand to benefit more from such recognition than their less wealthy counterparts.

There is some evidence of government willingness to address these instances of discrimination. The government has, for instance, proposed dropping the cohabitation rule[35] in the context of social welfare, (thus acknowledging the counter-productive nature of the rule in discouraging the cohabitation of parents). Likewise, the Parental Leave (Amendment) Act, 2006 extended to same-sex partners the right to obtain *force majeure* leave in respect of a partner's illness, thus remedying an apparent exclusion of same-sex partners from the earlier Parental Leave Act, 1998.[36] This move represents, it is suggested, an acknowledgment of the injustice involved in treating cohabiting couples differently based on sexual orientation.

Nonetheless, other recent legislative measures expose some considerable equivocation on the part of the state. In 2004, the Social Welfare (Miscellaneous) Provisions Act reintroduced, in legislative form, an administrative practice that discriminated between, respectively, the same-sex and opposite-sex partners of pensioners. While any person could avail, regardless of age, of a free bus pass for the purpose of accompanying his or her opposite-sex partner on public transport, this facility (along with a series of other social welfare measures) was, as a result of the Act, legislatively

---

33 Social Welfare (Consolidation) Act, 1993 s. 3(12) and 3(13) and S. 24 and Schedule 2 of the Social Welfare and Pensions Act, 2005.   34 Colker, 'Marriage', 3 *Yale Law J. of Law and Feminism* (1991) 321 at p. 326.   35 See Government of Ireland, *Government Discussion Paper: Proposals for supporting lone parents* (Dublin, 2006). See also Reid, 'Cohabiting welfare ban on single parents to be dropped', *Irish Times*, 29 December 2005, p. 1.   36 The impetus for this specific move appears to have been the enactment of the European Union's Framework Directive 2000/78/EC banning discrimination on the basis of (*inter alia*) sexual orientation in the

denied to same-sex partners.[37] Similar provisions serve legally to protect pension arrangements that confine benefits to widows and widowers, to the exclusion of unmarried surviving partners.[38] Although the Equal Status Acts, 2000–2004 generally preclude such treatment (a point that the Department of Social and Family Affairs appears initially to have accepted),[39] the latter Acts do not apply where discrimination is mandated by other legislative enactments.[40]

Nevertheless, a recent development suggests that the state may be willing to roll back on the 2004 Act. In October 2006, the Department of Social and Family Affairs (on foot of a complaint made through the Equality Authority) made an *ex gratia* social welfare payment of close to €10,000 to a person providing stay-at-home care for his same-sex partner, who is suffering from cancer.[41] Such payments are routinely made to opposite sex couples, whether married or unmarried. Although the department denied that the step constituted a precedent, it arguably acknowledges the fundamental injustices – not to mention the potential breach of Convention rights – arising as a result of the 2004 Act.

The pitfalls of incrementalism

Another less obvious infirmity arises as a result of the piecemeal nature of these reforms. It is arguable that these various reforms, far from consoli-dating the emergence of a legal concept of cohabitant, in fact serve to under-mine the development of a consistent and cohesive policy in this arena. Given the very disparate definitions of non-marital couples in the various Acts, the very distinct prospect arises that a couple may be afforded protection under one Act, while simultaneously being excluded under another. The risk thus arises that particularized solutions to specific legal issues will lead to diverse and inconsistent outcomes. For instance, the Domestic Violence Act allows a barring order to be taken out against a person where the applicant has lived with the respondent 'as husband or wife' for six of the previous nine months.[42] By contrast, the qualifying period for safety orders (in the same Act) is six of the previous twelve months,[43] while the

context of employment.   **37** For the rationale behind these changes see the comments of the then Minister for Social and Family Affairs, in 175 *Seanad Debates* cols. 1856–61 and the spirited response of Senator David Norris, ibid., cols. 1871–75. See also the criticisms levelled by Deputy Seán Crowe in 580 *Dáil Debates* cols. 1648.   **38** See the Pensions Acts, 1990–2005 s. 72(3) and recital 22 of the Framework Directive 2000/78/EC which permit differential treatment for married couples notwithstanding bans on discrimination based on sexual orientation (in the Directive and in Irish equality legislation) and marital status (in Irish equality legislation).   **39** Initially, the Department had accepted that its practice in excluding same-sex partners was discriminatory: see Equality Authority press release, 10 March 2004, www.equality.ie.   **40** See Equal Status Act, 2000, s. 14.   **41** See Hennessy, 'Gay carer payment not a precedent – Brennan', *Irish Times*, 13 October 2006, p. 3.   **42** Domestic Violence Act, 1996 s. 3.   **43** Ibid., s. 2.

period of cohabitation required under the Civil Liability Act is three years.[44]
The period stipulated under the Residential Tenancies Act, 2004, section 39
is six months *simpliciter*. To compound matters further, the Social Welfare
Act defines a cohabitant without reference to any minimum period of living
together.[45] Thus, although the category of cohabiting couple is gradually
being accorded legal recognition, reform has tended to proceed in a
piecemeal and disjointed fashion that does not lend itself to the development
of a comprehensive and coherent policy on non-marital couples.

That said, there may be some merit in achieving reform through an
incremental approach. The key benefit of incrementalism lies in its ability to
address specific legal problems on a case by case basis, offering ample opportunity to explore fully the complexities of particularized legal concerns.
Thus, sufficient time and attention may be devoted to what are sometimes
quite complex legal issues. The incremental approach also permits the
Legislature to maintain public focus on particular hardships caused by
legislation, a tactic that avoids the risk that debate will centre on ideological
rather than practical concerns. In short, it is easier to attract public support
for reform by reference to specific and particularized legal problems that face
real couples, rather than through the invocation of generalized or abstract
concepts. A further merit lies in the gradual nature of incremental reform,
each step appearing to represent a 'small' and thus more palatable change
than might be the case with 'all-encompassing' legislation.

Nonetheless, whatever the merits of a gradualist approach, the pace of
reform in Ireland has been painfully slow. The absence of all but the most
limited of reforms in the position of same-sex couples arguably militates in
favour of a comprehensive legislative remedy. A piecemeal and drawn out
response may ultimately prove inadequate.

The constitutional dimension

The legal difficulties noted above are copper-fastened in many respects by
the rigid, prescriptive terms of the Constitution of Ireland, 1937. While
Articles 41 and 42 thereof purport to guarantee the rights of the family, and
confirm the inalienability of parental rights and duties, these provisions are
definitively ring-fenced by the terms of Article 41.3.1, declaring that:

> The State pledges itself to guard with special care the institution of
> marriage, *on which the Family is founded*, and to protect it against attack.
> [emphasis added].

---

44 Civil Liability (Amendment) Act, 1996, s. 1.   45 Social Welfare (Consolidation) Act, 1993
ss 3(12) and 3(13) and s. 24 of the Social Welfare and Pensions Act, 2005.

Absent the highlighted words, Article 41 may well have been open to an interpretation inclusive of a diverse range of families. The interposition, however, of the words 'on which the Family is founded' (a statement that is notable for the self-evident tone in which it is expressed) necessarily implies that the Family to which the Constitution refers is that based on marriage alone. This point was affirmed in *State (Nicolaou) v. An Bord Úchtála*,[46] in which the Supreme Court denied the application of the family provisions to an unmarried man who fathered a child with his then non-marital partner. A similar conclusion prevailed in *K. v. W.*[47] and *W. O'R v. E.H.*,[48] the Supreme Court again confirming that the benefit of Articles 41 and 42 was confined to marital families.

The potency of Article 41.3.1 is ably demonstrated by the ruling in *O'Brien v. Stoutt*[49] a decision concerning the rights of non-marital children. Although the law has since been altered,[50] a child born outside of marriage at the time of the decision could not lay claim to a portion of the estate of an intestate parent. In this case, the plaintiff's father had died without making a will. While his other children, born inside marriage, were by law entitled to a portion of his estate, Ms O'Brien was denied such entitlement solely on the basis that she was not born within marriage. While the Supreme Court agreed that, *prima facie*, this amounted to unequal treatment, it concluded that, as a result of the constitutional preference for marriage, the measures in question were justified. The Supreme Court reasoned that, as a result of Article 41.3.1, the state was entitled to favour the institution of marriage, even if this resulted in the subordination of non-marital children.[51]

While the substantive law that led to this outcome has since been altered,[52] the implications are nonetheless severe. A flavour of the difficulties arising from the marital preference doctrine may be discerned from the later decision of *Ennis v. Butterly*,[53] where Kelly J denied the efficacy of a cohabitation agreement, on roughly similar lines. The agreement in question, it was claimed, sought to secure, in a case of relationship breakdown, a right to seek maintenance from a non-marital partner. Kelly J concluded that to the extent that such an agreement attempted to replicate for unmarried persons the legal consequences of marriage, it would be void for reasons of public policy. The clear public policy in favour of marriage prevented, the judge argued, the enforcement of arrangements that sought to 'mimic' marriage.

46 [1966] IR 567.   47 [1990] 2 IR 437.   48 [1996] 2 IR 248.   49 [1984] IR 316. On this point, see the commentary in Doyle, *Constitutional equality law* (Dublin, 2005) at pp 99–103.   50 See the Status of Children Act, 1987.   51 A similarly strong preference for the marital family and the maintenance of its privileged position is evident in a number of decisions on child custody disputes including *Re J.H.: K.C. and A.C. v. An Bord Uchtála* [1985] IR 375 and *N. and N. v. Health Service Executive* (the 'baby Ann' case) [2006] IESC 60. State intervention in the marital family, moreover, is strongly circumscribed. See *North Western Health Board v. H.W.* [2001] 3 IR 622.   52 Ibid.   53 [1996] 1 IR 426. See also Mee, 'Public policy for the new millennium?'

> [G]iven the special place of marriage and the family under the Irish
> Constitution, it appears to me that the public policy of this State
> ordains that non-marital cohabitation does not and cannot have the
> same constitutional status as marriage.[54]

It is certainly well-established that measures that favour non-marital
arrangements at the expense of marriage will more than likely be deemed
unconstitutional. Thus, in *Murphy v. Attorney General*,[55] taxation measures
were struck down on the basis that they served to place a higher tax burden
on double-income married couples than on similarly placed cohabitants.[56]
Whether the Constitution permits equal or equivalent treatment, however,
remains an open question. Indeed one of the greatest barriers to reform in
this area is posed by the uncertainty arising regarding the impact of the
constitutional preference for marriage. On the one hand, it might be
suggested that Article 41.3 simply precludes legal measures that treat non-
marital couples more favourably than married couples, a view favoured by the
Law Reform Commission[57] as well as the All-Party Oireachtas Committee on
the Constitution.[58] On the other hand, the argument may be made (and this
is supported in large measure by *dicta* in *Ennis*, noted above) that measures
that seek to equate marriage and non-marital unions necessarily undermine
marriage. After all, if there were to be no substantial differences between
marriage and non-marital status, in what sense other than the moral sense
would marriage be special in Irish law? Strangely, the latter argument might
militate in favour of measures that are confined to same-sex couples. As the
latter may not currently marry in Ireland, it might be argued that to accord
civil partnership status to couples of the same gender would not undermine
the currency of marriage, as the parties to same-sex specific civil partnership
would not have been able to marry anyway.

Whether the more liberal or conservative of these views would prevail has
yet to be seen. It may well be, given the current preference of the courts to
leave matters of social policy to the Legislature, that the courts will be
inclined to leave the balancing of rights to the Oireachtas.[59] Nonetheless, and
given the strong terms in which Article 41 is worded, the possibility of
cohabitation legislation being constitutionally stymied cannot be discounted.

(1997) 19 DULJ 149–60.   **54** Ibid., at 438.   **55** [1982] IR 241.   **56** See also *Hyland v. Minister
for Social Welfare* [1989] IR 624. On the other hand, measures that seek to privilege persons on
grounds related to their status as lone parents may be justified on the basis that one parent families
face particular social and financial difficulties when compared to married couples. See *Mhic
Mhathúna v. Attorney General* [1989] IR 504.   **57** Law Reform Commission, *The rights and duties
of cohabitees* (Dublin, 2004), LRC–32–2004, paras. 6.11–6.18.   **58** See All-Party Oireachtas
Committee on the Constitution, *Tenth progress report: The family* (Dublin, 2006) at 74–6.   **59** For
an interesting critique, see the discussion in Doyle, 'The duration of primary education: judicial
constraint in constitutional interpretation' (2002) 10 *ISLR* 222, and Doyle, *Constitutional equality*

Same-sex cohabiting couples: the dilemmas of 'equal treatment'

Particular complexities arise in respect of cohabiting couples of the same sex. One of the most interesting aspects of the current debate on non-marital couples in Ireland is the extent to which the agencies of law reform – including, in particular, the Law Reform Commission – have acknowledged the functional equality of opposite-sex and same-sex couples outside of marriage.[60] Although none of the law reform agencies have to date called for same-sex marriage in Ireland, the prevailing view among such agencies appears to be that insofar as non-marital relationships are concerned, legal distinctions should no longer be made between same-sex and opposite sex couples. This stance is in line with (and perhaps prompted in part by) the developing jurisprudence of the European Court of Human Rights. In *Da Silva Mouta v. Portugal*[61] the court held that the denial of custody to a father, solely by reason of his sexual orientation, contravened Articles 8 and 14 of the Convention on Human Rights. The father enjoyed, the court concluded, the right to a private and family life under Article 8. This right that had been undermined on the basis of his sexual orientation, a stance that amounted to discrimination under Article 14 in the application of convention rights. A similar conclusion arose in *Karner v. Austria*,[62] this time in the context of the right to respect for one's home life under Article 8. In that case, the European Court of Human Rights ruled that while states were entitled to take proportionate measures favouring the traditional family, housing legislation that distinguished between same-sex and opposite-sex couples outside of marriage contravened Convention rights, specifically the right not to be discriminated against on the basis of sexual orientation in relation to the right to respect for one's home life.

The Law Reform Commission, in its final report, on the *Rights and Duties of Cohabitants* took a similar line, defining 'qualified cohabitant', for the purposes of its report, in a manner that included both same-sex and opposite sex couples.[63] In the *Rights of De Facto Couples*, moreover (a report commissioned by the Irish Human Rights Commission), Walsh and Ryan[64] chose to follow suit, stating at an early juncture that 'the term de facto couple

---

law (Dublin, 2006) at chapter 2. **60** Law Reform Commission, *The rights and duties of Cohabitants*, LRC-82–2006, (Dublin: Law Reform Commission, 2006). See also Law Reform Commission, *The rights and duties of cohabitees*, LRC–32–2004 (Dublin, 2004). **61** (1999) 31 EHRR 47. **62** Application no. 400016/8, 24 July 2003. See also the decision of the House of Lords (Eng. & W.) in *Ghaidan v. Godin-Mendoza* [2004] UKHL 30. **63** Law Reform Commission, *The rights and duties of Cohabitants*, LRC–82–2006 (Dublin: Law Reform Commission, 2006). See also the Commission's earlier consultation paper, entitled *The Rights and Duties of Cohabitees*. **64** In the interests of transparency, it should be pointed out that Fergus Ryan, co-author of *The rights of de facto couples*, is also the author of this current paper. The views expressed in this current paper nonetheless should not be taken as necessarily representative of those of either Ms Judy Walsh or of the Irish Human Rights Commission.

for the purposes of this report is intended definitively to include both opposite sex and same-sex partners'.[65]

While welcome in many respects, this approach arguably poses a dilemma. Certainly, a strong argument may be made for the equal treatment of same-sex and opposite-sex couples outside of marriage. Adopting a functional approach to such relationships,[66] it is difficult to conclude otherwise than that these respective relationships should be accorded equal protection and recognition. In short, the functions performed by the respective parties to such relationships are similar in nature and impact. A consensus has thus developed that same-sex and opposite-sex couples should be treated, legally speaking at least, as equivalent (though, as discussed above, this consensus remains largely unreflected in current legislation).

Certainly, opposite-sex couples living together outside of marriage face significant legal disadvantages. Yet, however entrenched this legal quandary, there is in fact a very effective – though stark – remedy at their disposal. In general, opposite sex couples living together outside of marriage can get married. In this regard there are certainly exceptions.[67] Heterosexual cohabitants may, for instance, be precluded from marrying because one or other party is still married to another person, and not yet divorced. Given the four year living apart requirement for divorce under Irish law,[68] this situation is perhaps not susceptible to speedy remedy. Nonetheless, once the four year living apart requirement is met (a feat made substantially easier by the very broad interpretation accorded to the term 'living apart')[69] the parties are free

---

65 Walsh and Ryan, *The rights of de facto couples*, p. 10.   **66** On the functionalist approach to family law see further Glennon, '*Fitzpatrick v. Sterling Housing Association* – an endorsement of the functional family?' (2000) 14 *Intl. J. of Law, Policy and the Family* 226–55. See also the approach of Ward LJ in *Fitzpatrick v. Sterling Housing Association* [1998] Ch. 304 at 339. **67** For instance, marriage is not permitted within the prohibited degrees of relationship (consanguinity and affinity). See the Marriage Act 1835 (5 & 6 Wm. IV, c.54). Notably, however, in a recent decision, these measures were successfully challenged as infringing the right to marry. See Carolan, 'Couple fight for the right to be married' *Irish Times*, 26 May 2006 p. 4 and 'Woman can marry ex-spouse's brother', *Irish Times*, 18 October 2006 (*O'Shea v. Ireland, Irish Times Law Rep.*, 6 Nov. 2006). In that case, a divorced woman sued for the right to marry her former husband's brother, a marriage precluded by the Deceased Wife's Sister's Marriage Act 1907 and the Deceased Brother's Widow's Marriage Act 1921. Laffoy J ruled that the ban on marriage infringed the constitutional right to marry, there being no rational basis for such restrictions. (See also Maddock, 'Marriage to dead aunt's husband is valid', *Irish Independent*, 28 June 2001.)   **68** Constitution of Ireland, 1937, Article 41.3.2, and Family Law (Divorce) Act, 1996, s. 5. Technically the parties must have lived apart for four of the five years immediately preceding the commencement of divorce proceedings, there must be no reasonable prospect of reconciliation, and proper provision must be made for both spouses and for the children.   **69** 'Living apart' requires both a physical and a mental element of separation. A couple may live together even if they are not living in the same house: *Santos v. Santos* [1972] 2 All E.R. 246, *Pulford v. Pulford* [1923] P. 18. Correspondingly, a couple may be deemed to be living apart even if they are living under the same roof provided they are not sharing a

to divorce and remarry. A party might also complain that although she is willing to marry, her partner is not, thus posing a unilateral barrier to marriage. This difficulty, however, is not one for which legislators can bear any responsibility – the parties are still free to marry. The fact that one of the parties does not wish to do so is a matter for the parties themselves.

It is arguable, indeed, that non-marital couples of the same sex and those of the opposite sex are fundamentally different in several crucial respects. The first point – already noted above – centres on the radically different socio-cultural situations of same-sex and opposite-sex couples respectively. Arguably, the position of same-sex couples needs more urgently to be addressed because of the endemic experience of sub-ordination based on sexual orientation. While the sub-ordination of opposite-sex cohabitants is undoubtedly a point of concern that requires legal redress, the situation results solely from a choice as to legal status. By contrast, the experience of same-sex couples implicates a fundamental feature of human personality, namely sexual orientation. As such, while attempts to equate the difficulties faced by same-sex and opposite sex cohabitants are valid in certain respects, such an approach serves essentially to gloss important experiential differences.

An allied point of relevance is the ban on same-sex marriage. Many discussions and debates around non-marital couples, indeed, appear to proceed in ignorance of this 'elephant in the room'. Although marriage is not defined in the Constitution, both the Legislature and the Courts have concluded that marriage is a union of one man and one woman respectively. As far back as 1866, the Courts denoted that marriage was exclusively a heterosexual union,[70] a point underlined in several *dicta* from both the British[71] and Irish courts.[72] Although Irish legislation until very recently was silent on the point, the Civil Registration Act, 2004 (section 2(2)(e)) explicitly forecloses the option of civil marriage between two persons of the same sex.

---

household, and lives, in common: Judicial Separation Act, 1989 s. 2(3). See *Naylor v. Naylor*, [1961] 2 All E.R. 129; *Hopes v. Hopes* [1948] 2 All E.R. 920; *Fuller v. Fuller*, [1973] 2 All E.R. 650; *Holmes v. Mitchell* [1991] Simon's Tax Cases 25; *Smith v. Smith* [1939] 4 All E.R. 533; and *Bartram v. Bartram* [1949] 2 All E.R. 270. But cf. *Mouncer v. Mouncer* [1972] 1 All E.R. 289; *M. McA. v. X.McA.* [2000] 2 ILRM 48; see also Binchy (2000) 22 *DULJ* 216.   **70** *Hyde v. Hyde and Woodmansee* (1866) LR 1 PD 30 at 33.   **71** In *Talbot v. Talbot* 111 Sol. J. 213 (1967), for instance, the English and Welsh High Court declared that a marriage between two women (one being unaware of the true gender of her spouse) was void by reason of identity of sex. In *Corbett v. Corbett*, [1971] P. 83, moreover, the same court concluded that a marriage between a man and a post-operative male-to-female transsexual was void, on the basis that both parties were, in law, male.   **72** In *Murphy v. Attorney General*, [1982] IR 241, the Supreme Court suggested that marriage is the '… permanent indissoluble union of man and woman'. Likewise, in *B. v. R.*, [1995] 1 ILRM 491, Costello P observed that marriage in Irish law was 'the voluntary and permanent union of one man and one woman to the exclusion of all others for life' (ibid., 495) McKechnie J concurred in *Foy v. An tArd Chláraitheoir* [2002] IEHC 116 (9 July 2002), concluding that two persons of the same biological sex did not enjoy a constitutional right to

The Constitution, at first glance, is more equivocal on this point. Although marriage is accorded preferential status under Article 41.3, and deemed definitively (and exclusively) to be the foundation of family life in Ireland, nowhere in the Constitution is marriage expressly defined. Nevertheless, in its recent decision in *Zappone and Gilligan v. Revenue Commissioners*[73], the High Court concluded that for the time being, the term 'marriage' as used in the Constitution denotes only a marriage of persons of the opposite sex. As such, the Court concluded, there was no constitutional right either to marry a person of the same sex or to require recognition in Ireland of same-sex marriages celebrated abroad.

The plaintiffs in this case, a lesbian couple who had entered into a marriage in Canada, claimed that for the purpose of tax legislation they were entitled, under the Constitution, to be treated as a married couple. Although the couple accepted from the outset that the Constitution, as originally enacted, was not intended to embrace same-sex marriage, they argued that the Constitution was a 'living document'.[74] As such, ' ... by reason of the existence of a changing consensus', an 'updating construction' should be adopted favouring the inclusion of a right to marry a person of the same sex.

In rejecting this claim, Dunne J. observed first that '[m]arriage was understood under the 1937 Constitution to be confined to persons of the opposite sex.' Far from being 'some kind of fossilised understanding of marriage', Dunne J. noted that the ban on same-sex marriage had been affirmed in several recent judgments of the Courts.[75]

There was, moreover, insufficient evidence of any 'emerging consensus' to uproot the view that marriage as understood in the Constitution was thus confined. While acknowledging some limited support internationally for an alteration of the traditional understanding of marriage, she observed that ' ... in truth, it is difficult to see that as a consensus, changing or otherwise.' In fact, the legislative view that marriage is exclusively a heterosexual institution was confirmed, she added, as recently as 2004.[76]

Though expressing the hope that legislative changes granting recognition to same-sex couples ' ... will not be long in coming', the Judge ultimately

---

marry. See also Murray J in *T. v. T.* [2002] IESC 68 (14 October 2002) at para. 165: 'Nonetheless, marriage itself remains a solemn contract of partnership entered into between man and woman with a special status recognised by the Constitution.' **73** Unreported, High Court, Dunne J, 14 December 2006. **74** See O'Higgins CJ in *State (Healy) v. Donoghue* [1976] IR 325 at p. 347, Walsh J in *McGee v. Attorney General* [1974] IR 284 and McCarthy J in *Norris v. Attorney General* [1984] IR 36 at 96. See also the decision of the Privy Council in *Edwards v. Attorney General for Canada* [1930] A.C. 124 favouring an updating construction of the British North America Act 1867. **75** Such as *Murray v. Ireland,* [1985] IR 532, pp 535–536, *B v. R* [1995] 1 ILRM 491, *T.F. v. Ireland,* [1995] 1 IR 321 at p. 373, *T. v. T.,* [2003] ILRM 321, *Foy v. An t-Árd Chláraitheoir & Ors.,* [2002] IEHC 116 (9 July 2002). **76** Section 2(2)(e) Civil Registration Act 2004.

signaled that '… it is for the legislature to determine the extent to which such changes should be made.' Relying on the decision of the English and Welsh High Court in *Wilkinson v. Kitzenger*[77] Dunne J. further concluded that a failure to afford a right to marry a person of the same sex was not contrary to the European Convention on Human Rights. The case is, at the time of writing being appealed to the Supreme Court.

The decision in *Zappone*, though disappointing, is hard to fault from a strictly legal perspective. Indeed, given the overall tenor of the Constitution, the decision could hardly be characterized as surprising or unorthodox. The constitutional references to the position of marriage in Article 41 must be viewed in the overall context of the Constitution, a document that remains decidedly conservative and confessional. The Constitution, after all, begins with a reference to the 'Most Holy Trinity' followed by an acknowledgment of 'our obligations to our Divine Lord Jesus Christ'.[78] God is directly invoked in Article 6, all powers of government being designated as deriving 'under God, from the people' a formula that while affirming popular sovereignty, propounds that this sovereignty is enjoyed only as a result of the munificence of a higher power. Even the clauses protecting religious freedom directly acknowledge that 'homage of public worship is due to Almighty God' the state pledging 'to hold His Name in reverence' and 'to respect and honour religion'.[79] The Family provisions of the Constitution, moreover, owe their origins directly to Roman Catholic encyclicals on the family, as do the provisions on private property and the Directives of Social Policy.[80]

None of this necessarily precluded a result that favoured same-sex marriage. As the decision in *McGee v. Attorney General*[81] ably demonstrates, the Constitution is open to an 'updating' construction,[82] even if this involves a departure from Roman Catholic teaching. Drawing in part on natural rights theories that in themselves form an integral part of Roman Catholic theological heritage, the court in *McGee* struck down a law that precluded, *inter alia*, the importation of contraceptive devices.[83] Despite the Catholic Church's relatively consistent opposition to artificial methods of contraception,[84] the Supreme Court found that a married couple enjoyed a freedom

77 [2006] EWHC 2022. 78 Constitution of Ireland, 1937, Preamble. Indeed, in *Quinn's Supermarket v. Attorney General* [1972] IR 1, Walsh J cites the Preamble as evidence of the 'firm conviction that we are a religious people'. Later he observed, more explicitly that 'the Preamble acknowledges that we are a Christian people'. 79 Constitution of Ireland, 1937, Article 44.1. 80 See Whyte, *Church and State in modern Ireland*, 2nd ed. (Dublin, 1980). The property rights provisions, in particular, bear the hallmark of papal teaching: see Pope Pius XI, *Quadragesimo Anno* (1931). 81 [1974] IR 284. 82 See for instance the comments of Walsh J in *McGee v. Attorney General* [1974] IR 284 favouring a dynamic approach to constitutional interpretation. A similar line is taken by O'Higgins CJ in *State (Healy) v. O'Donoghue* [1976] IR 325. 83 Criminal Law (Amendment) Act, 1935 s. 17. 84 See Pope Paul VI, *Humanae Vitae* (25 July 1968) and Pope John Paul II, *Evangelium Vitae* (1995).

to choose whether or not to have children, and to realize this choice through the use of artificial contraception, or otherwise, as they saw fit.

On other occasions, however, the confessional nature of the Constitution has led to decidedly more traditionalist conclusions, in particular in *Norris v. Attorney General*,[85] where the christian churches' traditional opposition to homosexuality weighed heavily in the court's mind.[86] In the course of his judgment upholding laws that banned sexual activity between males,[87] O'Higgins CJ noted that '[h]omosexuality has always been condemned in Christian teaching as being morally wrong'.[88] As such, he concluded, a Constitution that affirmed, in such strong terms, a commitment to Christianity could not be interpreted as precluding the enforcement of a law that fully accorded with a great weight of Christian tradition:

> The preamble to the Constitution proudly asserts the existence of God in the Most Holy Trinity and recites that the people of Ireland humbly acknowledge their obligation to 'our Divine Lord, Jesus Christ.' It cannot be doubted that the people, so asserting and acknowledging their obligations to our Divine Lord Jesus Christ, were proclaiming a deep religious conviction and faith and an intention to adopt a Constitution consistent with that conviction and faith and with Christian beliefs.[89]

This being the case, the Chief Justice continued, it was inconceivable to believe that 'the people rendered inoperative laws which had existed for hundreds of years prohibiting unnatural sexual conduct which Christian teaching held to be gravely sinful'.[90]

> When one considers that the conduct in question had been condemned consistently in the name of Christ for almost two thousand years and, at the time of the enactment of the Constitution, was prohibited as criminal by the laws in force in England, Wales, Scotland and Northern Ireland, the suggestion becomes more incomprehensible and difficult of acceptance.[91]

While the passage of time may have blunted the full currency of such an approach, the prospect of a constitutional verdict in favour of same-sex marriage remained highly unlikely in the face of such a precedent.

---

85 [1984] IR 36.   86 See also *Maguire v. Attorney General* [1943] IR 238 and *Attorney General (SPUC) v. Open Door Counselling Ltd.* [1988] IR 593.   87 Specifically the offence of buggery under the Offences against the Person Act 1861, ss. 61 and 62, and the offence of gross indecency between males under the Criminal Law (Amendment) Act 1885, s. 11.   88 Ibid., at p. 63.   89 Ibid., at p 64.   90 Ibid.   91 Ibid.

Notwithstanding the failure to define marriage for constitutional purposes, the chances that a court would have taken an expansive approach – in the face of express legislative opposition to same-sex marriage – were slim. An originalist interpretation, if adopted, would undoubtedly have precluded such a conclusion.[92] Likewise, given the overall tenor of the Constitution, an approach that sought a harmonious interpretation of constitutional provisions would also have been unlikely to yield a result favourable to same-sex marriage. In the absence of any firm consensus for change – the matter remains highly controversial even in states that have adopted same-sex marriage – the prospects for recognition were slight.

That said, while *Zappone* confirms the view that the Constitution does not mandate same-sex marriage, it remains somewhat unclear whether it entirely excludes the prospect of legislative reform in favour of this option. The All-Party Oireachtas Committee on the Constitution, took the view that introducing same-sex marriage would indeed require a constitutional amendment. The Working Group on Domestic Partnership seems to have taken a similar stance.[93] It is indeed arguable that if *Zappone* is upheld, and marriage as understood in the Constitution deemed to denote solely a marriage between persons of the opposite sex, an attempt to extend marriage to persons of the same sex would probably require constitutional change. The otherwise likely conclusion is that measures establishing a right to same-sex marriage would run counter to the constitutional requirement to protect the privileged status of marriage as it is understood in the Constitution – namely *heterosexual* marriage. It may ultimately be the case that further judicial clarification will be needed.

Equalising outcomes: a reasonable alternative?

An alternative approach that may yet find favour would involve setting aside for the time being the laudable goal of same-sex marriage in favour of an approach that seeks to equalize the position of same-sex couples by reference to substantive outcomes. In other words, while marriage would remain confined to opposite sex couples, same-sex couples would, by means of an alternative civil partnership scheme, be afforded substantially similar legal outcomes. In effect, this is the approach that has found favour in the United Kingdom. The Civil Partnership Act 2004 introduced in the UK a scheme of formal registration that – while distinct from marriage – substantially replicates for same-sex couples the consequences of a legal marriage.[94] In

---

92 Though for an interesting critique of the difficulties involved in seeking out and relying upon original understandings see Doyle, *Constitutional equality law* (Dublin, 2005) chapter 3, pp 51–66.   93 Working Group on Domestic Partnership, *Options Paper* (Dublin: Department of Justice, Equality and Law Reform, 2006) at 7.20.1.   94 See Department of Trade and Industry, *Civil partnership: a framework for the legal recognition of same-sex couples* (London,

short, while the title may differ, the legal effects are substantially the same. The Act, indeed, is explicitly confined to same-sex couples, the UK Government arguing that heterosexual couples already enjoyed access to a similar scheme, namely marriage.

For same-sex couples, this approach affords an opportunity to access most of the substantial legal protections arising on marriage in a manner that largely sidesteps the ideological and religious controversy around same-sex marriage. It also arguably offers scope for the development of norms that address queer theoretical and feminist concerns regarding the oppressive potential of marriage. Yet in one fundamental respect the equality of outcomes approach falls short. As the present author has observed elsewhere,

> if it is impermissible to distinguish between same-sex and opposite-sex couples, how can it be appropriate to have two similar yet distinct systems for the civil recognition of these two like categories? As the US Supreme Court observed in *Brown v. Board of Education of Topeka*, 347 US 483 (1954), 'separate but equal' policies necessarily imply that the State does not really think that the subjects of the differentiation are alike.[95]

Indeed, this very difficulty has propelled one Californian judge to conclude that the ban on same-sex marriage in that state infringes the guarantee of equality.[96] In concluding that '… [n]o rational basis exists for limiting marriage … to opposite sex partners'[97] Kramer J. drew a compelling parallel between the anti-miscegenation statutes, banning inter-racial marriage, struck down by the US Supreme Court in *Loving v. Virginia*[98], and laws that banned same-sex marriage.

The only feasible argument that precludes a similar conclusion in respect of same-sex couples is that one of the purposes of marriage is procreation. Yet even this seemingly watertight argument, on closer examination, falls short. After all, a marriage will not be invalid on the basis that the parties cannot or do not wish to procreate.[99] Although a marriage may be voidable if unconsummated, a marriage cannot be avoided on grounds of infertility alone. Correspondingly, as the current extra-marital birth rate ably demonstrates,[1] one

---

2003) and Stonewall, *Get hitched* (London, 2004).   **95** Ryan, 'Casenote – *Ghaidan v. Godin-Mendoza*' (2005) 27:3 *Journal of Social Welfare and Family Law* 355 at 367–8. Cf. the 'separate but equal' doctrine posited in *Plessy v. Ferguson* 163 US 537 (1869). The case affirmed the constitutionality of providing racially segregated facilities, a decision subsequently reversed in *Brown*.   **96** *New York Times*, 15 March 2005.   **97** Ibid.   **98** 388 US 1 (1967).   **99** *Baxter v. Baxter* [1947] 2 All E.R. 886. See also *L. v. L. (orse. D.)* (1922) 38 T.L.R. 697 and Lord Stair's *Institutions* (1832) I tit 4, para. 6. See *M.M. (orse. G.) v. P.M.* [1986] ILRM 515.   **1** Indeed, while birth rates have generally slumped in recent decades, almost one-third of children born in Ireland between 1999 and 2005 were born outside marriage. This represents a ten-fold increase on the 1972 figure of three per cent. See, generally, the annual CSO, *Vital Statistics*

does need to be married to have children. As Lord Jowitt LC quite bluntly put it in *Baxter v. Baxter*:[2]

> [i]t is indisputable that the institution of marriage is not necessary for the procreation of children, nor does it appear to be the principal end of marriage as understood in Christendom.[3]

THE IMPETUS FOR REFORM

In a lecture delivered just over fifty years ago in Trinity College, Dublin,[4] Dr A.L. Goodhart, then Master of University College, Oxford, set forth in strong terms the need to ensure the relevance of the law to the lives of those governed thereby:

> The law must, as far as possible, mirror contemporary civilization and as that changes so must the law. If the law becomes too rigid and inflexible, then there is always the danger that it will be in conflict with the needs of the people, with all the unfortunate consequences to which such a conflict may give rise.[5]

'This is particularly true,' he continued, '… during the dynamic periods of history … for it then becomes essential for the legal system to adjust itself to the novel conditions of social life'.[6]

In this specific context, the 'novel conditions of social life' involve the incremental growth in the number and visibility of households not based on a marital union.[7] The 2002 census of population marked a watershed in this regard. The census enumerated 77,616 couples cohabiting outside of marriage, 8.4 per cent of all households in the state, 29,709 of them with one or more children.[8] This represented an increase of 31,300 on the figure for 1996. Indeed, while birth rates have generally slumped in recent decades, almost one-third of children born in Ireland between 1999 and 2004 were born outside marriage.[9] The census also specifically enumerated 1,300 same-sex cohabiting couples, an almost ten-fold increase on the 1996 figure of 150. The 2006 census, moreover, marked a further increase in the number and proportion of cohabiting couples, to just over 120,000 family units, 11.56% of all family units in the state.

(Central Statistics Office, Dublin, various years).   2 Ibid.   3 Ibid., at 890. See also Veitch, 'The essence of marriage – a comment on the homosexual challenge' (1976) 5 *Anglo-American Law Review* 41.   4 Goodhart, *Law reform – judicial and legislative* (11 May 1954), (Dublin, 1954).   5 Ibid., p.4.   6 Ibid.   7 On changes in the profile of the family generally see Fahy and Russell, op. cit., n.5, and Kennedy, *Cottage to crèche–family change in Ireland* (Dublin, 2004). 8 See *Census 2002, Volume 3, Household Composition and Family Status* (Dublin, 2004). Corresponding figures from the 2006 census have yet to be published.   9 This represents a

Thus, Archbold (referring in this case to family diversity in Northern Ireland) observes that:

> Marriage is no longer the only, or even the preferred life choice for enormous numbers of people … and if our legal system ignores these trends, it risks becoming irrelevant, and worse, providing no protection to people who may be in great need of it.[10]

Indeed, in Family Law generally, the centrality of the married state is gradually receding. Dewar notes that over the course of the last fifty years, the relationship of parent and child has replaced the relationship of husband and wife as the axis around which family law revolves.[11] O'Halloran too underlines the diminishing juridical significance of marriage, noting how:

> Marriage, marital status and the reciprocal obligations of spouses are no longer viewed as defining characteristics of Family law, integrating its parts and essential to its overall coherence. Whether or not the parents are married is, increasingly, beside the point.[12]

Although it is tempting to see these trends as evidence of a decline in the fortunes of the institution of marriage, the picture is in fact more complex.[13] Marriage remains quite a popular option in Ireland; since 1995, the marriage rate has actually increased from 4.3 per thousand of the population to 5.0 in 2005.[14] Indeed the figure for 2004 (5.1) is only marginally below the corresponding figure for 1951 (5.4) and above that for 1937 (5.0). While mass emigration in part kept marriage rates in check in the early part of the century, the 1960s and 1970s saw marriage rates (and correspondingly birth

ten-fold increase on the 1972 figure of three per cent. See, generally, the annual CSO, *Vital Statistics* (Central Statistics Office, Dublin, various years).   10 Archbold, 'Divorce – the View from the North' in Shannon (ed.), *The Divorce Act in practice* (Dublin, 1999) at p. 50.   11 Dewar, 'Policy issues in law and the family', in Wilson (ed.), *Frontiers of legal scholarship*, (Chichester, 1995), chapter 5, at pp 64–7.   12 O'Halloran, *Family law in Northern Ireland* (Dublin, 1997) at p. 3. 13 In September 2003, the *Economist* magazine reported that Ireland had the lowest marriage rate in the world. At '2.1 marriages per thousand of the population', Ireland apparently ranked, according to the *Economist*, worst in the world in the nuptial stakes, a shocking revelation sending media analysts and politicians into a something of a tailspin. Former Taoiseach, John Bruton, decrying the results, called on the Government to establish a Commission for Marriage to address the apparent decline: 'If marriage is in decline, the longterm social effects of this in Ireland are unknowable, but it is likely that they will be dramatic. The irreversible depletion of this form of social capital is not something that the Government should be indifferent to' (Fine Gael Press release, 'Ireland has lowest marriage rate in world – response from former Taoiseach', 25 September 2003). The report, however, was wrong. The normally erudite, informed and accurate *Economist* had based its figures on the number of marriages celebrated only in the first quarter of 2002. In fact, the marriage rate for 2002 as a whole stood at a respectable 5.1 per thousand, and the figures for 2003 at a similar and steady 5.1. In fact, marriage rates have been steadily climbing since 1997.   14 See www.cso.ie/ statistics/bthsdthsmarriages.htm (consulted 28 June 2006).

rates) rise to record levels. These figures tapered off in the 1980s and 1990s, but have risen again in the last ten years, plateauing at a respectable figure.

There is certainly some evidence that many cohabiting couples are delaying rather than eschewing marriage as an option – the increase in the average age of marriage for both women and men provides some support for this proposition.[15] In sum, these couples see no tension between an aspiration to marriage and an intention to cohabit. Nevertheless, a considerable diversification of family life is evident. Since 1998 at least, the rate of extra-and non-marital births has averaged over 30 per cent, a ten-fold increase on the figure for 1973.[16] Increases in marital breakdown and the introduction of divorce have led to more 'blended' and step-families, while same-sex couples make up a small but (it appears) rapidly increasing proportion of family units.

International developments have also added to the domestic impetus for reform in Ireland. In the past decade, a preponderance of EU states have introduced measures permitting the formalization of relationships outside of marriage.[17] In most cases, such measures have been confined to partners of the same sex, though some schemes have not been so confined.[18] Beginning with Denmark in 1989, a large number of western European States, as well as some notable new accession states, have introduced a variety of 'marriage-like' measures extending to unmarried couples many, and in some cases the vast majority of rights and obligations previously confined to marriage. Others have taken a step further by abolishing the identity of sex rule for marital purposes, thus permitting persons of the same sex to marry, under legislation that applies equally to opposite-sex and same-sex couples.

In this regard, the Netherlands led the way, introducing in 2001 a legislative amendment to its civil code stipulating that 'A marriage can be contracted by two persons of different sex or of the same sex'.[19] The comparatively more conservative states of Belgium and Spain followed suit in 2003 and 2005 respectively, introducing legislation permitting same-sex marriage on largely the same basis as applied to opposite-sex couples. Same-sex marriage is also a legal reality in Canada[20] and South Africa[21], with the highest court in Massachusetts also having ruled in favour of the civil right to marry, regardless of the respective genders of the parties.[22]

---

15 See *Marriages 2005* (Central Statistics Office, Dublin, 2006), indicating that the average age of marriage in 2005 was 33.1 for men and 31 for women, representing an increase of just over four years on the average figure for 1990.   16 See, generally, the annual CSO, *Vital Statistics* (Dublin, various years).   17 For further details see Appendix 1, 'Relationship recognition in European Union jurisdictions' in Walsh and Ryan, *The rights of de facto couples* at pp 139–41. 18 Belgium, Luxembourg, Netherlands and Portugal have extended civil partnership without distinction, to same-sex and opposite-sex couples alike.   19 Article 30(1), Book 1, Netherlands Civil Code, (September, 2000).   20 In June 2005, the Canadian Parliament enacted Bill C-38 permitting same-sex marriage throughout Canada.   21 *Fourie and Bonthuys v. Minister for Home Affairs* (Supreme Court of Appeal, 30 November 2004).   22 *Goodridge v. Massachusetts* (S. Court of Mass., 18 November 2003).

Yet perhaps the most significant international development of relevance in this context arose because of legal reform north of the border, in Northern Ireland. In December 2005, the UK's Civil Partnership Act 2004 came into force, permitting same-sex couples to enter into a civil partnership bearing most of the hallmarks of marriage.[23] Although technically distinct from marriage, the rights and duties attendant upon civil partnership differ only marginally from those that apply to married couples. By a quirk of bureaucratic fate, the first (full-notice) civil partnerships took place in comparatively conservative Northern Ireland, an event that brought into stark relief the absence of similar legislation in the Republic. This was not merely a cosmetic concern for politicians in the South. (Though some, no doubt, must have been embarrassed that certain minorities at least were better treated in Northern Ireland than in Ireland.) The Republic had after all, agreed, as part of the Good Friday Agreement of 1998, that human rights protections south of the border would be enhanced so that residents in the Republic would enjoy 'at least an equivalent level of protection of human rights as will pertain in Northern Ireland'.[24]

The Good Friday Agreement itself, of course, did not mandate civil partnership reform in either jurisdiction. Nonetheless, once measures had been taken in one jurisdiction, the equivalence requirement made the argument for reform in the other jurisdiction all the more compelling. On the basis of this requirement, Ó Cinnéide[25] concludes that the introduction of civil partnership legislation in Northern Ireland requires a similar (though not necessarily identical) response south of the Border:

> [T]he legislative recognition of the right to equality of treatment ... in Northern Ireland for transsexual people and lesbian and gay couples does appear to largely come within the scope of the equivalence requirement.[26]

Although the state is not obliged to replicate precisely all Northern Irish legislation, Ó Cinnéide notes that as the UK legislation constituted a response to unequal treatment of same-sex couples, designed to redress an imbalance in human rights protections for people who are gay and lesbian, Ireland was 'obliged under the equivalence requirement to introduce an equivalence of rights as introduced in Northern Ireland.'[27]

Ó Cinnéide further advises the state against the introduction of what he terms 'a watered-down version of the UK partnership legislation that will

---

23 It appears that it would also be possible to effect such a partnership in the British Embassy in Dublin, this being British territory.   24 *Agreement reached in the Multi-Party Negotiations* (Cm. 3883, 1998); 37 ILM 751 (1998), clause 9.   25 Ó Cinnéide, *Equivalence in promoting equality: the implications of the Multi-Party Agreement for the Further Development of Equality Measures for Northern Ireland and Ireland* (Dublin and Belfast, 2005).   26 Ibid., at 49.   27 Ibid.

inevitably have to be adjusted as the Strasbourg jurisprudence rapidly evolves in this area'.[28] This theme is further explored in Walsh and Ryan, *The Rights of De Facto Couples*, a report commissioned by the Irish Human Rights Commission.[29] The Report (of which the current author was co-author) highlights significant disparities between Irish law and international human rights standards as they apply to the family life of non-marital couples. In particular, the report addresses the gap between the legal protection provided to non-marital families in Ireland, and the requirements of the European Convention on Human Rights, which was recently incorporated into Irish domestic law as a result of the European Convention on Human Rights Act 2003. By contrast with the provisions of the Irish Constitution, Article 8 of the Convention (guaranteeing the right to a private and family life, home and correspondence) extends in its application to family units outside of marriage, including lone parents and their children[30] and non-marital couples.[31] Although the European Court of Human Rights initially proved reluctant to extend recognition to same-sex couples, the decisions in *Da Silva Mouta v. Portugal*[32] and *Karner v. Austria*[33] suggest that this exclusionary approach has been abandoned. *Da Silva Mouta* appears generally to preclude sexual orientation discrimination in the context of family life,[34] while *Karner* asserts an equal right to respect for the home life of same-sex couples.[35]

Indeed, insofar as same-sex couples are concerned, these decisions establish a principle of considerable significance, namely that in the application of the right to respect for one's private life, family life and home life, as required by Article 8 of the Convention, discrimination based on sexual orientation is proscribed. The Court has acknowledged that states continue to enjoy a margin of appreciation in relation to measures that privilege marriage over non-marital unions. Nonetheless, where non-marital couples are afforded legal protection, *Karner* in particular firmly establishes that measures that serve to distinguish between non-marital couples of the opposite-sex and of the same-sex respectively (such as the provisions of the Domestic Violence Act, the Civil Liability (Amendment) Act and the Residential Tenancies Act noted above) infringe Article 14 of the Convention, in that they discriminate between couples in relation to the respect accorded to the home life of same-sex couples. *Da Silva Mouta* suggests a similar conclusion in relation to the family life provisions of Article 8.

28 Ibid.   29 Walsh and Ryan, *The rights of de facto couples*.   30 *Marckx v. Belgium* (1979) 2 EHRR 330, *Keegan v. Ireland* (1994) 18 EHRR 342.   31 *Johnston v. Ireland* (1987) 9 EHRR 203.   32 [2001] 1 FLR 653, (1999) 31 EHRR 47.   33 Application no. 40016/98, 24 July 2003. 34 In *Da Silva Mouta* the European Court of Human Rights concluded that it was impermissible to refuse to grant custody to a father solely on the basis of his sexual orientation (the father being gay).   35 In *Karner* the Court concluded that the exclusion of same-sex couples from tenancy protections extended to opposite-sex couples outside of marriage infringed Article 14 in that it discriminated against same-sex couples in relation to the right to

Thus Walsh and Ryan conclude that to the extent that Irish legislative measures continue to favour non-marital couples of the opposite sex to the exclusion of same-sex couples, such measures infringe the terms of the Convention and must be reformed. Of course, even if such discriminatory measures were to be reformed, an obvious lacuna would remain. In the main, opposite sex couples may marry; same-sex couples may not. To date, the highest courts in Canada and South Africa, as well as those in Massachusetts, have taken the view that such treatment infringes the human rights standards set out in the respective constitutions of those jurisdictions. Nonetheless, international human rights standards do not, as things currently stand, require Ireland to introduce same-sex marriage. That said, as Walsh and Ryan note, the failure to extend marriage rights to same-sex partners, *when coupled with* a stance that reserves most rights and obligations to married couples alone, and most of the remainder to unmarried opposite-sex couples only, may in itself constitute a breach of international human rights standards:

> failure to accord *de facto* couples rights equivalent to those enjoyed by married couples implicates indirect discrimination on the basis of sexual orientation. Because same-sex partners are not entitled to marry each other, such couples are denied a variety of rights, privileges and duties that may in fact be accessed by heterosexual couples.[36]

Whilst acknowledging that this conclusion is tentative, the authors nonetheless point to a growing trend towards the proscription of sexual orientation discrimination, as well as the gradually shrinking margin of appreciation in favour of states that opt to preserve special treatment of the traditional family. The growth in the number of European states opting for civil partnership schemes is undoubtedly a factor of further relevance, a trend that may ultimately diminish the margin of appreciation afforded to states like Ireland. The approach of the European Court of Human Rights in *Goodwin v. United Kingdom*[37] is notable in this regard: the court's reversal in that case of previous jurisprudence on the legal recognition of gender reassignment was justified in part by the fact that the vast majority of convention parties (all but four) already recognized gender reassignment.

Official policy responses

A number of policy documents have, to varying degrees, added impetus to calls for the amelioration the position of non-marital partners.

---

respect for the home life of gay residents. **36** Walsh and Ryan, op. cit. at p. 130. **37** Application 28957/95, July 11, 2002. See the discussion in Ryan, 'Marriage at the boundaries of gender:

First out of the blocks was the Equality Authority in 2001. In its robust and wide-ranging report *Implementing Equality for Lesbians, Gays and Bisexuals*,[38] the Authority advised that a variety of laws and practices should be altered with a view to enhancing the position of same-sex couples. In doing so, it drew upon a report by Mee and Ronayne that it had commissioned, *The Partnership Rights of Same-Sex Couples*,[39] which had exposed significant deficiencies in the protections afforded to persons in same-sex relationships.

Partnership rights are foregrounded in Chapter 3 of the former report, the Authority noting that

> [t]he relative invisibility of lesbian, gay and bisexual people is perhaps most marked in the absence of official, statutory and legislative recognition of same-sex relationships. Few of the rights, responsibilities, commitments and benefits assigned to married heterosexuals are available to same-sex couples and only a few are enjoyed by non-marital heterosexuals.[40]

In this regard, the Authority directly addresses the issue of same-sex marriage, observing that the absence of a facility for marriage places gays and lesbians in a particularly vulnerable position.

In its response, the Authority propounded three core principles that, it asserted, should inform state policy:[41]

(1) Diversity – the Authority suggested that 'a legal framework should encompass a range of different kinds of partnerships for which couples or households should opt'.[42] In doing so, the Authority was clearly leaning against a one-size-fits-all, all-or-nothing stance in favour of offering a more multi-faceted range of options that would accord greater legal choice to families and households.

(2) Equality – Equality, the Authority advises, 'should be the core principle underlying any process of reform ...'[43] The Authority argued that '[r]ights and responsibilities currently conferred on married heterosexual couples in relation to pensions, residency, property, adoption, taxation and welfare entitlements ... should be equally conferred on lesbian and gay couples as well as heterosexual unmarried couples'.[44]

(3) Accessibility – the Authority asserts that 'all sections of the community' should have access to equal financial, property, inheritance

the "transsexual dilemma" resolved?' (2004) 1 *Irish Journal of Family Law* 15.   **38** Dublin: Equality Authority, 2001.   **39** Dublin: Equality Authority, 2000.   **40** *Implementing equality for lesbians, gays and bisexuals*, (Dublin, 2001) at p. 20.   **41** Ibid., pp 28–30.   **42** Ibid., at p. 28.   **43** Ibid.   **44** Ibid.

and social rights' by means that are 'simple, clear and comprehensible'.[45]

In addition, the Authority recommended a wide-ranging variety of specific reforms – for instance, in relation to taxation, immigration, domestic violence, property rights, succession rights, medical care and pensions – designed to eliminate discrimination against same-sex couples.[46] The Report is notable in that it addresses not only the need for legal and legislative reform but also for the adoption of best practice in relation to a range of administrative practices.

Building on the Authority's report, the National Economic and Social Forum in its report *Equality Policies for Lesbian, Gay and Bisexual People: Implementation Issues* proposed a range of reforms ameliorating the partnership rights of same-sex couples. The Forum focused particularly on affording rights of nomination, suggesting that same-sex partners should, for instance, have the right to nominate a partner as next-of-kin for medical purposes, as the successor to a pension or estate and as a co-parent or guardian of a child. The Forum furthermore recommended the extension of recognition for immigration purposes, thus permitting non-EU nationals to reside in Ireland with legally resident same-sex partners.

The recommendations of the Law Reform Commission are also worthy of note. Though its 2004 Consultation Paper[47] adopted a somewhat more cautious approach, the Commission's 2006 Report on *The Rights and Duties of Cohabitants*[48] recommended the introduction of a 'presumptive scheme' extending certain financial and proprietary remedies to 'qualified cohabitants'. For this purpose, a 'qualified cohabitant' is defined as a person cohabiting with another unrelated person in an intimate relationship, the qualifying period being two years where the parties have children, and three where the parties have none. Although this formula may militate in practice in favour of opposite-sex couples, (who are more likely to have children than same-sex partners) the Commission notably rejects any formal differentiation between gay and straight couples. In particular, the Commission recommends the extension to same-sex couples of measures currently confined to unmarried opposite-sex cohabitants, including the Civil Liability Act, 1961, the Domestic Violence Act, 1996 and the Residential Tenancies Act, 2004 as well as social welfare legislation. Similarly laudable reforms are suggested in

---

45 Ibid., at p. 29.   **46** In a similar vein, see the very robust recommendations of the Irish Council for Civil Liberties in *Equality for All Families* (Dublin, 2006).   **47** Law Reform Commission, *The Rights and Duties of Cohabitees*, LRC–32–2004 (Dublin: Law Reform Commission, 2004). On which, see further Ryan, 'Editorial', [2005] 1 *Irish Journal of Family Law* 2.   **48** Law Reform Commission, *The Rights and Duties of Cohabitants*, LRC–82–2006 (Dublin: Law Reform Commission, 2006).

relation to public service pension reform, the Commission recommending that qualified cohabitants be entitled to nominate partners as beneficiaries of a survivor's pension.

The Commission initially had opted, in its Consultation Paper, to exclude from the definition of 'qualified cohabitant' partners either of whom were already party to a valid subsisting marriage. Thus, a person would not have been treated as a 'qualified cohabitant' unless he or she was simultaneously free to marry.[49] In its final Report, however, the Commission relented on this stance, holding that those who were already married should also be entitled to redress as cohabitants, subject to the condition that the rights of any existing or former spouse would have to be fully taken into account in such cases.[50] This welcome change obviated the prospect of a great number of second unions following marital breakdown being excluded entirely from the suggested scheme, a situation that would have been made all the more invidious by the lengthy period of separation required as a prerequisite to divorce.[51] Indeed, where the parties are not free to marry, the case for civil recognition is arguably not weaker but decidedly stronger than might otherwise be the case. Unmarried cohabitants at least generally have a choice to get married; those still party to a pre-existing marriage do not.

The Commission, in its recommendations, appears to envisage the future introduction of civil partnership legislation extending rights to intimate partners on registration of their relationship. The Report however is confined in its application only to persons who do not marry each other or enter into a registered partnership (if and when such a facility becomes available) – in other words, it posits a presumptive scheme that will apply to persons who decline to marry or otherwise register their relationship.

In respect of such persons, the Commission recommends a two-pronged approach, the first limb of which proposes the adoption generally of 'a contract model', facilitating and encouraging cohabitants to enter into binding agreements addressing the financial arrangements of the parties in cases of

---

49 The apparent justification for this stance appeared to be that the Commission did not wish to interfere unduly with existing marital obligations. In fact, current Irish divorce law already affords remedies to former spouses that potentially impact on the legal position of existing spouses. For instance, a divorced person may claim maintenance from a former spouse, even if the latter is now married to another person, with resultant commitments and responsibilities, provided always that the maintenance *recipient* remains unmarried. See the Family Law (Divorce) Act, 1996, s. 13, which permits a former spouse to seek maintenance 'at any time after' divorce. In sum, a married person may find himself simultaneously supporting both a spouse and a person who is no longer his spouse.   50 The Commission also recommends that notice of any application for redress under the Commission's proposals should be served on any spouse or former spouse of either party.   51 The Constitution of Ireland, 1937, Article 41.3.2 and the Family Law (Divorce) Act, 1996 s. 5 stipulate that the parties to a divorce must have lived apart for four of the previous five years.

relationship breakdown or on the death of either party. The Commission suggests, moreover, that provision be made in legislation to ensure the validity and enforceability of such agreements.

The second prong of the Commission's recommendations addresses what it dubs 'the redress model' providing discretionary default protections – a 'safety net', as the Commission puts it – to persons unprotected by marriage or civil partnership legislation. While the Commission rejects any automatic right to redress for all cohabitants, it recommends that certain qualified cohabitants who are found to be 'economically dependent' should be entitled, on relationship breakdown, to seek from a court any of a range of orders against their partner. Such orders would include, the Commission suggests, a property adjustment order and a compensatory maintenance order, designed to restore the applicant to full financial independence. Pension adjustment and pension splitting orders would also be available. While such provisions reserve ultimate discretion to the courts, it is arguable that they would establish important safeguards for financially dependent cohabitants on relationship breakdown or on the death of a partner.[52] Such cases would benefit, moreover, from the *in camera* rule currently applicable only to married couples.

The Commission further suggests empowering a court to make out of the estate of a deceased person 'such provision as the court considers just and equitable' for a surviving qualified cohabitant of that person. Again such provisions are discretionary. As with similar provisions applying to the children of deceased persons,[53] the applicant would need to show a failure on the part of a deceased person to make adequate provision for the surviving qualified cohabitant.

In other respects, however, the Commission proved more cautious. In the context of immigration, for instance, the Commission appeared to 'kick to touch', opting to recommend no change, despite the very significant disadvantages faced by bi-national same-sex couples. It inclined, moreover, to the continuing exclusion of non-marital couples from the protective scope of the Family Home Protection Act, 1976. Similarly, although it favoured the extension to cohabitants of public pension entitlements, and a reclassification of cohabitants for Stamp Duty and Capital Acquisitions Tax purposes (thus increasing the CAT exemption available to persons inheriting or receiving gifts from a partner), the Commission opted against broader income tax reform. Its conclusion, effectively, was that non-marital couples should continue to shoulder a potentially heavier tax burden than applies to their marital counterparts.

---

52 The Commission recommends in its Report that such applications be brought within two years of relationship breakdown, a welcome extension from the six month limitation period suggested in its earlier Consultation Paper.   53 Succession Act, 1965, s. 117.

The Commission's recommendations appear to presuppose the introduction of civil partnership,[54] and thus are addressed only to the situation of parties who do not avail of marriage or, if and when available, civil partnership. The recommendations are thus confined to addressing what is commonly termed a 'presumptive scheme'. Such a scheme may usefully be contrasted with the alternative 'registration model'. While the former applies to any couple meeting the stipulated definition, the latter requires the parties definitively to 'opt-in' by registering their relationship in a prescribed manner. In other words, while a presumptive scheme extends benefits automatically, the registration approach requires that couples self-select by means of a formal process, often replicating in form the process of marriage.

The benefits of each are further explored by Walsh and Ryan in *The Rights of De Facto Couples*. The key advantage of a scheme requiring civil registration lies in the choice it affords to couples. As Walsh and Ryan observe,

> the opt-in facility furthers decisional autonomy and secures to couples the freedom to decide whether or not to accept the conferral of mutual rights and obligations.[55]

From the state's perspective, as well, the opt-in system affords considerable administrative certainty in determining who is (and correspondingly who is not) covered by the legislative scheme. A register provides clarity as regards the application of the relevant scheme, thus avoiding the complexities involved in determining whether a couple meet a stipulated definition based on the nature and duration of a relationship. A register also promotes administrative clarity in the state's dealings with families.

Though it has not always been so,[56] the status of marriage enjoys in this age a degree of certainty and clarity which cohabitative status clearly lacks.[57] Nowadays, at least, it can quite easily be established that a person is married.[58] Marriage sees its origin in a specific event (the wedding), an

---

54 A point confirmed in the Commission's press release 'Law Reform Commission launches *Report on Rights and Duties of Cohabitants*, December 1, 2006. 55 Walsh and Ryan, *The rights of de facto couples*, at p. 134. 56 Uncertainty as to marital status was a regular feature of social life in England and Wales prior to 1753. See Freeman, 'Marriage and divorce in England' in (1995–6) 29 *Fam. LQ* 549, Gillis, *For better, for worse: British marriages 1600 to the present* (Oxford, 1985) and Stone, *Uncertain unions: marriage and divorce in England, 1660–1857* (Oxford, 1995). 57 See the comments of the Constitution Review Group in their *Report* of 1996 (Pn. 2632) at 321–3 and those of the Commission on the Family, *Strengthening families for life* (Dublin, 1998) at p. 191. 58 Observing the history of marriage in these islands, it might well be said that this has not always been so. Prior to 1753, the marital status of many parties was not easily established in law. Some persons, indeed, were unsure as to their marital status. See Gillis, *For better, for worse* and Stone, *Uncertain unions*. In the civil law tradition generally, irregular marriages were formerly quite common. Parties could be deemed to be married through cohabitation alone without the need for a ceremony. See Clive, *The law of husband and*

explicit and public[59] exchange the result of which must be evidenced by signature of the Register of Marriages,[60] and kept on file by the state. Cohabitation, by contrast, possesses a much more open-textured status. It is not immediately clear, for instance, to what extent and for how long the parties should be living together or the degree of financial interdependency they must enjoy to be recognized as 'cohabiting'. Evidence of marriage then can avoid embarrassing inquiries of an intimate nature that must often be made to establish cohabitative status.[61] Clearly, then, a formal 'opt-in' registration system would alleviate many of these drawbacks.

On the other hand, as Walsh and Ryan note,

> an inherent problem with using registration as the sole means of ameliorating the position of *de facto* couples is that it neglects the position of people that are not party to a formalised relationship.[62]

In doing so, the law risks marginalizing economically dependent cohabitants who, for one reason or another, do not or cannot register their relationship (due for instance to the presence of a prior subsisting marriage or unilateral opposition on the part of one party alone).

The best approach, it is submitted, would involve a mixture of both models – the introduction of a robust scheme of registration for conjugal relationships complemented by a presumptive scheme that would afford some protection to people in unregistered arrangements. This approach was favoured by the All Party Oireachtas Committee on the Constitution, though the Committee suggests a presumptive scheme that would exclude same-sex

---

wife, 4th ed. (Edinburgh, 1997) at p. 40ff.   **59** In the case of Protestant and civil registry weddings there are strict rules regarding publicity prior to the marriage. A failure to observe these formalities, provided both parties know of such failure, will result in the marriage being null and void. See Ryan, 'Fundamentals of marriage', in Shannon (ed.), *The Family law practitioner* (Dublin, 2000). The Civil Registration Act, 2004 has introduced uniform rules for the celebration of marriage that likewise require that marriages occur in public (this portion of the Act has not yet been brought into force.)   **60** Although a failure to so register (or the entry of false details upon the register) will not affect the validity of the marriage: see *B. v. R.* [1996] 3 IR 549.   **61** That said, the authorities in many states are finding it increasingly necessary to peer behind the veil of marriage to establish, for instance, whether a marriage has been contracted with a view to obtaining favorable immigrant status. Recent court cases both in Ireland and the UK testify to the prevalence of 'green card' marriages. In one case a British woman had married seven times in the space of fourteen months, allegedly with a view to securing entry to the United Kingdom for her multiple spouses. See Amelia Gentleman, 'Serial bride faces jail over migrant scam', *The Guardian*, 5 November 1998. In the face of such incidents, the authorities in the United States, for instance, have begun to scrutinize the *bona fides* of immigrant spouses more rigorously. In the film *The Wedding Banquet* (Ang Lee, 1993) for instance the bride-to-be in a marriage of convenience is seen being drilled in the finer points of the life of her husband-to-be, right down to the intimate matter of 'boxers or briefs', the tutor being the latter's true lover.   **62** Walsh and Ryan, *The rights of de facto couples*, at p. 136.

couples, a point explored further below. While there would certainly be some ground for applying more extensive rights and duties to registered cohabitants,[63] on the basis that they have chosen that status, it is equally arguable that unregistered cohabitants may require limited protection, particularly where children and vulnerable adults are involved.

The political response

To date, the political response to issues of family diversity has been similarly reticent, although it is nonetheless evident that a clear consensus has developed in favour of civil partnership. In early 2006, following extensive consultations with the public and representatives of civil society, the All-Party Oireachtas Committee on the Constitution issued its Tenth Report entitled *The Family*.[64] Taking a stance that might most kindly be described as pragmatic, the Committee (by a majority) opted to leave unchanged the constitutional definition of the family.[65] In doing so, the Committee rowed back from the earlier recommendations of the 1996 Constitution Review Group which, while favouring the preservation of the special position of marriage, also recommended constitutional changes that would accord recognition to a greater diversity of family types. Although the All-Party Committee, in 2006, acknowledged significant changes in the profile of the family, and in particular in the number and visibility of alternative family forms, it nonetheless concluded that there was insufficient consensus in favour of change.[66] In particular, the Committee appeared to favour a stance that continued to afford exclusive recognition to the marital family, observing that

> it is not practicable to provide constitutional recognition for all family types while at the same time maintaining the uniqueness of one.[67]

---

63 Bala, for instance, argues that the different expectations and commitments involved (as between registered and non-registered cohabitants) may justify differential treatment, though such justification, he adds, may diminish in cases where informalised relationships are lengthy in duration and/or involve children. Bala, 'The evolving Canadian definition of family: towards a pluralistic and functional approach', (1994) 8 *Intl. J. of Law and the Family* 293–318 at 313. 64 All-Party Oireachtas Committee on the Constitution, *Tenth progress report: The family* (Dublin, 2006).   65 A minority report was also issued, favouring a constitutional addendum that would recognize family life outside the confines of marriage: 'The [S]tate also recognises and respects family life not based on marriage. All persons, irrespective of their marital status, have a right to family life. The Oireachtas is entitled to legislate for the benefit of such families and of their individual members.' See ibid., pp 128–9. The Committee did, nonetheless, recommend a change to the Constitution that would explicitly recognize the rights of children, though the report fell short of requiring that the children's rights should be treated as paramount in cases involving their welfare.   66 Ibid., at p. 121.   67 Ibid., at p. 122.

The prime motivating factor behind this stance appears to have been the Committee's profound fear of a divisive referendum campaign, and the prospect that such a referendum would not succeed:

> an amendment to extend the definition of the family would cause deep and long-standing division in our society and would not necessarily be passed by a majority. Instead of inviting such anguish and uncertainty, the Committee proposes to seek a number of other constitutional changes and legislative proposals to deal in an optimal way with the problems presented to it in its submissions.[68]

The populist nature of this conclusion is reinforced by a revealing observation in the introduction to the Report, in which the Committee notes the receipt of 7,989 submissions, 103 of which emanated from organizations and groups, the remainder from individuals, in addition to 16,143 petitions. 'The vast majority of these communications', the Committee noted, opposed reform.[69] One cannot avoid the conclusion that Oireachtas members cast their votes with one eye on the then forthcoming election.

While eschewing constitutional reform, the Committee did nonetheless lend its support to the inception of partnership legislation, though arguably in a manner that served only to compound the difficulties arising from the report. In short the Committee suggests two different schemes of recognition – a registration scheme that would apply to both same-sex and opposite-sex couples and a presumptive scheme that would apply only to the latter.[70] The Committee sought to justify such disparate treatment on the ground that while it was fair to assume that a man and woman living together were in a relationship, such a conclusion was less easily reached in the case of two cohabiting persons of the same sex. With respect, this conclusion appears somewhat naïve; it is arguable that were such a distinction to be made, much stronger grounds would be required should the state wish to avoid infringing the European Convention on Human Rights. Indeed, one of the strongest conclusions emanating from Walsh and Ryan's report on *The Rights of De Facto Couples* stresses the impermissibility (from a human rights perspective) of such differential treatment. As noted above, where non-marital couples are concerned, Articles 8 and 14 of the Convention, read together, appear to preclude the exclusion of same-sex couples from measures extending rights and duties to opposite sex non-marital couples. *Karner v. Austria*,[71] in particular, strongly militates against differential treatment based on sexual orientation, at least insofar as non-marital couples are concerned.

---

68 Ibid.   69 Ibid., at p. 11.   70 See Ibid., at pp 122–3.   71 Application No. 400016/98, 24 July 2003.

Despite the reserved nature of the Committee's recommendations, its support for legislative reform underscores a growing consensus in favour of civil partnership legislation. The government has indeed explicitly committed itself to civil partnership legislation, the Taoiseach on a number of occasions making reference to the need to provide specific legal recognition for same-sex couples.[72] The Minister for Justice, Equality and Law Reform also appears committed to legislative recognition, in principle at least.[73] To this end, in early 2006, the minister established a Working Group on Domestic Partnership to formulate options for reform in this area.[74] The latter, while consisting mainly of civil and public servants, nonetheless contained (as the sole representative of the NGO sector, it would seem) a representative of the Gay and Lesbian Equality Network,[75] a notable inclusion given that groups representing non-marital couples generally are not specifically represented. Indeed, the overall tenor of the Working Group's *Options Paper* of November 2006 appears to be heavily inclined to the situation of same-sex couples.[76] In the Paper, the Working Group outlines and critiques a number of legislative options, including same-sex marriage and a full civil partnership option replicating, in large part, the rights and responsibilities of marriage. Though commending the option of same-sex marriage as one that 'would underpin a wider equality for gay and lesbian people'[77] the Group warns that extending full marriage rights '… is likely to be vulnerable to constitutional challenge'.[78] While indicating that full civil partnership for heterosexuals '… is unlikely to be proposed as a viable legislative option',[79] the Group appeared much more favourable to this option for same-sex couples alone.

The devil, nonetheless, is in the detail and to date it is fair to say that the exact shape and tenor of the Government proposed scheme remains something of a mystery. Despite the plethora of reports, Government-sponsored legislation has not yet been published, let alone adopted. The public

72 For instance, at the official opening of the Gay and Lesbian Equality Network's offices (3 April 2006) the Taoiseach expressed his view that '[s]exual orientation cannot, and must not, be the basis of second class citizenship. Our laws have changed, and will continue to change, to reflect this principle'. See http://www.glen.ie/press/docs/press%20release%2021st%20April.doc (consulted 27 June 2006). 73 In his address at the opening of the Conference on the Legal Status of Cohabitants and Same Sex Couples, Royal College of Physicians of Ireland, May 26, 2006, see http://www.glen.ie/press/docs/Address%20by%20Minister%20McDowell%20260506.doc (consulted 27 June 2006) the Minister reiterated his view that the Government was 'unequivocally in favour of treating gay people as fully equal citizens in our society. That is why we have passed comprehensive equality legislation and put in place a strong equality infrastructure to ensure that people cannot be discriminated against on the basis of their sexuality.' 74 See http://www.justice.ie/80256E01003A21A5/vWeb/pcJUSQ6NRJWQ-en (consulted 28 June 2006). 75 See www.glen.ie. 76 Working Group on Domestic Partnership, *Options Paper*, (Dublin: Department of Justice, Equality and Law Reform, 2006). 77 Ibid., 7.20. 78 Ibid., 7.20.1. 79 Ibid., at 6.32.

pronouncements of the former Minister for Justice, Equality and Law Reform, moreover, suggest a relatively cautious, sometimes minimalist approach to reform. Although the minister had in principle committed the state to enacting civil partnership legislation, he has publicly intimated that equality of treatment with marriage is not the yardstick that will be applied. At the launch of the report for the Irish Human Rights Commission on the *Rights of De Facto Couples*, for instance, the minister expressed his preference for achieving 'fairness', in eliminating specific legal disadvantages, over a more generalized equalization of rights and responsibilities.[80] Most significantly, the Minister intimated a hope that whatever reforms were effected 'would be acceptable to the Catholic hierarchy' which hardly augurs well for those campaigning for robust and egalitarian civil partnership laws.[81] This is reflected also in the then minister's speech at the opening of the Conference on the Legal Status of Cohabitants and Same Sex Couples in May 2006. In his observations, the minister noted that 'if very significant legal change is to take place, it must have a fairly broad measure of support across society' a statement that appears to support the conclusion that equalization of rights and responsibilities is not on the cards. Indeed, it is worth noting that a Civil Partnership Bill proposed in 2004 by an independent senator[82] failed to attain government support. The Bill proposed a registration scheme for all non-marital couples that, if adopted, would have conferred substantially the same rights and obligations on civil partners as apply to married couples. An equally robust Labour Party Civil Unions Bill, put before the Dáil in February 2007, met a similar fate, the Government opposing the Bill partly on the basis that its largely egalitarian provisions went further than it considered prudent.

THE PITFALLS OF FAMILIALISM

Despite these potential pitfalls, there is no doubt that a consensus is developing around the need for civil partnership legislation. At first sight, it is hard to argue that this is anything but good for same-sex couples as well as for the LGBT community generally. The impetus for change in this regard is strong, a phenomenon that exhibits not only a sea-change in attitudes to diverse family forms but also underlines an increasing openness towards gay and lesbian citizens. Symbolically, civil partnership does more than simply alter the legal status of the parties. More generally, the introduction of civil

---

80 See Coulter, '"Equal" status for cohabiting couples ruled out', *Irish Times*, 13 May 2006, p. 7.   81 See Dowling, 'All couples "must get legal status" or State guilty of discrimination', *Irish Independent*, 13 May 2006, p. 12 and MacCárthaigh, 'Civil recognition for gay couples on the cards' *Irish Examiner*, 13 May 2006, p. 5.   82 For details, see www.senatordavidnorris.ie.

partnership denotes official sanction in respect of the phenomenon of same-sex relationships generally and, of necessity, an acceptance in law of the phenomenon of alternatives to heterosexuality. As Bourassa and Varnell observe:

> at the heart of the debate [about same-sex marriage] [is] not just the question of a small wording change to a marriage law, but more profound questions: 'Are individuals in same-sex relationships persons under the law or not?'; 'Do we form families or not?'; 'Are we deserving of dignity or not?'[83]

Nevertheless, a note of caution must be entered on two distinct fronts – one practical, one symbolic. First, from a practical point of view, some considerable danger arises in embracing family law models as a panacea for all ills. The discourse of equality for same-sex couples is arguably predicated on a view of marriage law that glosses the very real difficulties experienced by straight married couples in dealing with the family law system. Although space does not permit a lengthy discussion of these concerns, it is at least pertinent to refer to aspects of the family law system that compound and in some cases exacerbate the already difficult situation of parties to a family breakdown. The high costs and significant delays involved in litigating are clearly one factor. A further concern lies in the vagueness and uncertainty that attends litigation in this area. In particular, the very wide discretion that is afforded to judges in such cases makes it difficult to identify clear guiding principles in family law, posing particular challenges for those lawyers charged with advising clients on possible outcomes to litigation.[84] The adversarial nature of family proceedings is another particularly unattractive feature, an approach that promotes and rewards vigorous debate, mud-slinging and point-scoring over a genuinely conciliatory procedure.[85]

Indeed, Dewar[86] posits what might fairly be characterised as a post-modern view of family law as 'chaotic, contradictory or incoherent', fragmentary and

---

83 Bourassa and Varnell, 'It's a quiet thing: equal marriage is law' on www.samesexmarriage.ca.
84 On this point, see, generally, Martin, 'Judicial discretion in family law' (1998) 11 *ILT* 168, and Dewar, 'Reducing discretion in family law' (1997) *Austral. J. of Fam. Law.*   85 In this regard, it is important to note a growing trend in legal policy towards what might be termed 'dejuridification': encouraging and facilitating family law mediation and mutually agreed settlements as an alternative to court appearances. See, for instance, ss 5–7A of the Judicial Separation and Family Law Reform Act 1989, as well as ss 6–9 of the Family Law (Divorce) Act 1996. These provisions broadly require solicitors for both the applicant and the respondent in judicial separation and divorce proceedings respectively to certify that they have advised their clients on the alternatives to court proceedings, including the possibility of seeking reconciliation, mediation and of entering into a separation agreement. On mediation, see also Conneely, *Family mediation in Ireland* (London, 2002), and Blaney, 'Family mediation: a comparative overview' (1999) 2 IJFL 2.   86 In Dewar, 'The normal chaos of family law' (1998)

diffuse in its aims and objectives, and containing sometimes incompatible rules reflecting diverse and often irreconcilable priorities. That this is so, he observes, is merely to be expected. Family law 'engages the passion as no other part of our legal system does'.[87] It 'engages with areas of social life and feeling – namely love, passion, intimacy, commitment and betrayal – that are themselves riven with contradiction or paradox'.[88]

The avowed preference for family law models prevalent in modern discourses may in part reflect the socio-cultural promotion of unduly romantized views of the 'ideal' family. Modern discourses often promote the family as an idyllic counterpoint to the harshness of society, a haven of altruism from the ruthless world of commerce.[89] In practice, as Smart[90] observes, the family can equally be regarded as 'the focal point at which a range of ideological practices meet, [an] ideological and economic site of oppression which is protected from scrutiny by the very privacy which family life celebrates'.[91] There is, indeed, a great weight of evidence demonstrating that family life often falls far wide of the ideal. A myriad of research studies[92] for instance attest to the widespread occurrence of intra-familial violence and abuse, physical, sexual and emotional. Indeed, such is the extent and gravity of such maltreatment that it has become trite to report that a person is at greater risk of death or serious injury from a close relative than from a stranger.[93]

Thus it may be argued that in pushing for same-sex marriage, gays and lesbians are not challenging, but rather affirming and reinvigorating oppressive practices. As Ettelbrick observes,

61 *MLR* 467. See also Jameson, 'The antinomies of postmodernity', in *The seeds of time* (New York, 1994), who characterises modern family law as 'antinomic', that is, riven with internal contradictions and incoherence. See also Martin who blames the excessive discretion given to judges for facilitating doctrinal incoherence in Family Law: Martin, 'Judicial discretion in family law' (1998) 16 *ILT (n.s.)* 168.   87 Dewar, (1998) 61 *MLR* 467 at p. 484.   88 Ibid., at p. 468.   89 O'Donovan, *Family law matters* (London, 1993), at p. 22. See also Bates, 'The family and society: reality and myth' (1980) 15 *Ir. Jur. (n.s)* 195.   90 Smart, *The ties that bind*, (London, 1984) chapter 1.   91 See also Dewar, 'Family, law and theory', (1996) 16 *OJLS* 725 at p. 732, who notes that the 'stance of legal non-intervention has distinct consequences for women (and children), who are particularly vulnerable to the unrestrained exercise of power, and to uncorrected inequalities, in the private sphere'.   92 It is not possible to do justice to this topic here and it would be next to impossible to list even a moiety of the studies in this field. An excellent review of the literature is contained, however, in the Home Office Research Study No. 107 on *Domestic Violence* (London: HMSO, 1989). On Domestic violence generally see Casey, *Domestic violence: the women's perspective* (Federation of Women's Refuges and Women's Aid, 1993); Dobash and Dobash, *Violence against wives* (Shepton Mallet, Somt, 1980); Edwards, 'The real risks of violence behind closed doors' [1986] NLJ 1191; Ford, 'prosecution as a victim power resource', (1991) 25 *Law & Soc. Rev.* 313.   93 Dobash and Dobash, *Violence against wives*, at p. 247 conducted a survey of reported violent crimes recorded by the police authorities in Glasgow and Edinburgh in 1974. A striking 25% of all reported incidents involved violence against one's wife. All in all, 34.5% of all reported incidents involved intra-

Steeped in a patriarchal system that looks to ownership, property and dominance of men over women as its basis, the institution of marriage has long been the focus of radical-feminist revulsion.[94]

Whilst acknowledging the attraction for gays and lesbians in seeking to attain 'the imprimatur of social and personal approval that marriage provides,'[95] Ettelbrick ultimately concludes that

> marriage will not liberate us as lesbians and gay men. In fact, it will constrain us, make us more invisible, force our assimilation into the mainstream and undermine the goals of gay liberation ... Marriage runs counter to two of the primary goals of the lesbian and gay movement: the affirmation of gay identity and culture and the validation of many forms of relationship.[96]

An allied concern is that the equation of straight and gay relationships will stifle the creative and adaptive approaches of gays and lesbians in establishing models of family life that accord more effectively with the needs and patterns of life of the partners.[97] The risk arises that the imposition of a 'one-size-fits-all' model will fetter the development of a more multi-textured and diverse range of options for the modern family. The charge may be laid that instead of seeking to conform to 'straight norms', and to cleave to the constraints imposed by marriage, same-sex couples should be seeking to shape alternatives to marriage that better reflect the living arrangements of modern couples.

Others fear that the assimilationist tendencies exhibited in the calls for recognition are leading to the demise of aspects of gay culture, fostering a homogenization that has undermined the unique social and cultural contributions of people who are gay and lesbian. In *The Rise and Fall of Gay Culture*,[98] for instance, Harris charges that the assimilation of gays and lesbians into mainstream society has led to a 'cultural erosion', a systematic destruction of a uniquely gay outlook or 'sensibility'. Although Harris acknowledges that this assimilation marks the 'end of the oppression' of gays and lesbians,[99] 'liberation' (he asserts) has come with a price:

familial violence. Considering the under-reporting of intra-familial violence, the likelihood is that the true figure is much higher. Familiarity is also a significant factor in sexual crimes, especially rape. Over the three years prior to 1999, 87% of victims of rape reportedly knew their attacker: Reid, 'Rapists known by 87pc of victims, says Minister', *Irish Independent*, 27 November 1998.   94 Ettelbrick, 'Since when is marriage a path to liberation', *OUT/LOOK National Gay and Lesbian Quarterly* 6 (Fall 1989) and Browning, 'Why marry?', *New York Times*, 17 April 1986. See also Harris, *The rise and fall of gay Culture* (New York, 1997). 95 Ibid.   96 Ibid.   97 See for instance Browning, 'Why marry?' cited in Sullivan (ed.), *Same-sex marriage: pro and con: a reader* (New York, 1997).   98 Harris, *The rise and fall of gay culture*. 99 Indeed, in many respects, the culture of which Harris speaks largely arose as a response to

> a culture with unique traditions and rituals is submerged into the
> melting pot, its distinct characteristics dissolving into this grey,
> flavorless gruel as its members are accepted by society at large.[1]

An allied point is that the 'assimiliatory' processes spoken of above aid in the
construction by the state of what Stychin terms 'acceptable homosexualities'.[2]
Recognition and civil inclusion, he argues, 'come at a price in terms of the
demands of assimilation, normalization and disciplinarity ...'[3] In other
words, the civil recognition of same-sex couples serves to create a 'good
homosexual', a person responsive to the will of the state, a person duly
constrained by the demands of civil society and the market. The risk, in the
process, is that gays and lesbians who do not meet these ideals will be further
marginalized and discounted, even within their own communities.[4]

Certainly, for those anxious to identify with respectable society, the *social
status* that attaches to marriage is a very important motivating characteristic.
Marriage represents an identification with, and a symbolic reaffirmation of,
prevailing social understandings and moral norms. As Herma Hill Kay
comments,

> Even while we resist the regimentation that marriage entails we accept
> it as a sort of a 'gold standard' that signifies the desire for deep and
> permanent commitment. To be barred from marriage to one's chosen
> partner is to see one's individual relationship trivialised, one's personal
> commitment deemed unworthy of public recognition.[5]

It should not be assumed, however, that the introduction of same-sex
marriage or civil partnership will bring equal benefits to all. In fact, in many
respects, the landscape of civil partnership discourses remains largely middle
class. As Ruth Colker[6] observes, '[f]or poor people marriage[7] may offer few
economic advantages. It should not surprise us that marriage is a less popular
institution in poor communities than in middle-class communities'. In other

---

oppression, a defence mechanism in the face of the systematic attempts to obliterate gay life.
Much, though perhaps not all, of what Harris celebrates therefore as the 'gay sensibility' exists
in consequence of oppression rather than in spite of it, a point that the author himself appears
to acknowledge.   1 Harris, op. cit., at p. 4.   2 Stychin, '"A stranger to its laws": sovereign
bodies, global sexualities and transnational citizens' (2000) 27:4 *Journal of Law and Society* 601.
Cf. Yoshino, 'Covering' 111 *Yale LJ* 769 (2002).   3 Ibid., at 624.   4 A similar argument is
made in Kamikaze's 'I Used To Be An Activist ...' in O'Carroll and Collins (eds.), *Lesbian and
gay visions of Ireland in the twenty-first century* (London, 1995), pp 110–21. Kamikaze argues
that within the Irish gay community, an obsession exists '... with projecting a "respectable"
image of homosexuality' (ibid., p. 117). This, she argued, led to the marginalization of more
radical – and in particular radical feminist – perspectives.   5 Hill Kay, 'Private choices and
public policy: confronting the limitations of marriage' (1991) 5 *Austral. J. of Fam. Law* 69 at p. 85.
6 Colker, 'Marriage', 3 *Yale Law J. of Law and Feminism* (1991) 321 at p. 326.   7 Research

words, marginalized, and in particular poorer, members of the gay community may stand to gain comparatively less from the conferral of civil recognition than richer, more established gays and lesbians.[8] In fact (as noted above in the context of cohabitation and social welfare) poorer same-sex cohabitants ironically may stand to *lose out* if accorded legal recognition, by having the income of a partner combined with their own for the purpose of calculating entitlement to certain social welfare benefits.

CONCLUSION

These cautionary tales are not set out to discourage reform. Nor does the author wish to declare opposition to either same-sex marriage or civil partnership; quite the contrary in fact. Reforms in this arena are certainly long overdue, and much needed. Same-sex couples in modern Ireland currently remain adrift in an ocean of legal obfuscation, deprived of the rudder of legal recognition. A firm stand is required to redress the legal imbalance in this regard. Whether this involves advocating marriage or robust civil partnership is a matter of personal opinion, but it is indisputable that change is required to ameliorate the position of same-sex couples.

Nonetheless, it is equally important that in the rush to reform, the latent pitfalls of familial discourses are not ignored. Family law – as it applies to heterosexuals and homosexuals alike – requires root and branch reform both at a legislative and administrative level. It is hoped, moreover, that civil recognition will not blunt the subversive, inquisitive tradition of the gay movement, that gays and lesbians will continue to interrogate norms that subordinate classes of people based, in particular, on sexual orientation, gender and economic status.

suggests that judicial separation and divorce may have a like effect. A 1995 study showed how the facility of a 'barring order' (see Domestic Violence Act, 1996 and formerly the Family Law (Protection of Spouses and Children Act, 1981), is being used by many separated persons in lower-income groups as a substitute for a formal decree of separation: Fahey & Lyons, *Marital breakdown and family law in Ireland* (Cork, 1995) at p. 122. Fahey and Lyons thus allude to a two-tier family law system where, on marital breakdown, the economically comfortable proceed for judicial separation or divorce, and the economically disadvantaged rely on the largely inappropriate facility of a barring order. See also the Law Reform Commission, *Report on Family Courts*, LRC-52–1996 at p. 5ff and Coulter, 'District Court orders outnumber separations', *Irish Times*, 10 October 1995 who notes that '[m]ore than twice as many cases of marital conflict end in barring or maintenance orders in the District Courts as end in legal separation … District Court actions are the recourse of the poor, while the better-off are more likely to seek legal separation, the study found'. 8 Notably Stiers suggests that, generally, gay men appear to be more supportive of strategies promoting same-sex marriage than their lesbian counterparts,. Given the generally stronger earning potential of men, this may not be entirely co-incidental. See Stiers, Gretchen, *From this day forward: commitment, marriage and family in lesbian and gay relationships* (New York, 1999) at pp 184–5.

The debate around civil recognition of same-sex couples offers a timely window to address many of the problems noted above. On the one hand, it undoubtedly marks a maturation of gay discourses, a discursive shift towards a more familial perspective, one that values and celebrates commitment, mutual support and continuity. Yet in making these commitments same-sex couples have a unique opportunity also to challenge and recast social norms in a manner that redresses the dysfunctions noted above, to reform from the inside out. As Stiers has observed, same-sex couples may simultaneously 'use and contest traditional concepts of marriage'[9] in a postmodern recasting of family values that reaffirms the norms noted above while challenging some of the less savoury aspects of traditional marriage. Commenting on qualitative research conducted among gay and lesbian couples, Stiers notes that

> [w]hile many respondents were critical of the institutions of marriage and the family, the majority valued the ideals of love, commitment, monogamy and family life. At the same time they were supportive of these so-called traditional values, they also argued that marriage and the family needed to be redefined to reflect the families that people actually create.[10]

Thus, same-sex couples, while invoking the values of commitment, security, and continuity, may also 'create new truths about intimate lives'.[11] In conferring civil recognition, the state has a unique opportunity to recast family law in a way that re-affirms the affective values of commitment and mutual support without replicating the ills that in many cases characterise current family law norms. It is hoped that this opportunity will be grasped. If so, the benefits for *all* families may be considerable.

---

9 Stiers, *From this day forward: commitment, marriage and family in lesbian and gay relationships*, (New York, 1999). 10 Ibid., at 188. 11 Diduck, *Law's families* (London, 2003) at 31.

Form and substance in committed relationships in American law

LYNN D. WARDLE

FORM, SUBSTANCE, AND COMMITMENT IN ADULT INTIMATE RELATIONSHIPS

THERE HAS LONG BEEN A tension in family law between 'form' (meaning the structure, composition, formality, and conformity to customary cultural expectations) and 'substance' (meaning the essential nature or quality of a thing, its basic elements or internal constitutional qualities). Some people assert that form is irrelevant to or independent of the substance of a relationship; others argue that form and substance are inextricably connected. For family life and family law today many people believe that 'all you need is love' (to use the words of a famous Beatles song).[1] That assumption underlies, at least in part, the movement to extend marriage-equivalent legal status and benefits to other 'committed relationships.'

The desire to focus on substance instead of form in relationships is certainly understandable in this day when divorce rates have skyrocketed globally, and we constantly hear terrible stories of irresponsibility, dysfunction, abuse, abandonment, and domestic violence afflicting many formal relationships. The movement toward legal recognition for committed relationships also corresponds to a widely-felt yearning for privacy, independence and autonomy. The desire to be free of government-mandated rules, requirements and formalities in private relationships is very appealing in a day when government regulation of virtually other (public) aspects of our individual and social lives seems to be so totally pervasive. It also reflects a popular romantic egalitarianism – a belief in the equality of all committed relationships.

In this paper I consider whether 'substance' really is independent of and can be separated from 'form,' whether 'love is all you need' in domestic relationship law today. I also examine whether all 'committed relationships' really are substantially equal in terms of their consequences in the lives of couples, children, and for society.

1 All you need is love, <http://www.thebeatlesongs.com/all_you_need_is_love.htm> (seen 9 February 2004). See also 175 Songs of the Beatles (Lyrics and chords), <http://membres.lycos.fr /wilane/btls.html> (seen 9 February 2004). See generally, Lynn D. Wardle, 'All you need is love?' 14 *So. Cal. Rev. L. & Wo.'s Studs.* 51 (2004).

The focus of this book, which has brought together such distinguished legal experts, is 'committed relationships'. However, that is not a legal term of art. So, at the outset, it seems prudent to define what 'committed relationship' means.

The word 'relationships' include potentially many associations; but, in this context it is apparent that it refers to intimate relationships between consenting adults.[2] However, the modifying term 'committed' adds little specificity to the definition. The Oxford English Dictionary gives two definitions for 'committed' – '[e]ntrusted, delegated; put in prison; done, perpetuated,' and '[c]haracterized by commitment'.[3] The first definition is inapplicable in this context, and the second is of little practical value in resolving legal issues because 'commitment' has such a broad and indefinite meaning. Of the several different definitions given by the OED for 'commitment', three seem potentially relevant to the meaning of 'committed relationships'. The first is '[t]he committing of oneself, or being committed (to a particular course of conduct, etc.)',[4] This is unhelpfully circular ('committed' means 'characterized by commitment,' which means 'being committed'). The next OED definition suggests a factor showing commitment but does not answer the critical question–how much? It is 'an engagement; a liability; *pl.* pecuniary obligations'.[5] (Likewise, the American cases discussing 'committed relationships' often emphasize the assumption of mutual financial and social obligations and undertakings by the parties,[6] but specific types or amounts of financial obligations that must be assumed are not specified.) The third definition is 'an absolute moral choice of a course of action; hence, the state of being involved in political or social questions, or in furthering a particular doctrine or cause, especially in one's literary or artistic expression; moral seriousness or social responsibility in artistic productions.'[7] This rests on a moral consideration or motive, which is difficult to ascertain. Finally, in the American judicial opinions I have examined, the term 'committed relationship' is often used in conjunction with 'long-term' suggesting that it means an intimate relationship which has lasted or which

---

2 By 'intimate' I mean primarily sexual intimacy, relationships involving sexual relations. 3 The Oxford English Dictionary, *committed*, http://dictionary.oed.com/cgi/entry/50045048? query_type=word&queryword=committed&first=1&max_to_show=10&single=1&sort_type= alpha (seen April 23, 2005). 4 The Oxford English Dictionary, *commitment*, http:// dictionary.oed.com/cgi/entry/50045042?query_type=word&queryword=committed&first= 1&max_to_show=10&single=1&sort_type=alpha (seen 23 April 2005). 5 Id. 6 See, e.g., *T.B. v. L.R.M.*, 890, A.2d 1060, 2005 WL 697578, 2005 Pa. Super 114 (Mar 28, 2005); *Seymour v. Holcomb*, 790 N.Y.S.2d 858, 2005 N.Y. Slip Op. 25070 (N.Y. Sup., Feb 23, 2005); *Morrison v. Sadler*, 821 N.E.2d 15 (Ind. App. 2005); *Standhardt v. Superior Court*, 206 Ariz. 276, 77 P.3d 451 (Ariz. App. 2003); *Jegley v. Picado*, 349 Ark. 600, 80 S.W.3d 332 (2002); *Levin v. Yeshiva University*, 80 Misc.2d 829, 691 N.Y.S.2d 280 (1999); *Tanner v. Oregon Health Sciences University*, 157 Or.App. 502, 971 P.2d 435 (1998). 7 Id.

the parties expect to last for a long time.[8] But the term seems to be used as a conclusory label, not a test: 'How long' is required for a relationship to be deemed 'long term' or 'committed' is never indicated.

Thus, this conference is about the legal recognition of adult, consensual, intimate domestic relationships to which the parties have 'committed' themselves, and/or in which the parties have assumed some liability for financial obligations, and/or in which they have made a moral choice to further a political or social doctrine or cause, and/or which have lasted for a relatively 'long' time. That is not a very clear legal standard or practical measuring tool for lawyers and courts to work with. Not surprisingly, part of the dilemma of legal recognition of 'committed relationships' is the uncertainty about what they are and how to identify them.

COMMITTED RELATIONSHIPS IN AMERICAN LAW TODAY

For comparative purposes it may be helpful to review the legal status of committed relationships in American law today. That will lay the foundation for my discussion of the public policy issues that will follow. I focus on five points.

First, in the American federal system of government the *regulation of* domestic relations, including *committed relationships*, '[f]rom the earliest days of the Republic ... has unquestionably *belonged to the states*',[9] not the national government. The Supreme Court of the United States has declared that the '[r]egulation of domestic relations [is] an area that has long been regarded as a virtually exclusive province of the states'.[10] Thus, the regulation of committed relationships is left primarily to the states, and most of the applicable laws are state, not federal, laws, and state, not federal courts, hear most cases involving claims for legal recognition or benefits arising out of committed relationships. That means that there is not one uniform law concerning committed relationships for the entire United States, but there are fifty different state laws governing the subject, with different substantive

---

8 See, e.g., *Landiak v. Richmond*, 899. So.2d 535, 2005 WL 820545, 2005–0758 (La. Mar. 30, 2005) ('long-standing'); *T.B. v. L.R.M; Seymour v. Holcomb; Morrison v. Sadler; Standhardt v. Superior Court; Jegley v. Picado; Levin v. Yeshiva University; Tanner v. Oregon Health Sciences University; Baehr v. Miike*, 1996 WL 694235, 65 USLW 2399, 96 Daily Journal D.A.R. 14,647, 96 CJ C.A.R. 2041 (Hawai'i Cir.Ct., Dec. 3, 1996); *Lepar Realty Corp. v. Griffin*, 151 Misc.2d 579, 581 N.Y.S.2d 521 (N.Y. Sup. App.1991); *Ramirez v. Lewis*, 177 A.D.2d 296, 575 N.Y.S.2d 868 (N.Y. App. Div. 1991); *Rent Stabilization Ass'n of New York, Inc. v. Higgins*, 164 A.D.2d 283, 562 N.Y.S.2d 962 (N.Y. App. Div. 1990).   9 Anne C. Dailey, 'Federalism and Families', 143 *U. Pa. L. Rev.* 1787, 1821 (1995).   10 *Sosna v. Iowa*, 419 U.S. 393, 404 (1975); see also *Lehman v. Lycoming County Children's Services Agency*, 458 U.S. 502 (1982); *Moore v. Sims*, 442 U.S. 415 (1979); *Barber v. Barber*, 62 U.S. (21 How.) 582 (1859).

rules, legal procedures and court systems. Of course, there are many influences that tend to create uniformity or similarity in the laws of the American states, including strong national cultural influences in America (such as national television, newspaper, radio, professional organizations, religions, travel, educational standards, communications, etc.). Federal legislation also influences state family law because while Congress lacks authority to regulate family law, it has the authority to regulate such things as pensions, social security, taxes, immigration, interstate activities, which indirectly impacts upon state family law. Also, the Constitution of the United States is the 'Supreme Law' of the land, overriding conflicting state laws, and sometimes state family laws are invalidated for violating some constitutional provision or doctrine (such as equal protection, substantive or procedural due process of law, the privileges and immunities clauses, the full faith and credit clause, etc.). For these reasons, there are many similarities in the family laws of the fifty states. However, there are also still many significant differences. So a survey of the legalization of 'committed relationships' in American law calls for the examination of the laws of fifty different jurisdictions. What a court or legislature in, say, California, or Massachusetts, or New York may do may not be representative of what most courts and legislatures in most states are doing.

Second, the legal recognition of committed relationships historically in American *law has been limited almost exclusively to marriage or attempted marriage*. Marriage can be created formally or informally. All American states allow and prefer formal, licensed marriage. The requirements and formalities for marriage vary from state to state in the details (such as the age of marriage, the degree of consanguinity prohibited, the specific test for mental capacity, other impediments or prohibitions) but in general (with one notable exception) the American states define marriage as the consensual union for life of one adult man and one adult woman who are not closely related to each other and who have followed proper procedure to create their marriage.

The principal kind of informal marriage is 'common law' marriage which is allowed in only twelve American states.[11] However, all other states recognize common law marriages if entered into in one of the states where common law marriage is allowed by persons who are citizens or residents of that state. In the United States, 'common law marriage' is not merely a euphemism for nonmarital cohabitation, or some kind of alternative relational status for which a few marital benefits are available, but common law marriage is *real* marriage, with all of the legal incidents of formal

---

11 Marsha Garrison, 'Is consent necessary? An evaluation of the emerging law of cohitant obligation', 52 *UCLA L. Rev.* 815, 849 (2005) ('At one time, nearly two-thirds of the states recognized common law marriage; by 2002, only twelve did so, and two of the twelve had adopted strict limitations on its establishment').

marriage, differing from formal marriage only in the method of formation (creation) of the marriage, but not different in any way in the legal status or effects conferred upon the relationship.[12] Certain customary marriages (of persons living in Indian tribes or belonging to certain religions) are also recognized as informal (but real) marriages in some states.[13] In a few states, parties who have tried to enter into a valid marriage and in good faith believed that they were married will be treated as if they were married (for at least some economic benefits of marriage) under the 'putative spouse' or similar doctrines.[14]

Third, recently the term 'committed relationships' has begun to be used frequently in legal opinions in American courts. My research on Westlaw (April 2005) produced a list of 152 state and federal court opinions in which the term 'committed relationship' or 'committed relationships' was used.[15] The most recent was in a state court decision on 15 April 2005; the oldest case in that database was in a Federal Court of Customs and Patent Appeals on 1 October 1981. Eighteen of those opinions (approximately 12 per cent) were decided within the period 1 January and 15 April 2005; another 24 opinions (approximately 16 per cent) were rendered in the year 2004; and a total of 94 (approximately 62 per cent) have been rendered since January 1, 2000. Nearly 80 percent of these decisions, one hundred twenty (120) opinions or approximately 79 per cent of the total 152, have been rendered since the Hawaii trial court decision in *Baehr v. Miike*, ordering the state to give marriage licenses to same-sex couples (but never implemented).[16]

From my survey of the use of 'committed relationships' in American judicial opinions, three facts about legal recognition of 'committed relationships' in American courts are clear: First, the discussion of 'committed relationships' in American courts is a relatively new development, largely occurring within the past decade. Second, the discussion of "committed relationships in judicial opinions has become relatively common in a short period of time, and it is a very rapidly-expanding development. American

---

12 See ch. 3, 'Marriage formalities' in 1 *Contemporary Family Law* (1988). Common law marriage requires agreement, cohabitation, and public holding out as married but not licensing or solemnization.   13 See generally Ann Laquer Estin, 'Embracing tradition: pluralism in American family law', 63 *Md. L. Rev.* 540 (2004); 'Marriage formalities' § 3:13, in 1 *Contemporary Family Law* (1988) ('More than half of the states except certain religious and cultural gropus from some or all of the solemnization requirements').   14 See generally Monica Hof Wallace, 'The pitfalls of a putative marriage and the call for a putative divorce', 64 *La. L. Rev.* 71 (2003); John W. Carlson, 'Putative spouses in Texas courts' 7 Tex. Wesleyan L. Rev. 1 (2000); Raj Rajan, 'The putative spouse in California', 11 *J. Contemp. Legal Issues* 95 (2000); ch. 35, 'Putative marriages', in 4 *Contemporary Family Law* (1988).   15 On 23 April 2005 I searched in the 'allstates' and 'allfeds' databases of Westlaw for cases containing the term 'committed relationship!' ('!' is a universal character).   16 1996 WL 694235, 65 USLW 2399, 96 Daily Journal D.A.R. 14,647, 96 CJ C.A.R. 2041 (Hawai'i Cir.Ct., Dec 3, 1996).

courts have gone from using the term once every couple of years in the 1980s to about once-a-month in 1999, to about once-a-week in 2005. Finally, the vast majority of the cases discussing 'committed relationships' involve gay or lesbian couples seeking legal recognition of their same-sex relationship (which relates to the third OED definition of 'commitment' involving a choice to further a political or social doctrine or cause).

Fourth, with regard to recognition of *same-sex committed relationships*, American law is in a state of great controversy and flux. A socio-legal-political phenomenon of some significance is occurring in the United States of America. For purpose of our discussion, we can separate law regulating same-sex committed relationships into three categories: (1) same-sex marriage, (2) same-sex civil unions with all or most of the legal rights and incidents of marriage, and (3) extension of specific legal benefits to same-sex domestic partnerships or reciprocal beneficiaries.[17]

Only one state – Massachusetts – has legalized same-sex marriage. It did so by the undemocratic process of a November 2003 decree of the Massachusetts Supreme Judicial Court that took effect in May 2004.[18]

Supporters of same-sex unions have filed many lawsuits seeking to have courts mandate the legalization of same-sex marriage. Such law suits in the 1970s and 1980s met with unanimous rejection in all the courts.[19] However, in 1993, in *Baehr v. Lewin*, the Hawaii Supreme Court reversed the dismissal of claims for same-sex marriage holding that it appeared facially that the denial of marriage licenses to same-sex couples might violate the equality provisions of the state constitution.[20] Then in December 1996, a Hawaii trial court held that denial of same-sex marriage violated the equality guarantee of the state constitution and ordered the state to give marriage licenses to same-sex couples.[21] The judgment was stayed pending appeal to the Hawaii Supreme Court, and that decision legalizing same-sex marriage was subsequently overturned by an amendment to the state constitution which the voters in Hawaii passed in 1998 by a margin of 69 per cent to 29 per cent. Nonetheless, these Hawaii court rulings gave a great boost to the movement to legalize same-sex marriage.

Just a few months after the Hawaii trial court decision for same-sex marriage, a trial court in Alaska ruled in an interlocutory ruling that the denial of same-sex marriage appeared to violate the equality and privacy provisions of the Alaska Constitution.[22] Again, that ruling was effectively

---

17 *See* Lynn D. Wardle, 'Counting the costs of civil unions: some potential detrimental effects on family law', 11 *Widener J. Pub. L.* 401 (2002).   18 *Goodridge v. Department of Public Health*, 798 N.E.2d 941 (Mass. 2003); *In re Opinion of the Justices to the Senate*, 802 N.E.2d 565 (Mass. 2004).   19 Lynn D. Wardle, 'A critical analysis of constitutional claims for same-sex marriage', 1996 *B.Y.U.L.Rev.* 1.   20 *Baehr v. Lewin*, 852 P.2d 44, 67 (Haw. 1993).   21 *Baehr v. Miicke*, 196 WL 694235 (Haw. Cir. Ct. 1996).   22 *Brause v. Bureau of Vital Statistics*, No. 3AN-95–6562, 1998 WL 88743 at 6 (Alaska. Super. Ct., 27 Feb. 1998).

overturned when the voters that November ratified (by vote of 69 per cent to 31 per cent) an amendment to the state constitution barring same-sex marriage.

Since 1996, courts in a total of eight American states have ruled that same-sex unions must be legalized (though most like Hawaii and Alaska have been overturned, or are still on appeal).[23] Cases are currently pending in eight states seeking judicial legalization of same-sex marriage.[24] Parties seeking to legalize same-sex unions have invoked at least eight broad constitutional doctrines to support their claims,[25] and some courts have thus far accepted and relied upon at least six different constitutional doctrines in ruling in favor of same-sex unions.[26]

Many courts have rejected same-sex marriage claims in the past decade, as well. Appellate courts in the District of Columbia, Arizona, Indiana, and Oregon have all rejected same-sex marriage claims.[27] In New York four trial courts have rejected same-sex marriage claims, but recently one has ruled in favor of same-sex marriage.[28]

There has been significant social and political reaction to these lawsuits seeking and judicial rulings ordering same-sex marriage. Citizens in eighteen states have now ratified state marriage amendments (SMAs) to state constitutions to explicitly ban same-sex marriage. In the past year alone (July 2004–April 2005) voters in fourteen states ratified SMAs by overwhelming margins (from a low of 57 per cent to a high of 86 per cent, one-half passing with 70 per cent or greater popular support).[29] Proposed state marriage

23 These decisions have come in Hawaii, Alaska, Vermont, Massachusetts, Oregon, Washington, New York and California. Only the Vermont and Massachusetts decisions are final decisions recognizing same-sex unions.   24 The states are California, Connecticut, Florida, Maryland, Nebraska, New Jersey, New York, and Washington.   25 The constitutional doctrines courts have invoked to force same-sex unions are (1) equal protection, (2) substantive due process (privacy, right to marry, right of association), (3) due process standards of arbitrariness or irrationality, (4) privileges and immunities, (5) full faith and credit, and (6) the bill of attainder clause. Additionally, proponents of same-sex marriage have long invoked two other constitutional doctrines: (7) the free exercise of religion clause, and (8) the establishment of religion clause. For a list of cases and a sample of law review articles making these assertions, see Lynn D. Wardle, 'Tyranny, federalism, and the Federal Marriage Amendment', 17 *Yale J. L. & Femin.* 221.   26 See supra note 15, doctrines 1–6.   27 See *Dean v. District of Columbia*, 653 A.2d 307 (D.C. Cir. 1995); *Standhardt v. Superior Court*, 206 Ariz. 276, 77 P.3d 451 (App.2003); *Morrison v. Sadler*, 821 N.E.2d 15 (Ind.App. 2005); *Li v. State*, 110 P.3d 91, 2005 WL 852319, (Or., Apr 14, 2005).   28 See, e.g., *Seymour v. Holcomb*, 790 N.Y.S.2d 858 (Sup. Ct. N.Y., 2005); *Hernandez v. Robles*, 7 Misc.3d 459, 794 N.Y.S.2d 579 (Supreme Court, New York County, Ling-Cohan, J., 2005).   29 Arkansas 75–25%, Georgia 77–23%, Kentucky 75–25%, *Louisiana 78%–22%, Michigan 59–41%, Mississippi 86–14%, *Missouri 72%–28%, North Dakota 73–27%, Montana 66–34% Ohio 62–38%, Oklahoma 76–24%, Oregon 57–43%, Utah 66–34% (* means passed in an election in n2004 before the November election). Associated Press, (Nov. 4, 2004); see also Michael Fouse, *'Gay marriage' a loser, amendments pass in all 11 states, BP News,* http://www.bpnews.net/bpnews.asp?ID=19470 (Seen April 8, 2005); http://www.catholicexchange.com/vm/PFarticle.asp?vm_id=97&art_id =25942&sec_id=49657) (seen 8 April 2005). Earlier, voters adopted state marriage amendments

amendments are currently in mid-process (involved in multi-year amendment proposal-and-ratification processes) in three additional states,[30] and more than a dozen other state legislatures are considering proposing state marriage amendments.[31] In every state in which the people have been allowed to vote on a constitutional amendment to the state constitution to prohibit same-sex marriage, they have ratified such amendments by overwhelming majorities.

Additionally, in 26 other states the legislatures have enacted statutory prohibition of same-sex marriage.[32] Moreover, a proposed Federal Marriage Amendment is pending in the U.S. Congress, where, last year, well over half (55 per cent) of the House of Representatives voted for the amendment (short of the two-thirds vote required to move the amendment forward).[33] Clearly, a socio-legal-political phenomenon of profound significance is occurring in the United States of America.

Three states have created an alternative legal status for same-sex couples with substantially all of the legal effects and benefits of marriage. In 2000, the Vermont legislature, under order from the state supreme court, created 'civil unions' for same-sex couples with legal rights and benefits substantially equal to marriage.[34] In 2003, the California legislature, acting without judicial pressure, did the same but called them same-sex 'domestic partnerships' with legal rights and benefits virtually identical to marriage.[35] And on 20 April 2005, the Connecticut legislature voluntarily passed, and the governor signed, a law creating marriage-equivalent same-sex civil unions in that state.[36]

Many of the state marriage amendments ban not only same-sex marriage but also ban giving marriage-equivalent legal status or benefits to same-sex

in 1998 in Hawaii 69–29%, and Alaska 69–31%, in 1999 in Nebraska 70–30%, and in 2001 in Nevada 70–30%. See MarriageWatch.org, State Marriage Amendments, http://marriagelaw.cua.edu/Law/marriageamendments.cfm (seen April 14, 2005). Most recently, in April 2005, the latest state marriage amendment was approved by voters in Kansas 70–29%.
30 The states are Alabama, South Dakota and Tennessee. Senate Republican Policy Committee, *State-by-State Marriage Protection Update* (March 31, 2005) (copy in author's possession). See also www.stateline.org/stateline/?pa=story&sa=showStoryInfo&id=252058&columns-true. 31 Id. (identifying Arizona, Florida, Delaware, Illinois, Indiana, Iowa, Massachusetts, North Carolina, South Carolina, Texas, Vermont, Virginia, and Wisconsin). 32 Id. Only six states lack any constitutional or statutory protection for conjugal marriage. 33 Library of Congress, Summary of Bills Introduced in the 108th Congress, H.J. Res. 106, available at <http://thomas.loc.gov/cgi-bin/bdquery/D?d108:4:./temp/~bdBT8h::> (seen October 9, 2004). In 2004, both houses of Congress voted on earlier versions of this proposed marriage amendment; the proposal received well over a majority of votes in the House, just under a majority (50–48) in the Senate, but fell well short of the required two. thirds necessary to send the proposed amendment to the states in both houses. See Lynn D. Wardle, 'The proposed Federal Marriage Amendment and the risks to federalism in family law', 2 *St Thomas L. Rev.* 137 (2004). 34 *Baker v. State*, 744 A.2d 864, 867 (1999); Vt. Stat. Ann. tit. 15, §1201 (2001); Vt. Stat. Ann. tit. 13, §5301 (2001). 35 Calif. Ass. Bill. 205 (2003). See *Knight v. Superior Court*, 26Cal. Rptr. 3d 687, 2005 WL 745489 (Cal. App. 3 Dist., 2005). 36 *Connecticut Oks same-sex civil unions*, Newsmax.com, (21 April 20050 at http://www.newsmax.com/archives/articles/

couples, to prevent what happened in California from happening in those states. In California, voters approved by over 61 per cent an initiative defining marriage as 'the union of one man and one woman' only. The defiant legislature then passed a law providing effectively all of the same legal benefits of marriage to same-sex couples who registered for 'domestic partnerships', and California courts held that since the word 'marriage' is not used the law does not violate the voter-approved initiative banning same-sex marriage.[37]

Finally, two states (Hawaii and Vermont) also provide a small, selective portion of benefits (usually relating to property ownership and hospital benefits) to some heterosexual nonmarital couples and in Hawaii same-sex couples register for those 'reciprocal beneficiary status'. However, those have not proven to be very popular and few couples sign up for those 'RB' schemes. Additionally, eleven states and dozens of municipalities reportedly have extended some benefits (mostly health insurance and in some cases retirement and other benefits) to same-sex partners of public employees who register as 'domestic partners.'[38]

Fifth, heterosexual couples can participate in nonmarital committed relationships as well as same-sex couples. However, heterosexual couples who have sought legal recognition of their non-marital 'committed' relationships have had only sparse and limited success in getting American courts to give legal recognition or marital benefits to their 'committed relationships.'

In the 1970s, when California recognized 'palimony' claims of hetero-sexual nonmarital cohabitants in the seminal case of *Marvin v. Marvin*,[39] it appeared for a while that courts were going to give full, marriage-equivalent legal rights, benefits and protections to heterosexual nonmarital cohabitation in 'committed relationships', but despite the great publicity and popularity of that idea in some sub-cultures (especially in the academy and in the entertainment/media subculture), both courts and legislatures failed to deliver the expected revolution. Instead, because the burden of proof rests upon the nonmarital claimant to factually establish the existence and terms of the 'commitments' in those informal committed relationships, those claims often failed. Even the plaintiff in the famous *Marvin* case, Michelle Marvin, ultimately failed to recover on her palimony claim because she could not factually establish any legal or equitable basis for recovery.[40]

Likewise, because heterosexual couples can easily marry (including easily divorce and marry someone besides their current spouse),[41] courts and

2005/4/20/180352.shtml (Seen April 27, 2005).   **37** *Knight v. Superior Court.*   **38** Lambda Legal, *Issues, Domestic Partnerships*, www.lambdalegal.org (Seen April 2005).   **39** 557 P.2d 106 (Cal. 1976).   **40** *Marvin v. Marvin*, 122 Cal. App. 2d 871, 176 Cal. Rprt. 555 (1981). **41** Unilateral no-fault divorce laws throughout the United States make dissolution of an existing marriage a simple matter, so an existing marriage is rarely a significant obstacle to marrying another person. *See generally* Lynn D. Wardle, 'No-fault divorce and the divorce

lawmakers have been generally resistant to claims by male-female couples for marriage-equivalent legal recognition of their 'committed relationships.' For example, in *Irizarry v. Board of Education of the City of Chicago*,[42] a school system provided certain benefits to the married spouses and the same-sex (but not the heterosexual) nonmarital partners of its employees. An employee who had been cohabiting with a heterosexual partner without marriage for more than twenty years and had borne and raised two children with him brought suit to obtain the same benefits for her opposite-sex partner. The federal district court and the Court of Appeals for the Seventh Circuit rejected her constitutional claims that the discriminatory school policy violated equal protection or due process because heterosexual cohabiting couples can obtain the benefits by marrying but same-sex couples cannot. Respected federal appeals court judge Richard Posner succinctly explained:

> [T]he evidence that on average married couples live longer, are healthier, earn more, have lower rates of substance abuse and mental illness, are less likely to commit suicide, and report higher levels of happiness – that marriage civilizes young males, confers economies of scale and of joint consumption, minimizes sexually transmitted disease, and provides a stable and nourishing framework for child rearing – see, e.g., Linda J. Waite & Maggie Gallagher, *The Case for Marriage*: *Why Married People Are Happier, Healthier, and Better Off Financially* (2000); David Popenoe, *Life without Father*: *Compelling New Evidence That Fatherhood and Marriage Are Indispensable for the Good of Children and Society* (1996); George W. Dent, Jr., *The Defense of Traditional Marriage*, 15 J.L. & Pol. 581 (1999), refutes any claim that policies designed to promote marriage [by not giving similar benefits to heterosexual cohabitants] are irrational ... [T]he refusal to extend domestic-partner benefits to heterosexual cohabitators could be justified on the basis of the policy favoring marriage for heterosexuals quite apart from the reasons for wanting to extend the spousal fringe benefits to homosexual couples.[43]

---

conundrum', 1991 *B.Y.U.L. Rev.* 79. **42** As 251 F.3d 604, 607–8 (7th Cir. 2001). See generally *S.D. Myers, Inc. v. City & County of San Francisco*, 253 F.3d 461 (9th Cir. 2001); *Heinsma v. City of Vancouver*, 29 P.3d 709 (Wash. 2001); *Pritchard v. Madison Metro. Sch. Dist.*, 242 Wis. 2d 301, 625 N.W.2d 613 (2001); *Tyma v. Montgomery County*, 801 A.2d 148 (Md. 2002); Joshua K. Baker, 'Status, benefits, and recognition: current controversies in the marriage debate', 18 *BYU J. Pub. L.* 569, 622 (2004); but see *Devlin v. City of Philadelphia*, 862 A.2d 1234, 1251 (Pa. 2004). **43** *Irizarry v. Bd. Educ.*, 251 F.3d 604, 607–08 (7th Cir. 2001) (Posner, J opinion for the court). Judge Posner continued: 'Of course, self-selection is important; people are more likely to marry who believe they have characteristics favorable to a long-term relationship'. Lee A. Lillard & Constantijn W.A. Panis, 'Marital status and mortality: the role of health,' 33 *Demography* 313 (1996); Lee A. Lillard, Michael J. Brien & Linda J. Waite, 'Premarital cohabitation and subsequent dissolution: a matter of self-selection?', 32 *Demography*

Nevertheless, the movement to give nonmarital committed relationships legal benefits equivalent to marriage remains popular, especially in some elite circles. For instance, in May 2000 the prestigious American Law Institute approved a model set of family law reforms entitled *Principles of the Law of Family Dissolution*, which included provisions for recognition of nonmarital domestic partnerships (both heterosexual and homosexual, by both married and unmarried persons), and for the extension to such relationships of the same economic benefits which married spouses enjoy upon dissolution of the relationship.[44] These economic incidents of marriage are to be extended to same-sex and heterosexual cohabitants who 'for a significant period of time share a primary residence and a life together as a couple ...'[45] In proving that they shared their life and residence claimants are to be aided by two strong presumptions that arise after cohabitation for a minimal period.[46] Property acquired during the relationship 'should be divided according to the principles set forth for the division of marital property',[47] and 'a domestic partner is entitled to [alimony] on the same basis as a spouse ...'[48]

WHY IT MATTERS

These legal developments reflect the influence of a new theory of close relationships.[49]

---

437 (1995). But the Chicago Board of Education would not be irrational (though it might be incorrect) in assigning some causal role to the relationship itself. Linda J. Waite, 'Does marriage matter?' 32 *Demography* 483, 498–99 (1995), finds that cohabitants are much less likely than married couples to pool financial resources, more likely to assume that each partner is responsible for supporting himself or herself financially, more likely to spend free time separately, and less likely to agree on the future of the relationship. This makes both investment in the relationship and specialization with this partner much riskier than in marriage, and so reduces them. Whereas marriage connects individuals to other important social institutions, such as organized religion, cohabitation seems to distance them from these institutions. Irizarry and her domestic partner may, given the unusual duration of their relationship, be an exception to generalizations about the benefits of marriage. We are not aware of an extensive scholarly literature comparing marriage to long-term cohabitation. This may be due to the fact that long-term cohabitation is rare – only ten percent of such relationships last for five years or more, Pamela J. Smock, 'Cohabitation in the United States: an appraisal of research themes, findings, and implications,' 26 *Ann. Rev. Sociology* 1 (2000). But there is evidence that the widespread substitution of cohabitation for marriage in Sweden has given that country the highest rate of family dissolution and single parenting in the developed world. David Popenoe, *Disturbing the nest: family change and decline in modern societies* 173–4 (1988). It is well known that divorce is harmful to children ... Id. at 608.   **44** See generally American Law Institute, *Principles of the law of family dissolution: analysis and recommendations*, ch. 6 (2002).   **45** § 6.01(1).   **46** § 6.03(1)–(5).   **47** § 6.05.   **48** § 6.06(1).   **49** Dan Cere, *The experts' story of courtship* (Institute for American Values, 2000), at 15. Cere provides a pithy review of the 'close relationship' scholarly literature. Id. at 15–26.

Close relationship theorists argue that we need to bring a common theoretical and methodological approach to the study of all 'sexually based primary relationships.' They argue that, at the level of relational processes, alternative sexual lifestyles are not 'qualitatively other from what is known as the benchmark conventional nuclear family'. Close relationship theorists are convinced that the traditional nuclear family can no longer serve as a meaningful paradigm and focus for scholarly research ...

In the taxonomy of sexually based adult relationships, the presence or absence of a legally recognized bond, such as marriage, is a secondary consideration. Marriage is merely a 'de jure' category, not an actual scientific reality. In addition, the family itself largely fades away as a unit of analysis. For close relationship theorists, the only way effectively to understand a family system is to break it down into bi-directional dyadic pairs ...[50]

The movement to substitute adult personal relationships for marriage has begun to influence legislation and proposed legislation dealing with families, as the afore-mentioned ALI proposed *Principles of the Law of Family Dissolution* illustrates. Likewise, the Law Commission of Canada published a Discussion Paper entitled *Recognizing and supporting close personal relationships between adults*,[51] recommending that parliament reform existing law and to give equal support for all forms of intimate adult relationships. The paper began with two very questionable assumptions: 'A broad diversity of close adult personal relationships is a sign of a vibrant society. Permitting people to form relationships that matter to them and in which they can find happiness and comfort is the mark of pluralism and freedom.'[52] Those assumptions led the Law Commission Discussion Paper to the logical (and radical) conclusion that: 'All people should be able to freely choose their intimate partners and their legal relational status without penalty from the state or without financial inducement to abandon their choices ... The role of the law ought to be to support any and all relationships that further valuable social goals, and to remain neutral with respect to individuals' choice of a particular family form.'[53]

These proposals to treat all committed relationships equally in the law, regardless of form, appeal to powerful principles of pluralism, tolerance, and legal realism. But they mask some very serious problems for implementation as well as for the institution of marriage. I will briefly discuss those problems as they relate to proposals (1) to legalize same-sex marriage, (2) to create marriage-equivalent same-sex 'civil unions', (3) to extend some specific

---

50 Id. at 15–16.   **51** Http://www.lcc.gc.ca/en/forum/cpra (searched Jan. 15, 2001).   **52** Law Commission of Canada, *Recognizing and supporting close personal relationships between adults*, id. at 3.   **53** Id. at 38, citing B. Cossman & B. Ryder, *Gay, lesbian and unmarried heterosexual couples and the Family Law Act: accommodating a diversity of family forms* (Toronto, 1993), at 3, 5.

benefits to same-sex couples and (4) to give marital benefits to heterosexual couples in 'committed relationships.'

Same-sex marriage and concerns about preserving the institution of marriage

'Marriage is a vital social institution.'[54] The Supreme Court of the United States has frequently emphasized the importance of special protections given marriage because it is such a basic social institution. For example, in *Neilson v. Kilgore*,[55] in 1892, the court declared:

> Marriage is a civil institution, a *status*, in reference to which Mr Bishop has well said: 'Public interests overshadow private, – one which public policy holds specially in the hands of the law for the public good, and over which the law presides in a manner not known in the other departments.' 1 Bish. Mar. & Div. § 5.

As Justice Harlan put it in 1961 in his celebrated dissent in *Poe v. Ullman*, 'the institution of marriage [is] an institution which the State not only must allow, but which always and in every age it has fostered and protected.'[56]

Social institutions like marriage are based on shared understandings. The institution of marriage conveys powerful signals, scripting our most basic social and familial relations. Marriage links safe sex, responsible procreation and optimal child rearing. It bonds husband and wives, and connect parents (especially fathers) to children in the most beneficial way. It civilizes spouse, turning shallow young men into responsible husbands and fathers and turning superficial young women into committed wives and mothers. Institutions reinforce what cultural anthropologists call 'root paradigms,' that reflect the assumptions underlying the very nature of existence … They guide behavior of both individuals and groups in the crises of life, and often

---

54 *Goodridge v. Dep't. of Pub. Health*, 798 N.E.2d 941, 948 (Mass. 2003). 55 145 U.S. 487, 491(1892). See also *Williams v. North Carolina*, 317 U.S. 287, 298–99 (1942) ('each state by virtue of its command over its domiciliaries and its large interest in the institution of marriage can alter within its own borders the marriage status of the spouse domiciled there …'); *Cleveland v. U.S.*, 329 U.S. 14, 26 (1946) ('polygyny, like other forms of marriage, is basically a cultural institution rooted deeply in the religious beliefs and social mores of those societies in which it appears.'); *Orr v. Orr*, 440 U.S. 268, 281 (1979) (historical institutional discrimination against married women); *Lehr v. Robertson*, 463 U.S. 248, 257 ('The institution of marriage has played a critical role both in defining the legal entitlements of family members and in developing the decentralized structure of our democratic society.'); *Lawrence v. Texas*, 539 U.S. 558, 585 (O'Connor, J, concurring) ('Unlike the moral disapproval of same-sex relations – the asserted state interest in this case – other reasons exist to promote the institution of marriage beyond mere moral disapproval of an excluded group'). 56 367 U.S. 497, 553 (1961) (Harlan, J, dissenting). See also *Griswold v. Connecticut*, 381 U.S. 479, 499 (1965) (Goldberg, J, concurring).

require self-sacrifice on the part of individuals in the interest of group welfare.[57] Root paradigms 'are, at the socio-cultural level analogous to DNA and RNA at the genetic level'.[58] They crystallize the formative validity beliefs of society. The institution of marriage protects essential and ubiquitous 'root paradigm' of human societies.

Laws can reinforce, support and strengthen basic social institutions, and contribute to 'the shared public meanings' that constitute basic social institutions.[59] The law also can change, undermine, and weaken those common understandings and the institutions they sustain. A significant change in a 'root paradigm', a substantial alteration of the shared understanding that undergirds a social institution, may produce profound consequences for society.[60] As social institutions are weakened, their ability to express community values (and thus help educate the rising generation) also weakens as does their ability to channel members of society into responsible, socially beneficial, productive, and liberating behaviors and relationships[61]. Since marriage is one of the few mediating structures sheltering the individual from the growing and crushing powers of the state, the potential weakening of the institution of marriage is not a risk to be lightly dismissed.[62]

That is why Jennifer Roback Morse of the Hoover Institution expresses profound concerns about the weakening of the institution of marriage.

> Marriage is a naturally occurring, pre-political institution that emerges spontaneously from society. Western society is drifting toward a redefinition of marriage as a bundle of legally defined benefits bestowed by the state. As a libertarian, I find this trend regrettable. The organic view of marriage is more consistent with the libertarian vision of a society of free and responsible individuals, governed by a constitutionally limited state. The drive toward a legalistic view of

---

57 See Merlin G. Myers, 'The morality of kinship', the Virginia F. Cutler Lecture, Brigham Young University, Provo, Utah, 15 November 1983, in *BYU Speeches of the Year*, 1983–84, at 45 (hereinafter cited as 'Myers'). See also Victor Turner, *Dramas, fields and metaphors: symbolic action in human society*, 23–59 (1974) (examining how paradigms influences human behavior). See also B.C. Ray, Victor Turner, in *Encyclopedia of religion* 95 (ed. M. Eliade, 1987) (culture is a 'changing entity, influenced by 'root paradigms,' that is, by axiomatic frames, or deep myths, that propel and transform people and groups at critical moments'). 58 Myers, supra note 58, at 45. 59 Dan Cere, principal investigator, *The future of family law, law and the marriage crisis in North America* (Institute for American Values, Institute for the Study of Marriage, Law and Culture, and institute for Marriage and Public Policy, 2005) at 38. 60 See generally Monte Neil Stewart & William C. Duncan, *Marriage and the betrayal of Perez and Loving*, available at www.manwomanmarriage.org (copy in author's possession), (discussing the importance of marriage as the basic social institution of society). 61 Carl E. Schneider, 'The channeling function in family law', 20 *Hofstra L. Rev.* 495, 498, 503 (1992). 62 Cere, *The future of family law*, at 8.

marriage is part of the relentless march toward politicizing every aspect of society [...]

Government does not create marriage any more than government creates jobs [...] validates it!

The new idea about marriage claims that no structure should be privileged over any other. The supposedly libertarian subtext of this idea is that people should be as free as possible to make their personal choices. But the very nonlibertarian consequence of this new idea is that it creates a culture that obliterates the informal methods of enforcement. Parents can't raise their eyebrows and expect children to conform to the socially accepted norms of behavior, because there are no socially accepted norms of behavior. Raised eyebrows and dirty looks no longer operate as sanctions on behavior slightly or even grossly outside the norm. The modern code of sexual and parental tolerance ruthlessly enforces a code of silence ...[63]

The institution of marriage is so crucial to the organization of society and so powerful in effecting the transmission of social scripts and values that it has always been an appealing target for social and political movements. In the past two centuries at least two powerful social movements in America have 'captured' marriage for the purpose of mainstreaming their ideologies and promoting their political agendas. The White Supremacy movement and its successor the Eugenics movement both redefined marriage, adding require-ments to marry that were extraneous to the purpose and essential function of marriage. Indeed, the last vestiges of both the Eugenic movement and the White Supremacy movements' influence upon marriage law were only recently removed by the Supreme Court decision in *Loving v. Virginia*, declaring anti-miscegenation to be unconstitutional.[64]

The current effort to legalize same-sex marriage is the latest political movement seeking to capture (redefine) marriage. The movement to legalize same-sex marriage is the successor to those earlier social/political movements, and it poses exactly the same kind of threat to the institution of marriage, with the same potential for harm to society, as accompanied the capture and redefinition of marriage by those earlier (and equally popular) socio-political movements.[65]

⋆Legalizing same-sex marriage would profoundly alter the institution of marriage. It would shake the moral consensus regarding the meaning and responsibilities of marriage. That is because it would alter critical elements of the heart of the relationship.⋆

63 Jennifer Roback Morse, *Marriage and the limits of contract*. Ms. Morse is also the author of *Love and economics: why the laissez-faire family doesn't work.*   64 388 US1 (1967). See generally Stewart and Duncan, *Marriage and the betrayal of Perez and Loving.*   65 See generally id; see also Wardle, *Tyranny.*

The heterosexual dimensions of the relationship are at the very core of what makes 'marriage' what it is, and why it is so valuable to individuals and to society. The union of two persons of different genders creates something of unique potential strengths and inimitable potential value to society. It is the *integration* of the universe of gender differences (profound and subtle, biological and cultural, psychological and genetic) associated with sexual identity that constitutes the core and essence of marriage. In the same way the 'separate but equal' was a false promise, and that racial segregation is *not* equivalent to racial integration, same-sex marriage is not equal to real, heterosexual marriage. Thus, cross-gender uniting in marriage is not merely a matter of arbitrary definition or semantic word-play; it goes to the heart of the very *concept* or *nature* of marriage relationship itself.[66]

Men and women really are different and a union of a man and a woman really is different than a union of two men or two women. As Justice Ruth Bader Ginsburg stated for the Supreme Court in *Virginia v. United States*: 'Physical differences between men and women, however, are enduring: "[T]he two sexes are not fungible; a community made up exclusively of one [sex] is different from a community composed of both."'[67] As even the critical rationalist Judge Posner conceded: '[I]t would be misleading to suggest that homosexual marriages are likely to be as stable or rewarding as heterosexual marriages ... [P]ermitting homosexual marriage would place government in the dishonest position of propagating a false picture of the reality of homosexuals' lives.[68] Likewise, Professor Cere has written:

> A 'close relationships' culture fails to acknowledge fundamental facets of human life: the fact of sexual difference; the enormous tide of heterosexual desire in human life; the procreativity of heterosexual bonding; the unique social ecology of heterosexual parenting which offers children bonds with their biological parents; and the rich genealogical nature of heterosexual family ties and the web of intergenerational supports for family members that they provide.[69]

Moreover, marriage is not merely a private association; it is a public status, a public institution, involving significant public responsibilities in support of which are extended substantial public benefits. The argument that privacy considerations mandate extension of the public status, institutions and benefits of marriage to same-sex relationships confuses public and private realms and is nonsensical. Privacy might justify legal non-interference with truly private same-sex relations or bar public intrusion upon the private

66 Lynn D. Wardle, 'A critical analysis of constitutional claims for same-sex marriage', 1996, *B.Y.U. L. Rev.* 1.   67 *United States v. Virginia*, 518 U.S. 515, 533 (1996) (quoting *Ballard v. United States*, 329 U.S. 187, 193 (1946)).   68 Richard A. Posner, *Sex and reason* 312 (1992). 69 Cere, *The future of family law*, at 8.

realm adult committed relationships, but the privacy principles provides no justification for a claim to the public status, public responsibilities, and public benefits, of the public institution of marriage.

Likewise, the principle of tolerance fails to justify legalization of same-sex marriage. The law deals with relationships in three ways: (1) it prohibits some, (2) it tolerates others, and (3) it prefers and privileges others. Same-sex relationships historically were prohibited. In recent years, same-sex relationships have been decriminalized, and have moved from the category of 'prohibited' into the category of 'tolerated' – the law neither forbids same-sex relations, nor does it endorse them or give special preference to them; the law simply allows and tolerates them. However, marriage is the classic example of the most highly preferred, specially privileged relationship. Marriage is not merely tolerated, it is preferred and privileged, so the principle of tolerance does not support a claim for same-sex marriage. A claim for same-sex marriage is a claim for great preference and privilege, not a claim for mere tolerance.

Finally, part of the reason for the exceptional high and privileged status and benefits accorded the institution of marriage is because it is the institution in which most parenting is performed, and where parenting is performed best. That provides one of the sharpest distinctions between marriage and other 'committed relationships'. However, advocates of same-sex marriage (or civil unions) have been actively promoting the myth that there is 'no difference' for children between being raised by same-sex couples and being raised by married (conjugal) couples. That claim is blatantly misleading, in some respects demonstrably false, and logically absurd.[70]

Most of the studies that purport to show 'no difference' in children raised by homosexual parents are methodologically flawed, distorted, biased, and unreliable. Virtually all of the studies that purport to show 'no difference' have been criticized for invalidating bias, improper hypotheses, inadequate sample sizes, lack of or improper control groups, inappropriate testing techniques, incompetent interpretation, and conclusions that ignore the data.[71] As Lerner and Nagai reported: '[T]hese small studies claiming non-significant results must be treated as entirely inconclusive.'[72] Furthermore,

70 See generally Lynn D. Wardle, 'The potential impact of homosexual parenting on children', 1997 *U. Ill. L. Rev.* 833 (1997).   71 Robert Lerner & Althea K. Nagai, 'No Basis: What the Studies *Don't* Tell Us About Same-Sex Parenting' (Marriage Law Project, January 2001); Robert Lerner, and Althea K. Nagai, *Homosexual parenting studies: a methodological critique*, in 'Revitalizing the institution of marriage for the twenty-first century: an agenda for strengthening in marriage' (Alan. J. Hawkins, Lynn D. Wardle & David Coolidge (eds.), Greenwood Publishing Group 2002); Richard E. Redding, '*Sociopolitical diversity in psychology: the case for pluralism*', 56 *M. Psych.* 205, 207 (2001); David Kramer, 'Gay parents and their children: a review of research and practical applications', 64 J. *Counseling & Develop.* 506 (1986).   72 Lerner & Nagain, No Basis, at 108.

most of the studies that purport to show 'no difference' in children raised by homosexual parents fail to ask the hard questions, fail to examine the most important effects, evade the areas of greatest concern or risk regarding the potential impacts on children.[73] The 'no difference' myth is clearly false because even the biased, pro-lesbigay-parenting studies shows that children raised by lesbian or gay couples are more likely than children raised by conjugal couples or heterosexual parents to be drawn to a homosexual identity, homo-erotic attraction, and early, risky sexual behavior. The leading pro-lesbigay parenting study of Gollenbach and Tasker reveals, in the words of one reviewer, that 'there is a statistically significant difference between the two groups [children with heterosexual parents and children with homosexual parents] when one compares ratings of same-sex attraction.'[74] Many other 'no difference' studies also have produced data indicating 'some significant differences between children raised by lesbian mothers versus heterosexual mothers in their family relationships, gender identity and gender behavior.'[75] A notable but small critical study found substantial differences between children raised by lesbian mothers and children raised by single heterosexual mothers in terms of how many wanted to marry, how many wanted to have children, and in the sexual self-identities of the children.[76] Even the avowedly pro-lesbigay parenting report of Stacey and Biblarz acknowledged that there are differences between children raised by lesbigay parents and heterosexual parents relating to sexual orientation, gender-appropriate activities, and homoerotic behaviors.[77] Thus, the 'no difference' claim is demonstrably false concerning adolescent sexual orientation and behavior.

Furthermore, the claim that there is 'no difference' between raising children in a married heterosexual parent family and in a lesbigay parent family contradicts every theory of child development. Child development theories lead researchers to expect that children will imitate their caregivers (usually parents) in significant ways. The claim that children raised by adults engaged in a homosexual relationships will not follow their parents' example flies in the face of what we know about child development.

To extend marriage or comparable, equivalent legal status and rights to same-sex committed relationships could have the effect of 'de-coupling' the socially significant tie between marriage and parenting. By conveying the

---

73 See generally Lynn D. Wardle, 'Considering the impacts on children and society of *"lesbigay parenting"*', 23 *Quinnipiac L. Rev.* 541 (2004).   74 Warren Throckmorton, PhD, *Do Parents Influence the Sexual Preference of Children?*, <http://www.drthrockmorton.com/article.asp?id=39> (19 February 2004) (seen 25 March 2004).   75 Philip A. Belcastro et al., 'A review of data based studies addressing the affects of homosexual parenting on children's sexual and social functioning', 20 *J. Divorce & Remarriage* 105, 112, 119 (1993).   76 Id., 110 (1993).   77 Judith Stacey and Timothy J. Biblarz, 'How does sexual orientation of parents matter?', 66 *M Soc. Rev.* 159, 164–9 (2001).

message that 'fathers (or mothers) don't matter,' that two women or two men can raise a child just as well as a mother and a father, extending marriage-equivalent status and benefits to same-sex 'committed unions' could significantly weaken the socially important male link that children have to the community. Finally, those proposing a major change of legal policy regarding legal parenting have the burden of proof to establish clearly that there will not be significant potential harm for the children, and the research upon this issue is very preliminary at this point. Until the research clearly and honestly shows no significant increase in potential for harm of the children, it would be irresponsible to give legal status and benefits to other 'committed relationships' comparable to that accorded to married conjugal parents.

Concerns about legal recognition of marriage-equivalent 'civil unions' for same-sex committed relationships

The creation of a new legal status for 'committed relationships' with legal status and benefits that are tailored to the characteristics of such relationships seems reasonable on its face. However, extending the same status, rights, and legal incidents of marriage to same-sex committed relationships without calling them marriages would (a) still amount to same-sex marriage by another name, (b) pose a serious threat to marriage by confusing the concept and meaning of marriage, (c) send a false message to society concerning the qualities and characteristics of the relationships, and (d) result in excessive, unjust benefits disproportionate to the contributions of those relationships to society.

The prevailing model in America, as evidenced by the 'civil union' laws in Vermont and Connecticut, and the 'domestic partnership' law in California, has not been to tailor or customize the status and legal benefits of same-sex civil unions to the characteristics, circumstances, contributions and needs of the parties to such relationships. Rather, the approach that is heavily promoted in America is to simply 'copy and paste' all of the legal rights, benefits, and effects of marriage onto the new same-sex civil union status. The legal incidents are stunningly excessive and inappropriate, simply imported wholesale from marriage law rather than tailored to the characteristics of same-sex unions. That is problematic because the extension of specific benefits, rights, and responsibilities to married couples has occurred by incremental process over decades, centuries and millennia. That bundle of marriage rights and benefits has been customized to the characteristics, circumstances, contributions and needs of the parties in a marriage. Same-sex committed relationships do not share all of the same qualities that have led to the fashioning of all of the specific marital benefits and incidents.

While the creation of a carefully tailored, customized 'committed relationships' statute for same-sex couples has some appeal, it is impossible.

First, many gay advocates are offended by and oppose 'civil unions' because they are not marriage. For reasons ranging from a desire for the social validation to purely economic motives, they demand no less than the same benefits and status as marriage. (Thus, for example, even though same-sex couples had the same benefits as married couples in Canada, they continued to push until the courts ruled that they could marry.)

Second, it makes it easier for advocates of same-sex marriage or marriage-equivalent domestic partnership to convince courts that equal protection mandates giving full marital status and benefits to same-sex couples. The argument is simple: by enacting a civil union or law extending marriage-like benefits to same-sex committed relationships, the state has recognized the inequality of denying same-sex couples marital status and benefits; thus, equality is in order. However, the 'civil union' status the legislature created is not equal in status to marriage; the remedy is that the state must expand the benefits and status it created to provide label, status and benefits to same-sex couples fully equivalent to marriage. That is precisely the reasoning of the Massachusetts Supreme Judicial Court in 2004 in *Opinion of the Justices to the Senate* holding that a civil union bill extending all of the rights and benefits of marriage to same-sex couples without the label 'marriage' would be unconstitutional.[78]

Third, defenders of traditional marriage oppose the 'camel's nose' proposal, for they would foresee that it would lead to the creation of a marriage-equivalent status. It is just a small step from same-sex committed relationships to same-sex marriage.[79] Thus, even the enactment of a customized, limited 'committed relationships' status and benefit legislation would offend nearly everyone, invite litigation, and would evolve into an imitation-marriage form of civil union with full benefits and status equal to marriage – the very thing a carefully-tailored domestic partnership would be designed to avoid.

Fourth, legalizing same-sex civil unions with the same or substantially equivalent status and legal benefits as marriage is tantamount to legalizing same-sex marriage. Marriage is more than just a piece of paper or a word. Legally, it is a bundle of rights and responsibilities. If the same bundle of legal rights is conferred upon same-sex committed unions, even if those unions are called 'civil unions,' they effectively are marriages. Thus, legalizing same-sex civil unions raises the same set of concerns about weakening the institution of marriage as those accompanying the full legalization of same-sex marriage.[80]

---

78 802 N.E.2d 565 (Mass. 2004).   79 William N. Eskridge, Jr., 'Comparative law and the same-sex marriage debate: a step-by-step approach toward state recognition', 31 *McGeorge L. Rev* 641 (2000); see also Eskridge, *Equality Practice*, at 854.   80 See supra, Part III.A.

Concerns about legal recognition of heterosexual nonmarital committed relationships

Offering specific benefits to committed heterosexual nonmarital relationships that are tailored to the realities of those relationships has strong appeal to some. That would respect the autonomy of couples to order their adult intimate relationships (a great value in these days of intrusive and pervasive government regulation). The first problem, however as shown by the ALI *Principles* and the Canadian *Close Personal Relationship* report, is that rather than tailoring benefits to the actual characteristics and needs of nonmarital couples, policymakers and courts simply transfer wholesale the benefits tailored for married couples. That is irrational because nonmarital heterosexual cohabitation is very different from marriage.

A great deal of social science research clearly establishes heterosexual nonmarital couples have very different attributes, behavior patterns, and expectations than married couples. Even 'cohabitors themselves typically make a sharp distinction between marriage and [cohabitation]'.[81] For example, the financial expectations of parties who cohabit differ markedly from persons who marry. Cohabiting couples are less likely to join and co-mingle their finances than are married couples. Many people enter into nonmarital cohabitation to avoid marriage and particularly seek to avoid the economic responsibilities and obligations of marriage. Fear of the economic consequences of failure of a marriage is a major reason for people cohabiting as domestic partners rather than entering marriage.[82] Thus, the extension the same economic consequences of marriage to heterosexual parties who are cohabiting in 'committed relationships' is of dubious rationality, and not an accurate reflection of either the expectations or economic realities of those relationships.

The second problem with extension of some marriage-like legal benefits to cohabiting committed relationships is that it creates an incentive to enter those relationships. Empirical research has been done in the past twenty years on heterosexual nonmarital 'committed relationships' (cohabitation), and the picture that emerges of those relationships that emerges is troubling indeed. For example, in their thorough reviews of data on outcomes of nonmarital cohabitation in the United States, David Popenoe and Barbara Dafoe Whitehead, found that: '[V]irtually all research on the topic has determined that the chances of divorce ending a marriage preceded by cohabitation are significantly greater than for a marriage not preceded by cohabitation.'[83] Likewise, '[a]ccording to recent studies cohabitants tend not

---

81 Law Commission of Canada, at 37.   82 See Martha L. Fineman, 'Law and changing patterns of behavior: sanctions on non-marital cohabitation', 1981 *Wis. L. Rev.* 275, 325 (1981). 83 David Popenoe & Barbara Dafoe Whitehead, 'Should We Live Together? What Young Adults Need to Know about Cohabitation before Marriage, A Comprehensive Review of Recent Research at 3, 4' (The National Marriage Project: The Next Generation Series, 1999) <http://www. smartmarriages.com/ cohabit.html> (searched 12 June 1999).

to be as committed as married couples in their dedication to the continuation of the relationship … and they are more oriented toward their own personal autonomy.'[84] Most cohabiting relationships are relatively short lived.

In general, cohabiting relationships tend to be 'less satisfactory than marriage relationships'.[85]'Annual rates of depression among cohabiting couples are more than three times what they are among married couples. And women in cohabiting relationships are more likely than married women to suffer physical and sexual abuse. Some research has shown that aggression is at least twice as common among cohabitors as it is among married persons.'[86] Linda Waite's review of the National Survey of Families and Households data revealed that when cohabiting couples argue they are more than three times as likely to resort to physical violence than are married couples, a finding supported by several other studies.[87] Studies also indicate that in cohabiting couples there are 'far higher levels of child abuse than is found in intact families.[88] Child sexual abuse is much higher for children whose biological parent or parents are only cohabiting rather than married.[89] '[T]hree quarters of children born to cohabiting parents will see their parents split up before they reach age sixteen, whereas only about a third of children born to married parents face a similar fate.'[90] Likewise, '[w]hile the 1996 poverty rate for children living in married couple households was about 6%, it was 31% for children living in cohabiting households.'[91] Another study notes that cohabiting men are four times more likely than husbands to cheat on their partners, and cohabiting women are eight times more likely than wives to be unfaithful to their partners.[92] A recent study of the relationship of marital status and individual happiness reported that a strong positive relationship between marital status and personal happiness exists in sixteen of the seventeen nations examined.[93] The report found that being married increased happiness equally for men and for women in the nations examined,

84 Id. at 5.   85 Id. at 6. Popenoe and Whitehead note the 1980s data showing that about 80% of cohabitants married. In the 1990s, however, that rate of cohabitant marriage fell to about 35%. Forste, supra note 169.   86 Id. at 7.   87 Waite & Gallagher, supra note 69, at 155. Dean M. Busby, 'Violence in the family' in *Family Research, a 60-Year Review*, 1930–1990 at 361 (Steven G. Bahr, ed., 1991) ('Yllo and Straus (1981) … found that "cohabiting couples had higher rates of fiolence than married couples. Severe violence was almost five times as likely in cohabitation relationships [than in marriages".'); Faith Abbot, 'No Book', *Human Life Rev.*, Winter 1998, at 31, 43 (citing a 1993 British study by the Family Education Trust, using data on documented cases of child abuse and neglect between 1872 and 1877; found that – compared with a stable nuclear family – the incidence of abuse was 33 times higher when the mother was living with a boyfriend not related to the child. And even when the live-in boyfriend was the biological father of the children, the chances of abuse were still 20 times more likely); Popenoe & Whitehead, supra note 118, at 7 (aggression is at least twice as common among cohabitors as it is among married persons).   88 Popenoe & Whitehead, supra note 118, at 8.   89 Waite & Gallagher, supra note 69, at 159.   90 Popenoe & Whitehead, supra note 118, at 7.   91 Id. at 8.   92 *The Marriage Movement: A Statement of Principles*, <www.marriagemovement.org>, (June 29, 2000).   93 Steven Stack & J. Ross Eshleman, 'Marital status and happiness: a 17-nation study', 60 J. *Marr. & Fam.* 527 (1998).

and marriage was more than three times more closely associated with happiness than was nonmarital cohabitation.

Thus, if the law creates a new 'committed relationship' status with a substantially equivalent legal status and benefits as marriage, that equates that new status with marriage. That would send a false message about functional equivalence of domestic partnership and marriage. It would be a trap for the naive and unwary.

There are good reasons to believe that if 'committed relationships' are given significant legal recognition, many heterosexual couples would choose to enter 'committed relationships' and fewer couples would marry. For example, nonmarital cohabitation increased dramatically after the famous *Marvin v. Marvin* case and similar 'palimony' cases in courts in other states in the 1970s and early 1980s. Between 1970 (just six years before *Marvin*) and 1999 (just twenty three years after *Marvin*) the number of unmarried heterosexual couples living together rose more than 800 percent.[94] At the same time, the rate of marriage has fallen dramatically.[95] While cause and effect relations between legal changes and social changes are hard to pin down exactly, at least it can be reasonably expected that further legalizing of heterosexual cohabitation would result in more (dangerous) cohabitation and less (and less stable) marriage.

Scandinavian countries have extended marriage-equivalent legal benefits to heterosexual nonmarital cohabitants for nearly half-a-century (and also have recognized same-sex domestic partnership for more than a dozen years). The experience of those countries also suggests that legalizing domestic partnership will weaken marriage. As Judge Posner put it: '[T]here is evidence that the widespread substitution of cohabitation for marriage in Sweden has given that country the highest rate of family dissolution and single parenting in the developed world.'[96]

It appears that giving marriage-like status and/or benefits to nonmarital 'committed relationships' not only has a leveling influence upon marriage, but it also contributes to and crystalizes a significant weakening of the institution of marriage in society. When so weakened, the institution of marriage rarely recovers its position in society without great trauma.[97]

94 Statistical Abstract of the United States 2000 (U.S. Dept. of Commerce. Economics, and Statistics Admin., U.S. Census Bureau) at 55, Table No. 60 (from 1,589 in 1980 to 4, 486 in 1999); id. at 52, Table No. 57 (41.1% of women 15–44 in 1995 had cohabitated); id. at 51, Table No. 53 (24.1% of population in 1980 never married; 29.0% in 1999); Statistical Abstract 1995 at Table No. 60 (523,000 in 1970).   95 Statistical Abstract 2000 at 51, Table No. 53 (from 65.5% in 1980 to 59.5% in 1999); Statistical Abstract 1977 at 38, Table No. 48 (married population 71.7% in 1970, 69.6% in 1976).   96 *Irizarry v. Bd. of Educa.*, 251 F.3d 604, 608 (7th Cir. 2001), citing David Popenoe, 'Disturbing the nest: family change and decline in modern societies, 173–4 (1988).   97 William J. Goode, *World changes in divorce patterns* 318, 335–6 (1993).

THE MYTH OF EQUIVALENCE

Professor Daniel Cere warns of the growing 'marriage crisis in North America' that is the result of new 'competing models of marriage that are at odds in today's family law debates[.]'[98] We must remember that not all 'committed relationships' are of equal worth to society, to families, and to individuals. All committed relationships are not equal in terms of providing equally for the growth and stability of the adult couple and their mutual commitment and relationship. Not all 'loving' and 'committed relationships are equal in terms of providing financial security for the parties. Not all relationships produce equal fidelity and relationships satisfaction. Not all relationships provide equal protection against domestic violence. Conjugal marriage is the best in all these aspects. Likewise, not all relationships are equal in terms of providing opportunities for children. Not all relationships provide equal prospects for educational development of children. All relationships do not provide the same economic protection for children; marriage of their mother and father is best. All relationships do not provide the same protection against child abuse; marriage of man and woman provides the safest haven. All relationship do not provide the same protection against exposure to drug and alcohol abuse, and to other forms of dangerous environmental influences. Marriage between mother and father clearly provides the best, most promising environment for children to grow up and development in. Children deserve the best child rearing environment and unquestionably marriage provides that. While there are occasional individual deviations from the norm, the general experience is that conjugal marriage of the parents is the parenting form that is best for children in many ways. To fail to recognize the profound differences between various kinds of committed relationships is fatal to individuals, families, and society.

Marriage has an ethical or moral dimension lacking in other committed relationships that transforms it into a truly unique institution. 'Marriage is not just an inferior version of going steady, or a sexual barter, or a consumer good. Love is more than a style.'[99] The main weakness of close relationship theory that underlies the movement to give equal legal status to all committed relationships 'is that it radically relativises and privatises every possible dimension of human relationships, rejecting any criterion for relationship success other than the self's subjective assessment of the self's needs, denying any real connection between courtship and marriage, and obliterating any meaningful distinction between marriage and other sexually close relationships.'[1] It is simplistically reductionist, and in haste to see equivalence overlooks and eliminates the essence of what makes marriage valuable for couples and for society.

98 Cere, *The future of family law*, at 5, 7.   99 Ibid., at 31.   1 Ibid., at 30.

Certainly some committed relationship (including same-sex relations) may make some contributions that are valuable to society and that justify legal recognition for some specific social purposes. In appropriate circumstances those specific contributions should be socially acknowledged and legally recognized. Extension of specific legal benefits linked with those contributions (such as hospital visitation, medical decision-making, and perhaps tailored asset co-ownership) is not unreasonable. However, neither 'committed relationships' in general, nor same-sex unions in particular, make overall contributions toward the social purposes of marriage that are comparable to the contributions of heterosexual marriage. Thus, the status and same or substantially equivalent package of legal benefits and incidents of marriage itself or marriage status benefits ought not to be extended to nonmarital heterosexual and same-sex unions.

CONCLUSION: FORM REFLECTS SUBSTANCE, AND LOVE IS NOT ALL YOU NEED

The connection between form and substance, between formal premises and actual behavior is ... of quite dreadful importance today. We face a world which is threatened not only with disorganization of many kinds, but also with the destruction of its environment, and we, today, are still unable to think clearly about the relations between an organism and its environment.[2]

The proposal to treat as equivalent all committed relationships reflects apathy or ignorance about our social environment, and rests upon very confused thinking about the interconnection between domestic relationships and our social environment. Since at least the time of Aristotle, we have understood that life is created when form and matter are combined.[3] The quality of life reflects and varies with the form and substance of domestic relationships. The relationships between the substance and form of marriage and of other committed relationships differ, and those differences justify treating those relationships differently in law.

'The extent to which substance and form are linked is a complex one.'[4] In family relations, the connection between form and substance are deep and

2 Gregory Bateson, *Form, Substance, Difference*, http://www.rawpaint.com/ library/bateson/ formsubstancedifference.html (seen 23 April 2005), from Steps to an Ecology of Mind (1972).
3 Aristotle on Substance, Matter, and Form, http://faculty.washington.edu/smcohen/320/ zeta17.htm (seen 23 April 2005) ('Matter underlies and persists through substantial changes. A substance is generated (destroyed) by having matter take on (lose) form ... An animal is generated when matter (contributed by the mother) combines with form (contributed by the father)').   4 Jay M. Feinman, 'Un-making law: the classical revival in the common law', 28

profound. Form reflects substance. The legal form of domestic relationships should reflect the reality and substance of those relations. To confer the 'form' of marriage upon committed relationships that in substance are quite different from marriage would be misleading, distorting, and detrimental to the basic unit of society. The form would communicate a false message about the substance of the relationship. Mere wishful thinking, the wish that all committed relationships would be like marriages, is not a good reason to confer the legal status and benefits of marriage on relationships whose substance differs markedly and materially from marriage. The movement to give heterosexual nonmarital and same-sex committed relationships legal status and benefits substantially equivalent to marriage reflects the discredited Kelsenian myth of positivist legal alchemy – that we can change the substance of relationships by merely altering their legal form.

Human experience teaches that mere 'commitment' is highly ambiguous, unreliable, and largely indiscernible by judges. Subjective feelings or intentions like 'commitment' are unreliable measure of love.[5] Love is best measured by behavior. Human experience indicates that mere nostalgic feelings or sentiments in the heart, or good intentions (commitments) in the mind of the lover pale and fade away; whereas acts of care, concern, sacrifice, and the deliberate undertakings of clear legal obligations endure and substantiate love and commitment.

Commitment as action, manifest in interconnnected form and substance is what matters in life, domestic relationships, and in the law. Relationships that are truly committed reflect that commitment in form (marriage) as well as substance. The form and substance of marriage are truly unique among committed relationships. Thus, ultimately, love is *not* 'all you need', but loving commitment manifest in both the form and substance of conjugal marriage is what is needed for families to flourish, individuals to enjoy fullness and liberty, and societies to prosper.

Seattle U. L. Rev. 1, 53 (2004). Id. (Thomas Grey ... suggests, 'the new formalism is just the old legal pragmatism, now mostly in the hands of conservatives rather than Progressives ... .'). '[A]lmost all questions of interpretation implicate the tension between form and substance.' Avery Weiner Katz, *The Economic of Form and Substance in Contract Interpretation*, at 1 (Preliminary version, February 2002), eScholarship Repository, University of California, http://repositories. edlib.org/berkeley_law_econ/spring2002/4, available at http://repositories.cdlib.org/cgi/ viewcontent.cgi?article=1027&context=berkeley_law_econ (seen April 23, 2005). *See generally* Duncan Kennedy, 'Form and substance in private law adjudication', 89 *Harv. L. Rev.* 1685, 1685 (1976) (comparing the costs and benefits of strict legal rules and looser standards). **5** As Susan Bandes has written: 'Of what use is an emotion to law if it doesn't manifest itself in action? ... How can a trier of fact ascertain what emotion an offender feels?' Susan A. Bandes, 'Introduction' in *The passions of law*, 12 (Susan A. Bandes, ed. 1999). See generally Lynn D. Wardle, 'All you need is love?' 14 *So. Cal. Rev. L. & Wo.'s Studs.* 51 (2004).

Marriage or 'civil partnership' for same-sex couples: will Ireland lead or follow the United Kingdom?

ROBERT WINTEMUTE*

IN THE EUROPEAN UNION IN 2007, discrimination in the criminal law against sexual activity between men or between women is not permitted, thanks to the case law of the European Court of Human Rights, including the landmark cases brought by Jeffrey Dudgeon in Northern Ireland and by David Norris in the Republic of Ireland.[1] National legislation must ban discrimination based on sexual orientation in public and private sector employment and higher education, thanks to a European Community Directive.[2] The focus of groups working for full legal equality for lesbian, gay, bisexual and transgender ('LGBT') individuals at the national level has therefore shifted to the rights of same-sex couples, including equal access to legal marriage[3] and joint adoption of children. In the Irish context, this topic raises six questions I would like to address:

I   Is there an historical trend towards full LGBT equality in every country?
II Are there any strong arguments against allowing same-sex couples to marry?

* This chapter is based on a series of presentations on this topic, at three events in Ireland and one in Austria: Conference on 'ECHR Act Review and Human Rights in Committed Relationships', Irish Human Rights Commission and Law Society of Ireland, Dublin, 16 October 2004; Conference on 'Legal Recognition of Committed Relationships', School of Law, Trinity College Dublin, 30 April 2005; Meeting with 'Working Group on Domestic Partnership', Department of Justice, Equality and Law Reform, Dublin, 18 May 2006; 'Against Sexual Apartheid: A ceremonial act to celebrate 15 years for the Right to Love – 15 years *Rechtskomitee Lambda*', Austrian Federal Parliament (debating chamber of the lower house, the *Nationalrat*), Vienna, 2 October 2006.   1 See the judgments of the European Court of Human Rights ('ECtHR') in *Dudgeon v. United Kingdom* (22 Oct. 1981), and *Norris v. Ireland* (26 Oct. 1988). All judgments and admissibility decisions of the ECtHR are available at http://www.echr.coe.int (HUDOC).   2 Council Directive 2000/78/EC (in force 2 Dec. 2003). Ireland's legislation predates, and provides more extensive protection than, the EC Directive. See Unfair Dismissals (Amendment) Act, 1993, No. 22, s. 5(a), adding 'sexual orientation' to Unfair Dismissals Act, 1977, No. 10, s. 6(2)(e); protection extended to other aspects of employment by Employment Equality Act, 1998, No. 21, s. 6(2)(d); extended to education, goods, services, housing by Equal Status Act, 2000, No. 8, s. 3(2)(d).

III Is 'civil partnership' enough to provide full LGBT equality?
IV Is 'civil partnership' a necessary intermediate step towards full LGBT
     equality?
 V Must the Irish Constitution be amended to permit same-sex couples to
     marry?
VI Should Ireland follow Belgium and Spain, or the United Kingdom?

IS THERE AN HISTORICAL TREND TOWARDS FULL LGBT EQUALITY IN EVERY COUNTRY?

On 21 December 2005, I was a guest at one of the first 'civil partnership'
ceremonies held in England, at Chelsea Town Hall in London, under the
new law creating a 'separate but equal' institution of 'civil partnership' for
same-sex couples only.[4] My friends Adnan Ali from Pakistan, and Eric
Stobbaerts from Belgium-Morocco-Portugal, asked me to give a short speech
at their reception. I thanked them for allowing their guests to be part of
history, and reflected on how far same-sex couples have come. As late as 1860,
two men who loved each other in London (or in Dublin or Belfast), and
expressed their love physically, risked being executed by hanging.[5] In 2005,
145 years later, two men or two women who loved each other in London or
Belfast (but not yet in Dublin), became eligible to register their partnerships
at the town hall.

Roughly the same historical progression can be seen in many countries in
Europe, North America, Southern Africa, and Australasia: from the death
penalty to demands for equal access to legal marriage. Indeed, as Austrian
human rights lawyer Helmut Graupner has pointed out,[6] the first country in
the world to begin the process of law reform, by abolishing the death penalty
(decapitation) for same-sex 'carnal knowledge', was Austria in 1787. Once a
country has taken this step, others have followed, initially quite slowly, but
later at an accelerating pace.

---

3 I will generally refer to 'legal marriage' (a marriage with legal but not religious consequences)
and 'religious marriage' (a marriage with religious but not legal consequences), rather than
'civil marriage' (a marriage performed by a state official with legal but not religious
consequences). In some European countries, like the Netherlands, Belgium and France, 'civil
marriage' and 'legal marriage' are synonymous, because a religious marriage can never be a
legal marriage (have legal consequences). This is not true in Ireland, the United Kingdom,
Canada and the United States, where a marriage performed by a religious official (eg, in a
Christian church) can be simultaneously a legal marriage and a religious marriage.   4 Civil
Partnership Act 2004.   5 Paul Crane, *Gays and the law* (London, 1982).   6 See Helmut
Graupner, 'The first will be the last: legal recognition of same-sex partnerships in Austria' in
Robert Wintemute (ed.) & Mads Andenæs (hon. co-ed.), *Legal recognition of same-sex
partnerships: a study of national, European and international law* (Oxford, 2001), p. 549.

In England and Wales, it took 106 years, from 1861 when the death penalty was abolished,[7] to 1967, to decriminalize sexual activity between men,[8] and until 2000 to equalize the age of consent to sexual activity.[9] The first legislation against private sector discrimination in employment and higher education entered into force in 2003,[10] followed by laws on 'civil partnership' and joint adoption in 2005.[11] But same-sex couples are stilled denied equal access to legal marriage. In a few countries or states, where same-sex couples may marry and adopt children jointly, the long struggle for full legal equality is largely over: the Netherlands,[12] Belgium,[13] Spain,[14] Canada,[15]

---

7 Offences against the Person Act 1861, s. 61.   8 Sexual Offences Act 1967.   9 Sexual Offences (Amendment) Act 2000.   10 Employment Equality (Sexual Orientation) Regulations 2003.   11 See Robert Wintemute, 'Sexual orientation and gender identity' in Colin Harvey (ed.), *Human rights in the community* (Oxford, 2005) (survey of situation in the UK); Civil Partnership Act 2004 (all of UK, in force 5 Dec. 2005); Adoption and Children Act 2002, ss. 50, 51 (second-parent and joint adoption, England and Wales only, in force 30 Dec. 2005). s. 144(4) of the 2002 Act defines a 'couple' as including 'two people (whether of different sexes or the same sex) living as partners in an enduring family relationship'.   12 Act of 21 December 2000 amending Book 1 of the Civil Code, concerning the opening up of marriage for persons of the same sex (Act on the Opening Up of Marriage), *Staatsblad* 2001, nr. 9, in force 1 April 2001: Article 30: '1. A marriage can be contracted by two persons of different sex or of the same sex. 2. The law only considers marriage in its civil relations'.   13 *Loi du 13 février 2003 ouvrant le mariage à des personnes de même sexe et modifiant certaines dispositions du Code civil* (Law of 13 Feb. 2003 opening up marriage to persons of the same sex and modifying certain provisions of the Civil Code), *Moniteur belge*, 28 Feb. 2003, Edition 3, p. 9880, in force 1 June 2003: Art. 143. – 'Deux personnes de sexe différent ou de même sexe peuvent contracter mariage.' ('Two persons of different sex or of the same sex may contract marriage.') The 2003 law did not permit married same-sex couples to adopt children jointly. This exception was removed by the *Loi du 18 mai 2006 modifiant certaines dispositions du Code civil en vue de permettre l'adoption par des personnes de même sexe* (Law of 18 May 2006 modifying certain provisions of the Civil Code so as to permit adoption by persons of the same sex), *Moniteur belge*, 20 June 2006, Edition 2, p. 31128.   14 *Ley 13/2005, de 1 de julio, por la que se modifica el Código Civil en materia de derecho a contraer matrimonio* (Law 13/2005, of 1 July, providing for the amendment of the Civil Code with regard to the right to contract marriage), *Boletín Oficial del Estado* no. 157, 2 July 2005, pp 23632–4 (in force 3 July 2005): Article 44 (new second para.): '*El matrimonio tendrá los mismos requisitos y efectos cuando ambos contrayentes sean del mismo o de diferente sexo*' ('Marriage shall have the same requirements and effects whether both parties are of the same or different sex').   15 Civil Marriage Act, Statutes of Canada 2005, chapter 33 (in force 20 July 2005): s. 2: 'Marriage, for civil purposes, is the lawful union of two persons to the exclusion of all others.' See also Robert Wintemute, 'Sexual orientation and the Charter: the achievement of formal legal equality (1985–2005) and its limits', (2004) 49 *McGill Law Journal* 1143, http://www.journal.law.mcgill.ca/abs/vol49/4winte.html.

South Africa,[16] and the US state of Massachusetts[17] (apart from federal law).[18]

I would argue that the success of this slow, painful march towards full LGBT equality (see Tables 1 and 2 below)[19] is inevitable, as a matter of social justice, and will eventually be repeated in every country in the world.[20] It is as inevitable as the process of abolishing slavery, and granting the vote to women, which began in a few countries and then spread. This should give us the courage we will need to fight laws that still criminalize same-sex sexual activity in over one-third of the member states of the United Nations, especially those that permit the death penalty (as in, for example, Iran, Saudia Arabia, and some states of Nigeria).[21]

conclusion

16 Constitutional Court of South Africa, Case nos. CCT60/04, CCT10/05, *Minister of Home Affairs v. Fourie, Lesbian and Gay Equality Project v. Minister of Home Affairs* (1 Dec. 2005) (9–0 on constitutional violation) (the common-law definition of marriage as different-sex only is discrimination contrary to the Constitution of South Africa). The Court's order (at para. 162 of Justice Sachs' judgment) gave the South African Parliament until 1 Dec. 2006 to pass legislation allowing same-sex couples to marry. Parliament did so through the Civil Union Act, No. 17 of 2006, which was signed by President Thabo Mbeki on 29 Nov. 2006 and entered into force on 30 Nov. 2006. The Act permits any couple to contract a 'civil union', which shall be known as a 'marriage' or a 'civil partnership' according to the couple's choice. Ironically, South Africa has retained a small element of segregation or apartheid. The 'legal marriage waiting room' has two doors, one marked 'All Couples' (the Civil Union Act) and one marked 'Different-Sex Couples Only' (the Marriage Act, No. 25 of 1961, which Parliament decided not to amend so as to make it available to same-sex couples). Once inside the waiting room, the rights and obligations attached to legal marriage, and the name 'marriage', are available to all couples.   17 See the two decisions of the Supreme Judicial Court of Massachusetts: *Goodridge v. Department of Public Health*, 798 N.E.2d 941 (18 Nov. 2003) (4–3) (Massachusetts Constitution requires equal access to legal marriage for same-sex couples); *In re the Opinions of the Justices to the Senate*, 802 N.E.2d 605 (3 Feb. 2004) (4–3) (a separate law establishing 'civil unions' for same-sex couples only is not sufficient) (the two decisions took effect on 17 May 2004).   18 See the federal Defense of Marriage Act of 1996.   19 Tables 1 and 2 were inspired by the more detailed tables in Kees Waaldijk, 'Towards the recognition of same-sex partners in European Union law: expectations based on trends in national law' in Wintemute (ed.), *supra* n. 6; and William N. Eskridge, Jr., *Equality practice: civil unions and the future of gay rights* (New York, 2002), 234–5.   20 Robert Wintemute, 'From "sex rights" to "love rights": partnership rights as human rights' in Nicholas Bamforth (ed.), *Sex rights* (Oxford, 2005).   21 See http://www.ilga-europe.org/europe/publications/non_periodical/rights_not_crimes_april_2005. 22 National legislation or, for the public sector, Council Directive 2000/78/EC (in force 2 Dec. 2003).   23 Perhaps excluding certain parental rights (access to joint adoption or medically assisted procreation).   24 Laws in the *comunidades autónomas* (regions).   25 The Dutch government plans to remove the exception for intercountry adoption in 2007.   26 This law recognizes de facto cohabitation by same-sex couples, but does not allow them to register.

Table 1

EU (first 15 member states) (year law passed)	blanket ban on male-male sexual activity repealed (equal age of consent)	ban on discrimination (employment[22] or services)	same-sex couples: second-parent adoption (child of partner)	same-sex couples: joint adoption (unrelated child)	same-sex couples: register + some rights	same-sex couples: register + equal rights[23]	same-sex couples: register + equal rights + name (marriage)
Spain	1822 (1988)	1995	2005	2005	1998–2003[24]	2005	2005
Belgium	1792 (1985)	2003	2006	2006	1998	2003	2003
Netherlands	1811 (1971)	1991	2000	2000[25]	1997	1997	2000
Sweden	1944 (1978)	1987	2002	2002	1994	1994	committee
UK	1967, 1980, 1982 (2000)	2003					—
Denmark	1930 (1976)	2003	2002	2002	1989	2004	—
Finland	1971 (1998)	1987	1999	—	2001	1989	—
Germany	1969 (1994)	1995	2004	—	2001	2001	—
France	1791 (1982)	2003	—	—	1999	—	—
Luxembourg	1792 (1992)	1985	—	—	2004	—	—
Portugal	1945 (?)	1997	—	—		—	—
Ireland	1993 (2006?)	2003	—	—	2001[26]	—	—
Italy	1889 (1889)	1993	—	—	—	—	—
Austria	1971 (2002)	2003	—	—	—	—	—
Greece	1950 (?)	2003	—	—	—	—	—

Table 2

Canada + USA (year law passed or year of court decision)	blanket ban on male-male sexual activity (or 'sodomy') repealed	ban on discrim- ination (employment or services)	same-sex couples: second-parent adoption (child of partner)	same-sex couples: joint adoption (unrelated child)	same-sex couples: register + some rights	same-sex couples: register + equal rights	same-sex couples: register + equal rights + name (marriage)
Québec	1969	1977	1991	1991	2002	2002	2004[27]
Ontario	1969	1986	1995	1995	2003	2003	2003
British Columbia	1969	1992	1995	1995	2003	2003	2003
Massachusetts	1974[28]	1989	1993	1993	2003	2003	2003[29]
Vermont	1977	1991	1993	1993	1999/00[30]	1999/00	—
Connecticut	1969	1991	2000	2000	2005	2005	—
California	1975	1992	2003	2003	1999	2003[31]	—
New York	1980	2002[32]	1995	1995	—	—	—
Texas	2003[33]	—	—	—	—	—	—
Florida	2003	—	—[34]	—	—	—	—
Mississippi	2003	—	—[35]	—	—	—	—
Utah	2003[36]	—	—[37]	—	—[38]	—	—

27 The 2003 and 2004 judgments of the Courts of Appeal of Ontario, British Columbia and Québec were extended to all 10 provinces and 3 territories by a federal law, supra n. 15, in 2005. 28 Invalid as applied to 'consensual conduct in private between adults'. See *Commonwealth v. Balthazar*, 318 N.E.2d 478 (Mass. 1974), as clarified by *Gay & Lesbian Advocates & Defenders v. Attorney General*, 763 N.E.2d 38 (Mass. 2002). 29 First ceremonies on 17 May 2004. State recognition of same-sex couples generally does not apply at the federal level, especially with regard to immigration law. See *supra* n. 18. 30 *Baker v. State*, 744 A.2d 864 (Vermont Supreme Court 1999), Act 91 of 2000 ('civil unions'). 31 'Domestic partnership' now identical to legal marriage? See http://www.eqca.org. 32 But legislation was passed by New York City in 1986. 33 *Lawrence & Garner v. Texas*, 539 US 558 (2003). The Texas law prohibiting black-white marriages had to be struck down by the US Supreme Court in *Loving v. Virginia*, 388 US 1 (1967). *Lawrence* and *Loving* both applied to Florida and Mississippi. 34 See Florida Statutes ch. 63.042, s. 3 (added in 1977): 'No person eligible to adopt under this statute may adopt if that person is a homosexual'. 35 See Mississippi Code Annotated s. 93–17–3(2) (added in 2000) provides that '[a]doption by couples of the same gender is prohibited'. 36 *Lawrence* applied to Utah, but not *Loving*. Utah Code Annotated s. 30–1–2, repealed in 1963 only four years before *Loving*, prohibited marriages: '(5) Between a negro and a white person. (6) Between a Mongolian, member of the Malay race or a mulatto, quadroon, or octoroon, and a white person'. 37 Utah expressly bans individual adoption by 'a person who is cohabiting [residing with another person and being involved in a sexual relationship with that person] in a relationship that is not a legally valid and binding marriage under the laws of this state'. See Utah Code Annotated ss. 78–30–1(3)(b), 78–30–9(3) (added in 2000). 38 Utah Constitution, Article I, s. 29 (added in 2004): '(1) Marriage consists only of the legal union between a man and a woman. (2) No other domestic union, however denominated, may be recognized as a marriage or given the same or substantially equivalent legal effect'.

ARE THERE ANY STRONG ARGUMENTS AGAINST ALLOWING SAME-SEX COUPLES TO MARRY?

The first argument is often one of tradition: the definition of legal marriage as between one man and one woman has existed for thousands of years, and has served society well. It is for 'the common good', as Professor William Binchy has put it. But, as I replied to him,[39] which part of society and whose good has this definition served? Quite simply, the good of the heterosexual majority, who have no desire to marry a person of their own sex, not the good of the LGBT minority. The traditional definition of legal marriage cannot be viewed in isolation. It is part of a long history of discrimination against a despised minority by a powerful majority, and is merely one of the final forms of legal discrimination to be addressed. The history of this despised minority includes the fact that the Nazi regime in Germany (1933–1945) established a *Reichszentrale zur Bekämpfung der Homosexualität und der Abtreibung* (Reich Office for the Combating of Homosexuality and Abortion), and made one of the categories of prisoner in their concentration camps that of *Homosexuell*, indicated by a pink triangle on the prisoner's uniform.[40]

There is thus a strong analogy between discrimination based on sexual orientation and discrimination based on race, religion or sex.[41] This analogy has been recognized by the European Court of Human Rights,[42] the Supreme Court of Canada,[43] and the drafters of the constitutions of South Africa, Fiji, Ecuador, and Portugal,[44] as well as the drafters of Article 21 of the EU's Charter of Fundamental Rights, which expressly mentions sexual orientation alongside race, religion and sex.

The second argument is that legal marriage is intended for couples with the capacity to procreate without assistance from third parties. Only

---

39 Conference on 'ECHR Act Review and Human Rights in Committed Relationships', Irish Human Rights Commission and Law Society of Ireland, Dublin, 16 October 2004 (discussion period). 40 See Günter Grau, *Hidden holocaust? Gay and lesbian persecution in Germany, 1933–45* (London, 1995), at 86–130. 41 Robert Wintemute, *Sexual orientation and human rights: the United States Constitution, the European Convention, and the Canadian Charter* (Oxford, 1997); Robert Wintemute, 'Sex discrimination in *MacDonald* and *Pearce*: why the law lords chose the wrong comparators' (2003) 14 *King's College Law Journal* 267. 42 See the ECtHR judgments in *Smith & Grady v. UK* (27 Sept. 1999), para. 97 (race); *Salgueiro da Silva Mouta v. Portugal* (21 Dec. 1999), para. 36 (religion, implicit in citation to *Hoffmann*); *S.L. v. Austria* (9 Jan. 2003), para. 37 (sex). 43 *James Egan & John Nesbit v. Canada*, [1995] 2 S.C.R. 513, paras. 5, 173–175 (sexual orientation is an 'analogous ground' of discrimination under s. 15(1) of the Charter). 44 See the express inclusion of 'sexual orientation' in the following constitutional prohibitions of discrimination: Constitution of the Republic of South Africa Act (No. 200 of 1993), s. 8(2) (transitional Constitution) ('sexual orientation'); Constitution of the Republic of South Africa (No. 108 of 1996) (final Constitution), s. 9(3); Fiji Islands, Constitution Amendment Act 1997, s. 38(2)(a); Ecuador, Constitution, 1998, Article 23(3); Portugal, Constitution (as amended in 2004), Article 13(2).

different-sex couples have this capacity, therefore only they can marry. This argument collapses under close scrutiny. Different-sex couples are allowed to marry whether or not they have any capacity to procreate without assistance, whether or not they are willing to exercise their capacity, and whether or not they are raising children. Same-sex couples are not allowed to marry, even if they have procreated with assistance, or are otherwise raising children. The European Court of Human Rights made it clear in 2002 that the procreation argument cannot be accepted in Europe. The court said, with regard to a transsexual woman with no capacity to procreate, who wished to marry a non-transsexual man, that: 'the inability of any couple to conceive or parent a child cannot be regarded as … removing their right to [marry]',[45] under Article 12 of the European Convention on Human Rights.

The third argument is that marriage is both a legal and religious institution. Because many religious bodies are unwilling to marry same-sex couples, the State must not do so either. To accept this argument is to ignore the separation of law and religion, and to impose the religion or religions of the heterosexual majority on the LGBT minority.[46] The state may decide to marry same-sex couples and, in countries where religious marriages can count simultaneously as legal marriages, allow religious bodies that wish to do so to perform legal marriages of same-sex couples. But the human right to freedom of religion will protect any religious body that chooses not to marry same-sex couples. Canada's 2005 legislation makes this clear.[47] Eventually, there will be no need for this exemption, because all religions that discriminate against LGBT individuals and same-sex couples will acknowledge their error and stop doing so. But it could take hundreds of years for all religions to catch up with the standards of secular human rights, and grant same-sex couples equal access to religious marriage, so we must not wait before changing the law on access to legal marriage.

Why are so many members of the heterosexual majority, especially those who have strong religious convictions, opposed to allowing same-sex couples to marry? Increasingly, I think that the simple answer is a lack of empathy on their part: they must try to put themselves in the position of a lesbian woman or a gay man. If you are heterosexual, imagine waking up tomorrow in a society with a lesbian and gay majority, in which heterosexuals are a minority of 2 to 10 percent. You are told that even though you are a man who is attracted to women, falls in love with women, and wants to spend his life with a particular woman, you must fight these impulses and seek treatment, because your feelings are wrong, immoral, sinful. You must marry another man, because that is what is right for the majority of men (who are gay),

45 *Christine Goodwin v. UK* (11 July 2002) (ECtHR judgment), para. 98.   46 Robert Wintemute, 'Religion vs. sexual orientation: a clash of human rights?', (2002) 1 *Journal of Law and Equality* (University of Toronto) 125, http://www.jle.ca/files/v1n2/JLEvln2art1.pdf.

whether or not it is right for you. Heterosexual women are told the same thing.

In addition to thinking about what it would be like if the majority and minority positions were reversed, heterosexual individuals who oppose full LGBT equality should also think about what it is like to be lesbian or gay. It is very easy. A heterosexual woman need only think about the good feelings of love, and physical attraction and pleasure, she can experience with a man. A lesbian woman experiences exactly the same feelings with another woman. And a gay man experiences exactly the same feelings with another man as a heterosexual man does with a woman. Why would you want to deny expression of these very positive feelings to one of your fellow human beings?[48]

DOES 'CIVIL PARTNERSHIP' PROVIDE FULL LGBT EQUALITY?

In a growing number of countries or states, the heterosexual majority has said to same-sex couples: 'Yes, we understand that it is unjust to deny you access to the rights and obligations attached to legal marriage. You can have them all (or all except access to adoption and donor insemination). But you'll have to take them without the name 'marriage'.' Laws allowing same-sex couples, and only same-sex couples, to enter a new, 'separate but equal' institution, known as 'registered partnership', 'civil union' or 'civil partnership', have been passed in Denmark (1989), Norway (1993), Sweden (1994), Iceland (1996), Finland (2001), the United Kingdom (2004), and Switzerland (2004),[49] as well as the US states of Vermont (2000), Connecticut (2005) and New Jersey (2006).

While politicians often think that same-sex couples should be satisfied with this compromise, Canadian appellate courts responsible for applying constitutional principles of equality found it inadequate in two 2003 judgments. A unanimous three-judge British Columbia Court of Appeal concluded that '[a]ny other form of recognition of same-sex relationships, including the parallel institution of [registered domestic partnerships], falls short of true equality'.[50] A unanimous three-judge Ontario Court of Appeal stressed that '[S]ame-sex couples are excluded from a fundamental societal institution – marriage ... Exclusion perpetuates the view that same-sex

---

47 See footnote 15 above.   **48** For an expanded version of this discussion of empathy, in relation to heterosexual individuals with strong religious convictions, see Robert Wintemute, 'Same-sex marriage: when will it reach Utah?' (2006) 20, *Brigham Young University Journal of Public Law* 527 at 541–4 (forthcoming).   **49** The law was approved by 58% of voters in a referendum on 5 June 2005, and entered into force on 1 Jan. 2007.   **50** *EGALE Canada Inc. v. Canada (Attorney General)* (1 May 2003), 228 DLR (4th) 416, para. 156.

relationships are less worthy of recognition than opposite-sex relationships.'[51]

In 2004, four of seven judges of the Massachusetts Supreme Judicial Court advised the legislature that creating 'civil unions' for same-sex couples only would not discharge the State's constitutional obligation to allow them to marry: 'Segregating same-sex unions from opposite-sex unions cannot possibly be held rationally to advance ... the [State's] legitimate interests ... The history of our nation has demonstrated that separate is seldom, if ever, equal ... '[C]ivil union' ... is a considered choice of language that reflects a demonstrable assigning of same-sex ... couples to second-class status ... The bill would have the effect of maintaining ... a stigma of exclusion ... [and] an unconstitutional, inferior, and discriminatory status for same-sex couples ...'[52]

In her dissenting opinion, Justice Sosman asked 'what's in a name?', and described the difference between the names 'marriage' and 'civil union' as 'insignificant'.[53] I wonder what Justice Sosman would think if male judges in Massachusetts were called 'judges', and female judges were called 'senior legal secretaries', but enjoyed exactly the same pay and benefits as male judges. Would that be an 'insignificant' difference?

Legal marriage is a public institution. LGBT persons can never be fully equal if they do not have equal access to all of the same public institutions as heterosexual persons. A sign saying 'Same-Sex Couples May Not Enter' is a form of segregation or apartheid, whether the sign appears in front of the legislature, the national museum, a local public library, or the waiting room for civil marriages at the town hall. In the United Kingdom, some town halls have made the segregation almost invisible. The 'civil partnership' ceremony of my friends Adnan and Eric was virtually identical to a civil marriage: the official, the room, the music, the flowers, the readings, the love and the tears were the same, and the vows were almost identical. But the certificate they received at the end read 'civil partnership', not 'marriage'. This insistence on withholding a word seen as belonging to the heterosexual majority is both amazingly petty, and extremely harmful. It is harmful even if the majority of same-sex couples prefer a different name, and do not want access to legal marriage. It is enough that there is even one same-sex couple who would like to have the same option to marry as different-sex couples, whether or not they ever choose to exercise it.

---

51 *Halpern v. Canada (Attorney General)* (10 June 2003), 65 O.R. (3rd) 161, para. 107.   52 *In re the Opinions of the Justices to the Senate*, 802 N.E.2d 565, at 569–570 (Mass., 3 Feb. 2004).

IS 'CIVIL PARTNERSHIP' A NECESSARY INTERMEDIATE STEP
TOWARDS FULL LGBT EQUALITY?

In the beginning, this might have been true. Sometimes fear of change on the part of the majority or dominant group causes it to grant partial equality to a minority or subordinated group. In 1918, the United Kingdom granted the vote only to women aged 30 or more, whereas men could vote at 21.[54] It took another ten years to equalize the voting age at 21.[55] Thus, the Netherlands might not have become the first country to allow same-sex couples to marry in 2001, without the 'Scandinavian experiments' (the registered partnership laws passed by Denmark in 1989, Norway in 1993, and Sweden in 1994), and the Netherlands' own registered partnership law passed in 1997.

However, I would argue that this intermediate step (a 'civil partnership' law prior to a marriage law) is no longer required. We know now that the sky does not fall once same-sex couples are allowed to marry. In five of the six territories where same-sex couples were permitted to marry in December 2006, the legislature at the national, federal or state level, which had the sole power to grant equal access to legal marriage to same-sex couples, had not created any 'separate but equal' institution before exercising this power. This is true of Belgium (where the 'statutory cohabitation' law[56] did not grant equal rights), Spain, Canada, South Africa and Massachusetts. In the Netherlands, a 'separate but equal' institution of registered partnership had been created before same-sex couples were allowed to marry, but it was made available to all couples.[57] To date, none of the countries that have created a 'separate but equal' institution for same-sex couples only has allowed them to marry. But once they are permitted to marry, the question will arise: 'What should we do with the 'separate but equal' institution: abolish it or extend it to all couples?' Sweden will probably be the first country to face this question.[58]

Examining the sequence of changes in different countries brings into focus a key feature of all 'civil partnership' laws, both laws for same-sex couples only (as in Sweden) and laws for all couples (as in the Netherlands). To date, all of these laws have been passed for a very negative reason: avoiding the opening up of legal marriage to same-sex couples.[59] To date, no

---

53 802 N.E.2d at 573. 54 Representation of the People Act 1918, s. 4. 55 Representation of the People (Equal Franchise) Act 1928, s. 1. 56 *Loi du 23 novembre 1998 instaurant la cohabitation légale* (Law of 23 November 1998 establishing statutory cohabitation), *Moniteur belge*, 12 Jan. 1999, p. 786. 57 Act of 5 July 1997 amending Book 1 of the Civil Code and the Code of Civil Procedure, concerning the introduction therein of provisions relating to registered partnership (*geregistreerd partnerschap*), *Staatsblad* 1997, nr. 324. 58 For the latest information, see http://www.homo.se. 59 An exception was 'An Act instituting civil unions and establishing new rules of filiation', Statutes of Québec 2002, chapter 6 ('civil unions' are available to all couples, as in the Netherlands), because Québec's legislature did not have the constitutional power to allow same-sex couples to marry.

'civil partnership' law has been passed by a country that already allowed same-sex couples to marry. There may be a strong, positive case for an alternative registration system (called 'civil partnership', 'civil union' or 'registered partnership') that is open to all couples who object to the word 'marriage'. But this is an entirely separate question, and does not answer the equality claim of same-sex couples who seek access to legal marriage. Indeed, the best way to avoid the creation of an alternative registration marriage open to all couples (which might draw many different-sex couples away from legal marriage) could be to allow same-sex couples to marry.

MUST THE IRISH CONSTITUTION BE AMENDED TO PERMIT SAME-SEX COUPLES TO MARRY?

What is the impact of the Irish Constitution on the question of equal access to legal marriage for same-sex couples? In relation to any national, federal or state constitution, there are four main possibilities.

⚹ (a) **The constitutional text** *expressly prohibits a decision by the legislature* **voluntarily to grant equal access.** Among the 27 member states of the European Union, there are only two examples. In Poland, the 1997 Constitution's Article 18 states: '*Marriage*, being *a union of a man and a woman*, as well as the family, motherhood and parenthood, shall be placed under the protection and care of the Republic of Poland [emphasis added].' In Latvia, the Constitution's Article 110 (as amended on 15 Dec. 2005) states: 'The State protects and supports *marriage – a union between a man and a woman*, family, rights of parents, and children [emphasis added].' It is no coincidence that these two countries are both among the poorest in the EU, and among the most homophobic, as demonstrated by the fierce opposition to attempts by their LGBT communities to hold marches or demonstrations for 'equality' or 'pride', as Article 11 of the European Convention on Human Rights permits them to do.[60] ⚹

(b) **The constitutional text is ambiguous or silent as to the sexes of the spouses, and is interpreted as** *permitting but not yet requiring a decision by the legislature* **voluntarily to grant equal access,** as in Canada, in Spain, and under the current interpretations of the European Convention on Human Rights and the EU Charter of Fundamental Rights. In Canada, the Supreme Court refused to interpret the single word 'Marriage', in the federal legislative power over 'Marriage and Divorce' (Constitution Act, 1867, Section 91(26)), as freezing the meaning of

---

60 See http://www.ilga-europe.org/europe/publications/non_periodical/prides_against_ prejudice_a_toolkit_for_pride_organising_in_a_hostile_environment_september_2006.

'marriage' in 1867 as meaning 'different-sex'.[61] In Spain, the 1978 Constitution's Article 32(1) (captioned 'Marriage, Matrimonial Equality') provides: 'Man [*el hombre*] and woman [*la mujer*] have the right to contract matrimony with full legal equality.' A case pending before the *Tribunal Constitucional* (Constitutional Court) asks whether Article 32(1) permits the 2005 law allowing same-sex couples to marry. Most observers expect the court to interpret 'man' and 'woman' as stressing the equal rights of men and women in legal marriage, and not as specifying that men and women must marry each other.

The text of Article 12 of the European Convention on Human Rights resembles the Spanish text: 'Men [*l'homme*] and women [*la femme*] of marriageable age have the right to marry and to found a family, according to the national laws governing the exercise of this right.' In *Christine Goodwin v. United Kingdom*, the European Court of Human Rights held that a transsexual individual must be allowed to contract a different-sex legal marriage (different-sex after legal recognition of their gender reassignment), and left the door open for a future interpretation of Article 12 as requiring equal access to legal marriage for same-sex couples.[62] In particular, the court cited Article 9 of the Charter of Fundamental Rights of the EU: 'The right to marry and the right to found a family shall be guaranteed in accordance with the national laws governing the exercise of these rights.' According to the official commentary on Article 9: 'This Article neither prohibits nor imposes the granting of the status of marriage to unions between people of the same sex.'[63]

(c) The constitutional text is ambiguous or silent as to the sexes of the spouses, but the *equality provision is interpreted as requiring equal access*, as in Massachusetts and South Africa.[64] In Canada, the Ontario and British Columbia Courts of Appeal interpreted Section 15(1) of the Canadian Charter of Rights and Freedoms as requiring equal access.[65] However, the Supreme Court of Canada declined to confirm their reasoning, and instead merely interpreted the Charter (and the rest of the federal Constitution) as permitting the federal Parliament to grant equal access voluntarily.[66]

(d) The constitutional text is ambiguous or silent as to the sexes of the spouses, but is interpreted by the highest court as *implicitly prohibiting a voluntary decision by the legislature* to grant equal access. To date, this question has arisen concretely, rather than hypothetically, in only four countries, where the legislature acting voluntarily had passed, or was proposing to pass, a bill granting equal access, without a prior

61 *Reference re Same-Sex Marriage* (9 Dec. 2004), [2004] 3 S.C.R. 698. 62 (11 July 2002), paras. 98–101. 63 See http://ec.europa.eu/justice_home/unit/charte/index_en.html. 64 Supra nn. 16–17. 65 Supra nn. 49–50. See also *EGALE Canada Inc. v. Canada (Attorney General)* (1 May 2003), 225 DLR (4th) 472 (B.C. Ct. App.). 66 Supra n. 60.

determination by the highest court that it was required to do so: the Netherlands, Belgium, Spain, and Canada. To date, in none of these four countries has the highest court interpreted the national or federal constitution as prohibiting a passed or proposed bill granting equal access. The same is true, at least in Europe, in the case of 'civil partnership' laws that apply only to same-sex couples. In 2002, Germany's Federal Constitutional Court (*Bundesverfassungsgericht*) upheld Germany's legislation against a challenge by three German states claiming that it was unconstitutional because it was too close to legal marriage.[67]

In view of its text, which of categories (a), (b), (c), and (d) above applies to Ireland's 1937 Constitution? Article 41 on 'The Family' provides: '3. 1 *The State pledges itself* to guard with special care the institution of Marriage, on which the Family is founded, and *to protect [the institution of Marriage] against attack* [emphasis added].' Despite having no knowledge of the case law interpreting Article 41, I would argue that Article 41 falls into category (b), ie, its text is ambiguous or silent as to the sexes of the spouses, and should be interpreted at least as *permitting but not requiring a decision by the legislature* voluntarily to grant same-sex couples equal access to legal marriage.

Whether or not Article 41 permits or prohibits a voluntary decision by the legislature to grant equal access remains a purely hypothetical question until the legislature actually takes this step. Thus, the legislature should not see itself as inhibited by Article 41, no matter what hypothetical (and therefore *obiter*) statements the Supreme Court of Ireland has made (in its case law to date) to the effect that 'Marriage' in Article 41 means 'different-sex marriage only'. Faced with a bill passed by the Oireachtas, and referred by the President, I doubt that the Supreme Court would choose to become the first in the world to interpret an ambiguous constitutional provision as precluding a voluntary decision by the legislature to grant equal access to legal marriage to same-sex couples, and therefore as requiring a referendum on a constitutional amendment. Whatever 'the institution of Marriage' means in Article 41.3.1, a voluntary decision by the Irish legislature to allow loving same-sex couples to marry would by no means be an 'attack' on the 'institution of Marriage'.

Does the Irish Constitution fall into category (c)? At the moment, it seems unlikely that the Supreme Court of Ireland would interpret the equality provision (Article 40.1) as *requiring* equal access to legal marriage for same-sex couples. This is for the simple reason that, to date, no appellate court in

---

67 *Urteil des Ersten Senats vom 17. Juli 2002*, [Cases] 1 BvF 1/01, 1 BvF 2/01, upholding Law of 16 Feb. 2001 on Ending Discrimination Against Same-Sex Communities: Life Partnerships (*Gesetz zur Beendigung der Diskriminierung gleichgeschlechtlicher Gemeinschaften: Lebenspartnerschaften*), [2001] 9 *Bundesgesetzblatt* 266 (which does not yet grant all the rights attached to legal marriage, because of political opposition in the *Bundesrat*, the upper house of the German Parliament).

Europe has been willing to interpret a national constitutional provision as requiring equal access, and the Supreme Court will probably not choose to be the first. To date, all judicial decisions requiring equal access have come from Canada, the USA, and South Africa.[68] In Europe, equal access has come from the legislature in the Netherlands, Belgium and Spain. Trial courts considering this question are therefore likely to be especially cautious.[69]

SHOULD IRELAND FOLLOW BELGIUM AND SPAIN, OR THE UNITED KINGDOM?

With regard to equal treatment of same-sex couples, the main models for the Republic of Ireland (in view of the current disparity with Northern Ireland) are:

(a) Belgium and Spain (two countries with Roman Catholic majorities), ie, grant same-sex couples equal access to legal marriage; and

(b) the United Kingdom, ie, create a new, 'separate but equal', alternative registration system for same-sex couples only.

In view of my analysis above, I would make the following proposals for Ireland.[70]

68 The Supreme Court of Israel's 2006 decision to require registration (but not necessarily full legal recognition) in Israel of Canadian same-sex marriages is not comparable, because it would appear that it could be overruled by ordinary legislation. It is also a result of the fact that, in Israel, all legal marriages are religious marriages. Civil marriages do not exist. See http://www.tau.ac.il/law/aeyalgross.   69 Both *Gilligan & Zappone*, 14 December 2006 (HC), and *Wilkinson v. Kitzinger*, [2006] EWHC 2022 (Fam) (England and Wales High Court) involved attempts to have Canadian same-sex marriages recognized in Ireland and the UK. But, in these cases, it was not really possible to stress the distinction between the (possibly easier) question of recognising a foreign same-sex marriage under principles of private international law (only a few same-sex couples would every qualify), and requiring equal access for all same-sex couples to legal marriage in Ireland or the UK, under Ireland's Constitution or European Convention on Human Rights Act, 2004, or under the UK's Human Rights Act 1998. This was because neither couple were long-term residents of Canada moving to Ireland or the UK for the first time, and because same-sex couples may marry (e.g., in British Columbia or Ontario) without any period of notice or residence (depending on flights, they could stay in Canada for less than 24 hours). This means that, if Gilligan and Zappone, and Wilkinson and Kitzinger, had succeeded in having their Canadian marriages recognized, any same-sex couple in Ireland or the UK could take a holiday in Canada, marry, and demand recognition of their marriage as a legal marriage (not just a 'civil partnership') in Ireland or the UK.   70 Cf. 'Options Paper: Presented by the Working Group on Domestic Partnership to the Minister for Justice, Equality and Law Reform, Mr Michael McDowell', Nov. 2006, http://www.justice.ie (Search, 'domestic partnership').

Proposal 1: The dynamic new Ireland should lead the UK (and other EU countries) by adopting the Belgian-Spanish model, rather than the UK model. This means equal access to *all* of the rights and obligations of legal marriage, including joint adoption of children and medically assisted procreation, and to the name 'marriage'. Because, as I have argued above, it is inevitable that every EU member state will eventually grant equal access to legal marriage to same-sex couples, it would be a matter of national pride for Ireland if the Republic could be the fourth EU member state to do so (there is still a chance to pip Sweden to the honour), and especially if the Republic could do so before the UK.

Proposal 2: In addition to adopting Proposal 1, Ireland could consider creating a new alternative registration system (with a name like 'civil partnership', 'civil union' or 'registered partnership') for all couples who object to the name 'marriage', providing all the same rights and obligations as legal marriage, or a lesser package (depending on whether it is considered desirable to retain an incentive to marry).

Proposal 3: In addition to adopting Proposal 1, and whether or not Proposal 2 is adopted, Ireland: (i) *must* equalize legal recognition of unmarried different-sex and same-sex couples under *Karner v. Austria*,[71] especially through legislation granting rights to couples 'living as husband and wife'; and (ii) *should* extend its recognition of unmarried different-sex and same-sex couples, so as to provide all the same rights and obligations as legal marriage or 'civil partnership', or a lesser package (depending on whether it is considered desirable to retain an incentive to marry or register). This is to avoid injustices to different-sex and same-sex couples who have chosen or would choose (unilaterally or bilaterally) not to marry or register, or who have neglected or would neglect to marry or register.[72]

If Ireland were to adopt all three of my proposals, it would achieve what I consider the ideal legal situation, and the possible culmination of the international trends with regard to legal recognition of couples (see Table 3).

---

71 (24 July 2003) (ECtHR judgment).   72 The Irish government should bear in mind that in providing rights or benefits to couples (whether married, registered or unmarried/ unregistered), it is not required by the European Convention on Human Rights to extend the same rights or benefits to non-couple cohabitants, such as older unmarried heterosexual sisters who live together. See *Burden v. United Kingdom* (12 Dec. 2006) (ECtHR judgment) (4–3) (Grand Chamber hearing on 12 Sept. 2007). Their relationships are qualitatively different from those of couples (who are having, have had, or could have a sexual relationship). Any granting of benefits or imposition of burdens must be in the context of a looser relationship, so that the older unmarried heterosexual sisters do not have to divorce each other if one of them meets a nice fellow at the bingo parlour!

Table 3 – Equal choices for all couples

	Different-sex couples	Same-sex couples
legal marriage (civil or religious, if religious institution agrees and has state authorisation)	Yes: Netherlands, Québec, Ireland, UK	Yes: Netherlands, Québec No: Ireland, UK
alternative registration system (for couples who object to the name 'marriage')	Yes: Netherlands (registered partnership) Québec (civil union) No: Ireland, UK	Yes: Netherlands (registered partnership) Québec (civil union) UK (civil partnership) *No: Ireland (behind UK)*
unregistered cohabitation (for couples who choose not to marry or register or who neglect to do so)	Yes: Netherlands, Québec Limited recognition: Ireland, UK (*Ireland less than UK?*)	Yes: Netherlands, Québec Limited recognition: Ireland, UK (*Ireland less than UK?*)

CONCLUSION

We know now that full equality for LGBT individuals and same-sex couples can be achieved in countries with Roman Catholic majorities, such as Belgium and Spain. I would express the same hope for Ireland that I have for Austria:[73] that Ireland will have the courage to recognize the inadequacy of the 'separate but equal' compromise of 'civil partnership', will grant all couples the same choices (see Table 3 above), and will therefore lead rather than follow the United Kingdom, by granting same-sex couples equal access to legal marriage. As Prime Minister Zapatero said before the final vote on Spain's historic legislation in June 2005: 'We are not legislating for people living far away. We are increasing opportunities for happiness for our neighbours, work colleagues, friends and relatives. And at the same time, we are building a more decent country. Because a decent society is one that does not humiliate its members.'[74]

73 Author's presentation at 'Against sexual apartheid: a ceremonial act to celebrate 15 years for the Right to Love – 15 years *Rechtskomitee Lambda*', Austrian Federal Parliament (debating chamber of the lower house, the *Nationalrat*), Vienna, 2 October 2006. 74 Author's translation of statement in Spanish. See *Cortes Generales, Diario de Sesiones del Congreso de los Diputados* (30 June 2005), No. 103, p. 5228, http://www.congreso.es/public_oficiales/L8/CONG/DS/PL/PL_103.PDF.

A question of definition: same–sex marriage and the law*

NEVILLE COX

THE LEGALITY OF GAY MARRIAGE

SURPRISING AS IT MAY SEEM, homosexual marriage is and probably always has been lawful in Ireland. It is true that some aspects of what may loosely be termed the consummation of a gay marriage were unlawful in the past[1], but it was never unlawful for two homosexuals to marry, or more accurately to declare themselves to be married. The perception that this *was* unlawful or indeed impossible, derives exclusively from the mistaken belief that the term 'marriage' has only one definition – a definition which covers civil marriages and religious marriages and beyond which marriage does not exist.

In fact this is a misunderstanding. Nobody 'owns' the definition of marriage. It seems fairly clear that the term generally tends to be used with considerable gravitas, and for most persons the fact that their relationship is called a marriage means that they intend to create ties that are unlike those created in any other relationship. Nonetheless, it is also true both that the word can mean different things to different people (and quite clearly it does), and also that there is no legal basis for preventing groups or individuals from acting on the basis of their definition of the term.

I may, to put it glibly, declare that I am married to a tree in my back garden, and whereas people might quite correctly assume that I had certain emotional issues with which to grapple, nonetheless the less as far as I am concerned, I am married to my tree. I may mark this relationship with a ceremony (possibly a religious one) and a reception to which my friends and family are invited. Indeed if I can find a publication that will carry my message, I may announce details of this marriage – and more importantly, I can tell people that what has occurred *is* a marriage. And there is nothing that

* I am grateful to Dr Oran Doyle, Sharon Smith and Blaithin Kinsella for their helpful comments in respect of this paper.   1 In *Norris v. AG* [1984] IR 36 the Irish Supreme Court upheld the constitutionality of laws (ss. 61 & 62 of the Offences against the Person Act 1861 and s. 11 of the Criminal Law (Amendment) Act 1885) which had the effect of rendering illegal all sexual activity between male homosexuals. The effect of these laws was eventually abolished by the Criminal Law (Sexual Offences) Act 1993.

the state or the church or any other person can do to prevent me from announcing or more importantly from *believing* the fact that I am married to my tree, according to my lights and in line with *my* private definition of the term 'marriage'. This definition – my definition – is my own business, and no one else has any rights over it no matter how ludicrous or laughable they regard it to be (and nor, frankly do I have any rights over their definition of the term 'marriage' which, presumably, would exclude human–tree relationships). It is, quite simply a matter in which freedom of conscience reigns supreme.

And, in its application to an infinitely more serious and deserving set of circumstances, this principle is the reason why *gay* marriage was never illegal. Homosexual couples can marry, indeed they could *always* marry, in the sense that they could determine that their relationship conformed to *their* definition of marriage and as such, *was* a marriage. And dissident churches which shared that definition could always perform grand public ceremonies to celebrate such a marriage, and could always claim that they were performing a marriage ceremony. And again there could be a reception to mark this marriage ceremony and details thereof could be publicized. And it would be arrogant and (in literal terms) inaccurate to say of such a couple that they are 'not married', for of course on one definition of marriage (theirs) they are – just as it would be arrogant and inaccurate of that couple to say that a definition of marriage endorsed by another private body which *excluded* homosexual relationships from its ambit was thereby invalid.

It is true, of course, that one (private) definition of marriage tends to attract vastly more support than any other, both for historical reasons and also because it is a variant of this definition which the state adopts as *its* definition of marriage. This definition – which owes its prominence in Western society to the impact of Judaeo-Christian teaching – envisages marriage as a permanent relationship between monogamous heterosexuals. Indeed until recently, it may be said that this definition also saw procreation as the purpose of marriage, and marriage as the only appropriate context in which to raise children. But it remains important to realize that despite the fact that it is a definition that has substantial support and indeed conforms to the ideal of marriage in fairy tales, romantic novels and other social indicators, this *is* merely one definition of marriage, and others do exist and are equally sincerely held. Thus a polygamist will see the institution as involving more than two people. A gay couple may well (although not necessarily) view the institution as not necessarily confined to persons of opposite genders. Perhaps most prevalently, in the divorce era, many, many people do not regard the institution as inexorably permanent. Different definitions for different people.

Moreover, even within the prevalent norm discussed above there will be more minor and nuanced differences of definition as to what the institution means to the participants, in terms of matters such as gender based differences in the roles of the parties, whether and to what extent procreation will occur, whether the marriage is to be 'open' in the sense of parties consenting to each other having sexual liaisons with other people and so on. Equally, as long as such definitions are framed sincerely and as long as the parties getting married consent to the terms of the marriage as they define them, they are all legitimate, and basic human rights notions of free speech, freedom of religion and freedom of conscience commit us to this view.

This reality – that there are many definitions rather than only one definition of marriage – means that the terminology traditionally used within the 'gay marriage' debate is in fact both inaccurate and inappropriate. The point is that when the Catholic Church, for example, teaches against the notion of gay marriage it will tend to say that there is no such thing as gay marriage, or that *the* definition of marriage excludes same-sex relationships. Yet the use of the definite article in this phrase involves a subtle yet inaccurate replacement of what should be subjective with what is objective. When it says that marriage is by definition a relationship between people of opposite genders, what it is in fact saying is that *its* definition of the term does not include same-sex relationships. And when two gay men get married or say that *the* definition of marriage includes same-sex relationships, what they are *in fact* saying is that their definition of the term is different from that of the Church. And just as the Church cannot demand that the homosexuals change their view of what marriage is to conform with its definition, so also the homosexuals cannot demand that the church change its definition to encompass their situation.

Of course, in both cases, the relevant parties may seek to persuade and to cajole and to convince the other that its definition should be altered, but in as much as there is no one definition of the institution but rather a myriad of different definitions, neither body can say that by adopting a definition different from that which *it* endorses the other body is actually wrong. It would be as literally inaccurate as trying to convince an ardent football supporter of one team that she or he is wrong to support this team because objectively one *should* support another team. Moreover, the fact that what is at stake is a clash of subjectivities further means that no one private definition of marriage can affect another. In other words, the fact that the Catholic church and I take different views on whether our definitions of marriage include human/tree relationships does not in any sense undermine either of our views. I will continue sincerely to believe one thing and the church will continue sincerely to teach another.

The reason why neither of these parties has a right over the other party's definition is because both are 'private' bodies, in the sense that they are not connected to the state. Indeed until the state is asked to get involved the expression of marriage is essentially private.[2] Where, however, the state definition of marriage is concerned – when the individual participants in the marriage ask the state to regulate and govern its relationship through the law – on the other hand, all members of society have a stake. In this context, whereas the interests of all need not necessarily be accommodated, they are all relevant and should all be considered.[3] In other words, all members of a society have a right over the *public* definition of marriage, even if, as a result of the manner by which the state is administered in a democracy, this right may not come to very much in practice.

And this leads, it is submitted, to the single biggest problem with the debate on gay marriage, and the reason why this debate is in danger of becoming as fractured and bitter as the debate on abortion, namely that it proceeds from a fallacious and flawed starting point that leads to the wrong questions being asked and, as a result, answers being given which govern the debate without actually being relevant thereto. In simple terms, the debate currently proceeds on the basis that what is at issue is some cataclysmic threat to *all* definitions of marriage, when what is, *in fact* at stake, is the question of whether *one* such definition (the state's definition) can and should be widened.

THE WRONG QUESTION IS BEING ASKED

If we wish to deal with the reality of the question of gay marriage, rather than score cheap and easy political points, then our starting point should not be to ask 'Should gay people be *allowed* to marry?' or 'should gay marriage be *legal* or *illegal*'. Rather we should ask the less emotionally loaded question 'Should the civil definition of marriage be expanded to encompass the definition of marriage to which proponents of gay marriage would subscribe, namely one that includes same-sex relationships?' This approach (which has the politically unattractive effect of framing the debate in terms which are not amenable to use of snappy sound bites) may seem like semantics, but it is assuredly more than that, if for no other reason than because it makes it clear that whereas historically in Ireland, the state's definition of the term was based in large measure on the definition provided by Judaeo-Christian teaching, equally the state's definition of marriage and the church's definition of marriage are *distinct entities*. For the church, marriage is a sacred relationship where what is key is that the couple are joined *by God*. For the

2 Lee, 'Finding marriage amidst a sea of confusion: a precursor to considering the public purposes of marriage', 43 *Catholic Law* 339 (Fall 2004).   3 In *Goodridge v. Department of Health* 440 Mass 309, 798 N.E.2d 941 (17 November 2003) the Massachusetts Supreme Court saw the 'right to marry' as essentially a right to receive community endorsement.

state, marriage is not sacred and is merely a particular relationship where what is key is that the couple in question are joined by a terms of a legally binding contract recognized by the state. And this distinction is most clearly manifest in the fact that those who oppose church teaching or cannot bring themselves within it will still have rights over the civil definition.

The separation of church and state as far as the definition of marriage is concerned, is, moreover, equally beneficial for both church *and* state. After all, those who operate from a religious view point may prioritize the church's definition of the term over the state's. And most importantly, this prioritization means that if such persons disagree with the breadth of the state's definition of the term, they may continue to take solace in the fact that changes in the state's definition does not alter the status of *their* marriages in the least, for they will continue to live out their marriages according to *their* definitions of the term. Therefore, changes in the public definition of marriage simply do not alter any private definitions thereof, and thus persons living out their marriages according to the terms of such private definitions remain unaffected.

What the civil recognition of gay marriage would do then, is not to change any individual views of what marriage is, and not to undermine any such private views. Especially, it would not (for it could not) undermine any perceptions of marriage as a sacred institution, but would merely mean that the public definition of marriage encompassed yet one more private definition thereof.

THE INTRODUCTION OF DIVORCE AND THE SEPARATION OF DEFINITIONS

That this is the case is exemplified by the introduction of divorce into Irish law. Previously, and partially, though not exclusively, because of the historical links between Roman Catholic social teaching and the Irish state, the Judaeo-Christian definition of marriage 'fitted' Irish society nicely. Marriage was the norm for couples in settled relationships, many of whom tended to the view that this was the only acceptable context in which such relationships could be lived out. Moreover, it is at least arguable that whereas historically the religious and the civil definitions of marriage were one and the same, equally for many people it was the religious marriage that was the more important. Yet with some exceptions, for example in the context of older Irish nullity law, this was a superficial prioritization, because the church and state definition of marriage were in reality, identical. And marriage was permanent (a permanent sacrament in the religious tradition and a legally binding contract in perpetuity in the secular) such that divorce was impermissible.

On the other hand, in more recent times, many people in Ireland tended to the view that the religious definition of marriage no longer fitted the social reality. This view did not hold that the religious definition should change, but rather that it should no longer be the sole model adopted by the state. And the state through the people endorsed this view and divorce was introduced into the Irish constitution and Irish law. For present purposes, the significance of this change lies in the fact that at this point, the state definition and the church definition of marriage separated (or more accurately, the state definition separated *from* the church definition), and the separation involved created a gulf of unparalleled proportions between the two. Indeed, it must surely be true that the change in the state's definition of marriage that would be wrought by expanding this definition to include same-sex relationships would be nothing like as enormous as the change thereto that was caused by the introduction of divorce.

The point is that the central focus of the religious definition of marriage and hence of the traditional civil definition of the institution – that is to say the single factor that marked it out as different to any other relationship – was *not* the fact that it involved people of opposite genders (for many relationships can exist between such people) but rather that it could only be terminated by the death of one of the parties. Heterosexual couples can, after all, seek fulfillment in many different types of relationships with varying degrees of commitment and in so doing, they can procreate, can decide to abstain from sex or not, can own property and so on. But traditionally, marriage was unique (indeed in a sense, it was defined), because, and only because it involved parties signing up to a contract that would be binding for life.[4] And thus the Catholic position, whereby marriage is *still* 'for life' and the state's position, whereby it is not, are now distinct – and distinct at the precise point of definition of the Church's concept of the institution. Yet vitally, this cataclysmic change in the state's definition did not and could not hurt or undermine the church's definition, nor could it 'de-sanctify' the relationship of those who viewed their marriage as gaining legitimacy because they were celebrated in the religious tradition, because, once again, the public definition of marriage is but one such definition; it is not the *only*

---

4 I confess that my view of liberalism (both social and economic) commits me to the view that if parties wish to do this then they should be allowed to do so. I regard it as profoundly illiberal that the state, by introducing divorce (a) retrospectively invalidated thousands of such contracts in perpetuity and (b) precluded couples in the future from entering into such contracts – or more accurately expressly refused to enforce such contracts if they *were* entered into. From a contract lawyer's point of view, I would suggest that the introduction of divorce represented a strange and unreasoned recasting of the rules in respect of *force majeure*. From a social standpoint, it is one of the great paradoxes of the divorce referendum that those in favour of divorce spoke of the right to 'choose' yet the impact of he referendum was to reduce by one the number of types of relationship that people *could* choose.

such definition, and other definitions can exist independently of it and remain immune from changes effected to it and within it.

The introduction of divorce as an aspect of the civil definition of marriage is important to the ongoing marriage debate then for three reasons.

- First it separated the church and state definitions of this term at the most fundamental possible level such that they are now irretrievably cleaved. In other words, it was the clearest possible statement that more than one definition of marriage could be operative in Irish society, and that the civil definition could and would change to meet the perceived needs of members of society, even if the church's definition could not, would not, and need not.

- Secondly, because the institution of marriage survived a change which struck at the heart of the definition by which it was traditionally understood, it must now surely be clear that it will also survive more minor changes in this respect. The implication of this for gay marriage is obvious.

- Thirdly, the introduction of divorce as it coincides with the ongoing relevance to many of the Roman Catholic definition of marriage, is instructive. The point is that post-divorce in Ireland, many, many people still commit to and still live out lifelong marriage relationships irrespective of the change in the civil definition of the term. Their definitions of marriage, like the church's, are not altered one jot by the changes in the state's definition. Indeed in a secular sense, they continue to see their relationship as one to which they are permanently contractually bound because such is the terms of their agreement with each other and with God.

The question of recognition of gay marriage then is not about disturbing other relationships, or undermining traditional religious teaching. It is not about changing *the* definition of marriage. It is quite simply a question of whether the state should effect a further amendment of *its* definition of the term to include same-sex relationships.

In this respect, moreover, it should be recognized, it is submitted, that marriage *is* a public institution. Hence questions of public policy and, arguably, public morality[5] will feed into both the manner in which the state defines marriage *and* the practical consequences which the state affords to

---

5 Hence it may be argued that the decision of the US Supreme Court in *Lawrence v. Texas* 539 US 558 (2003) whereby it was held that the individual right to liberty was sufficiently strong that laws restricting liberty purely in the interests of morality were constitutionally invalid, does not necessarily mean that there is a constitutional right to gay marriage (as had been suggested by Scalia J speaking in dissent). While civil marriage undoubtedly has a strong grounding in public morality, there are also important public policy considerations that are not moral in essence with which it is connected. Generally see Tribe, '*Lawrence v. Texas*: the "fundamental right" that dare not speak its name' 117 *Harv L Rev* 1893 (2004), Ball, 'Gay rights after *Lawrence v. Texas*' 88 *Minn L Rev* 1184.

those who bring their relationships within the state's definition of the term. In other words, it is not merely a question of the individual getting what the individual wants – nor is it in any sense an extension of an individual right based on privacy or liberty to engage privately in gay sex. Arguments for gay marriage (or for the state's definition being widened to include same-sex relationships) which are grounded exclusively in liberal philosophy, or the right to privacy will, it is submitted, be inadequate.[6] Rather it is necessary that societal interests (of which individual rights, like public policy and public morality are one very important aspect) justify expanding the state's definition of this public institution, or at the very least that such societal interests do not justify rejecting such an expansion.

In order to explore very briefly this question of whether, in 21st century Ireland the state should extend its definition of marriage to include same-sex relationships, the following issues are considered:

- The societal interests in the civil definition of Marriage
- The traditional reasons for opposing gay marriage
- The reasons for suggesting that the state *should* expand its definition of marriage to cover same-sex relationships.

SOCIETAL INTERESTS IN THE CIVIL DEFINITION OF MARRIAGE

It is generally accepted that traditionally there are four main categories of societal interests in having laws that distinguish and privilege 'marriage' from other relationships,[7] namely

- Society's interest in promoting procreation and responsible parenting
- Society's interest in fostering a particular moral atmosphere
- Society's interest in promoting the well being of its members by facilitating the kind of intimate relationships that promote individual fulfillment
- Society's interest in the equitable distribution of economic and other tangible benefits.

Clearly then, one's view of the appropriate definition of civil marriage and particularly on whether this definition will include same-sex relationships will depend on the utterly value-laden question of how one prioritizes these interests. Thus proponents of same-sex marriage will tend to focus on the

---

6 See 'Inching down the aisle' 116 *Harv L Rev* (2004).   7 See Worthern, 'Who decides and what difference does it make?: defining marriage in 'Our Democratic, Federal Republic' *8 BYU J. Pub. L. 273* (2004).

third and fourth of these interests, highlighting the distributional function of marriage, as far as *inter alia* taxation, succession and social welfare benefits are concerned, and also the importance of marriage as a means of ensuring that gay people are able to live lives as fulfilling as possible. On the other hand, those opposed to gay marriage tend to stress the fact that a homosexual couple cannot procreate without external assistance, and also, and more perniciously to argue that by expanding the civil definition of marriage to cover same-sex relationships, the state is opening up a moral can of worms where any kind of sexual deviance can become the norm[8] – where I will shortly be knocking on the door of the state asking for tax relief on the basis of my marriage to my tree, for example. We need therefore to consider whether either of these two interests justify the state in continuing to restrict its definition of marriage to exclude same-sex relationships.

Marriage and procreation

The first of these arguments, which is considered in more detail in other chapters of this book, works at a literal level (marriage is for procreation and, ideally procreation is for marriage) at a 'natural law' level (marriage means the sexual complementarity of man and woman (and ensures the proper regulation of heterosexual sexual activity) which finds expression in either procreation or attempts to procreate) and at a utilitarian level (marriage is a good place in which to conceive and raise children and hence society should promote the view that marriage is about procreation).

It is submitted that the first two of these levels of argument does not have huge force for a variety of reasons. First of all, whereas many heterosexual married couples *do* procreate, equally many don't or can't yet this fact does not make them any less married.[9] We would never say, for example, that if owing to some calamity (or indeed the onset of advancing years) one or both of a married couple lost the capacity to procreate, this meant that they were no longer properly married. Indeed the fact that many plainly post-menopausal women (a) get married and (b) are allowed to do so indicates in turn (a) that marriage can be about more than procreation and (b) that the civil definition of the term accepts this fact. Most importantly, it is not a term of the contract of a civil marriage that a couple must, or must try to have children. Secondly, it seems clear that such a view of marriage (as the only bastion of acceptable sexual or procreative activity) is simply and utterly out

---

8 See Cahill, 'Same-sex marriage, slippery slope rhetoric, and the politics of disgust: a critical perspective on contemporary family discourse and the incest taboo', 99 *Northwestern University Law Review* (2005).   9 Culhane, 'Uprooting the arguments against same-sex marriage', 20 *Cardozo L. Rev* 1119 (1999). This was one of the central reasons why the Massachusetts Supreme Court rejected the procreation argument in *Goodridge v. Dept of Public Health* 798 N.E 2d 941 (18 November 2003).

of line with contemporary social reality, and unlike the Church, it is incumbent on the state to make its laws relevant to its own society.

The utilitarian argument, however, has more force. For any number of reasons it may be wise for the state to adopt the view that because, at its best, a traditional marriage unit is the best context in which to have and to raise a child, thus this unit should be privileged above other forms of relationship.[10] Thus as Cordy J pointed out, dissenting in *Goodridge v. Department of Public Health*,

> As long as marriage is limited to opposite-sex couples who can at least theoretically procreate, society is able to communicate a consistent message to its citizens that marriage is a (normatively) necessary part of their procreative endeavour; that if they are to procreate, then society has endorsed the institution of marriage as the environment for it and for the subsequent rearing of children; and that benefits are available explicitly to create a supportive and conducive atmosphere for those purposes.

It will be submitted later that by *including* committed same-sex relationships within the definition of marriage, the state will in fact be communicating another and more currently vital message to society about tolerance, non-discrimination and equality. Moreover, what Cordy J's view commits us to is the notion that procreation is about marriage – not that marriage is about procreation. In other words, it is more profoundly an argument about preventing people who are not married from having children than it is about preventing people who cannot or will not have children from getting married. As such, and because, self-evidently, gay couples cannot procreate without external assistance, the utilitarian argument in respect of procreation, understood in this sense, does not apply here.

At its height the argument from procreation may in fact be an argument about the well being of children – with the state saying that marriage because of its quasi permanent status, provides a stability that is conducive to the good upbringing of children, because it allows them to be confident in the 'sureness' of their family setup. Again, however, it is ludicrous to suppose that the well being of children is enhanced merely by ascribing the definition of 'marriage' to the relationship of those charged with their upbringing. After all, marriages can be abusive, violent and unhappy places and they do

10 This was the conclusion of the dissenting judges in *Goodridge v. Department of Public Health*. It would seem that the best view is that (as the dissenting judges in the case accepted), there is simply not enough evidence to take a definite stance on whether children raised in same-sex units will be inherently disadvantaged as compared to children raised in a traditional marriage unit. See for example Reville, 'Evidence is clear that traditional family is best', *Irish Times* 19 October 2006.

break up, whereas non-marital relationships can be blissfully happy entirely stable and do survive.

More to the point, it is impossible to comment on whether homosexual relationships would provide an equally certain stability for a growing family, and unfair to suggest that they could not do so, in that, because the state has not extended the definition of marriage to cover gay couples, the theory simply cannot be tested.[11] On the other hand, it cannot be denied that empirical evidence currently tends to the view that a happy stable homosexual relationship is an appropriate (if not necessarily the ideal) environment in which to raise a child.[12] Hence the suggestion that the privileging of heterosexual marriage (as traditionally understood) is justified on the basis that – at its best – it may be a slightly better location for children to be raised is simply insufficient and at worst an entirely disproportionate reaction to uncertain statistics which ignores the current reality – namely that in many, many cases, a marriage is a most unstable and unsatisfactory thing wherein children will suffer rather than develop.

The definition of marriage and public morality

Of more concern is the notion that the restrictive definition of marriage promotes or sustains a particular moral atmosphere within the state.[13] It is at least arguable that many if not most of the traditional arguments against gay marriage (which operate with religious undertones) focus to some extent on this concept. They proceed from the notion that marriage is in large part a moral institution which means, and has always meant, a certain thing and hence there is something inappropriate about a situation in which it is not reserved for heterosexual couples. Put bluntly, the view is that homosexual relationships do not fit within what the president of the United States likes to term a 'sacred relationship' – even where the relationship in question is seeking civil rather than religious approval. That this line of reasoning is so important to those opposed to gay marriage is supported by the widespread use of moral terminology in the debate.

This is a point of enormous concern, in that at its core it implies or indeed bluntly expresses the notion that marriage is an important moral institution within society[14] and that a homosexual relationship cannot approach the level

11 Sosman J, dissenting in *Goodridge v. Department of Public Health* noted that 'Gay and Lesbian couples living openly together and official recognition of them as their children's sole parents comprise a very recent phenomenon, and the recency of that phenomenon has not yet permitted any study of how those children fare as adults and at best minimal study of how they fare during their adolescent years'.   12 Dent, 'Traditional marriage: still worth defending', 18 *BYU J. Pub. L.* 419 (2004).   13 Ibid., for the view that 'By recognizing marriage the law gives it honour, thereby encouraging people to marry and stay married'. Dent points out that such an action does not entail an illiberal judgment that homosexual acts or relationships are illegal or immoral.   14 See for example Devlin, *The enforcement of morals* (Oxford, 1965), Mitchell,

of sacrosanctity necessary for it to come within the civil definition of marriage.[15] This in itself is of course a value judgement, and one which, it is submitted, has its roots in the view that gay love is not love at all but rather illness or perversion. It is also, it is submitted, a value judgment based in large part on what has been termed the 'sexualization' of gay relationships – in other words the characterization of the totality of the homosexual relationship in terms of the sexual activities of the parties thereto.

SEXUALIZATION OF HOMOSEXUAL RELATIONSHIPS

In its seminal decision of *Lawrence v. Texas*,[16] the US Supreme Court *per* Kennedy J used the broad concept of liberty contained within the 14th amendment to the US constitution to strike down a Texas statute (and by implication all American state laws) that criminalized homosexual sodomy. The decision undoubtedly has its flaws, on a number of different levels.[17] Nonetheless one of the key elements of Kennedy J's opinion (yet strangely one that was not actually necessary to his conclusion) was his view that it was both wrong and demeaning to classify the homosexual relationship purely in terms of gay sex.[18]

No one after all, would suggest that a heterosexual relationship – perhaps most of all a heterosexual marriage – could be defined in this fashion. Yet this is the manner in which gay relationships tend to be defined.[19] Thus for example, President Bush during the second presidential debate prior to the 2000 presidential election was asked about his stance on gay marriage. Having commented that he opposed gay marriage, seeing marriage as a sacred institution between a man and a woman, the then governor of Texas went on to say that despite this view, 'I don't think it's any of my, you know, any of my concern how you conduct your sex life. And I think that's a private matter.' In other words, as far as the then governor was concerned, the

---

Law, morality and religion in a secular society (Oxford, 1967).   **15** Dent argues that 'Because gay couples do not bear children and not have traditional religious and cultural encouragements to marry, and because the majority of gays who are male tend to be promiscuous, many gay marriages would be marriages of convenience entered into primarily for tangible benefits … [such marriages] would be views as particularly offensive examples of a noxious theme': Dent, 'Traditional marriage: still worth defending', 18 *BYU J. Pub. L.* 419 (2004).   **16** 123 S.Ct. 2472 (2003). See Tribe, '*Lawrence v. Texas*: the "fundamental right" that dare not speak its name'. 117 *Harv. L. Rev* (2004) 1893.   **17** Most of these flaws are commented upon at some length in Scalia J's dissent in the case.   **18** On the impact of the *Lawrence* decision for gay marriage see Ball, 'Same-sex marriage in the aftermath of *Lawrence v. Texas*'. 88 *Minn. L. Rev* 1184, Strasser, '*Lawrence* and same sex marriage', 69 *Brooklyn L. Rev*, 1003 (2004). Generally see Wardle, 'A critical analysis of constitutional claims for same sex marriage', 1996 *BYUL Rev* 1.   **19** Generally see Ross, 'The sexualisation of difference: a comparison of mixed-race and same gender marriage' Summer (2002) 37 *Harv C.R-C.L.L. Rev* 255.

totality of the homosexual relationship could be reduced to the sexual act. Indeed, anecdotally, in the many conversations I have had with people in researching this paper, in which I have asked for views and opinions on the subject of gay marriage, the responses have tended either to support gay marriage ('It's people's own business who they have sex with') or to oppose it ('It isn't natural', 'Marriage is about procreation' etc.). In other words, by and large (and from both sides of the argument) a common reaction to homosexuality and what may be termed 'the homosexual question' is to see what is at stake as being sexual intimacy and nothing more. Yet plainly any marriage (and nearly every relationship) is about more than sex,[20] and hence this sexualisation is devaluing in the extreme.

The most insidious effect of the sexualization of gay relationships is that it makes it easy to overlook the fact that heterosexual relationships and homosexual relationships have far more in common than they have in difference. Both categories of relationship will have stresses and worries, mortgages to pay, bereavements to overcome, romance, bitterness, companionship, joy and pain. And above all, it is submitted, both will involve love (and possibly hate, or worse, indifference). And because love is present, and in the context of marriage is declared in the intense solemnity of a binding perpetual contract, both deserve to be taken seriously. The only major point of distinction is sex (and naturally the concerns in respect of procreation derive from sex) and not necessarily the *nature* of the sex but rather the identity and biological makeup of the participants. Hence the sexualisation of gay relationships is designed to and has the effect of ensuring that gay relationships become associated with the major if not the only point whereby they are different to straight relationships. Were homosexual relationships to be associated with all the other (more abundant and generally more important) elements of such relationships – the elements that are common to all relationships, gay or straight – it would, I believe be easier for persons who support what may be termed gay rights also to support gay marriage.

Sexualization, gay marriage and racism

In this respect, the links between the arguments in respect of gay marriage in this era and those in respect of *interracial* marriage in the past are striking,[21] not least in the fact that interracial marriages were also sexualized by those who opposed the concept. Thus the laws in the US that made mixed race marriage illegal were part of a package of laws that also criminalized sex

---

20 See Culhane, 'Uprooting the arguments against same-sex marriage', 20 *Cardozo L. Rev* 1119 (1999).   21 Ross, 'The sexualisation of difference, 255, Trosino, 'American wedding: same sex marriage and the miscegenation analogy', *73 BUL Rev* 93 (1993), Hutchinson, 'Ignoring the sexualisation of race', 47 *Buffalo L. Rev* 1 (1999), Culhane, 'Uprooting the arguments against same-sex marriage'.

between people of different unions. Sociologists and journalists as late as the mid-1960s spoke of the *thought* of a white woman having sex with a black man as 'a vulgar thing, a perverse thing'.[22] And radical opponents of interracial marriage canvassed supporters by presenting the allegedly repulsive (and self-evidently so) vista of their (white) daughter having sex with a black man. In other words, opposition to these loving and caring relationships was garnered by reducing them to the level of sex, and worse, by defining them in terms of sex. As has been pointed out, 'the obsession with sexuality played a key role in maintaining the racist power imbalance and the continued second-class treatment of certain relationships'.

In the current era, where racism is less widespread or at least, less overt, the notion that any reasonable and thoughtful person would take seriously the viewpoint that an interracial relationship could be somehow defined by the sexual activities of its protagonists is a nonsense. In other words, interracial relationships have been elevated – have been 'desexualized'. It is submitted that it would behoove this generation, in the interests of fairness, and of truth to do the same for homosexual relationships. Indeed it may be in time that the homosexual choice may be explained by a phrase more holistic and more accurate than 'sexual orientation' – a phrase which, despite its superficial neutrality simply does not have any genuine resonance for heterosexuals.

Beyond sexualization; gay marriage and racism

Before leaving this theme, it is perhaps worth noting that, quite apart from sexualizing interracial relationships, in the comparatively recent days when the laws of some American states criminalized interracial marriage, the arguments that tended to be put forward in support of such laws mirror to a fascinating degree the arguments proffered in opposition to homosexual relationships today;[23] such arguments included

- Religious arguments such as 'Almighty God created the races black, white, yellow, Malay and red and he placed them on separate continents. And but for the interference with his arrangement there would be no cause of such marriages. The fact that he separated the races shows that he did not intend for the races to mix'.[24] On the other hand, it is a fair point that the level of Judaeo-Christian teaching against homosexual behaviour, while neither absolute nor complete,[25] is far greater both quantitatively and qualitatively than that against interracial marriage.

---

22 Hernton, *Sex and racism in America* (1965) at 90.   23 Generally see Ross, 'The sexualisation of difference' at 262ff. For the opposing view see Dent, 'Traditional marriage: still worth defending'.   24 Comments from the trial judge in *Loving v. Virginia*, 388 US 1 (1967).   25 At the trial of the action in *Norris v. AG* a Church of Ireland cleric, Roy Warke (later bishop of Cork) had testified that, in his view, the condemnation of homosexuality was in fact profoundly unchristian.

- Natural law arguments – i.e. the notion that interracial relationships were 'unnatural' and should be prohibited as such.[26]
- Arguments from tradition (i.e. that marriage has always been a particular way and meant a particular thing the state should not be forced to change an institution which historically has lain at the heart of society at the behest of those whose (immoral) relationships do not come within the definition of the term)
- Arguments in respect of procreation. Thus in 1883 Judge Henry of the Missouri Supreme Court explained that an interracial couple were actually incapable of producing children.[27] (and there is no typographical error in that sentence). Others have suggested that the progeny of interracial couples would inevitably be genetically inferior[28] to that of a couple from the same race.
- Arguments in respect of children. Thus it was suggested that children raised in an interracial setting might be lured into thinking this was a good thing and might be tempted to 'fall prey' to interracial activity when they hit adolescence[29].

It is not necessarily true that because such arguments now appear nonsensical in the context of interracial relationships they must by definition be nonsensical when applied to homosexual relationships. Nonetheless the fact that these arguments which are now addressed against gay relationships and the legalization of civil gay marriage were once addressed at interracial relationships and, which we can now see were patently founded either on ignorance or on prejudice and racial hatred must surely give us pause for thought.

THE IMPACT OF GAY MARRIAGE ON HETEROSEXUAL MARRIAGE

A further argument *against* gay marriage and deriving from a concern with public morality is to say that without making any judgement against homosexual relationships, marriage, that important social institution, is reserved for heterosexual relationships (for any number of reasons) and that such traditional marriage would be undermined (both morally and socially) by the legalization of gay marriage.[30] In other words the view is that marriage is by definition a man/woman thing and to speak of a 'same-sex marriage' is a contradiction in terms[31] and one with distinctly negative side effects.

First of all, and for the reasons discussed at the outset, it is surely true that the definition of what the state regards as a marriage is not set in stone.

26 *State v. Gibson* 36 Ind 389 (1871).   27 *State v. Jackson*, 80 Mo. 175, 179 (1883).   28 *Scott v. Georgia*, 39 Ga321(1869).   29 A variant of this argument had been used by O'Higgins CJ in *Norris v. AG* as an argument against recognizing a constitutional right to engage in gay sex.   30 Dent, 'Traditional marriage: still worth defending'.   31 Culhane, 'Uprooting the arguments against same-sex marriage'.

Traditionally after all, marriage was above all a 'permanent' thing, yet in the divorce era we can still speak of marriage without being accused of contradicting ourselves. Moreover, as mentioned, having survived the impact of divorce, civil marriage can withstand any other less foundational change to which it may be subjected. Finally, the argument that marriage is defined in a particular way and cannot be extended to accommodate others is itself undermined by the fact that marriage is defined by those who have had access to the institution. It is like men saying that women could not be horse trainers because by their definition a horse trainer was a man.[32]

Furthermore, the conclusion that heterosexual marriage would be undermined by the recognition of gay marriage is also flawed, and again for the reasons set out at the beginning of this essay.[33] What would happen should the state accept the notion of gay marriage would of course result in a very visible and high profile opening up of a gap between the church and the state definition of this term but this need not be of any concern for those who regard their marriage as being sacred in the religious sense. After all, as mentioned earlier, no one has any rights over the Christian or religious definition of marriage.[34] So if gay marriage was recognized by the state, this would not alter the religious definition of the term one iota, and people who derived comfort and validity for their relationship from the religious definition or as has been stressed, *from their own definition* of the term could continue to do so. In other words they could continue to prioritize the fact that they are married in the eyes of God and the church over the fact that they are married in the eyes of the law, or they could merely view themselves as operative within an institution that is defined on their own terms. Moreover, as far as the state definition of the term is concerned, the fact that an additional class of relationship is permitted to enjoy the benefits both tangible and intangible of marriage would in no sense reduce the level of entitlement enjoyed by those who fit within a more traditional definition of the term.[35]

On the basis of all of the above, then, it is submitted that the traditional and contemporary societal arguments against the extension of the civil definition of marriage to cover homosexual relationships are simply not of

---

32 *Nagle v. Feilden*, [1966] 2 QB 633. See Cox & Schuster, *Sport and the law* (Dublin, 2004). 33 Culhane, 'Uprooting the Arguments against same-sex marriage'.   34 It is submitted that comments about how the church should alter its teaching on homosexuality or feminism or contraception, in order to come into line with changing social conditions are facile in the extreme. After all, religion sees itself as setting an agenda for society rather than as following an agenda set by society for it. If people do not wish to follow religion then they are perfectly entitled not to do so. On the other hand, they are not entitled to demand that, in as much as they do not wish to follow religious teaching on a particular issue, that religious teaching should alter to comply with what they want.   35 Thus the Massachusetts Supreme Court in *Goodridge v. Dept of Public Health*, 798 N.E.2d 941 (Mass.2003) concluded that same-sex marriage '... will not diminish the validity or dignity of ... marriage any more than [interracial marriage] did'.

the force argued by their proponents, nor do they justify the continued restriction of this definition. The next question then is whether there are sufficient societal arguments that would justify such a change.

IS GAY MARRIAGE NECESSARY?

A very common argument for those who support gay rights but oppose gay marriage is to say 'I support gay unions and they should be recognized by law, but I would not go so far as to recognize gay marriage'. In other words, perhaps because the shadow of the religious definition still hangs so significantly over common perceptions of what marriage is, to the point that an inaccurate understanding exists that there is only one definition of marriage, there is a reticence towards gay marriage.[36] It is felt that gay couples should be treated equally to their straight counterparts where economic distribution and social benefits are concerned. It is indeed occasionally felt that gay couples should be allowed to adopt[37] – in that empirical evidence from North America indicates (albeit in a limited context) that despite common assumptions, and accepting the fact that the ideal for child raising is in a situation where both biological parents are present and are committed to each other,[38] children do well in stable relationships whether gay or straight, and that homosexuality is not a disease that can be transmitted over the family dinner table.[39] But there is still the viewpoint that marriage *per se* is a bridge too far. Most importantly, it is felt that there is no particular *reason* to call a recognisable same-sex union a marriage, in that the legal recognition of same-sex unions would have exactly the same effect for gay couples as would the legal recognition of gay marriage.

The arguments have force – and are I believe considerably more tenable than was the conclusion of the Massachusetts Supreme Court in *Goodridge v. Dept. of Public Health*[40] to the effect that the distinction between a civil

---

36 Generally see Dent, 'Traditional marriage: still worth defending'.   37 It is notable that in Massachusetts at the time of *Goodridge v. Dept of Public Health*, whereas it was not possible for a gay couple to marry it *was* possible for such persons to adopt.   38 See Dent, 'Traditional marriage: still worth defending'.   39 See Becker, 'Family law in the secular state and restrictions on same-sex marriage' 2001 *U. Ill L. Rev* 1; Wardle, 'The potential impact of homosexual parenting on children' 1997 *U.Ill. L. Rev* 833 (1997) Ball & Pea, 'Warring with Wardle: morality, social science and gay and lesbian parents', 1998 *U.Ill. L. Rev* 253 (1998); Ball, 'Lesbian and gay families', 2003 31 *Cap UL Rev* 691. Generally see 'Parents patriarchy: adoption eugenics and same sex couples', 2003 40 *Cal. W.L.Rev* 1; Culhane, 'Uprooting the arguments against same-sex marriage' 20 *Cardozo L. Rev* 1119 (1999). Indeed in the American context it has been argued that '... given the desirability of legal stability for the hundreds of thousands of children being raised by same-sex couples, using the parenting rationale to deny same-sex marriage would seem counterproductive'. Weiser, 'The next normal – developments since marriage rights for same-sex couples in New York',13 *Columb. J. Gender and Law*, 48 (2004). 40 798 N.E. 2d 941 (Mass. 2003).

union and marriage was mere semantics. Indeed it has been pointed out that by severing marriage from any consequential values the court 'undermined the one consequential value – public acceptance – that it sought to advance'.[41] Equally I would offer three tentative arguments as to why it does make sense for the state to expand its definition of marriage to cover gay relationships.

Overcoming prejudice and underpinning a new morality

It may be argued that it simply constitutes good social policy to give gay relationships the ultimate seal of approval by terming them marriages.[42] After all the alternative involves saying that such seal of approval cannot be given, exclusively because of the gender of the two parties to the relationship – a discrimination that may foster a stigma that may lead to persecution. It is true that in the wake of the decision of the Massachusetts Supreme Court in *Goodridge v. Department of Public Health*[43] it was pointed out, on the other hand, that the effects of such a social statement will in light of the reality of the situation be frankly illusory. Nonetheless it may be that civil recognition of gay marriages is simply a necessary corollary of our obligations to homosexuals under Irish and EU equality laws. This would be less so if the issue of gay marriage was not 'on the table'. But on the table it undoubtedly now is, and the deliberations of courts and parliaments around the world on this topic must take cognizance of the fact that what is decided therein will represent a clear statement as to the state's view of the legitimacy of homosexuality and homosexual relationships generally.[44]

Moreover, the recognition of gay marriage may enable the institution of state marriage to do in the twenty-first century what it had done in the past. Traditionally, after all, society was seen as being to some extent based on the institution of marriage,[45] or more accurately, the institution of marriage was seen as an important repository of public morality. Yet society and social mores have changed. For a society that seeks to be underpinned by notions of equality, human rights, respect and tolerance, it may be that the recognition of gay marriage would actually ensure that marriage regains it status as an essential element of social morality, upon which society is rooted, simply because it is such an emphatic manifestation of these core values.

The practicalities of social distribution

It has long been argued that the benefits accorded to marriage should be extended to non-marital but committed relationships. Yet this does pose

---

41 See case note 117 *Harv L. Rev*, 2441.   42 See Cox, 'The lesbian wife: same sex marriage as an expression of radical and plural democracy', 1997 33 *Cal.WL Rev* 155.   43 798 N.E.2d 941 (Mass. 2003).   44 Culhane, 'Uprooting the arguments against same-sex marriage'. 45 Mitchell, *Law, morality and religion in a secular society*' (Oxford, 1967).

difficulties in terms of trying to draw a line for determining *when* a relationship has become sufficiently serious that it merits economic protection. If marriage is a statement of commitment, then this provides such a line (both for heterosexuals and homosexuals). This is not to say that non-married couples should have no rights under the law to tax relief and other forms of economic benefits, but merely that in terms of economic distribution, succession and indeed the impact of family law generally, the introduction of gay marriage may actually prove a help rather than a hindrance.

Why do people get married?

The final argument may be the most forceful, but is certainly the least empirical, and it relates to the question of why people get married at all.[46] Of course some people get married for an array of reasons not connected with the desire to commit to a loving relationship (as far as possible) in perpetuity. But many persons (and it is to these people that the social benefits of marriage are most idealistically aimed) cling to old ideals about marriage as a public statement of love, loyalty and solidarity. And for many, the need to make this statement is almost transcendent, and certainly is not susceptible to rational explanation. People propose and accept marriage proposals and they get married without being able to explain precisely why they needed to do so, especially as the consequences are so onerous. But despite not knowing why they are getting married they *do* get married. For these people (and clearly this is not a universal condition) the act of getting married represents the only expression at the time which properly conveys the nature of their relationship. In this context, and however pointless, idealistic or nonsensical this may seem to other people, for these individuals marriage is simply the ultimate expression of the inexpressible. And naturally this is because of what marriage has come to mean because of its history, but this does not devalue either the institution or the deep desires of persons who wish to enter into it.

This is why people who have days left to live marry their sweethearts.[47] This is why the breakup of marriage is so painful. This is why fairy tales so often end in marriages with the ideal that the participants will indeed live happily ever after. Socially, publicly, privately, for some people marriage expresses some deep sense of belonging that cannot be expressed in any other

46 See Lee, 'Finding marriage amidst a sea of confusion: a precursor to considering the public purposes of marriage', 43 *Catholic Law* 339 (Fall 2004).   47 'At the end of his life, Paul was living in Susan's house. For the last five years, Susan had seen Paul in the midst of a very noble, very heroic, very holy struggle, and she had wanted to share it with him even if that meant suffering pain herself. As Paul struggled with his helplessness and total dependence on others in the final stages of the disease, he said to Susan, "I don't have anything I can give you," and Susan responded, "I want to marry you." What Susan wanted was to give words to the relationship that already existed between them'. See Lee, 'Finding marriage amidst a sea of confusion'.

way. And it is not the permanency, nor the intention to create legally binding contractual relations (and for many people it is not even the religious aspect of the thing) that is important. It is simply that marriage and all that it means and has come to mean to twenty-first century Irish society is important *in and of itself* – as a statement, as a commitment and as a source of identity. And Irish society buys into this view of marriage (rightly or wrongly) and sees in it (again rightly or wrongly) certain tangible social benefits, and as such it rewards the making of that statement or rather the motivation behind it, by elevating the status of marriage, so that it is in its eyes the highest form of loving relationship available, and one to which it provides the maximum of comfort and support.[48]

For myself the single greatest argument in favour of expanding the civil definition of marriage to cover gay marriage is that it is quite simply unfair that something so important both socially and personally and, at its best, so wonderful, should be denied to people simply because their love in order to be properly expressed and explained is directed towards someone of the same gender.[49] Nor do I see any reason why gay relationships if they are intended to be permanent should be denied the social approbation that goes along with the civil definition of this institution. Nor do I see what social harm would be done by expanding the civil definition of marriage while leaving untouched all other private definitions of the term.

48 Culhane, 'Uprooting the arguments against same-sex marriage'.   49 Thus Marshall CJ in *Goodridge v. Department of Public Health* accepted that 'Each plaintiff attests a desire to marry his or her partner in order to affirm publicly their commitment to each other and to secure the legal protections and benefits afforded to married couples and their children'.

Moral argument and the recognition of same-sex partnerships

ORAN DOYLE

WRITING IN THE US CONTEXT, Carlos Ball attempts to justify the use of moral argument by a gay rights advocate. He begins by noting how such arguments have traditionally been eschewed by gay rights advocates:

> For most of the history of the gay rights movement in the United States, it has been possible and even advisable for its supporters to avoid engaging questions of morality directly. Arguments based on notions of morality have been used primarily by opponents of gay rights to justify the differential treatment by society of lesbians and gay men. It is the purported immorality of a gay and lesbian sexuality, for example, that justifies in the minds of some denying same-gender couples the right to marry ... In response to these and other familiar arguments raised by opponents of gay rights about the immorality of gay and lesbian sexuality and relationships, most supporters of gay rights (including political activists and academics) prefer to sidestep moral arguments altogether and instead rely on what are taken to be morally neutral (and largely liberal) arguments based on considerations of privacy, equality and tolerance.[1]

Ball refers to this avoidance of moral arguments as 'moral bracketing' – a 'strict separation of moral, philosophical, and religious views ... from considerations of justice'.[2] This moral bracketing, sometimes phrased as a right to privacy in matters of sexual intimacy, well served the political objective of the decriminalisation of homosexual activity.[3] Ball argues, however, that most of the controversies over homosexuality are moral controversies. Correctly, in my view, he argues that 'even the paradigmatic

---

1 Carlos A. Ball, *The morality of gay rights* (London, 2003), at 1.   2 Ibid.   3 Ball also argues that moral bracketing even, in the form of neutral equality arguments, provided the basis for obtaining from the state the protection afforded by anti-discrimination legislation. I am not as convinced on this point as, I think, any detailed examination of the 'relevance' criterion that tends to inform such legislation shows that it is not neutral and, indeed, imports moral arguments. Given Ball's later comments on moral argument in general, I suspect that he might agree with this observation.

right to privacy in matters of sexual intimacy … is most convincingly grounded on a moral conception of the potential for human flourishing that inheres in the exercise of self-determination or autonomy'.[4] Claims that the state should provide recognition for same-sex partnerships necessarily require some argument as to why such recognition *should* be provided: these are moral arguments.[5] Intellectual honesty and political expediency combine: gay rights advocates must rely on moral arguments.

Now I do not conceive of myself as a gay rights advocate, although perhaps that is (part of) what I am. More particularly, my purpose in this paper is not to construct the most convincing moral argument in support of the recognition of same-sex partnerships. Rather my purpose is to examine a number of moral arguments advanced in support of and against such recognition. My selection of arguments is, as will quickly become apparent, far from exhaustive. I focus on natural law arguments against partnership recognition and egalitarian arguments in favour of recognition. My basis for focusing on natural law arguments is my intuition that arguments against the recognition of same-sex partnerships are at root moral arguments that rely on some natural law type account of human sexuality. My basis for focusing on egalitarian arguments is my intuition that equality provides the most compelling basis on which to argue for partnership recognition. Clearly my argument is incomplete, but my hope is to make some contribution to those aspects of this debate that I have chosen, somewhat arbitrarily, to focus on. Within these limits, the purpose of this paper is ultimately two-fold: first, to assess whether some recognition of same-sex partnerships is morally permissible or required; secondly and if so, to assess which form of recognition best reflects the moral argument that justified recognition in the first instance.

Two points that generally cause difficulty must be clarified. First, as noted above, I agree with Ball's contention that rights to privacy, whereby the state allows to the individual a zone of personal autonomy within which to make her own choices, are themselves moral propositions. Notwithstanding that the substance of the right is the non-imposition of the state's moral code within that zone of autonomy, the belief that the state should not impose its moral code is itself a moral belief. It is a moral belief about the importance of individual autonomy in certain areas. Some advocates of such a right might agree with this characterisation; others might not. For the purposes of this paper, whether one agrees with the characterisation or not is irrelevant. Privacy rights rest on moral beliefs about the appropriate limits on the actions of the state.

---

4 Carlos A. Ball, *The morality of gay rights*, at 5.   5 Although it is possible to argue that recognition should be provided to all relationships *unless* there is a good reason not to, this does not seem a particularly attractive proposition. In any event, it requires moral argument to support the proposition that recognition should presumptively be provided to all relationships. In the context of positive state action (at the very least), moral arguments are unavoidable.

Secondly, the word 'moral' is itself, in a very literal way, ambiguous. This becomes clear if one considers how the word 'moral' is the opposite of two other words: 'amoral' and 'immoral'. 'Amoral' is essentially a descriptive word, connoting (although this meaning may have been hijacked) 'having nothing to do with issues of right or wrong'. 'Immoral' is an evaluative word, connoting 'against a code of what constitutes right or wrong'. Thus the word 'moral' itself must have two meanings: one descriptive, one evaluative. Used in the descriptive sense, a 'moral' proposition is one that purports to provide a reason for behaving or not behaving in a particular way. Used in the evaluative sense, a 'moral' proposition is one that truly does provide a reason for behaving or not behaving in a particular way. The purpose of this essay is to assess moral (in the descriptive sense) arguments in order to identify the moral (in the evaluative sense) position on the recognition of same-sex partnerships.

I shall begin with an examination of Finnis's natural law theory and his particular application of that to the question of partnership recognition. Although there are many variants of natural law theory, I focus on Finnis for the reason that he advances a natural law argument that unequivocally rejects the civil recognition of same-sex partnerships. If I can show Finnis's argument to be unfounded, my case is stronger than if I had undermined a natural law theory that was more moderate in its approach. Having considered Finnis's argument, I shall consider egalitarian arguments in favour of partnership recognition. In doing so, my primary concern (in this paper) is to defend egalitarian arguments against the general claim that there are no valid egalitarian arguments. I shall conclude with an assessment, in the light of egalitarian arguments, of various forms of partnership recognition currently under discussion.

THE NATURAL LAW ARGUMENT

Outline of the natural law argument against partnership recognition

Finnis articulates a natural law argument against the recognition of same-sex partnerships.[6] In outline, this argument is as follows: marriage (that is, the presumptively procreative union of a man and a woman) is a basic good; it is impermissible to intend to destroy, damage, impede or violate any basic human good or to prefer an illusory instantiation of a basic human good to a real instantiation of that or some other human good; accordingly, the state should not recognize and thus legitimize same-sex partnerships, as these partnerships are illusory representations of the basic good of marriage and

6 John M. Finnis, 'Law, morality and sexual orientation', 69 *Notre Dame Law Review* 1049 (1994).

thus inimical to that basic good. In order to understand and evaluate this argument, it is necessary to understand the broad outlines of Finnis's natural law argumentation.

Finnis's theory of natural law

Finnis asserts that there are seven basic values or goods: life, knowledge, play, aesthetic experience, sociability (friendship), practical reasonableness and religion. These goods are not themselves moral propositions, but are rather basic facts about human nature on which moral argument is based. In establishing that something is a basic good or value, Finnis seems to place most importance on two discrete observations. The first is the observation of an inclination; the second is the observation of the grasp of value. Finnis considers these in the context of knowledge. He notes that 'curiosity' is a name for the inclination that we have when, just for the sake of knowing, we want to find out about something.[7] However, there is more to this than just inclination for, on reflection, one can perceive that there is a good in this inclination:

> Commonly one's interest in knowledge, in getting to the truth of the matter, is not bounded by the particular questions that first aroused one's desire to find out. So readily that one notices the transition only by an effort of reflection, it becomes clear that knowledge is a good thing to have (and not merely for its utility), without restriction to the subject-matters that up to now have aroused one's curiosity.[8]

Thus, basic goods are identified by both inclination and grasp of value. It is not sufficient that there be a common urge to do a particular thing, there must also be a sense of the worthwhileness of doing that thing. Finnis undertakes a similar, although abbreviated exercise, in respect of the other basic goods.

Three points must, in particular, be noted about the basic goods. First, they are self-evident. Finnis asserts, for instance, that the good of knowledge is 'self-evident, obvious'; it cannot be demonstrated, but equally it needs no demonstration. This does not mean, however, that it is self-evident to everyone:

> On the contrary, the value of truth becomes obvious only to one who has experienced the urge to question, who has grasped the connection between question and answer, who understands that knowledge is constituted by correct answers to particular questions, and who is aware of the possibility of further questions and of other questioners

---

7 John M. Finnis, *Natural law and natural rights* (Oxford, 1980), at 60.   8 Ibid., at 61.

who like himself could enjoy the advantage of attaining correct answers.[9]

This self-evidence is a proposition of rationality, not psychology. The soundness of the assertion that knowledge is a self-evident good is not addressed by any inquiry into the physical, biological or psychological conditions under which a person might make such an assertion. The issue of value is not addressed by such factual inquiries. Conversely, one should not commit the naturalistic fallacy and attempt to derive value from purely factual observations:

> [I]f one is to go beyond the felt urge of curiosity to an understanding grasp of the value of knowledge, one certainly must know at least the fact that questions can be answered. Moreover, one certainly will be assisted if one also knows such facts as that answers tend to hang together in systems that tend to be illuminating over as wide a range as the data which simulate one's questions. But one who, thus knowing the possibility of attaining truth, is enabled thereby to grasp the value of that possible object and attainment is not inferring the value from the possibility. No such inference is possible. No value can be deduced or otherwise inferred from a fact or set of facts.[10]

Similarly one cannot infer the value of knowledge from the mere fact that all people desire to know, nor from the mere fact that all people not only desire to know but also affirm the value of knowledge. Conversely, the mere fact that not all people desire to know or that not all people affirm the value of knowledge is not sufficient ground for denying the self-evident good of knowledge. The self-evidence of the goodness of knowledge boils down to the following: it can be denied, for it is not a principle of logic conformity to which is essential if one is to mean anything, but to deny it is 'to disqualify oneself from the pursuit of knowledge'; it is as 'straightforwardly unreasonable as anything can be'.[11]

The second point to be noted about basic goods is that they are *basic*. That is, they are not instrumental to other goods; they are irreducible. Thus, when Finnis speaks of knowledge, he is more precisely speaking about speculative knowledge. That is, he speaks of knowledge for its own sake rather than

---

9 Ibid., at 65. This amounts to little more than a declaration that those who consider knowledge important think knowledge important, thus offering little independent support for the contention that knowledge is a basic good. However, this perhaps misses the point: the whole point of self-evident goods is that they cannot be justified by reference to something else. They are *self*-evident.   10 Ibid., at 66.   11 Ibid., at 69. Again, however, the circularity is plain: why does it matter if one disqualifies oneself from the pursuit of knowledge unless one first accepts that knowledge is a basic good?

knowledge as instrumental to some other end, such as money-saving, personal advancement or, indeed, other goods such as environmental protection or the preservation of life. This is not to say that knowledge for other ends is not a good, but simply that it is not an instantiation of knowledge as a basic good.

The third point to be noted about basic goods is that they are not moral propositions. They do not of themselves and in the abstract possess moral force; they do not of themselves and in the abstract direct that certain things should be done or not done, allowed or disallowed. It is through the good of practical reasonableness that the basic goods are brought to bear on particular situations. This represents the (moral) natural law method of working out the natural law from the first (pre-moral) principles of natural law.

In working out such a stance, Finnis identifies a number of basic requirements of practical reasonableness. I propose only to outline these here in order to provide a rough sense of the character of moral reasoning, as envisaged by Finnis. First, one should adopt a rational and coherent plan of life: this requires one to view one's life as a whole.[12] Secondly, one should adopt no arbitrary preference amongst the basic values. Although any coherent plan of life requires one to concentrate on one or some of the basic goods, such a commitment is rational only if it is made on the basis of one's assessment of one's capacities, circumstances and tastes. It would be unreasonable to concentrate one's efforts in this way as a result of a devaluation of one of the basic goods.[13] Thirdly, one should not have arbitrary preferences among persons. Fourthly and fifthly, one must maintain a certain detachment from one's projects (such that one would not consider one's life as devoid of meaning if one project were to fail) and yet, at the same time, one should be committed to one's projects, having undertaken them. Sixthly, the consequences of particular courses of actions have a certain, though limited, relevance for the morality of choosing one course of action over another; efficiency can be taken into account to a limited extent.

Seventhly – and of particular importance for Finnis's later arguments in relation to the recognition of same-sex partnerships – 'one should not choose to do any act which *of itself does nothing but* damage or impede a realization or participation of any one or more of the basic forms of human good'.[14] This injunction applies, Finnis argues, because the only reason for doing such an act would be that its good consequences outweighed the damage done in and through the act itself. Such reasoning involves a necessarily arbitrary and delusive, and hence inappropriate, consequentialist weighing. As the goods are equally basic and do not share any common essence, they are incommensurable: they cannot be weighed against each other in the manner required by consequentialist logic.

12 Ibid., at 103–5.   13 Ibid., at 105–6.   14 Ibid., at 118. Emphasis original.

There is a distinction, Finnis argues, between acts which promote one basic good but indirectly damage another basic good and acts which do nothing but damage basic goods.[15] The latter are prohibited; the former may be permitted:

> [T]o indirectly damage any basic good (by choosing an act that directly and immediately promotes either that basic good in some other aspect or participation, or some other basic good or goods) is obviously quite different, rationally and thus morally, from directly and immediately damaging a basic good in some aspect or participation by choosing an act which in and of itself simply (or, we should now add, primarily) damages that good in some aspect or participation but which indirectly, *via* the mediation of expected consequences, is to promote either that good in some other aspect or participation, or some other basic good(s).[16]

Clearly, the key problem here is how to differentiate between those acts which indirectly damage a basic good and those acts which directly damage a basic good. Finnis describes this as a problem of individuating acts. If an act is individuated, it follows that its consequences are also individuated acts. If an act is not individuated, it follows that its consequences can be seen as part of the one act, and hence as indirect effects. We decide whether an act is individuated by reference to 'those factors which we gesture towards with the word "intention"':

> Fundamentally, a human act is a that-which-is-decided-upon (or -chosen) and its primary proper description is as what-is-chosen. A human action, to be humanly regarded, is to be characterized in the way it was characterized in the conclusion to the relevant train of practical reasoning of the man who chose to do it. On the other hand, the world with its material (including our bodily selves) and its structures of physical and psycho-physical causality is not indefinitely malleable by human intention. The man who is deciding what to do cannot reasonably shut his eyes to the causal structure of his project; he cannot characterize his plans *ad lib*.[17]

---

15 Such indirect damage is inevitable given that, for example, time expended promoting one basic good (for instance, knowledge) is time taken away from the promotion of another basic good (for instance, life). These moral propositions amount, I think, to what is commonly referred to as the doctrine of indirect effect. Finnis notes that this raises the problem of individuating actions; i.e. if one characterizes an action as individual, one implicitly treats the consequences of that action as individual and as actions in themselves. Accordingly, the consequences cannot be seen as indirect effects of a morally good action. On the other hand, if an action is not individuated, its consequences can be seen as indirect effects and therefore permissible. Ibid., at 119.   16 Ibid., at 120.   17 Ibid., at 122. Internal cross-references omitted.

Eighthly, one must favour and foster the common good of one's community. Ninthly and finally, one must follow one's own conscience: thus if one decides to do what one believes is wrong, one breaches a requirement of practical reasonableness.

For Finnis, morality is the product of these requirements. Each of these requirements provides a reason for acting or not acting in a particular way. Put together, they constitute morality. Therefore, it is not permissible to rely on one of the requirements, say efficiency, to the expense of the others. Morally sound judgments can only be reached if all the requirements of practical reason are taken into account.

Finnis and the criminalization of same-sex activity

Finnis identifies a particular position on homosexuality (at the time described as the 'modern [European] position',[18] although this description might now require change) whereby criminalization of homosexual activity or conduct is considered wrong and unreasonable discrimination by public bodies against homosexuals is prohibited. However, the other side of this position is that it does not outlaw discrimination by private persons against homosexuals and it discourages the promotion of forms of life which both encourage homosexual activity and present it as a valid or acceptable alternative to committed heterosexual union. Although this position might at first appear contradictory as to the moral character of homosexual activity, it is explicable – in Finnis's view – by reference to the concept of subsidiarity. Thus the position identified by Finnis unequivocally views homosexual activity as morally wrong, but also considers that 'the state's proper responsibility for upholding true worth (morality) is a responsibility *subsidiary* (auxiliary) to the *primary* responsibility of parents and non-political voluntary associations'.[19] Under this account, the state does not assume a directly parental disciplinary role in relation to consenting adults. On the basis of this, a distinction is drawn between supervising the truly private conduct of adults and supervising the public realm. The public realm is particularly important as it is there that the young are educated and assisted in avoiding bad forms of life.[20] The supervision of that public realm is an important 'part of the state's justification for claiming legitimately the loyalty of its decent citizens'.[21]

---

18 Finnis, 'Law, morality and sexual orientation', at 1051.   19 Ibid., at 1052. Emphasis original.   20 Although Finnis provides other grounds for the different roles afforded to the state in the public and private realms respectively, this ground may prove problematic or at least more complicated and in need of greater explanation. There are families in which for morally unsound reasons (on Finnis's terms), younger members of the family are encouraged to view homosexual activity and same-sex relationships as acceptable and praiseworthy. It is unclear whether the principle of subsidiarity is capable of supporting the public/private distinction in this context.   21 Finnis, 'Law, morality and sexual orientation', at 1053.

Thus Finnis advances an avowedly moral argument against the recognition of same-sex partnerships that does not extend to the criminalization of same-sex activity or conduct. This argument, although based on sophisticated moral reasoning, employs as a determining criterion the public/private distinction. As such, it is not far removed from liberal arguments for privacy and individual autonomy, although it adopts a position on what constitutes a morally acceptable exercise of individual autonomy that would probably find little favour with most who classify themselves as liberals. For present purposes, however, it suffices to note that Finnis's argument against the recognition of same-sex partnerships, although based to a certain extent on the immorality of same-sex conduct, does not extend to the criminalisation of such conduct. Although this point is important in itself, it also demonstrates that Finnis's argument cannot plausibly be criticized on the grounds that it represents an unwarranted interference with personal liberty.

Same-sex partnerships, marriages and basic goods

Imagine an unsophisticated political debate about homosexuality and, in particular, about the recognition of same-sex partnerships. An unsophisticated supporter of such recognition might rely on hazy propositions of equality and personal freedom. An unsophisticated opponent of recognition might adopt a position against homosexual activity on the basis of its unnatural (by which is meant non-procreative) characteristics. On the basis of this, she argues, the state should prohibit such activity or, at the very least, deny recognition to relationships in which such activity (we assume) will take place. Our supporter of such recognition responds by arguing that non-procreation is also a feature of much heterosexual activity (even in the absence of contraception) and of many heterosexual marriages, at least for certain periods, whether through choice or capacity. Accordingly, she concludes, the non-procreative characteristic of same-sex activity does not justify a position criminalizing same-sex activity or denying the recognition of same-sex partnerships. Our opponent of recognition, not to be outdone, responds that marriage is not just about procreation, however; it is also about care and companionship. Aha, our supporter concludes, same-sex partners can also demonstrate care and companionship: if that is the basis for recognition of heterosexual marriage, we should also recognize same-sex partnerships.

This is in many ways an unsatisfactory argument. The supporter of recognition fails to specify or justify the appropriate default position for the debate: recognition or non recognition? In particular, the positive arguments in favour of such recognition are not clearly spelt out. The opponent of recognition, on the other hand, probably commits the naturalistic fallacy in deriving moral propositions from observations of biological facts. Finnis, in particular, would make no such claim. As already discussed, his moral argumentation consists of the exercise of practical reason in choosing to act – or not act – in order to promote one of the basic goods. For these reasons, I am not identifying the position of any theorist with the arguments put forward by my imagined supporter and opponent of recognition. However, their discussion does highlight a feature in this debate. A natural law theorist, if she is to justify non-recognition of same-sex partnerships at the same time as recognition, in the form of marriage or otherwise, of heterosexual partnerships, cannot rely simply on the basic good of life (or procreation) as that would seem to preclude recognition of some marriages – it is an under-inclusive rationale. However, if she relies on the basic good of friendship, it would seem to include recognition of same-sex partnerships – it is an over-inclusive rationale. If the recognition of marriage is justified in terms of either of these basic goods (in other words, if marriage is viewed as a secondary good, instrumental to one or more basic goods), the moral position against the recognition of same-sex partnerships and, indeed, against same-sex activity is undermined.

I have set out this argument in some detail because I see Finnis's argument against the recognition of same-sex partnerships as being a response to it, although he does not state it as explicitly as I have done. For Finnis articulates a position against the recognition of same-sex partnerships that is based on none of the basic, self-evident goods identified in *Natural Law and Natural Rights* but rather on the new basic good of marriage:

> [I]n sterile and fertile marriages alike, the communion, companionship, *societas* and *amicitia* of the spouses – their being married – *is* the very good of marriage, and is an intrinsic, basic human good, not merely instrumental to any other good. And this communion of married life, this integral amalgamation of the lives of the two persons ... has as its intrinsic elements, as essential *parts* of one and the same good, the goods and ends to which the theological tradition, following Augustine, for a long time subordinated that communion ... Parenthood and children and family are the intrinsic fulfilment of a communion which, because it is not merely instrumental, can exist and fulfil the spouses even if procreation happens to be impossible for them.[22]

Thus marriage is itself a basic good; it is – contrary to earlier church teaching – neither subordinate nor instrumental to other goods, such as life (procreation) or friendship. Such goods are intrinsic and essential parts of marriage, but marriage is itself a primary good. By this stage, it should be obvious that, marriage being a basic good, other forms of relationship will be deemed

22 Ibid., at 1054–5. Emphasis original.

morally dubious. Nevertheless, it is worth considering Finnis's argument in some detail as it throws light on a number of other issues.

Procreation and friendship are essential elements of marriage: they make marriage what it is. But marriage itself is a basic good: the sexual union of wife and husband within marriage makes them one reality and allows them experience their real common good, their marriage. Outside of marriage, sexual union does not allow for the experience of such common good, because there is no common good being served by the union. This, for Finnis, is particularly the case in respect of the sexual acts of same-sex partners:

> [T]hose acts cannot express or do more than is expressed or done if two strangers engage in such activity to give each other pleasure, or a prostitute pleasures a client to give him pleasure in return for money, or (say) a man masturbates to give himself pleasure and a fantasy of more human relationships after a gruelling day on the assembly line ... [T]here is no important distinction in essential moral worthiness between solitary masturbation, being sodomized as a prostitute, and being sodomized for the pleasure of it.[23]

Sexual acts can only be 'unitive' in their significance if they are marital. This is not a licence for non-procreative sexual acts within marriage, however, as owing to the good of marriage having two essential elements (procreation and friendship) sexual acts are not marital unless they are acts both of friendship and of procreative significance. 'Procreative significance' does not mean being capable of generating or intended to generate but rather means being acts of the reproductive kind. Acts of procreative significance would thus, presumably, include unprotected vaginal intercourse between a woman and a man (even if one or both parties is sterile), but not (artificially?) protected vaginal intercourse or any other types of intercourse.

Finnis's assertions here must be understood in their proper context. He relies on no empirical, anecdotal nor, presumably, experiential basis for his comments about the characteristics of same-sex activity. His assertions, I think, do not purport to be factual descriptions in that sense. This is not to say, however, that his assertions are counter-factual. Rather, his assertions are evaluative descriptions of a world in which marriage is a basic good. The described characteristics of homosexual activity cannot be taken as independent support for his moral views, let alone for his assertion that marriage is a self-evident good. If nothing else, this would infringe Finnis's own injunction against reliance on the naturalistic fallacy. Rather, the described characteristics are incidents of a reality in which marriage is a self-evident good. Although both the status of marriage as a self-evident good

23 Ibid., at 1067.

and the characteristics of homosexual activity are important parts of Finnis's overall moral position, only the former is of argumentative significance, as it is the former that determines the latter. Finnis's argument, that is, turns on the status of marriage as a self-evident good and not (directly at any rate) on his described characteristics of homosexual activity.

Communal self-delusion and false instantiation of basic human goods

The final step in Finnis's argument is that non-marital sexual unions represent illusory instantiations of a basic human good. It is a moral principle, as seen earlier, that one may never intend to destroy, damage, impede, or violate any basic human good, or prefer an illusory instantiation of a basic human good to a real instantiation of that or some other human good. It is this proposition that transforms same-sex partnerships into something specifically and radically immoral, something that no state, attempting to achieve the common good of its citizens, should countenance. Same-sex partnerships are not simply inimical to those who take part in them (as private same-sex activity might arguably be):

> [The deliberate genital coupling of persons of the same sex] treats human sexual capacities in a way which is deeply hostile to the self-understanding of those members of the community who are willing to commit themselves to real marriage in the understanding that its sexual joys are not mere instruments or accompaniments to, or mere compensations for the accomplishment of marriage's responsibilities, but rather enable the spouses to *actualize and experience* their intelligent commitment to share in those responsibilities, in that genuine self-giving.[24]

In Finnis's view, one can only view homosexual acts as acceptable if one views sexual capacities, organs and acts as instruments for gratifying the individual selves who have them. In his view, such an acceptance is itself inimical to marriages:

> A political community which judges that the stability and protective and educative generosity of family life is of fundamental importance to that community's present and future can rightly judge that it has a compelling interest in denying that homosexual conduct – a 'gay lifestyle' – is a valid, humanly acceptable choice and form of life, and in doing whatever it *properly* can, as a community with uniquely wide but still subsidiary functions, to discourage such conduct.[25]

---

24 Ibid., at 1069. Emphasis original.   25 Ibid., at 1070.

Problem with Finnis's argument: marriage as a self-evident good

As noted above, in 1980 Finnis identified only seven self-evident goods, not including marriage. Although he noted that the list was not exhaustive, he did make a number of important methodological points about any tendency to recognize further self-evident basic goods. These methodological points provide good reasons not to identify marriage as a basic, self-evident good and thus require further consideration.

Finnis recognizes that, as well as the seven self-evident basic goods, there are countless objectives and forms of good. But he suggests:

> [T]hese other objectives and forms of good will be found, on analysis, to be ways or combinations of ways of pursuing (not always sensibly) and realizing (not always successfully) one of the seven basic forms of good, or *some combination of them.*[26]

He accepts that there might be more than seven self-evident basic goods and that people might reasonably not accept his list, still less his nomenclature – the words 'life', 'knowledge' and so on simply gesture 'towards categories of human purpose that are each, though unified, nevertheless multi-faceted'.[27] But again he makes the point:

> Still, it seems to me that those seven purposes are all of the basic purposes of human action, and that any other purpose which you or I might recognize and pursue will turn out to represent, or be constituted of, some aspect(s) of some or all of them.[28]

Thus Finnis strongly, although not dogmatically, maintains that there are only seven self-evident basic goods. He further suggests that any inclination to identify other forms of good as further self-evident basic goods is probably mistaken for one of two reasons. Either the new form of good is a means to achieving a basic self-evident good. Or the new form of good is a representation or combination of a number of basic self-evident goods. Neither of these propositions means that the new form of good is no longer good nor worth pursuing. Rather, their import is simply that the good should not be perceived as a basic, self-evident good in its own right.

Each of these injunctions seems apposite to Finnis's subsequent identification of marriage as a basic, self-evident good. His reasoning on this, as set out above, is that marriage is a good comprised of both life and friendship. However, applying Finnis's own reasoning from *Natural Law and Natural Rights*, one should probably reject that as a basis for the assertion of marriage

---

26 Finnis, *Natural law and natural rights*, at 90. Emphasis added.   27 Ibid., at 91.   28 Ibid., at 91.

as a self-evident good. That assertion is either the mistaken elevation of an instrumental good into a basic good or the mistaken characterisation of a combination of two goods as a unitive basic good. These contentions are born out by Finnis's own comments about marriage in *Natural Law and Natural Rights*.

As noted above, the first requirement of basic reasonableness is to have a coherent life plan. In analysing this requirement, Finnis notes a number of projects which one might adopt in order to achieve particular basic goods:

> Commitment to the practice of medicine (for the sake of human life), or to scholarship (for the sake of truth), or to any profession, or to a marriage (for the sake of friendship and children) ... all require both direction and control of impulses, and the undertaking of specific projects.[29]

I am taking this passage out of context. Nevertheless, it demonstrates Finnis's understanding, in *Natural Law and Natural Rights*, that marriage is in some way instrumental to the goods of friendship and children (life/procreation) in much the same way as the practice of medicine is in some way instrumental to the good of life and scholarship is instrumental to the good of knowledge. Such an understanding is consistent with Finnis's overall methodology, set out above, but not with his argument as set out in 'Law, Morality and Sexual Orientation'.

Finnis's argument in 'Law, Morality and Sexual Orientation' is also problematic with regard to other aspects of his general theory of natural law. In *Natural Law and Natural Rights*, he makes a number of other general points about the basic goods:

> More important than the precise number and description of these values is the sense in which each is basic. First, each is equally self-evidently a form of good. Secondly, none can be analytically reduced to being merely an aspect of any of the others, or to being merely instrumental in the pursuit of any of the others. Thirdly, each one, when we focus on it, can reasonably be regarded as the most important. Hence there is no objective hierarchy amongst them.[30]

The second point in the above paragraph goes a little further than the point already made: basic goods are not instrumental or derivative in any sense, not even to or of other basic goods. The third point in the above paragraph is that there is no objective hierarchy between the goods. Finnis's argument against the recognition of same-sex partnerships, principally the assertion

---

29 Ibid., at 104. Ellipsis original.   **30** Ibid., at 92.

that there are eight basic goods including life, friendship and marriage, is profoundly problematic in the light of these requirements of natural law theory. The problem with Finnis's argument against the recognition of same-sex partnerships, apart from its treatment of marriage as a basic good comprised of other basic goods, is that it necessarily introduces a ranking of basic goods. In his characterisation of same-sex partnerships as inimical to the good of marriage, notwithstanding the ignored extent to which they are instrumental to the basic good of friendship, Finnis effectively ranks the good of marriage above that of friendship. Finnis might respond, however, that this arises not because of a preference for marriage over friendship, as basic goods, but rather because of the fact that marriage is a basic good whereas same-sex partnerships are, at best, only instrumental to a basic good.

This response, however, points up the crux of the problem. It would perhaps be permissible to rank marriage – as an instrument – above same-sex partnerships as the former promotes two basic values (life and friendship), whereas the latter promotes only one (friendship).[31] However, when the instrument of marriage is characterized as a basic good, against all the methodological injunctions set out in *Natural Law and Natural Rights*, any such ranking becomes an implicit ranking of the goods themselves. This becomes clear if one considers something that might be instrumental to marriage, such as tax breaks for married couples. If marriage is a self-evident good, such an instrument could plausibly be seen as a secondary good. However, that which is instrumental to friendship, such as same-sex partnerships, is deemed illegitimate. This implies a ranking of the good of marriage over the good of friendship.

A response to this argument is to maintain that the basic goods are not being ranked. Instead, this response argues, same-sex partnerships are bad not because marriage is more important than friendship but rather because same-sex partnerships harm marriage whereas tax breaks for married couples do not damage any basic good. However, it is not the case that natural law theory prohibits all acts that harm basic goods. As noted earlier, natural law theory prohibits acts that are intended to do nothing but harm to a basic good. When one act, objectively speaking, both serves one basic good and damages another basic good, one determines its legitimacy by focusing on intention. This emerges from Finnis's discussion of the doctrine of indirect effect. As noted above, Finnis argues that it is permissible indirectly to damage a basic good in one's pursuit of another basic good, but it is impermissible directly to damage a basic good. This substantive distinction imposes a methodological need to distinguish between individuated and non-individuated acts. One does this through reference to the intention with which the acts are performed:

31 Even if this argument is sound, it is unclear that it applies to other heterosexual partnerships. At the very least, further arguments would have to be found.

Fundamentally, a human act is a that-which-is-decided-upon (or -chosen) and its primary proper description is as what-is-chosen. A human action, to be humanly regarded, is to be characterized in the way it was characterized in the conclusion to the relevant train of practical reasoning of the man who chose to do it. On the other hand, the world with its material (including our bodily selves) and its structures of physical and psycho-physical causality is not indefinitely malleable by human intention. The man who is deciding what to do cannot reasonably shut his eyes to the causal structure of his project; he cannot characterize his plans *ad lib*.[32]

On this basis, it is difficult to see how choosing a same-sex partnership can be morally unacceptable. Even if marriage is a basic good, and even if that basic good is damaged by same-sex partnerships, such damage is inflicted indirectly. That is, such damage is an incidental side-effect of the person's efforts to pursue the good of friendship. This respects the person's own characterisation of her action, the reason why she has acted in this way. Perhaps Finnis could avoid this problem, and thus maintain his position against the recognition of same-sex partnerships, by characterising marriage as a more important good than friendship, but such a move is wholly incompatible with his basic position that there is no hierarchy as between the basic goods. In short, Finnis has provided no basis on which a position against the recognition of same-sex partnerships can be reconciled with his general natural law theory.

Based on these observations, one can develop two responses to Finnis's overall argument against the recognition of same-sex partnerships. The first, which is of limited use and value, amounts to little more than a personalized attack on Finnis himself. This response would argue that the tension between *Natural Law and Natural Rights* and 'Law, Morality and Sexual Orientation' illustrates that, for Finnis, the category of supposedly basic and self-evident goods is infinitely expandable to meet the demands of whatever moral conclusion is desired in a particular context. This argument is, I think, of limited value as it seeks to draw inferences about Finnis's state of mind from his writings. Although this might be a worthwhile focus of inquiry for a psychologist or a biographer, it is of little assistance to the working out of moral justifications. For even if the argument is sound – and I am unsure as to whether it is – it provides no direct response to the argument actually advanced in 'Law, Morality and Sexual Orientation'. Finnis and, *a fortiori*, anyone else would still be entitled to stand over that argument. For these reasons, this response is argumentatively useless for those concerned to rebut the moral propositions advanced by Finnis in 'Law, Morality and Sexual Orientation'.

---

32 *Natural law and natural rights*, at 122. Internal cross-references omitted.

The second and, I think, stronger argument is that *Natural Law and Natural Rights* provides compelling reasons, from natural law theory itself, as to why the natural law argument against the recognition of same-sex partnerships is deeply flawed. That argument, at least as advanced by Finnis, fundamentally relies on the characterization of marriage as a basic, self-evident good. For it is only that characterisation that allows same-sex partnerships to be viewed as an illusory (and therefore damaging) instantiation of a basic good, rather than as an instrument to promote another basic good, that of friendship. This characterization of marriage as a basic good, however, constitutes unsound natural law theorizing in that it either mistakes an instrument for a basic good or it creates a new basic good out of a combination of two other basic goods. The proposition that marriage is a basic good, essential to Finnis's argument, is not a valid proposition of natural law theory. The argument must therefore fail.

PRIVACY ARGUMENTS IN FAVOUR OF SAME-SEX
PARTNERSHIP RECOGNITION

As noted at the outset of this article, most of the early political objectives in the gay rights movement were secured through reliance on privacy arguments. The typical structure of such arguments is that the state should not interfere in each individual's zone of personal autonomy, leaving the individual to make her own moral judgments within that zone. Such arguments, although often presented as being amoral (that is, as being neutral as between competing moral visions) do themselves reflect a particular moral position, namely that the state should not impose any moral vision (even one preferred by a majority of its citizens) within that zone of personal autonomy.

Privacy arguments are not the preserve of liberals. Even Finnis, as noted above, endorses a form of the privacy argument in accepting, on the grounds of subsidiarity, the decriminalization of the homosexual activity that he strongly argues to be wrong. The overall argument of Finnis, however, amply demonstrates the limited value of privacy arguments from the perspective of a gay rights advocate. For it is entirely possible for one to advocate privacy, as Finnis in a sense does, while maintaining a moral position against some of the activities that persons engage in within that private zone. (Despite the criticisms that I have made of Finnis's moral argument against partnership recognition, his privacy position is, in the abstract, a tenable moral position.) Same-sex partnership recognition, however, is on any account a matter in the public zone: it is all about the public recognition to be given by the state to a private relationship. Thus privacy arguments, however successful they may have been in relation to the decriminalisation of homosexual activity, provide no support for the recognition of same-sex partnerships.[33]

---

33 For a slightly more detailed consideration of this issue, see Nicholas Bamforth, 'Same-sex

EGALITARIAN ARGUMENTS IN FAVOUR OF SAME-SEX
PARTNERSHIPS

The possibility of a strictly egalitarian argument

Bamforth contends that egalitarian arguments do not provide a sound basis
for same-sex partnerships. He makes a number of tactical arguments, which
do not concern this paper, but also suggests that egalitarian arguments are
question-begging and incapable of supporting a case for partnership
recognition. He reasons:

> For to say that two persons (or couples) are morally equal, we need to
> explain *why*, in normative terms, they deserve to be viewed in this way.
> The concept of equality cannot, in and of itself, provide us with an
> answer – for at root, the term 'equality' is simply a descriptive label
> telling us *that* two persons (or couples) deserve analogous treatment,
> rather than *why* such treatment is deserved.[34]

Bamforth argues that an argument deeper than equality is needed in order to
answer that 'why?' question. This scepticism of equality arguments in the
context of same-sex partnerships reflects a general scepticism, on the part of
some philosophers and legal thinkers, of the worth of equality arguments.
Bamforth cites two in particular: Peter Westen and Joseph Raz. Westen states
the position as follows:

> [T]o say that people who are morally alike in a certain respect 'should
> be treated alike' means that they should be treated in accord with the
> moral rule by which they are determined to be alike. Hence 'likes
> should be treated alike' means that people for whom a certain treatment
> is prescribed by a standard should all be given the treatment prescribed
> by the standard. Or, more simply, people who by a rule should be
> treated alike should by the rule be treated alike. So there is its: equality
> is entirely circular. It tells us to treat like people alike; but when we ask
> who 'like people' are, we are told they are 'people who should be treated
> alike'. Equality is an empty vessel with no substantive moral content of its
> own. Without moral standards, equality remains meaningless, a formula
> that can have nothing to say about how we should act.[35]

partnerships and arguments of justice' in Robert Wintemute and Mads Andenaes (eds.), *Legal
recognition of same-sex partnerships: a study of national, European and international law* (Oxford,
2000). **34** Bamforth, 'Same-sex partnerships and arguments of justice', at 40. **35** Peter Westen,
'The empty ideal of equality', 95 *Harvard Law Review* 537, at 547 (1982). The closest philosophical
forerunner of Westen is probably Richard Flathman, 'Equality and generalization: a formal
analysis' in *Nomos 9: Equality* (J. Roland Pennock and John Chapman eds, New York, 1967), p. 38.
For a brief discussion, see Oran Doyle, *Constitutional equality law* (Dublin, 2004), at 3–4.

Westen essentially argues that equality is an entirely formal concept, requiring only that rules which are stated to apply to a particular class should be applied to all members of that class. As such, it provides no independent basis on which one could criticize a particular rule: equality does not tell us what is a good rule; equality only reminds us to apply rules impartially. Put in other words, equality provides no guidance as to what is a just distribution of goods in society. I shall consider Westen's argument in more detail below. Before doing that, it is necessary to address Raz's argument.

Raz's argument

Raz distinguishes between strictly egalitarian principles and rhetorically egalitarian principles.[36] He considers the following as the paradigm of a strictly egalitarian principle:

> All Fs who do not have G have a right to G if some Fs have G.[37]

This principle is sensitive to existing inequalities among members of the relevant group with respect to the relevant benefits. Under this strictly egalitarian principle, it is not the case that all people are entitled to G. Nor is it the case that all Fs are entitled to G. An F is entitled to G, only if other Fs actually have G. One can secure compliance with this strictly egalitarian principle either by giving G to those Fs who do not yet have G, or by depriving G from those Fs who already have it. In the language of constitutional law, one can level up or level down. Theories which are dominated by such principles are, in Raz's language, strictly egalitarian theories.[38]

There are, however, other theories and principles that may produce equalities or that may make use of the language of equality but are not themselves strictly egalitarian. For instance, principles of entitlement generate equality in some respect in that all who have equal qualification under them have an equal right. As an example, say that unemployed people are each entitled to €200 a week from the state. This principle produces an equality of treatment for unemployed people but it is not, according to Raz, a strictly egalitarian principle because a strictly egalitarian principle is not the basis for the treatment. In such principles, egalitarian ideas may serve a useful argumentative function, but they do not identify the normative basis of the principle. In contrast, a strictly egalitarian theory is one in which strictly egalitarian principles provide the normative basis for the argument and, in so doing, dominate all other distributive principles.

---

36 Joseph Raz, *The morality of freedom* (Oxford, 1986), chapter 9.   37 Ibid.   38 By dominated, Raz means that the principles are rarely or never overridden by other considerations and that the principles apply to the main cases to which the theory applies. Ibid., at 233.

Raz observes that a theory consisting entirely of egalitarian principles would have absurd consequences:

> The only intrinsic goods and ills such principles admit of are relational ones. If they constitute the entire foundation of morality then the happiness of a person does not matter except if there are other happy people. Nor is there any reason to avoid harming or hurting a person except on the ground that there are others who are unharmed and unhurt. The absurdity of this view is seen by the fact that we only have reason to care about inequalities in the distribution of *goods* and *ills*, that is of what is of value or disvalue for independent reasons. There is no reason to care about inequalities in the distribution of grains of sand, unless there is some other reason to wish to have or avoid sand.[39]

Now it is the final sentence and a half of this proposition on which Bamforth relies to argue that egalitarian principles, whatever their argumentative assistance, provide no normative basis for recognition of same-sex partnerships:

> In relation to the legal entitlements of lesbian and gay individuals or couples, such a reason can only be found in a deeper justification for granting legal protection, suggesting that it is that justification which should – in the interest of clarity – be used in the first place.[40]

But this reads too much into what Raz actually says. For Raz's criticism – if that is the word – is not of egalitarian principles *per se* but rather of theories which rely solely on egalitarian principles. In referring to the distribution of grains of sand he does not, at least at this point, mean to indicate that egalitarian principles are of no relevance to distributional issues, but rather that it would be nonsensical to have a theory consisting solely of egalitarian principles. Indeed, his idea of a strictly egalitarian theory, as noted above, is one in which egalitarian principles dominate non-egalitarian principles. In such a theory, one must rely on other principles to identify what constitute goods and ills. However, egalitarian principles are the dominating force on the distribution of those goods and ills.

These general observations about the structure of egalitarian arguments can be applied to the partnership recognition debate. If one accepts that partnership recognition is a good, it seems to follow that everyone should be entitled to partnership recognition. This, however, is not a strictly egalitarian argument. For the normative basis for this entitlement is not egalitarian but rather the status of partnership recognition as a good.[41] There may be an

---

39 Ibid., at 235.   40 Bamforth, 'Same-sex partnerships and arguments of justice', at 40.
41 Bamforth suggests autonomy as a basis on which partnership recognition might be a good; I shall return to this argument later.

egalitarian by-product of this argument: partnership recognition being accorded to everyone. One could even introduce egalitarian rhetoric into the argument: 'equal partnership recognition for all!' But the normative basis of the argument is not equality. In order for a partnership recognition argument to be strictly egalitarian, the egalitarian principle must be dominating. It is possible to formulate a partnership recognition argument in such terms. For one can – in theory at least – subordinate the good-identifying argument to Raz's paradigm of an egalitarian argument.

This argument can be loosely formulated as follows. Partnership recognition is a good. However, if some people are entitled to partnership recognition, all people must be entitled to partnership recognition. This second distributional principle dominates the first good-identifying principle for the following reasons. As noted above, the paradigmatic strictly egalitarian principle can be achieved either by levelling up or by levelling down. It is this characteristic that marks it as strictly egalitarian because by this characteristic the strictly egalitarian principle can defeat a good-identifying principle, holding that it is better for none to have the good than for some to have it. Thus the dominating egalitarian principle in the current argument could be satisfied either by according partnership recognition to all or by denying partnership recognition to all. As partnership recognition is identified as a good, it follows that recognition for all is preferable to recognition for none. However, as the egalitarian principle dominates, recognition for none is preferable to recognition for some. If it were otherwise, the egalitarian principle could not be said to dominate and this would not be an egalitarian theory. In this light, one can rephrase the point of strictly egalitarian principles in the following way. The import of a strictly egalitarian principle on the distribution of a good is that it is better for none to have a good than for only some to have it. Or one can look at the same proposition from the other side: if an argument holds that it is better for none to have a good than for some to have it, then such an argument is strictly egalitarian.

This illustrates that one can have an egalitarian argument in support of partnership recognition. However, it is necessary to note briefly a number of reservations one should have about the egalitarian argument just formulated. First, I have indicated only the structure of such an argument. This leaves open the question of whether the good of partnership recognition really should be subordinated to the strictly egalitarian principle. Secondly, the argument is loose as to what is meant by the good of partnership recognition. Does the slogan 'partnership recognition is good' mean that people should have partnerships recognized, regardless of whether they seek recognition for the partnerships that they have formed? There is no necessary reason why this proposition should not be the case. However, if one thinks that there must be a desire for recognition (on the part of both parties) in order for recognition to be a good, then one must identify more precisely what one means by 'partnership' and what one means by 'desire for recognition'. For the time being, I shall assume that the good of partnership recognition incorporates the idea of desire for recognition (in the form of a joint desire to have that relationship recognized by the state).[42] Thirdly, the argument does not specify what groups are connoted by the words 'all', 'some' and 'none'. This raises another crucial issue about egalitarianism which I shall consider below.

Before doing that, however, it is necessary to consider Raz's argument further, as it has subtleties not alluded to by Bamforth. He posits two further distinctions: one between satiable and insatiable principles; the other between diminishing and non-diminishing principles. The demands imposed by satiable principles (e.g. 'Everyone's needs should be met') can be completely met, and diminish as they are met. The demands imposed by insatiable principles (e.g. 'Everyone should have as much pleasure as they can enjoy') can always (in principle) be satisfied to a higher degree. However, some insatiable principles may be non-diminishing and some may be diminishing. Principles with no distributive implications – such as 'It is good if each has as much wealth as can be secured' – are non-diminishing, insatiable principles. A person is not less entitled to more wealth simply because she already has wealth. This produces unacceptable consequences in the cases of conflict; strict egalitarian principles can be seen as an attempt to modify the non-diminishing insatiable principles in order to ensure that the unacceptable consequences do not arise. Raz argues, however, that non-diminishing, insatiable principles are invalid principles of justice: fundamental principles of justice are all diminishing. As such, strictly egalitarian principles add nothing to a theory of justice on that front as there are no valid non-diminishing principles the effects of which must be mitigated. I do not, in this paper, wish to disagree on that point.

Raz also argues that there is no case for relying on egalitarian principles to modify diminishing principles because such principles themselves provide guidance in cases of conflict. The fact that the force of the principle diminishes as it is satisfied means that, in cases of conflict, the principle itself will tend to resolve the conflict in a way which produces egalitarian results, although such results are a by-product, and do not directly reflect the normative basis for the distribution. Thus, egalitarian principles add nothing to satiable, diminishing principles. As such, strictly egalitarian principles – although valid in form – can add nothing to any theory of justice and should be rejected.

Raz's conclusion on this point turns fundamentally on the proposition that strictly egalitarian principles can add nothing to a theory of justice as the

---

42 When I later consider the form of partnership recognition, I shall have to address questions such as whether the relationship must be sexual in nature and whether consent is an important pre-requisite for recognition.

only valid principles in such a theory are diminishing principles and such principles do not need to be regulated by egalitarian principles. He reasons as follows:

> Do [egalitarian principles] have any role in regulating the operation of [diminishing principles]? Only if they identify a source of concern which, even though it does not affect the outcome, improves our understanding of why the outcome is the right one. There is no way of conclusively proving that egalitarian principles fail to identify such a concern. But wherever one turns it is revealed that what makes us care about various inequalities is not the inequality but the concern identified by the underlying principle. It is the hunger of the hungry, the need of the needy, the suffering of the ill, and so on. The fact that they are worse off in the relevant respect than their neighbours is relevant. But it is relevant not as an independent evil of inequality. Its relevance is in showing that their hunger is greater, their need more pressing, their suffering more hurtful, and therefore our concern for the hungry, the needy, the suffering, and not our concern for equality, makes us give them the priority.[43]

It seems to me that this reasoning has reached its conclusion too quickly. As Raz notes, the strictly egalitarian principle can be satisfied in one of two ways: levelling up or levelling down.[44] However, he later suggests that levelling down would be inconsistent with any plausible theory of justice:

> Egalitarian principles would be indifferent between achieving equality through taking away from those who have and giving to those who have not. The implausibility of such a view points to the existence of additional fundamental principles which at least establish a preference for the non-wasteful option.[45]

Raz is too quick to label this proposition 'implausible'. It may be implausible with regard to tangible goods, such as bread, water or dwelling places. However, it is far from clear that it is implausible with regard to intangible goods, such as partnership recognition.[46] Consider the following. Let us assume that the electoral franchise is a good. It follows, on Raz's reasoning, that it is better for more people to have this good than for fewer people to

---

43 Raz, *Morality of freedom*, at 240.   44 Ibid., at 226.   45 Ibid., at 235.   46 I think that partnership recognition can be classed as a satiable, diminishing good because it is clearly something that one can acquire fully (unlike Raz's example of pleasure) and it is diminishing because the more partnership recognition one has (in this case, one either has it or one does not), the less reason there is to give one more of it. In this regard, Raz notes that satiable principles are invariably diminishing principles.

have it. However, is it better for nobody to have the franchise than for a limited group of people to have it? That is, is a system of government such as North Korea's dictatorship better than that of Apartheid-era South Africa? It does not seem implausible to argue that a dictatorship is better than 'democracy' with a racially limited franchise. This is not to argue that a dictatorship is a good form of government: far from it – it denies the electoral franchise which is conceded to be a good. However, it is to argue that a democracy with a racially limited franchise is worse than a dictatorship.

The only way, I suggest, in which such a proposition can make sense is if one concedes a role to strictly egalitarian principles in regulating the operation of diminishing principles of justice – that is, if one concedes that the argument in favour of the electoral franchise can, in some cases, be regulated (made subordinate to) strictly egalitarian principles. Raz might respond that the very notion of the electoral franchise incorporates the idea that it is a franchise for all: as such, Apartheid-era South Africa was not a valid instantiation of an electoral franchise and the comparison with North Korea's dictatorship proves nothing. But I do not think that this objection is sound. It is not inherent in the idea of electoral franchise that it is a franchise for all.[47] Such a view can only derive from the incorporation of egalitarian principles within the good in the first place. Such incorporation would again concede vitality to egalitarian principles but at a conceptual level adds little, if anything, to the concept of egalitarian principles regulating the operation of diminishing principles of justice.

There is a further way in which one can perceive independent force for egalitarian principles. Raz's satiable and diminishing goods are themselves insensitive to different distributions. Imagine that in a situation of equal hunger, there is enough bread to relieve the hunger of 90 per cent of the population. Of itself, the satiable and diminishing good is indifferent to whether the 10 per cent who do not receive the good are selected randomly or on the basis of some other criterion, such as race, religion or sexual orientation. If there is force to the contention that the distribution that singles out members of a particular racial or ethnic group for starvation is *worse* than a distribution that randomly selects the same number of people to starve, that force can only derive from some egalitarian principle that has independent vitality.

Raz is thus wrong to conclude that strictly egalitarian principles have no role to play in a theory of justice. At the very least, strictly egalitarian principles have a potential role to play in regulating the operation of

---

47 It may follow from the acceptance of the electoral franchise as a good, that it is a good which should be provided to all (subject to whatever restrictions can be objectively justified). However, this does not mean that it is inherent in the character of that good that it be available to all. On that analysis, bread would not be bread unless everybody had it.

diminishing principles of justice, where those principles identify intangible goods, such as the electoral franchise. However, once it is established that strictly egalitarian principles have independent force in one context, one must concede the possibility that they have independent force in other contexts, even if they would in those other contexts lead to the same result as the diminishing principles of justice themselves. That is, there is no requirement to limit one's theory of justice to exclude strictly egalitarian principles.

A number of points may be made about these strictly egalitarian principles. First, although they have most force with relation to goods and ills, they may have application to the distribution of items which are not themselves goods or ills. For instance, one might have reason to object to a law which provides that white people are entitled to grains of sand, but black people are not, even if grains of sand are not considered to be a good nor an ill. Secondly, strictly egalitarian principles appear concerned with the results of distribution, not the process of distribution. That is, it is not conscious decisions to discriminate that are wrong, but rather inequality in the actual distribution of goods. An unequal distribution that occurs by accident is as much a concern as an inequality that occurs intentionally. Thirdly, although one identifies the independent existence of such principles where they have a levelling-down effect, this does not mean that they only have force in such a situation. That is, having been obliged by one context to concede independent force to such principles, one must concede the possibility of independent force in all contexts. For instance, one must concede at least the possibility that the slogan 'Partnership Recognition for All!' relies on strictly egalitarian principles as well as on the diminishing principle of partnership recognition. Fourthly, if one considers a number of restrictions on the electoral franchise, it is quickly apparent that some unequal distributions of the good cause more concern than others. For instance, an exclusion of black people from the franchise causes more concern than an exclusion of children. Any account of the substance, as opposed to the form, of egalitarian principles must be sensitive to this phenomenon.

For these reasons, I do not think it is strictly necessary to demonstrate that partnership recognition is itself a good that is subordinate to strictly egalitarian principles in the same way as the electoral franchise. The electoral franchise example indicates a good that is subject to strictly egalitarian principles, thereby indicating the independent vitality of such principles. If those principles have independent vitality in one context, it follows that they may have vitality in other contexts, even if they support the same conclusion as the diminishing principle of justice itself. In such a situation, one might say that the theory is egalitarian, but not strictly egalitarian, in that it could be based either on strictly egalitarian principles or on diminishing principles of justice. Nevertheless, I shall argue that partnership recognition, as a good, is regulated by strictly egalitarian principles and that, as a result, the most coherent arguments in favour of partnership recognition are strictly egalitarian arguments.

Westen's argument

Although these arguments deal with Raz's points, they do not address those of Westen. Thus, Bamforth could possibly defend his position, along the lines advocated by Westen, by focusing not on the good and the reason for its distribution (which can be egalitarian) but on the differentiations between persons. Westen's point is that equality cannot itself tell us who is alike and who is unalike. As such, Westen argues, the only function of equality is to remind us that rules should be applied to all to whom they are stated to be applied. The logically anterior question of who is actually 'alike' is a substantive question of rights, and not a matter of equality at all. Bamforth might modify his argument along these lines to suggest that, while an argument for partnership recognition could have an egalitarian structure, the determination of who is alike for the purposes of recognition cannot be a matter of equality, because equality only tells us to treat like persons alike; it does not tell us who is alike.

However, there appears to be little reason why one should accept that arguments as to which equality is more important are not egalitarian arguments. Westen's conclusions on this point follow from his purely formal definition of equality. He derives this from Aristotle's proposition on equality:

> Equality in morals means this: things that are alike should be treated alike, while things that are unalike should be treated unalike in proportion to their unalikeness.[48]

Based on Aristotle's statement of equality, Westen advances his own idea of equality as a formal concept:

> [E]quality is an entirely formal concept: it is a 'form' for stating moral and legal propositions whose substance originates elsewhere, a 'form' of discourse with no substantive content of its own.[49]

It may be that this purely formal conception of equality follows from Aristotle's proposition, although it is surely worth noting that Aristotle himself did not view his propositions on equality as being limited to formal equality.[50] However, Westen's conception of formal equality does not follow

---

48 Aristotle, *Nicomachean Ethics* V.3.1131a–1131b (W. Ross trans. 1925), extracted in Peter Westen, 'The empty idea of equality' 95 *Harvard Law Review* 537, at 543 (1982).   49 Westen, 'The empty ideal of equality', at 577–8. References omitted.   50 See Wolfgang von Leyden, *Aristotle on equality and justice: his political argument* (London, 1985).

from the strictly egalitarian principles identified by Raz. Those principles are again formal in the sense that they potentially capture a number of different arguments as to why it is wrong to provide a good to some persons unless that good is provided to other persons who are equally entitled to it. However, there is no reason to refuse to describe such substantive reasons as 'egalitarian'. We know that they are not simply substantive entitlements (or rights) because the whole point of an egalitarian principle, as demonstrated above, is that it potentially overrides a right. But if such substantive reasons are not derived from substantive entitlements and if we are not allowed to call them 'egalitarian', how are we to describe them? Most people would intuitively describe these arguments as 'egalitarian'; indeed, 'egalitarianism' is the heading in political philosophy under which such arguments, given their form, most readily fall. It may be that work is needed to relate the intuitive understanding of such arguments with a coherent philosophical position, but this is no reason why they should not be called 'egalitarian'. Westen's position on this issue is only defensible if equality is, as Westen defines it to be, inherently formal. But this is the rub: Westen's position is only true by definition. If an alternative, philosophically credible interpretation exists, there is no reason to accept Westen's definition.

Bamforth's autonomy argument

Bamforth, having rejected egalitarian arguments, ultimately argues for the recognition of same-sex partnerships on the basis of autonomy. He argues that sexual/emotional desires, feelings aspirations and behaviour are of central importance for human beings.[51] He then considers the effects of laws and social practices which (implicitly) deny that autonomy:

> Laws and social practices which target any social group as a recipient deserving of unfavourable treatment could be said to objectify members of that group: the members, unlike non-members, are stigmatized as being undeserving of full consideration as human beings because of a characteristic or characteristics which they are assumed to possess by virtue of their actual or perceived group membership. A group will typically be singled out for hostile treatment where some element of social sensitivity or controversy attaches to it.[52]

If this is not an egalitarian argument, it is difficult to see what is. It is the differential restriction of autonomy – as distinct from restriction of autonomy *simpliciter* – that seems to concern Bamforth.

---

51 Bamforth, 'Same-sex partnerships and arguments of justice', at 41.   52 Ibid., at 43.

Conclusions

The discussion on egalitarian principles can be summarized as follows. Many theorists have asserted that justice claims should not be formulated in terms of equality. Some, such as Westen, argue that equality is a purely formal concept and involves no more than the impartial application of rules. Others, such as Raz, argue that the very form of egalitarian principles can add nothing to a theory of justice. From these different perspectives, both Westen and Raz agree that substantive goods – not equality – are the stuff of a theory of justice. However, it has been demonstrated that strictly egalitarian principles provide a form of justice argument that is not expressed by theories of substantive goods. For this reason, egalitarian arguments have some vitality in justice theories. Although the form of such egalitarian arguments leaves open many questions – most crucially that of equality between whom – there is no reason why those questions should not be viewed as egalitarian questions. They certainly cannot be viewed as solely questions about the relative importance of substantive goods. For these reasons, egalitarian arguments are relevant to any discussion of partnership recognition.

EQUALITY ARGUMENTS AND PARTNERSHIP RECOGNITION

The most important feature that an equality argument must capture in order to be convincing is the way in which inequalities as between some persons or groups is of more concern than inequalities as between other persons or groups. Very broadly speaking, there are two competing accounts of equality on this point: process equality and substantive equality. Under process equality, what is important is the process of differentiation which amounts to unequal treatment. Such a process must rationally take account of only relevant differences between different persons or groups. Provided it does so, equality is observed. Under substantive equality, what is important is the relative position of groups in society. Where one group is unjustly subordinated, it would be wrong to exacerbate that position of relative subordination; further, one should act to remedy the situation.[53]

There is much academic debate as to which of these constitutes the better understanding of equality. This perhaps misses the point: both capture values that we consider important. I have argued in a different context that we should be more concerned to advance substantive equality than process equality because currently substantive inequality is much more entrenched than process inequality. For present purposes, however, I wish to make a

---

53 For discussion on the parameters of these conceptions of equality, see Doyle, *Constitutional equality law* (Dublin, 2004), at 201–31. The account I provide there is mediated somewhat by limits on judicial power. No such limits apply in this context.

different point. If one accepts that partnership recognition is a good and that the relevance of a strictly egalitarian principle is that it provides an independent basis for arguments as to how that good should be distributed, it seems that one's conception of equality should be more sensitive to the actual distribution of goods than to the process through which such goods are distributed. That is, one should favour a substantive conception of equality over a process conception. I shall operate on this basis for the purposes of this paper.

I have elsewhere outlined a substantive conception of equality that turns on status groups and the need to avoid the unjust subordination of already unjustly subordinated groups. On this analysis, gay people are a status group in that they, to varying extents, conceive of themselves as a group, are conceived of by others of a group and their status is tied to their membership of that group. They are subordinated within society in a number of ways. Of most relevance to the present issue is the denial of partnership recognition to them. That is, although gay people can have partnerships recognized by the state – i.e. they can get married – they can only do so by denying what they are and opting into heterosexual marriage.[54] In this way, the basic structure of subordination of gay people in current times is much the same as it has always been: acceptance and respect within society is possible, but only to the extent that one pretends to be what one is not. The closet lives on. This focus on status ties this conception of equality quite closely to the context in which, considering Raz's arguments, we considered that egalitarian principles most clearly had force: the distribution of intangible goods. For the reason why people want intangible goods is because of what such goods say about a person's place in society, their status. To deny an intangible good is to deny status. It is to say: although this good costs us nothing to give, we deny it to you simply because you are not worthy – you are inferior to us.

Now it is of crucial importance to this conception of equality that it only prohibits the *unjust* subordination of already unjustly subordinated social groups. This does not mean that one must find an argument, outside of equality, as to why the subordination is unjust, but rather that one may conclude that inequality for some groups or in some circumstances, is justified. For this reason, it must address arguments to the effect that, although the denial of partnership recognition amounts to subordination, it is not unjust either because it is just to subordinate homosexuals generally or because it is just to subordinate homosexuals in this particular way. Although many moral arguments have been put forward to this effect, I propose here to deal with those advanced by Finnis and discussed earlier in this article.

---

54 Indeed, as a matter of Irish law, it is questionable whether gay people have the requisite capacity to form valid heterosexual marriages. See *C v. C* [1991] 2 IR 330. As a side issue, this raises the possibility that, in Ireland, it is not simply the case that gay marriage is not allowed but rather that gay people are excluded from all marriage. This changes slightly the contours of the debate.

In this regard, the justice arguments for the subordination of homosexuals generally and for the subordination of homosexuals particularly through the denial of partnership recognition run in parallel. For the general subordination argument appears to turn on the fact that sex is an act directed to the production of human life (a good) and non-procreative sex is inimical to that good of human life. This is similar in form to the more particular argument that marriage is a basic human good and any form of partnership which purports to be marriage but does not have that unique synthesis of friendship and life-production is inimical to that basic good of marriage. I have already outlined the flaws with the marriage argument: it simply posits marriage as a basic good, in contravention of the general methodology of the natural law. As such, it provides no reason, beyond bald and questionable assertion, as to why same-sex partnership recognition would be wrong. There are similar flaws with the general sex argument for unless one makes life subordinate to the good of marriage (and, quite apart from the problems of recognising marriage as a basic good, natural law methodology again prevents this), non-marital sex would have to be regarded as a legitimate means of advancing a good while non-procreative marital sex would be illegitimate. The position against homosexual acts can only be maintained by introducing other distinctions that are unacceptable for the natural law theorist. In this way, the justice arguments for both the general subordination of homosexuals and the particular subordination through the denial of partnership rights both founder on the insuperable difficulties of developing a coherent and justified set of distinctions which endorse marital non-procreative sex, but prohibit non-marital procreative sex. Non-procreative marital sex is of course a good thing: it is instrumental to the good of friendship (and, indeed, play). By the same token, homosexual sex is instrumental to the good of friendship, a good that is also served by the recognition of same-sex partnerships. For all these reasons, I suggest that there is no basis in justice for the denial of partnership recognition to gay couples.

THE FORMS OF PARTNERSHIP RECOGNITION

In the light of these various moral arguments about partnership recognition, it is appropriate to consider the various forms of partnership recognition that are currently proposed. This is not intended as a detailed discussion of current proposals, but rather an attempt to clarify the moral implications of various forms of partnership recognition.

Retrospective partnership recognition (the presumptive scheme)

In many ways, this is not partnership recognition at all. Under this approach, the state retrospectively recognizes non-marital partnerships when the partnership comes to an end, either through death or through dissolution. When the partnership comes to an end, the state makes such property adjustment orders as appear just and could provide tax breaks equivalent to those afforded to married couples in relation to their property. This could be done either on a generic or a case-by-case basis.

Typically, the trigger for such retrospective partnership recognition is a certain amount of time lived together. For instance, if two persons have lived together for three years (leave aside for present purposes the character of that relationship) and one dies without having made a will, the intestacy rules might be amended to be more favourable to the other party. The advantage of such an approach is that even people who do not formally enter into a relationship receive some protection. Others, however, construe this as a disadvantage in that people may become subject to obligations that they have not voluntarily undertaken. More seriously, people who have consciously decided not to seek recognition from the state may find themselves unwillingly saddled with such recognition. This objection could be overcome, however, by making the scheme presumptive only, i.e. by allowing people to opt out of it.

Of more relevance to the current concerns, however, are the egalitarian implications of such a stance. As suggested above, one can divide partnership recognition into two aspects: symbolic and practical. The practical impact of retrospective recognition is important: persons are protected from unfortunate events and, depending on the extent of legal measures possible upon retro-spective recognition, could be put into effectively the same situation as heterosexual, married couples where a marriage comes to an end, either through death or separation. The symbolic impact of retrospective recognition is, however, much less. For the state is effectively saying that non-marital partner-ships are only deserving of recognition once they are over. Most people who want their partnership recognized would, I suggest, want it recognized while still in existence. This lack of symbolic impact is of particular concern for egalitarian principles which turn on comparative recognition. Retrospective recognition of partnerships effectively denies non-marital partnerships the intangible elements of recognition for as long as there is anything there that can be meaningfully recognized.

General partnership recognition (contractual)

Under this approach, any two people could, upon application, have their partnership recognized by the state. One can imagine various procedures and substantive requirements that would have to be met, but these are unimportant for present purposes. This recognition would thus be available to heterosexual and homosexual partnerships, but also to non-sexual partnerships, such as that between two sisters who have lived their lives together in one house. It is difficult to deny the justice of the claims of that latter group of people. For why should the state, in its formal recognition of people's personal relationships, confine itself to sexual relationships? There are other types of relationships, very important for those involved in them. Any reconfiguration of partnership recognition laws should make some provision for people in long-term personal but non-sexual relationships who would like such relationships recognized by the state.

However, one wonders how many people in non-sexual relationships would want their relationship recognized in this way. Such an approach would cause difficulties if one person were to meet someone else and wish to marry that person. Presumably one could not be married and in a civil partnership at the same time. Would one have to divorce your sister, for example, in order to get married? This points up the issue that the relationships between elderly sisters, although raising mutual moral rights and duties and although they should be protected and recognized in some way by the state, are not really the same as sexual relationships. Most importantly, I suggest, people in such relationships do not aspire to the same exclusivity that is generally accepted as the ideal in sexual relationships. Thus, although non-sexual long-term relationships deserve protection, it is doubtful whether a contractual civil partnership scheme, broadly analogous to marriage, is the best method of providing that protection.

From the perspective of egalitarian principles, one would also have reservations about the limits of this approach. For, although not as blatant as blanket non-recognition for same-sex relationships, it could be seen as a form of the closet in that it would allow the state (or society) to pretend that homosexual relationships have more in common with asexual relationships than with heterosexual relationships. The ultimate in state recognition – marriage – would be reserved for heterosexual relationships. In this way, the state would again provide practical benefits for same-sex couples while still denying status to such couples. For these reasons, while there are merits to a general partnership recognition scheme of this type, if it leaves marriage as an option for hetero-sexuals and implicitly equates homosexual relationships with asexual relation-ships, it would be objectionable on egalitarian grounds. The primary objection here is not to non-sexual relationships being equated with homosexual relation-ships, but rather to heterosexual relationships being elevated above homosexual relationships. That said, the combination of the two amounts to a powerful statement against homosexual relationships: such relationships will only be recognized by the state because the state can pretend that they are not really sexual relationships. The sexual relationships of homosexuals are not recognized for what they are; homosexuals themselves remain invisible to the law.

Civil recognition scheme for same-sex partnerships

Such an approach would address some of the egalitarian concerns with retro-spective recognition and general partnership recognition. However, it would still implicitly elevate marriage (and by extension heterosexual relationships) over homosexual partnerships. Even if precisely the same benefits were afforded to each type of relationship, the implicit statement of the state, given the generally positive cultural associations with the word 'marriage', would again be that homosexual relationships are inferior to heterosexual relationships. This would be an inequality for which no justification has been shown.

Civil recognition scheme for all partnerships, in addition to opposite-sex marriage

This form of recognition poses the same egalitarian concerns, although considerably diluted, as civil recognition only for same-sex partnerships. Again, the implicit statement of the State is that homosexuals are less worthy than heterosexuals as only the latter are entitled to the ultimate good of partnership recognition in the form of marriage. However, the force of this statement is in this case mitigated as it is provided that heterosexuals may also choose civil recognition as an alternative to marriage. Thus, heterosexuals are still held up as being more worthy than homosexuals, but the sting of this statement is lessened by the fact that civil recognition is not deemed to be an option beneath heterosexuals.

Gay marriage

It might follow from the discussion thus far that the most egalitarian solution to the partnership recognition issue is to allow gay people to get married. However, the institution of marriage raises egalitarian concerns of its own. This is because of the extent to which it is gendered, i.e. the extent to which it ascribes presumptive gender roles to the partners. Those who choose to marry choose an institution in which the following roles are presumptively assigned according to gender: child-rearing, wage-earning, meal-cooking, lawn-mowing, lightbulb-changing, blocked-drain-cleaning, clothes-washing, rodent-killing, etc. These roles are not rigid; many married couples can and do negotiate (in a loving way) the roles that each partner will play. However, such negotiation takes place against a background of what is assumed appropriate for each partner, given their sex.

It would be wrong to single out the institution of marriage as being responsible for these gender roles. To a certain extent, marriage probably reflects general societal ideas of what is appropriate work for men and women. To that extent, presumptive gender roles might persist in heterosexual civil partnerships. However, marriage remains more marked in this respect, for marriage explicitly and unashamedly celebrates ascribed gender roles in its very essence: marriage is a union of 'husband' and 'wife'. For this reason, the presumptive gender roles in marriage are stronger than the presumptive gender roles in a heterosexual civil partnership.

Why should this matter? What is wrong with ascribed gender roles? The problem is that ascribed gender roles form the basic structure of the subordination of women. Whereas the structure of subordination of gay people turns on self-denial and public denial, the structure of the subordination of women turns on role differentiation as between men and women. Women as a subordinated group in society have traditionally lost out through the division of labour as between men and women. The relative emancipation of women has largely consisted of challenges to that division of labour.

As an institution, marriage reinforces that role differentiation and – in so doing – reinforces the subordination of women. Same-sex relationships challenge role differentiation as between men and women because it is necessary (and not just possible) that at least one partner adopt a role that is traditionally ascribed to the opposite sex. In this way, same-sex relationships can be a wider egalitarian force in society, helping to dismantle generally accepted ideas of appropriate gender roles. This egalitarian potential could be undermined, however, if same-sex partnerships were to be recognized through the form of marriage. For by labelling one member of a same-sex partnership 'husband' and the other 'wife', the partners would not only indicate their willingness to conceive of their relationship in terms of wholly inappropriate gender roles but also undermine the challenge that same-sex relationships in general pose to ascribed gender roles. For these reasons, it can be argued that gay marriage is an appropriate, egalitarian response to the question of same-sex partnership recognition.[55]

Against this, however, it could be argued that nothing would undermine gender roles within marriage more than opening it up to same-sex couples. Although in the short-term there might be a tendency to 'gender-ise' the same-sex partners, in the long-term the more likely impact would be to 'de-gender-ise' the opposite sex partners within marriage. Given this potential, and given the unique and generally positive cultural resonance of marriage, the only truly egalitarian approach is to allow gay people to marry.

Civil partnership recognition for all!

If one continues to have egalitarian reservations about marriage, however, a scheme of civil partnership open to all, combined with the abolition of state marriage, would be the most appropriate egalitarian response to this issue. Given the abolition of state-recognized marriage for heterosexuals, there would be no inegalitarian concerns in making such civil recognition available to non-sexual, personal relationships, as well as to homosexual and hetero-

---

55 There is a symmetry between this position and that advocated by Finnis. The difference is that Finnis believes that homosexuals would be bad for marriage because marriage is for partners of the opposite sex. I am suggesting that marriage would be bad for homosexuals because marriage is for partners of opposite gender.

sexual relationships. On the other hand, one could give different names to the recognition of sexual and non-sexual relationships. As each is a new institution, there would be no implicit denigration of the form of relationship recognized by the other.

Such an approach would not prevent individuals or communities (religious or otherwise) adopting their own definitions of marriage. Thus a couple could choose to get married in the Catholic church, for example, and also have their relationship recognized by the state in the form of a civil partnership. However, the state would not deem this form of relationship to be more worthy than any other committed relationship, whether a heterosexual partnership not sanctified by a church or a homosexual partnership.

Conclusions

In the current political context, it is most unlikely that Ireland will opt for the abolition of state recognition for marriage coupled with a civil partnership scheme of this type. In that context, I suggest that a civil recognition scheme open to all sexual relationships and incurring all the rights and obligations of marriage would be the most egalitarian solution politically possible. At the same time, there should be a retrospective, presumptive scheme that would provide minimal, but significant, rights to people who lived together in a relationship of mutual support. The benefits would be provided retro-spectively, i.e. after the relationship ends. Such an approach would meet the needs of non-sexual couples without inappropriately preventing them from forming sexual relationships; it would not impose stringent rights or obligations on people without the consent of those people. Conversely, if people in sexual relationships want those rights and obligations, they always have the option of having their partnership recognized.

CONCLUSION

This paper has tried to assess a number of moral arguments concerning the recognition of same-sex partnerships. This was done in the belief that this is an essentially moral issue. My suggestion is that natural law arguments, traditionally most opposed to the very idea of homosexuality, do not provide a coherent basis for opposing same-sex partnerships. I accept that there are other arguments, apart from natural law arguments, against same-sex partner-ships. For this reason, the conclusions I draw are open to critique on other grounds. That is work for another day. Nevertheless, I have argued that egalitarian principles provide a compelling basis for arguments in favour of same-sex partnership recognition. When one considers the precise form that such recognition should take, one encounters competing egalitarian concerns. Nevertheless, an approach that is sensitive to the iniquity of differential recognition provides the most compelling analysis of the issue.

Autonomy, commitment
and marriage

WILLIAM BINCHY

IN IRELAND TODAY, as in the western world generally, a great debate is taking place about the nature of marriage. I welcome this debate because of its radical character. In contrast to the past three decades or so, in which the rhetoric of no-fault divorce predictably, but to some degree insidiously, transformed the meaning of marriage, without exposing the philosophical core of the issue for public discussion, today we are grappling openly with the crucial issues. What does marriage mean? Is a procreative dimension essential? Does marriage necessarily involve a commitment that is, 'in principle',[1] lifelong? Must spouses be of differing sexes?

Broader questions relate to identifying the best models of interpersonal relationship for rearing children and to how society can most effectively encourage these models to be chosen and to flourish. Debate on these questions involves a complex conjunction of empirical and normative considerations. The empirical issues range over such matters as whether divorce impoverishes women and children, whether a liberal law weakens marital stability and whether married or unmarried cohabitation is a preferable environment in which to rear children. The normative considerations relate to the extent to which society is entitled to encourage people to choose particular models of relationship (by tax breaks or by the denial of legal recognition to particular relationships, for example) and the extent to which the common good should trump the values of privacy and autonomy and the principle of pluralism.

I shall not seek to address the empirical issues although they are, of course, crucial in the determination of future social policy on marriage and on committed relationships generally. Instead I shall restrict myself to considering a narrower question. In the light of the values of dignity, privacy, autonomy and pluralism, which have gained a certain ascendancy in contemporary culture, can a case be made out for the legal recognition of irrevocable lifelong commitment? I shall not here be arguing for the abolition of Article

---

1 *D.T. v. C.T. (Divorce: Ample Resources)* [2002] 3 IR 334, at 405 (Supreme Ct, *per* Murray J). See further Byrne & Binchy, *Annual Review of Irish Law 2002*, pp 263–82, especially p. 267.

41.3.2 of the Constitution, which prescribes a divorce jurisdiction.[2] Rather shall I be offering for consideration the argument that the law should respect the option of lifelong commitment as an alternative to the option of marriage subject to access to divorce.

It has to be acknowledged that, in the years before the constitutional amendment of 1995 providing for divorce, some people felt that our law was unnecessarily restrictive in recognizing[3] only one model of interpersonal relationship – irrevocable lifelong commitment. This single model, while seeking to accomplish important social goals relating to encouraging a secure environment for the rearing of children, scarcely reflected a high degree of respect to the value of pluralism. Yet, what was done in 1995 was the replacement of one model by another model: marriage subject to divorce. The only way in which people can receive legal recognition for their interpersonal relationship in this state is by entering into a commitment which the law insists must be revocable in character. Even as spouses commit to marry until death do them part, the law hears their commitment differently and treats them as having made a commitment of a quite different character. Whatever force the arguments in favour of divorce may have, the values of privacy, autonomy and pluralism are sacrificed by the adoption of a single model of relationship which contradicts the free choice of those who seek legal support for an irrevocable commitment.

2 Article 41.3.2 provides as follows:

> A Court designated by law may grant a dissolution of marriage where, but only where, it is satisfied that
> i. at the date of the institution of the proceedings, the spouses have lived apart from one another for a period of, or periods amounting to, at least four years during the previous five years,
> ii. there is no reasonable prospect of a reconciliation between the spouses,
> iii. such provision as the Court considers proper having regard to the circumstances exists or will be made for the spouses, any children of either or both of them and any other person prescribed by law, and
> iv. any further conditions prescribed by law are complied with.

3 The concept of legal *recognition* of a particular relationship is complex. It can refer to the ascription of a *name* ('marriage' for example) or the *conferral by the State of legal benefits* on a particular category of relationship or the ascription of *a range of mutal rights and obligations* – a legal status, in effect – to that relationship. Names are important. They carry a clear message of social approval (or disapproval) – and legitimization (or delegitimisation). As to the ascription of legal benefits in the context of marriage, it is worth noting that the Irish Constitution has been interpreted as *requiring* the State only to desist from discriminating *against* marriage (*Murphy v. Attorney General* [1982] IR 241, *Muckley v. Ireland* [1985] IR 472, *Hyland v. Minister for Social Welfare* [1989] IR 624, *Greene v. Minister for Agriculture* [1990] 2 IR 17), while *entitling* the State to discriminate *in favour* of marriage (*O'B v. S*, [1984] IR 316). See further, Hogan & Whyte eds, *J.M. Kelly, The Irish Constitution* (4th ed., 2003), paras. 7.6.14–7.6.27. The question whether marriage should involve a State-prescribed range of rights

HUMAN DIGNITY, PRIVACY, AUTONOMY AND PLURALISM

As a first element in my argument, I wish to consider briefly the four norms of human dignity, privacy, autonomy and pluralism. Each of these norms celebrates the unique value of every human person. Together, they seek to cherish the inherent worth of the individual and the moral power of free human choice.

Human dignity

Human dignity[4] is the core value of international human rights instruments.[5] The Preamble to the Charter of the United Nations in 1945 and the Preamble to the Universal Declaration on Human Rights in 1948 both refer to 'the dignity and worth of the human person'. Both the International Covenant on Civil and Political Rights and the International Covenant on Economic, Social and Cultural Rights recognize 'the inherent dignity and ... the equal and inalienable rights of all members of the human family' as the foundation of freedom, justice and peace in the world. Dignity is a value underlying the Irish Constitution.

The concept of human dignity is of an ancient pedigree.[6] Its philosophical origins may be found in Greek philosophy and in Judeo-Christian insight into the unique value and equal worth of every human being.[7]

This insight sadly is not a constant feature of human understanding. Every generation loses its capacity to appreciate the value and worth of some human beings, white or black, men or women, heterosexual, gay or bisexual.

and obligations raises major issues for debate in the context of autonomy, gender equality and paternalism. I shall merely note here that Irish law, which formerly contained significant gender inequalities at a formal level, failed until 1976 to provide effective protection to wives living with husbands who did not support them, to wives whose husbands beat them or to wives whose husbands sold the family home over their head. Even today, wives have no automatic entitlement to a share in the family home, the Supreme Court having invoked natural law principles, quite unconvincingly, to strike down as unconstitutional a fairly modest legislative initiative: see *In re Article 26 and the Matrimonial Home Bill 1993* [1994] 1 IR 305, analyzed by Hogan, 16 *DULJ* 175 (1994). **4** See D. Kretzmer & E. Klein (eds.), *The concept of human dignity in human rights discourse* (2002); Feldman, 'Human dignity as a legal value' [1999] *Public L* 682 [2000] *Public L* 61. **5** See Dicke, 'The founding function of human dignity in the Universal Declaration of Human Rights', in D. Kretzmer & E. Klein (eds.), op. cit., 111. **6** See Canick, 'Dignity of man' and *'Persona'* in Stoic anthropology: some remarks on Cicero, *De Officiis I*, 105–107, in D. Kretzmer & E. Klein (eds), op. cit., 19. **7** Cf. Starck, 'The religious and philosophical background of human dignity and its place in modern constitutions', in D. Kretzmer & E. Klein (eds.), op. cit., 179, at 180–1 (footnote references omitted):

The recent affirmation of human dignity in constitutions and international declarations is a product of a relatively secular age. Yet the development of the underlying idea – the concept of what a human being is – closely parallels the development of Christian thought. Both the Old and New Testaments state that the basis of human dignity is the fact that humans were created in the image of god (Gen. 1, 27; Eph. 4. 24). If follows that every human being has inalienable value in his or her own right, which is why no human being may be treated as a mere object or as a means to an end.

The Preamble to the UN Charter speaks of reaffirming '*faith* in human rights, in the dignity and worth of the human person ...'[8] The use of such a term with its religious connotations is important in reminding us that our journey from empirical to normative insight does require some internal decision of commitment to the moral significance of human existence.[9]

The Irish Constitution refers to the subject in the Preamble where the 'people of Éire', 'seeking to promote the common good, with due observance of Prudence, Justice and Charity, so that the dignity and freedom of the individual may be assured ...', adopt the Constitution. The Preamble does not enlarge on the nature of 'the dignity and freedom of the individual'.

In *Molyneux v. Ireland*[10] the plaintiff, who was charged with assault under section 28 of the Dublin Police Act 1842, argued that the Act was inconsistent with the Constitution on the basis that it violated the guarantee of equal treatment given by Article 40.1 since that Act gave a power of arrest which had no counterpart outside the Dublin area. Costello P rejected this argument, stating:

> The preamble to the Constitution declares that by enacting it the people of Ireland were, *inter alia*, seeking to promote the common good so that the 'dignity and freedom' of the individual might be assured, and it required by Article 40.1 that all citizens 'as human persons'

A second strand of the concept of human dignity finds its origins in classical antiquity. Philosophers in this period recognized characteristics of human beings that distinguish them from animals, namely their capacity for rational thought and free will, and from this starting point, began to recognize human dignity in citizens. Later, their theory was extended in a more cosmopolitan context to all human beings.

A strong social component characterizes the classical and Christian concepts of freedom which the notion of human dignity underpins: human beings were always seen as interdependent, social creatures. This is evident from the concepts of the *polis*, of the community of believers, of general fraternity and of solidarity. Human freedom was anchored in divine law, in natural law and in moral law.

Christian life and belief, in which human beings depend (*religio*) on God, on Jesus Christ as intercessor and saviour and on the Christian community, led by the Holy Spirit, transcend the physical world. In this context, it is usual to speak of metaphysics. Thus, human beings have a metaphysical anchor, which provides the basis for their freedom, and for their equality and fraternity: all human beings are, in equal measure, the image of God. Human dignity does not mean unlimited self-determination, but self-determination which is exercised on the basis that everyone – not simply the person claiming the right to self determination – is of value in his or her own right.

8 Emphasis added.   9 Just as the Charter uses the word faith in its non–doctrinal connotation, so do I. There is need for our society to acknowledge the entitlement of religious language and concepts to be heard, and heeded, in philosophical, ethical and political debate; that entitlement should not rest on any necessary acceptance of the empirical validity of any doctrinal proposition of any particular religion but rather on the philosophical depth and ethical force of the language and concepts. Cf. Byrne & Binchy, *Annual Review of Irish Law 1995*, 174–7; R. Dworkin, *Life's dominion* (1993).   10 High Ct, 25 February 1997.

should be held equal before the law. The concepts thereby enshrined are ones which, quite literally, are universally recognized. The 1948 UN Declaration of Human Rights refers in its preamble to 'the inherent dignity of all members of the human family' and declares in Article 1 that 'all human beings are born free and equal in dignity and rights'. Innumerable laws are enacted in every state which treat differently one group or category of persons from other groups or categories of persons by imposing detriments or conferring benefits on one group or category and not on others. Every law which so provides does not of course breach the concept contained in Article 40.1 of the Constitution or Article 1 of the Universal Declaration ... The Supreme Court has explained why. The guarantee in the Constitution is not a guarantee of absolute equality for all citizens in all circumstances, but is a guarantee of equality as human persons relating to their dignity as human beings and a guarantee against inequalities based on the assumption that some individuals because of their human attributes, ethnic, racial, social or religious background are to be treated as inferior or the superior of other individuals in the community.[11]

This perception of dignity as inhering in the human person rather than being contingent on particular external realities is undoubtedly in harmony with the natural law philosophy grounding the Constitution.

In the *In re Ward of Court (No. 2)*,[12] dignity was treated in a radically new way by Denham J. For the first time she identified a *right* to dignity, in contrast to the perception of dignity as a quality inhering in the human person. She stated:

An unspecified right under the Constitution to (sic) all persons as human persons is dignity – to be treated with dignity. Such right is not lost by illness or accident. As long as a person is alive they have this right. Thus, the ward in this case has a right to dignity. Decision-making in relation to medical treatment is an aspect of the right to privacy; however, a component in the decision may relate to personal dignity. Is the ward, as described by Brennan J in his dissenting judgment in *Cruzan v. Director, Missouri Department of Health*,[13] 'a passive prisoner of medical technology'? If that be so, is it in keeping with her right as a human person to dignity? Just as 'the individual's right to privacy grows as the degree of bodily invasion increases'[14], so too the dignity of a person is progressively diminished by increasingly invasive medicine.[15]

11 Pages 3 to 5 of Costello P's judgment.   12 [1996] 2 IR 79.   13 497 US 261 (1990).   14 *In re Quinlan*, 355 A. 2d 647 (1976).   15 [1996] 2 IR, at 163.

Denham J considered that a range of factors had to be taken into account by the court in determining where the best interests of the ward lay. These included the wards 'constitutional right to ... (e) Dignity in life. (f) Dignity in death.'[16]

Denham J did not seek to analyze the constitutional 'right to dignity' further. So far as one can see from her brief description of the right, she appeared to regard a person's dignity as being capable of being diminished by invasive medicine; the greater the degree of invasiveness, the greater the consequent diminution of the person's dignity. Dignity would appear thus to be determined by reference to the extent to which the values of autonomy and privacy are compromised by external factors. Dignity, on this view, is not the inherent and equal worth of every person but rather a more fragile and contingent phenomenon, dependent on how others, or even fate, may treat us.[16a]

In the same sense O'Flaherty J described the ward's life as 'technically ... life, but life without purpose, meaning or dignity.' Like Denham J, O'Flaherty J did not appear to regard dignity as a value inhering in the person but rather as a quality that can depart from the person by virtue of external circumstances.

It seems that these strands of judicial perception of dignity as not inhering in every human being are inconsistent with the understanding of dignity that underlies the international human rights instruments, in which dignity has such a prominent positon, as well as being hard to harmonize with the Preamble to the Constitution, which seems clearly premised on the inherent character of dignity.

An aspect of human dignity on which I seek to place emphasis is the freedom of the will. It is part of our essence as human beings[17] that we can exercise moral choice, not based on mere emotional preference but rather by reference to a normative system which we acknowledge as having binding force. We have the freedom to adhere to the norms of this system or to act inconsistently with them: in short, to act well or badly. Respect for human dignity does not seek to relieve us of this freedom or to deny the reality that we are moral agents. If society denies its citizens the opportunity to exercise moral freedom or pretends that people are incapable of making such choices, it contradicts our human dignity in a profound way.

Privacy

The right to privacy is recognized under our Constitution as a personal right of the citizen. The manner of its recognition is curious. In *Norris v. Attorney General*,[18] the majority of the Supreme Court held that any putative right to

16 Id., at 167. 16a See p. 180 below. 17 Of course not every human being has the capacity to exercise free choice: mental incapacity can be of such a character as to render a marriage invalid. The jurisprudence on this area of the law of nullity of marriage is less than fully satisfactory: see Byrne & Binchy, *Annual Review of Irish Law 2002*, pp 293–303. 18 [1984] IR

privacy was trumped by a range of contervailing factors which rendered consistent with the Constitution the nineteenth-century criminal prohibitions on private male homosexual conduct. It is the minority judgments, however, which have provided the philosophical grounding of the right to privacy.

Henchy J stated:

> That a right of privacy inheres in each citizen by virtue of his human personality, and that such right is constitutionally guaranteed as one of the unspecified personal rights comprehended by Article 40, s. 3, are propositions that are well attested by previous decisions of this Court. What requires to be decided – and this seems to me to be the essence of this case – is whether that right of privacy, construed in the context of the Constitution as a whole and given its true evaluation or standing in the hierarchy of constitutional priorities, excludes as constitutionally inconsistent the impugned statutory provisions.
>
> Having regard to the purposive Christian ethos of the Constitution, particularly as set out in the preamble ('to promote the common good, with due observance of Prudence, Justice and Charity, so that the dignity and freedom of the individual may be assured, true social order attained, the unity of our country restored, and concord established with other nations'), to the denomination of the State as 'sovereign, independent, democratic' in Article 5, and to the recognition, expressly or by necessary implication, of particular personal rights, such recognition being frequently hedged in by overriding requirements such as 'public order and morality' or 'the authority of the State' or 'the exigencies of the common good', there is necessarily given to the citizen, within the required social, political and moral framework, such a range of personal freedoms or immunities as are necessary to ensure his dignity and freedom as an individual in the type of society envisaged. The essence of those rights is that they inhere in the individual personality of the citizen in his capacity as a vital human component of the social, political and moral order posited by the Constitution.
>
> Amongst those basic personal rights is a complex of rights which vary in nature, purpose and range (each necessarily being a facet of the citizen's core of individuality within the constitutional order) and which may be compendiously referred to as the right of privacy. An express recognition of such a right is the guarantee in Article 16, s. 1, sub-s. 4, that voting in elections for Dáil Éireann shall be by secret ballot. A constitutional right to marital privacy was recognized and implemented by this Court in *McGee v. The Attorney General*,[19] the

---

36 (Supreme Ct, 1983), critically analyzed by Gearty, (1983) 5 *DULJ* 3 (ns) 264, Quinn, 'The lost language of the Irish gay male: textualization in Ireland's law and literature (or the most hidden Ireland)', (1995) 26 *Columbia Human Rts L Rev* 553.   **19** [1975] IR 284.

right there claimed and recognized being, in effect, the right of a married woman to use contraceptives, which is something which at present is declared to be morally wrong according to the official teaching of the Church to which about 95% of the citizens belong. There are many other aspects of the right of privacy, some yet to be given judicial recognition. It is unnecessary for the purpose of this case to explore them. It is sufficient to say that they would all appear to fall within a secluded area of activity or non-activity which may be claimed as necessary for the expression of an individual personality, for purposes not always necessarily moral or commendable, but meriting recognition in circumstances which do not engender considerations such as State security, public order or morality, or other essential components of the common good.'

The last sentence captures the essence of the right. The 'secluded area of activity or non-activity' is not limited to physical seclusion: it clearly has metaphorical force. At the heart of the concept of the right to privacy is the *expression of an individual personality*: thus the rights of autonomy and dignity are inevitably engaged. Henchy J openly acknowledges – as Walsh J did in relation to the right to marital privacy – that the purposes for which the right is exercised need not necessarily be moral or commendable. The limiting factors are 'considerations such as State security, public order or *morality*, or other essential components of the common good.'[20] Formally, it could be argued that Henchy J's limiting factors are no less extensive than those proferred by O'Higgins CJ, but the right of privacy recognized by Henchy J has a reality and power which contrasts with the ghostly lack of substance of that right in the perception of the Chief Justice.

An argument that might at first appear attractive is that the right to privacy should confer on parties in intimate relationships the entitlement to

20 Emphasis added. It is worth noting that elsewhere in his judgment in *Norris*, Henchy J invoked the values of dignity and pluralism in support of the principle of legal deference to variations among individuals' moral codes. The fact that homosexual conduct was contrary to the standards of morality advocated by the Christian Churches in the State should not, in Henchy J's view, be treated as a guiding consideration: 'What are known as the seven deadly sins are authorized as immoral by all the Christian Churches, and it would have to be conceded that they are capable, in different degrees and in certain contexts, of undermining vital aspects of the common good. Yet it would be neither constitutionally permissible nor otherwise desirable to seek by criminal sanctions to legislate their commission out of existence in all possible circumstances. To do so would upset the necessary balance which the Constitution posits between the common good and the dignity and freedom of the individual. What is deemed necessary to his dignity and freedom by one man may be abhorred by another as an exercise in immorality. The pluralism necessary for the preservation of constitutional requirements in the Christian democratic State envisaged by the Constitution means that the sanctions of the criminal law may be attached to immoral acts only when the common good requires their proscription as crimes'.

conduct those relationships completely beyond the scrutiny of the law. The implication is that the right to privacy would be advanced by the dejuridification of marriage and the withdrawal of the law from its role in policing family relationships. Further reflection makes it clear that the concept of the right of privacy does not necessarily imply the absence of legal engagement. On the contrary, parties wishing to exercise their right to privacy are entitled to call on society through its laws to facilitate those choices that are integral to this right.

What does this mean for marriage and divorce? I would suggest that the following important implication is of direct relevance to the thesis that I am seeking to advance. Spouses who wish to marry for life should be let do so by our legal system. This does not mean that the law should be indifferent to that irrevocable commitment: still less does it mean that the law should positively interpret that commitment as being revocable (which is precisely what it is not). The spouses, in the exercise of their right to privacy, are entitled to have the law respect their choice fully by giving it legal effect.

One question that arises from the language of Walsh J in *McGee* and Henchy J in *Norris* has to be confronted. Both judges are strongly of the view that conduct judged by society to be immoral should nonetheless not be criminalized if it falls within the range of the exercise of the right to privacy. Does this mean that the right to privacy includes the right to act contrary to *one's own* value system? If it does, then it might be argued that, whereas respect for human dignity and autonomy entitles (or perhaps requires) the state to hold a person to his or her promise, the right to privacy requires the state to let the person break the promise without sanction. On that basis, the state would not be entitled to deny access to divorce to a promise-breaking person who had committed to a lifelong marriage. Apart from the inherent constitutional inconsistency that this argument involves, two points can be made in reply. First, neither Walsh J nor Henchy J gave a clear blessing to conduct inconsistent with the actor's value system. Secondly, both were speaking in the context of the imposition of a criminal sanction. This is quite different from that of marriage where the only 'sanction' that lifelong marital commitment involves is integral to the promise undertaken and not imposed by an external agency.

Autonomy

Autonomy is a value that has been recognized in Irish constitutional jurisprudence. It is clearly relevant to the question of committed relationships. At the heart of the notion of autonomy is the entitlement of the human person to fashion his or her own future destiny in accordance with that individual's values and existential vision rather than simply complying with a normative system imposed from on high by the state. The value of autonomy is closely linked to the values of dignity, liberty and privacy. All of these emphasize the unique worth and identity of every person and the need to preserve that identity from oppressive intrusions by the state.

Of course, autonomy cannot be permitted to trump other values, notably the protection of others and the common good. I have already indicated that in this paper I do not intend to engage in any process of assessing where the common good lies in the context of marriage. That important question is for another day.

The idea that society should interpret the expression of lifelong commitment as an expression of revocable commitment is surely at odds with respect for the value of autonomy. If the spouses on marrying make it plain beyond argument that they are committing themselves to exclude the option of future resort to divorce, society would not be truthfully responding to that exercise of autonomy by purporting to hear the commitment as less than lifelong in character. Society may, of course, choose to provide a model of marriage based on revocable commitment with a facility for divorce but this does not mean, in respect of those who have autonomously elected for lifelong commitment, that society should override their autonomy. The entitlement to act freely in accordance with one's value system is a clear instance of the exercise of autonomy, not its contradiction.

Pluralism

Pluralism is a value that seeks to accommodate diversity to the greatest extent possible, consistent with the common good. Our courts[21] have recognized the pluralist character of our Constitution, which is not based on any single religious perspective. Our society is composed of people with different traditions, philosophies, religious and world views. This diversity should be a source of celebration rather than concern.

SOME OBSERVATIONS ON THE NATURE OF COMMITMENT

It may be useful at this point of the argument to make some brief observations on the nature of the commitment. The title of this book refers to the legal recognition of *committed* relationships: when, we may ask, is a relationship a committed one?

It may be suggested that commitment relates to the moral order. It is not reducible to emotions or to a particular psychological condition. It involves a

---

21 Cf. *McGee v. Attorney General* [1974] IR 284, at 318; *The State (Keegan) v. Stardust Tribunal* [1986] IR 642, at 658; *Coughlan v. Broadcasting Complaints Commission* [2000], 3 IR 1.

positive disposition of the will, a free choice by a morally free being. On a determinist hypothesis, in which freedom of the will is an illusion, commitment here would be sucked dry of its moral component and measured exclusively in terms of the presence and intensity of particular psychological and emotional states, judged by empirical criteria relating to their continuity, actual and predicted. What a person said about his or her commitment would be but one (albeit important) piece of the data rather than presumptively representing the external aspect of an act of will.

Let us consider the question of the levels of commitment that a committed relationship can involve. It could be an unqualified and irrevocable one: I take you as my partner, in sickness or in health, no matter how wonderful or disappointing you – or the experience of being with you – may turn out, for as long as we both shall live. This is, of course, the essence of matrimonial commitment where marriage is lifelong in character.

The commitment could, however, be qualified to a limited or substantial extent: I take you as my partner for as long as you are kind to me, or for as long as I find the relationship fulfilling.[22]

Depending on the nature of the qualification, a question arises as to whether the commitment can truly be so described at all. Where, for example, the person making the commitment considers himself or herself free to walk away from the relationship if he or she no longer finds it fulfilling, one can enquire what the true content of commitment is in such a case. Commitment involves applying oneself to a particular goal, restricting or excluding present and future choices and acts that would otherwise have been entirely legitimate. In the delicate area of a personal relationship, where people are called on to exercise testing moral qualities – including patience, generosity, kindness and forgiveness – it seems questionable whether one can speak meaningfully of commitment when the proviso or qualification to the commitment made does not in fact restrict the person's range of choice in the future.

THE CENTRAL THESIS RECONSIDERED

Let me now attempt to reconsider the central thesis of the paper, in the light of the values of human dignity, autonomy, privacy and pluralism which I have adumbrated. What I am trying to encourage is a new beginning, in which the historical accretions of our culture are for the moment ignored and which does not seek to make a prudential assessment of where the common

---

22 Cf. Stanton Collett, 'Recognizing same-sex marriage: asking for the impossible', 47 *Catholic U.L. Rev.* 1245, at 1255 (1998).

good may direct socio-legal policy on committed relationships. Of course, we are not deracinated individuals with no concern for what is good for our society, but the time has surely come for removing the clutter of old debates from our minds and openly assessing the issue in the light of values that have gained a particular prominence in contemporary society but have not, perhaps, yet been fully analyzed. When subjected to that analysis, they show themselves to be the friends, not the enemies, of the deepest moral choices for good that human beings are capable of making.

Whilst many of the most potent emotive arguments in favour of divorce appeal ostensibly to facts – notably the fact of the dead marriage relationship – they contain premises rooted in distinct and identifiable values. These values derive principally from one of two competing sources. The first is that of determinism, which regards human decisions as resulting from a complex combination of social, economic, physical and psychological stimuli rather than as involving free choice. If human beings have no freedom of the will, then it would be cruelty to inflict on them the consequences of decisions that they may have believed at the time were freely made but which were not in fact so. The second, opposing, value does acknowledge freedom of the will but elevates the exercise of choice to a supreme position. On this approach, the exercise of autonomy takes priority over the constraints of moral claims by others for solidarity or support or to the constraints of an earlier exercise of autonomy by the same autonomous being. According to this approach, if I choose to commit myself in one way today, I should be free to commit myself in the opposite way tomorrow. I should be no more the slave of my own past choices than I should be the slave of another person.[23]

The introduction of divorce in 1995 has replaced a single definition of marriage by another single definition of marriage. There are several difficulties with this approach.

First, the new definition of marriage as not involving a lifelong mutual commitment contradicts the actual commitment made by many couples when they marry. Of course, some couples may marry in the new sense of giving a qualified commitment intended to be capable of being contradicted at some time in the future but others will marry on the basis of making an unqualified lifelong commitment. The new law purports to mishear the public expression of their commitment and treats it as exactly what it is not, namely a commitment with a qualification denying its lifelong character.

The new single definition of marriage created in 1995 clearly conflicts with the principle of pluralism. Whether one approaches the issue from the standpoint of religious or secular values it is plain that the denial of a model

---

23 I have already argued that this is an impoverished understanding of autonomy, in failing to recognize the human capacity to exercise autonomy to choose to act in accordance with one's normative system.

of lifelong marriage to those who would wish to commit themselves in that way is anti-pluralist in its intent and effect.

The new single definition of marriage also offends against the value of autonomy. Even if it were considered that this definition is the one that best serves most citizens, individual citizens should be free to make up their own mind on the question and act in accordance with what they perceive to be appropriate to their needs and values. The whole point of respect for autonomy is that society steps back and lets the individual fashion her or his future without being told by the state what is the best (and, in this context, only) legally recognized course of action to follow.

In *In re a Ward of Court* (*withholding medical treatment*) (*No. 2*),[24] the Supreme Court accepted that respect for individual autonomy means that society must stand by and not intervene in cases where an autonomous individual chooses to die by refusing necessary medication. In *North Western Health Board v. H.W. and N.W.*,[25] the Supreme Court held that respect for family autonomy requires society to stand by in many cases where parents make medically unjustifiable decisions which risk causing some injury to their child. If autonomy means that one can make the awesome choice to die when society might regard this as being a grievously mistaken one, it is hard to see why respect for autonomy should not permit a couple legally to commit themselves to each other for life. It is surely a matter for reflection that a decision to end one's life can be a constitutionally protected choice but a decision to marry for life should be treated as contrary to public policy so far as it would call for the support of the law.

We should test the new definition of marriage against a further constitutional value: that of marital privacy. The right to marital privacy was recognized by the Supreme Court in *McGee v. Attorney General*.[26] In this decision – arguably the most important in Irish constitutional jurisprudence[27] – the Supreme Court held that a married couple had the entitlement to have access to contraception which could not be denied them by the law. Walsh J. stated:

---

24 [1996] 2 IR 79. For analysis, see Byrne & Binchy, *Annual Review of Irish Law 1995*, 156–81; Whyte, 'The right to die under the Irish Constitution' [1997] *European Public Law*; O'Carroll, 'The right to die: a critique of Supreme Court judgment in "the Ward' case" (1995) 84 *Studies* 375; Feenan, 'Death, dying and the law' (1996) 14 *ILT* (ns) 90; Hanafin, 'Last rites or rights at last: the development of a right to die in Irish constitutional law', (1996) 18 *J of Social Welfare & Family L* 429; Tomkin & McAuley, '*Re a Ward of Court*: legal analysis', (1995) 2 *Medico-Legal J of Ireland* 45; Iglesias, 'Ethics, brain-death and the medical concept of the human being', id., 51, especially at 56–7; Kearon, '*Re a Ward of Court*: ethical comment', id., 58; Mason & Laurie, 'The management of the persistent vegetative state in the British Isles' [1996] *Juridical Rev* 263, especially at 270–2. Much of the commentary, even by some of those sympathetic to the outcome in the case, is critical of the court's analysis. Dr John Keown, writing in the *Cambridge Law Journal*, observed that, '[i]f this is the sort of reasoning a written Constitution produces, long may we remain without one': 'Life and death in Dublin', [1996] *Camb. L.J.* 6, at 8. **25** [2001] 3 IR 622. **26** [1974] IR 284.

> It is outside the authority of the State to endeavour to intrude into the privacy of the husband and wife relationship for the sake of imposing a code of private morality upon that husband and wife which they do not desire.
>
> In my view, Article 41 of the Constitution guarantees the husband and wife against any such invasion of their privacy by the State.[28]

The import of this statement is that married couples should be permitted to prescribe the terms of their relationship in accordance with their own particular values without state intrusion. If the spouses mutually prescribe a marital relationship based on lifelong commitment, that should be their prerogative.

Let us now consider the concept of marriage as an exercise of the constitutionally protected freedom of expression.[29] The whole purpose of protecting freedom of expression is that the state is not concerned with prescribing the content, philosophy or values forming the basis of that expression. The richness of the right consists of the fact that the expression constitutes the outward communication – to other individuals or society in general – of something to which the communicator attaches value.

There is surely truth in the observation that:

> [c]ivil marriage is a unique symbolic or expressive resource, usable to communicate a variety of messages to one's spouse and others, and thereby to facilitate people's constitution of personal identity …
>
> First and foremost, civil marriage is nearly always an act and expression of commitment. Marital commitment is expressed not simply by ceremonies, rings and gifts. It is also expressed by the act of undertaking and continuing to live under the responsibilities of civil marriage, and by letting it be known that one is living as a part of a civil marriage. One's statements of marital commitment gain additional credibility for the civil status. A proposition of (civil) marriage is an invitation to a partner to join a publicly valued institution, not simply to maintain a relationship in the realm of the private.[30]

---

27 The decision explores the relationship between the law and private morality, the impact of fundamental values of justice and charity on constitutional analysis and the potential for constitutional analysis to change in the light of changes in dominant values in society. The latter issue was an important element in the Supreme Court decision of *Attorney General v. X* [1992] 1 IR 1, critically analyzed by Byrne & Binchy, *Annual Review of Irish Law 1992*, 154–208.   28 [1974] IR, at 313.   29 Article 40.6.1.1 of the Constitution.   30 Cruz, '"Just don't call it marriage": the First Amendment and marriage as an expressive resource', 74 *S. Calif. L. Rev.* 925, at 928, 932 (1999).

This relationship between private acts and public expression is crucial to an understanding of marriage in society. It is important that the relationship be based on truth. Society is entitled to require that those who seek to engage with society and its laws by making a public commitment to each other for life should mean what they say and not mislead society as to the true nature of their mutual intent. Thus, in *H.H. (otherwise H.C.) v. J.F.F.D.S.*[31], where a spouse sought a declaration of nullity of marriage on the basis that the spouses when entering the marriage had secretly intended to divorce, Carroll J. of the High Court refused to grant the decree and this judgment was affirmed by the Supreme Court.

Part of the necessary cement of society is the general principle that public commitments should not be subverted by freely chosen private reservations. Whereas it is entirely proper that apparently freely made public commitments should be capable of being revealed as having been vitiated by duress, mistake or mental illness, for example, a freely made public commitment, intended to be understood and treated as such by other members of society, should arguably be held binding, even in the face of a later revelation that it was contradicted by a private reservation. The basis of this approach is that society must be able to rely on a presumed consistency between public and private commitment. Indeed that is one of the reasons why marriage is adorned with such ceremonial and unambiguous social markers. The converse of this, of course, is that spouses who make a lifelong commitment should be entitled to have society respect their choice. If, in a society with a divorce jurisdiction, the spouses make it perfectly clear that the nature of their commitment excludes the option of divorce, society should not insist on defining marriage inconsistently with their choice.

A further reason why the new single model of revocable marriage may be considered to fail to protect the constitutional and human rights of citizens is its interference with the constitutionally protected right to marry. Such a right has long been recognized in Irish constitutional jurisprudence[32]. When

---

31 High Ct., Carroll J, 19 December 1990, affirmed *sub nom. H.S. v. J.S.*, Supreme Ct., 3 April 1992. For analysis, see Byrne & Binchy, *Annual Review of Irish Law 1990*, 301–6; *Annual Review of Irish Law 1992*, 347–9.   32 Cf. Kelly, op. cit., paras. 7.6.12–7.6.13; J. Casey, *Constitutional law in Ireland*, 425–7 (3rd ed., 2000); *Ryan v. Attorney General* [1965] IR 294; *Murray v. Ireland* [1985] IR 532. An important question of characterisation arises here. If the right to marry is rooted exclusively in Article 41 it may be more difficult to convince a court that such right is not contingent on, and determined by, the contours of the legal institution of marriage prescribed by Article 41, namely (since 1995) one that does not involve a legally supported lifelong commitment. If, however, the right to marry is based (either exclusively or in addition to Article 41) on Article 40.3, it may be easier to argue that the right extends to one involving permanent commitment. In *Murray*, Costello J considered that the right to marry fell under Article 40.3. In *Foy v. An t-Árd Chláraitheoir*, High Ct., McKechnie J, 9 July 2002, counsel for the respondents conceded that the right to marry was founded on Article 40.3. There is no right to divorce under the European Convention on Human Rights: *Johnston v. Ireland* 9

its existence was first acknowledged, and re-affirmed subsequently in several decisions, divorce was prohibited under Article 41.3.2. That is, of course, no longer the case. But does this mean that the right to marry in the sense of making a mutual lifelong commitment has, as a result of the change to Article 41.3.2, ceased to exist? Is the constitutionally protected right to marry now only the right to marry without a legally recognized lifelong commitment?

To answer yes, one would have to repudiate the human rights basis for recognition of the right to marry and adopt an unashamedly positivist philosophy whereby rights are traced not to inherent human dignity and capacity but to the external, contingent state of positive law. It would mean that, if the law abolished the right to marry, the human right to marry would thereby cease to exist. One would need to be a very doctrinaire proponent of legal positivism to make such a claim.

What is the solution to this conflict? In order to give due respect to these values it may be considered necessary that people should be permitted to make legally recognized mutual lifelong commitments if they so choose as an aspect of their human dignity, and in the autonomous exercise of their free will. This does not mean that others, who wish to marry on the basis of retaining the option of divorce, would be prevented from doing so under the existing constitutional dispensation.

LIBERTY AND SERVITUDE

Let us now consider two arguments that could be marshalled against the idea that irrevocable lifelong committed is entitled to legal support. One speaks the language of liberty; the other, of servitude.

Liberty

It may be argued that the essential characteristic of liberty is the right to change one's mind: having chosen one course of action, to choose another; having committed, to resile from that commitment. To foreclose future options is to deny one's essential freedom of choice. Thus, to commit oneself never to act contrary to one's present desires is to engage in a process of thought and action which must always be open to the possiblity of future, inconsistent, thought and deed.

EHRR 203 (1986). Under the same Convention, the right of transsexuals to marry persons of their former sex was recognized in *Goodwin v. United Kingdom*, [2002] 2 FLR 487, analyzed by Probert, 'The right to marry and the impact on the Human Rights Act 1998', [2003] *Internat'l Fam. L.* 29; Bessant, 'Transsexuals and marriage after *Goodwin v. United Kingdom*', [2003] *Fam. L.* 111. In *Foy v. An t-Árd Chláraitheoir*, *supra*, decided very shortly before *Goodwin*, McKechnie J rejected the argument that transsexuals had the constitutional right to marry.

How sound is this argument? Does it survive an analysis of the nature of commitment as a free human choice? If one can meaningfully speak of commitment as being within the range of human moral capacity, then the libertarian argument is in some difficulty, since the inhibition on the entitlement to act in the future inconsistently with the commitment one has made *springs from the nature of the commitment itself.* To commit is, in essence, to foreclose present and future options. If I commit irrevocably to do X, the denial of my liberty now and at some future time to act inconsistently with that commitment is integral to the commitment rather than something separate from it. To argue that the value of liberty trumps irrevocable commitment is to make a normative argument – that liberty *should* trump it – rather than to *demonstrate* that irrevocable commitment is defeated by liberty. The contours of liberty are not ncessarily shaped in such a way as to defeat irrevocable commitment. On the contrary, since liberty is an aspect of human choice, it may be argued that liberty is at its most profound and free when a human being knowingly and freely chooses to restrict the scope of his or her range of future choice.

Servitude

The argument against irrevocable commitment based on the notion of servitude is that people should not be entitled to turn themselves into slaves by denying their own liberty. Just as one should not be entitled to place oneself in actual bondage to a slave-owner, similarly one should not be permitted to foreclose one's future options to such an extent as to deny oneself essential liberty of action. This argument is somewhat less ambitious than the liberty-based argument just considered: it does not reject the foreclosure of any future option as being inconsistent with one's freedom but instead contends that at some point the restriction of future choice becomes so oppressive as to constitute servitude.

Let me readily acknowledge that concern for avoiding servtitude does indeed justify placing some limits on the exercise of personal automony. No one would seek to defend a law that permitted people to place themselves – even for some initial financial consideration – into slavery. But is the promise, traditionally made when marrying, to commit to one's spouse 'for better, for worse, for richer, for poorer, in sickness and in old age' truly so oppressive as to constitute servitude? Undoubtedly some people think so and would not wish to make a commitment of this character; others, who take a different view, should be denied legal support for that choice only where it is clear that the commitment in question is truly oppressive. That may involve consideration of empirical data, which I have sought to avoid in the present paper, but I would suggest that there is much evidence that human beings can make this commitment without becoming slaves in the process.[33]

33 It is worth noting that Article 4 of the European Convention on Human Rights, which

One should retain a sense of realism. The sanction for breach of a lifelong commitment is simply the denial to one who makes the commitment of the entitlement to obtain from the law a divorce decree with the consequent possibility of having the name of marriage attributed to a subsequent relationship during the lifetime of one's spouse. People are free to leave their partners, even partners to whom a lifelong commitment has been made.

NO NEED FOR LEGAL RECOGNITION OF LIFELONG COMMITMENT?

Could it be argued that there is simply no need for special legal recognition to be afforded to lifelong commitment? After all, nothing in the present constitutional dispensation prevents any spouse from making such a commitment and keeping it. Providing access to divorce does not make it compulsory. Forcing the other spouse to keep his or her promise may be considered to interfere with his or her autonomy.

I acknowledge the truth of the first part of this argument but I would suggest that it is not the whole truth. The distinctive character of marriage as a legal concept is that it represents an engagement by the spouses with society. Marriage is not simply a private phenomenon: society is implicated. The spouses when marrying communicate with society and call on society to pay attention to what they are doing. Under our present constitutional regime, marriage as a legal concept links the spouses to society by rendering their mutual promises eligible for respect by society, subject only to the entitlement to divorce on the conditions set out in Article 41.3.2 of the Constitution and the Family Law (Divorce) Act 1996. It would, of course, be possible to remove any connection between marriage and society by abolishing the legal concept of marriage; but, as long as marriage remains a legal concept, society has an interest in what the spouses actually promise. If the particular promise by both spouses is to exclude their future resort to divorce, each of the spouses has a legitimate entitlement to expect that society, having been engaged, will heed the nature of the spouses' promises and not actively frustrate their fulfilment. As to the suggestion that the exclusion of the other spouse from access to divorce represents an interference with that other spouse's autonomy by the first spouse, it may be pointed out that the inhibition is inherent in that other spouse's exercise of autonomy when making the irrevocable commitment.

prohibits holding anyone in slavery or servitude, has not been invoked to strike down lifelong marriage. The potential dissonance between *F. v. Switzerland*, 10 EHRR 411 (1988) and *Johnston v. Ireland* 9 EHRR 203 (1986), on the scope of the right to marry under Article 12, and the relationship between Articles 8 and 12, should be noted.

LIFELONG MARRIAGE AND THE PRESENT
CONSTITUTIONAL DISPENSATION

Let me now consider briefly the important question whether it is possible under the present constitutional dispensation to make an irrevocable lifelong commitment that has legal recognition and support. I should point out that, whatever the answer to this question may be, it does not affect the strength or weakness of the central thesis of this paper which is that the commitment of this type *should* have such recognition and support.

I suspect that the initial response of a court to the argument that lifelong commitment has legal recognition and support at present would be that this simply cannot be the position. The whole purpose of the divorce referendum of 1995 was to change the nature of marriage by removing the lifelong element from its definition. If people could sidestep this fundamental change, they might be considered to be violating the policy underlying the amendment to the Constitution.

It is perhaps worth reflecting on what is at stake here: could it be that lifelong marriage has become contrary to public policy? That stark consequence was not prominent in the advocacy in favour of the constitutional change.

What arguments would those seeking legal protection for the option of lifelong marriage be likely to advance? The most obvious is that they have a constitutional right to waive their right of access to the courts for divorce.

Irish jurisprudence on waiver of constitutional rights is at an early stage of development.[34] All we have are relatively unconsidered judicial statements, often lacking the cautious qualifications[35] or depth of analysis which the seriousness of the issue demands.

It seems that one may waive one's parental rights in respect of one's children.[36] If one can do this – with its stark and irrevocable consequences – the case against waiver of one's constitutional rights to divorce may not seem particularly radical.

A decision that is of some interest in this context is *Egan v. Minister for Defence*.[37] Here a commandant in the Air Corps sought to retire prematurely from it in order to take up a financially more attractive position. The

---

34 See Kelly, op. cit., paras. 7.1.16–7.1.78. **35** Thus in the Supreme court decision of *The State (Nicolaou) v. An Bórd Uchtála* [1966] IR 567, at 644, Walsh J (for the court) observed that there is no provision in Article 40 which prohibits or restricts the surrender, abdication, or transfer of any of the rights guaranteed in that Article by the person entitled to them. It scarcely is the case that waiver of one's right to bodily integrity against torture or, more radically, that waiver of one's right to life is unproblematic. **36** This subject raises large jurisprudential issues. I will limit myself to noting that it is possible, consensually, to lose one's parental rights through adoption and that the process of adoption prescribed by the Adoption Act 1988 contains a concept of 'abandonment' of parental rights that appears to extend to consciously chosen waiver. **37** High Ct., 24 November 1988.

Minister, exercising his functions under section 47(b) of the Defence Act 1954, refused him permission. Barr J rejected an attack on the constitutional validity of the statutory provision as violating the commandant's asserted right, under Article 40.3 of the Constitution, to use his labour as he saw fit and to transfer his service, subject to contract, from one employer to another. Barr J observed:

> If a constitutional right in the form postulated by the applicant exists (and I make no finding in that regard) it could not apply in his circumstances because ... he had entered into a voluntary contract to serve in the permanent defence force until the retirement age applicable to his ultimate rank and he was bound to remain in the army for that period. Accordingly, the right to transfer his labour to a civilian employer does not arise until the period of his service comes to an end by effect of time or otherwise, or he is given permission by the Minister to retire early.[38]

It seems, therefore, that one may waive one's constitutional right to transfer one's employment. The analogy with marriage is not perhaps a very romantic one but the point is nonetheless important. A person can choose to exclude a constitutional entitlement and to foreclose constitutionality supported choices over an extended period into the future. Of course, the commitment made by Commandant Egan had not the intimate character of marriage and was not for life, but these differences do not render the case irrelevant to the general question of waiver.

The courts could take the attitude that access to divorce is not simply a constitutional right, which may possibly be waived, but rather is part of the fundamental machinery of the social structure relating to personal status. In another context it has been observed that:

> [p]erhaps the best solution is to regard the right to jury trial not merely as a right which is simply personal to the accused, but rather as a mandatory constitutional rule ('a constitutional imperative') which is not susceptible of waiver by the accused.[39]

It may be that the courts would similarly regard the institution of divorce, which is associated strongly with the question of legal status. Our courts have already shown themselves opposed to the idea that the estoppel principle should deny recognition to a foreign divorce otherwise capable of recogntion under the rules of private international law. Estoppel differs from waiver in that estoppel results in the denial of recognition to a factually true situation

38 Page 16 of Barr J's judgment.   39 Kelly, op. cit., para. 7.1.76.

whereas waiver involves an act of choice which does not contradict reality in any way. Nevertheless there is a common denominator between the two in that both raise an issue as to whether facts relating to the parties' conduct *inter se* should trump public reality. This suggests that the estoppel cases could have some influence in the context of our discussion.

It seems, therefore, that, while it is possible that courts would apply the waiver principle in respect of the right to divorce, they are by no means certain to do so. If they were impressed by strong arguments based on dignity, privacy and autonomy, in conjunction with the philsophy of moral freedom on which the edifice of our legal system is constructed, the courts would – and, I suggest, should – look with favour on the entitlement of spouses to make legally enforceable lifelong commitments to each other.

SAFEGUARDS FOR ENTERING LIFELONG MARRIAGE

If lifelong irrevocable marriage were to be recognized as a lawfully supported option, it would seem sensible for the law to have very stringent safeguards to encourage the parties to reflect in depth and at length on the awesome nature of the commitment that they are contemplating, to ensure that they have been fully informed of the consequences – personal and legal – of this choice. There is evidence that spouses entering marriage overestimate the prospects of its success. This depressing reality must be conveyed clearly to the spouses. The couple must not only be completely informed on all of these implciations; it is essential that they should have the mental capacity and maturity to enter into this kind of commitment.

Translating these desiderata into practice suggests that there should be a prescribed period of some considerable duration in which the parties, before marrying, would be informed and counselled and engage in the appropriate professional consultations to seek to ensure that they have the maturity that this challenge requires. Parties could not reasonably complain that these state-imposed inhibitions interfered with their autonomy: the whole point about these inhibitions would be to respect the free exercise of autonomy.

CONCLUDING OBSERVATIONS

The purpose of this paper has been provocative: to encourage engagement, contradiction and further progress in the debate on marriage. Few people are likely to have a strong prejudice in favour of the argument I have presented. Those who associate the benefits of marriage with the common good will be cautious about the emphasis on individualist norms, which in much discourse are regarded as competing with common good considerations; those who favour autonomy and privacy may regard the emphasis on free choice to act in accordance with one's normative system as a species of closet moralism. To the first of these groups, I would point out again that this paper has purposely excluded from its scope all consideration of the common good, not because it is not of importance – it is in fact crucial – but simply in order to purify the analytic focus of the thesis. To the second group, the challenge is to address the nature of human dignity and freedom of the will and to rejoice in the repertoire of choice to which we, as human beings, can aspire.

16a One should here acknowledge that the word 'dignity' can be used to describe the characteristic of human valour and self-composure in adverse or hostile circumstances. Denham J is clearly correct in noting that people have a right to be treated with dignity in the sense that others – even society – should not subvert their self-respect. These usages of the term 'dignity' are, however, separate from the dignity to which the Irish Constitution and the several international human rights instruments refer.

Cohabitation, civil partnership and the Constitution

JOHN MEE*

THIS CHAPTER CONSIDERS THE IMPACT of the Constitution on the possible introduction of a civil partnership scheme for unmarried couples in Ireland. The starting point for this reflection is an assessment of the contribution to the debate of two law reform documents published in 2006: the Report on the Family by the Oireachtas All-Party Committee on the Constitution[1] ('the Oireachtas Report') and the Options Paper produced by the Working Group on Domestic Partnership, chaired by Anne Colley[2] ('the Options Paper'). These two documents are, of course, not the only important documents which have been generated by the current law reform process in Ireland. In 2004, the Law Reform Commission (LRC) produced a Consultation Paper on the *Rights and Duties of Cohabitees*.[3] This dealt with the possibility of introducing a 'presumptive' scheme which would apply by default to cohabiting couples who satisfied certain qualifying criteria. The LRC, however, did not consider the introduction of a civil partnership scheme which unmarried couples could choose to enter. The LRC's *Report on the Rights and Duties of Cohabitants*[4] was published in December 2006, a few days after the publication of the Options Paper. The LRC Report again

* I am grateful to my colleagues, Dr Mary Donnelly and Dr Conor O'Mahony, and to Dr Oran Doyle, for their comments on an earlier draft of this chapter. Responsibility for any errors remains with the author.   1 Tenth Progress Report (Dublin: Stationery Office), published on January 24 2006; full text available at www.constitution.ie/ reports/10th-Report-Family.pdf. 2 Presented to the Minister for Justice, Equality and Law Reform, November 2006; full text available at www.justice.ie/80256E01003A21A5/vWeb/flJUSQ6VYKDA-en/$File/OptionsPaper.pdf. 3 LRC CP 32–2004 (April 2004). For detailed comment, see Mee, 'A critique of the Law Reform Commission's proposals on the rights and duties of cohabitees' (2004) 29 *Irish Jurist* (ns) 74. Note also the Consultation Paper subsequently published by the Law Commission of England and Wales, *Cohabitation: the financial consequences of relationship breakdown* (Consultation Paper No. 179, May 2006).   4 LRC 82–2006 (December 2006); full text available at www.lawreform.ie/Cohabitants%20 Report%20Dec%201st%202006.pdf. In relation to the difference in terminology in the titles of the Consultation Paper and the Report (i.e. the switch from 'Cohabitees' to 'Cohabitants'), note the *obiter* comment of Minister Michael McDowell shortly after the publication of the Consultation Paper: '"Cohabitees" does not mean anything to me. ... Maybe I am old-fashioned but I just do not like it.' See 176 *Seanad Debates* 777 (5 May 2004).

concentrated on the idea of a default scheme, on this occasion preferring the term 'redress model' rather than 'presumptive scheme' to describe the relevant proposal.[5] Since neither of the LRC publications dealt directly with civil partnership, this chapter does not consider them in depth. However, the work of the LRC is clearly part of the broader picture in relation to possible law reform in this jurisdiction and will be referred to where appropriate throughout the discussion in this chapter.[6]

Part I of the chapter will consider the contribution made by the Oireachtas Report. A key decision of the Oireachtas Committee was to reject the possibility of a referendum to change the current constitutional provisions in relation to the family (on the grounds that such a referendum would be divisive). Instead, the Committee favoured legislative reform.[7] Unfortunately, the Report failed to engage to any extent with the specifics of possible legislative reform. While the Committee's remit clearly related to the Constitution, rather than to the shape of legislative reform, it was unreal to conduct an analysis of the possible need for constitutional change without considering how the provisions of the Constitution might impact upon possible legislative reform. Having considered the Report, the chapter goes on in Part II to consider the proposals made in the Options Paper in relation to civil partnership.[8] Taking these proposals as useful illustrations of the possibilities, Part III of the chapter will argue that, as the Constitution currently stands, there are serious constitutional constraints on the available options in terms of a legislative civil partnership scheme. The difficulties are most serious in relation to the creation of civil partnership schemes for opposite sex couples but there are also issues to be considered in relation to same-sex couples. In its Conclusion, the chapter offers some observations on

---

5 The phrase 'presumptive scheme' is not a felicitous one. The LRC in its Consultation Paper note 30 above, p 3 explained that '[t]he term 'presumptive' is used because once the necessary facts are established the parties are presumed to be cohabiting.' This explanation risks circularity, since a central aspect of the 'necessary facts' regarded by the LRC as triggering the presumption is that the parties *are* cohabiting, i.e. living together in a marriage-like relationship. The Options Paper note 2 above, which was published just before the LRC Report, continues to refer to the option of a 'presumptive scheme' and, notwithstanding the author's reservations about the term, it will be simplest to follow this usage in this chapter. See also text following footnote note 33 below.   6 Note also two other relevant reports published in 2006: Walsh and Ryan, *The rights of de facto couples* (Irish Human Rights Commission, March 2006), available at www.ihrc.ie/_fileupload/banners/DeFactocouples.pdf; Irish Council for Civil Liberties, *Equality for all families* (April 2006), available at http://iccl.ie/DB_Data/publications/EqualityForAllFamilies1.pdf.   7 The Report did recommend constitutional changes not directly relevant to the subject matter of this chapter. See note 1 above, p. 124 (the rights of children should be enshrined in Article 41) and ibid., p. 127 (Article 41.2 in relation to the role of woman in the home should be modified to provide gender-neutral recognition of the role of parents).   8 Given its topicality, some consideration is also given to other aspects of the Options Paper, notwithstanding this chapter's primary focus on the civil partnership issue.

the best way forward in light of the issues considered in the chapter. It will be suggested that the focus should be on the immediate introduction of full civil partnership for same-sex couples, with a more measured approach to the possible introduction of other major reforms.

PART I: THE REPORT OF THE OIREACHTAS COMMITTEE

An overview of the report

The Oireachtas Report begins with a detailed consideration of 'Changes in the demographic and social context of the family'.[9] This interesting survey, contained in Chapter 1, takes up more than a quarter of the body of the report.[10] Chapter 2 then considers the definition of the family in the Constitution.[11] As is well known, the courts have interpreted the provisions of Article 41 of the Constitution as providing protection only for the family founded on marriage.[12] The pre-eminence of marriage in the constitutional scheme is underscored by Article 41.3.1 which states that '[t]he State pledges itself to guard with special care the institution of Marriage, on which the Family is founded, and to protect it against attack.' The Committee's general consideration of the definition of the family is followed by individual chapters on six major areas of concern which were seen to arise from the sub-missions made to the Committee: cohabiting opposite sex couples; same-sex couples; children; the natural or birth father; lone parents; and the status of the 'woman in the home'.[13] All of these chapters (including Chapter 2 on the definition of the family) consist to a large extent of the presentation in sequence of extracts from the conflicting submissions made to the Committee, with no real analysis being provided by the Committee.

In Chapter 3, which deals with cohabiting opposite sex couples, the Committee concludes that, while an extension of constitutional protection to cohabiting opposite-sex couples would be welcomed by 'both the families themselves and the agencies that deal with them', it is 'clear that legislation could extend to such families the broad range of marriage-like privileges without any need to amend the Constitution.'[14] Chapter 4 concludes in similar terms in respect of same-sex couples.[15] Unfortunately, however, the relevant chapters of the Report offer no reasoning to justify these con-clusions. In its concluding chapter, the Report states that the Committee was

---

9 Note 1 above, pp 19–53.   10 Excluding the extensive appendices (consisting primarily of the text of submissions to the Committee).   11 See generally Hogan and Whyte, *J.M. Kelly: the Irish Constitution* (4th ed) (Dublin: 2003), p 1825ff.   12 *The State (Nicholau) v. An Bórd Uchtála* [1966] IR 567.   13 It is beyond the scope of this chapter (which is concerned with cohabiting opposite and same-sex couples) to comment on the Report's treatment of the last four of these topics.   14 Note 1 above, p. 76.

faced with a 'strategic decision' as to 'whether or not to seek a change in the definition of family life so as to extend constitutional protection to all forms of family life'.[16] The Committee acknowledges that, while the 'installation of the traditional family based on marriage in the Constitution suited the demography and ethos of the day',[17] there has been considerable change in demography and ethos since then. Nonetheless, the Committee saw no consensus in favour of constitutional change in respect of the definition of the family. Instead, there was a sharp division of opinion in the submissions received. The Constitution Review Group in 1996 had proposed a 'comprehensive reworking of Article 41 which would provide constitutional protection for all forms of family life while preserving the special character of the family based on marriage.'[18] However, this kind of proposal 'encounters the strong belief of many people that it is not practicable to provide constitutional recognition for all family types while at the same time maintaining the uniqueness of one.'[19]

The committee pointed out that 'Irish experience of constitutional amendments shows that they may be extremely divisive and that however well-intentioned they may be they can have unexpected outcomes.'[20] This led to the conclusion that:

> [A]n amendment to extend the definition of the family would cause deep and long-lasting division in our society and would not necessarily be passed by a majority. Instead of inviting such anguish and uncertainty, the committee proposes to seek through a number of other constitutional changes and legislative proposals to deal in an optimal way with the problems presented to it in the submissions.[21]

The committee recognized that the result of its approach would be that cohabiting opposite sex couples would not be given any constitutional protection for their family life. Instead, the problems faced by such couples would have to be addressed at a legislative level. The committee recommended 'legislation to provide for cohabiting heterosexual couples by either a civil partnership scheme or a presumptive scheme such as the Law Reform Commission suggests'.[22] Under the LRC's proposed scheme, a range of rights and duties would automatically apply to 'persons who, although they are not married to one another, live together in a 'marriage like' relationship

15 Ibid., p. 87.   16 Ibid., p. 121.   17 Ibid.   18 Ibid.   19 Ibid., pp 121–2. A minority of the Committee concluded that constitutional change was necessary in relation to the definition of the family and proposed (pp 128–129) an addendum to Article 41, expressing the state's recognition of and respect for family life not based on marriage. The proposed amendment would also have stated that the Oireachtas was entitled to legislate for the benefit of such families and their individual members.   20 Ibid., p 122.   21 Ibid.   22 Ibid.

for a continuous period of three years or where there is a child of the relationship for two years.'[23]

In relation to same-sex couples, the Committee also took the view that reform should proceed at legislative level. The Report states that '[s]ince a presumptive scheme would not be appropriate, this provision might be made by way of civil partnership legislation'.[24] The following conclusion is then stated:

> The committee recommends that civil partnership legislation should be provided for same-sex couples.
>
> The committee would recommend similar legislation to meet the needs of other long term cohabiting couples.[25]

Assessing the specific recommendations in the report

In relation to opposite sex couples

Although this is remarkable in a Report of such importance, it is difficult at the most basic level to make sense of the Committee's recommendations in relation to opposite sex couples. As has been mentioned, the recommendation in respect of opposite sex couples was for *either* civil partnership legislation *or* a presumptive scheme.[26] On the next page of the Report, in relation to same-sex couples, the recommendation is for civil partnership.[27] However, it is then stated that '[t]he committee would recommend similar legislation to meet the needs of other long term cohabiting couples'.[28] This seems to amount to a definitive recommendation of civil partnership legislation for opposite sex couples, since such couples appear to be the only 'other long term cohabiting couples' besides same-sex couples. However, this interpretation would involve the Committee having changed its mind decisively between page 122 and page 123 of its Report and having overruled the earlier recommendation in its section on opposite sex couples in a subsequent section dealing with same-sex couples. One could seek to explain away the inconvenient recommendation of civil partnership for those in 'other long-term cohabiting couples' as referring to those in non-sexual relationships and therefore as having no bearing on opposite sex couples, although this seems rather implausible in light of the use of the word 'couples'. Whether one adopts this approach, or simply regards the inclusion of the troublesome recommendation as some form of oversight, the most persuasive interpretation appears to be that the Committee wished to

---

23 LRC Consultation Paper note 3 above, p 1. The LRC subsequently favoured a more flexible approach in its Report note 4 above, pp 34–5, whereby cohabitants who did not meet the specified thresholds would be permitted to apply 'where serious injustice would result if no right of application were granted'.   24 Note 1 above, p. 123.   25 Ibid.   26 Ibid., p. 122.
27 Ibid., p. 123.   28 Ibid.

recommend legislative intervention in relation to opposite sex couples, with no indication as to whether this should take the form of a civil partnership scheme or a presumptive scheme and with no guidance as to which of the many possible variations on these two themes would be the best option.

In relation to same-sex couples

As has been mentioned, the recommendation in relation to same-sex couples was in favour of the introduction of a civil partnership scheme. This recommendation differs from that in relation to opposite sex couples in that the alternative of a presumptive scheme is not contemplated. The Report simply states, with no justification or explanation, that 'a presumptive scheme would not be appropriate' for same-sex couples.[29] By way of contrast, the LRC in its Consultation Paper on *Rights and Duties of Cohabitees*[30] had no reservations about recommending the inclusion of same-sex couples within its proposed presumptive scheme[31] (and this approach was maintained in the subsequent LRC Report on *Rights and Duties of Cohabitants*[32] and also in the Colley Options Paper.[33]) Judging from media coverage in the wake of the publication of the Report, the Oireachtas Committee's conclusion may have been based on the view that it would be inappropriate to presume from the fact that two men or two women had been living together for a certain period that they were involved in a sexual relationship. If this was the reasoning, then the Committee was labouring under a fundamental misunderstanding. In the context of a 'presumptive' scheme, there is no question of presuming a sexual relationship from the mere fact of sharing a home; the LRC's presumptive scheme would only be triggered if the parties were living together in a 'marriage-like' relationship,[34] so that the existence of a sexual relationship, generally being a feature of a marriage, would be one of the facts triggering the presumption rather than being something presumed from other facts.[35]

Conclusion on the Report

On the basis of the preceding discussion, it can be concluded that little of real substance is to be found in the Report in relation to possible legislative reform. The concern of the majority of the Oireachtas Committee was to avoid 'the anguish and uncertainty' associated with a referendum to change the constitutional definition of the family. The idea of legislative reform

29 Ibid.   30 LRC CP 32–2004 (April 2004).   31 See the discussion ibid., pp 11–14 and the conclusion at p. 18 (inclusion of same-sex couples within the scheme 'does not violate the Constitution and complies with the EHCR [European Convention on Human Rights]'). 32 Note 4 above.   33 Note 2 above.   34 Note that the LRC in its Report note 4 above, pp 26–7 replaced 'marriage-like relationship' with 'intimate relationship' in its definition of cohabitants. 35 See also note 5 above, noting the difficulties with the term 'presumptive scheme'.

appears to have been seized upon as a justification for avoiding a referendum on this point. One might be forgiven for suspecting that some of the 'anguish and uncertainty' mentioned by the Committee might be suffered by politicians who could find it hard to predict the possible electoral damage caused by a particular stance on the difficult issues involved. It is arguable that the 'uncertainty' associated with a referendum would, assuming that the amending provision was carefully drafted, largely be removed once the result was known. If, however, one were to proceed to introduce legislative reform without modifying the current constitutional provisions, a constitutional challenge could, in principle, arise at any time in the future. If a piece of legislation conferring rights on cohabiting couples were to be introduced and subsequently was struck down as unconstitutional, thus triggering the need for a referendum, it seems likely that passions on both sides would be more inflamed than if the issues were tested in a referendum which had been deliberately planned and did not stem from an intervention of the courts. Thus, if the Constitution actually does present a potential obstacle to legislative reform, it would promote certainty to tackle that obstacle before enacting legislation.

A central question is therefore whether the Constitution is likely to present difficulties for any of the main legislative options. The Report itself is not exactly coherent on this question. At the end of Chapter 3, the Committee concluded that 'it is clear that legislation could extend to [cohabiting opposite sex couples] the broad range of marriage-like privileges without any need to amend the Constitution'.[36] A similarly definitive conclusion is reached at the end of Chapter 4 in relation to same-sex couples.[37] However, by the concluding chapter of the Report, the Committee was taking a more cautious tack:

> The preponderance of the Article 41 case law would seem to suggest (although this is admittedly far from certain) that the Oireachtas may legislate to provide 'marriage-like' privileges to cohabiting heterosexual couples provided they do not exceed in any respect those of the family based on marriage.[38]

Thus, what was previously 'clear' has now become 'far from certain'. One is surely entitled to ask which it is. If the constitutional position is indeed 'far from certain', then why does the Committee feel entitled to suggest legislation which might come unstuck at some unpredictable point in the future?

It must be concluded that the Report adopted an approach which was intellectually untenable, even if perhaps politically expedient. It rejected the

36 Note 1 above, p 76. 37 Ibid., p 87. 38 Ibid., p 122. See also ibid., p 123 in relation to same-sex couples.

option of a referendum to change the definition of the family without undertaking any proper inquiry into whether or not the relevant constitutional provisions would cause difficulties for plausible reform options.

The next Part of this chapter will turn to a consideration of the Options Paper which, amongst other things, discussed a number of variants of civil partnership. This will prepare the ground for a subsequent analysis of how the current provisions of the Constitution might impact on possible civil partnership legislation.[39]

PART II: THE OPTIONS PAPER

General observations

In December 2005, the Minister for Justice, Equality and Law Reform, Michael McDowell, announced his plan to establish a Working Group on Domestic Partnership, although its composition was not announced until April 2006. The Working Group was chaired by Anne Colley, a solicitor, outgoing Chairperson of the Legal Aid Board and former Progressive Democrats TD. The Working Group describes its composition as 'diverse'[40] but this appears to mean primarily that its members were drawn from a variety of different government departments and agencies. Besides the Chair, eight of the eleven other members of the Working Group[41] were civil servants, with two drawn from the Department of Justice, Equality and Law Reform and one from each of the Department of Finance, the Department

---

[39] Important constitutional issues also arise in relation to the LRC's proposal for what was termed in its Consultation Paper a 'presumptive scheme' and is now referred to in its Report as the 'redress model'. Notably, the LRC took the view in its Consultation Paper note 3 above, pp 9–11 that the Constitution would require the exclusion from its proposed presumptive scheme of couples where one or both parties was legally married to a third party. The current author argued in 'A critique of the Law Reform Commission's proposals on the rights and duties of cohabitees' (2004) 29 *Irish Jurist* (ns) 74, 83–89 that such a restriction would fatally weaken the proposed scheme and is not, in fact, demanded by the Constitution. This point was taken on board by the LRC in its final Report note 4 above, pp 32–34, which drops the restriction in question (although the Options Paper note 2 above, pp 12–13, apparently written without the benefit of the LRC's new analysis, supported the position taken in the LRC Consultation Paper). It is not proposed to revisit this issue in detail in this chapter. It should be mentioned however that, from a constitutional point of view, an important feature of the 'redress model' is that it does not attempt to create a new status in the law for qualified cohabitants (as stressed in the LRC Report note 4 above, p. 33) nor does it provide the parties with an alternative means, beside marriage, of making a public commitment to each other. Therefore, any constitutional objections to the 'redress model' on the basis that it competes with marriage are likely to be considerably weaker than those against the creation of (opposite sex) civil partnership, which are discussed later in this chapter.   [40] Options Paper, p. 2.
[41] See Options Paper, p. 61 for a list of the members.

of Health and Children, the Department of Social Welfare, the Attorney General's Office, the Equality Authority and the General Register Office. In addition, there was one representative from the Gay and Lesbian Equality Network and one from the Family Lawyers Association, as well as an economist. The terms of reference of the Working Group were as follows:[42]

> The Group is charged with preparing an Options Paper on Domestic Partnership for presentation to the Minister for Justice, Equality and Law Reform by 20 October 2006, within the following terms of reference:
>
> 1 to consider the categories of partnerships and relationships outside of marriage to which legal effect and recognition might be accorded, consistent with Constitutional provisions, and
>
> 2 to identify options as to how and to what extent legal recognition could be given to those alternative forms of partnership, including partnerships entered into outside the State.
>
> The Group is to take into account models in place in other countries.

The creation of the Working Group meant that, somewhat confusingly, two different official bodies were considering the question of law reform in relation to cohabitants. The LRC had published its Consultation Paper in April 2004[43] and, at the time of the establishment of the Working Group, was still working on its final report. However, the LRC had declined to consider the question of civil partnership in its Consultation Paper, concentrating instead on the possibility of a presumptive scheme which would afford rights across a wide range of legal areas. The LRC felt that 'the question of registration [of civil partnerships] involves major policy considerations, a detailed discussion of which would require a Paper of its own.'[44] The current author has previously been critical of this stance on the part of the LRC, since (particularly from the perspective of same-sex couples) it is not possible to assess the merits of a proposal for a presumptive scheme/redress model unless one knows if this scheme is to operate instead of, or alongside, a registration scheme.[45] The most practical approach probably would have been to begin with a consultation paper dealing with constitutional and policy issues surrounding both types of scheme and then, following consideration of the responses to the initial consultation, move on in later papers to address more specific issues. Even though this approach was not

---

42 Options Paper note 2 above, p. 2.   43 Note 3 above.   44 Ibid., p. 4. This view limited the extent to which the LRC found it necessary to consider the impact of the Constitution on possible reform in this area. See the discussion ibid., pp 7–12. The LRC, ibid., p. 7, also saw no need to consider the proposals by the Constitution Review Group in 1996 for changes to the relevant constitutional provisions: see *Report of the Constitution Review Group* (Dublin, 1996). 45 See Mee note 39 above, 78–9.

taken initially, it would still have been possible to charge the LRC with a consideration of the civil partnership issue. However, the new Working Group was given this task instead. Moreover, the Working Group also addressed, in the 'limited time available to complete its task',[46] the presumptive scheme option. One consequence of this overlap in subject matter was that, within a week of each other, the LRC and the Working Group published documents containing divergent recommendations on the latter option. Unfortunately, since both documents were published at essentially the same time, one had the worst of both worlds from the point of view of clarity, with neither body having the opportunity to address and comment on the final proposals of the other.

Another interesting question concerning the Options Paper relates to the extent to which it is actually an 'options' paper. At the outset of the Options Paper, it is confirmed that the Working Group 'was not mandated to make recommendations'.[47] However, the difficulty for the Working Group was that the task of simply identifying possible law reform options would not have been a particularly difficult one. Anyone who has studied the area reasonably closely could immediately have produced a list of the main options: same-sex marriage; civil partnership resembling marriage; more limited civil partnership; a presumptive scheme. Of course, this list would only be a starting point, since there could be an infinite number of versions of 'limited' civil partnership and of a presumptive scheme.[48] Thus, the task of identifying options is not an easy one – depending on how you look at it, it is arguably either too trivial to be worthwhile or too open-ended to achieve.

One possible solution for the Working Group might have been to focus on the aspect of the terms of reference which referred to identifying options 'consistent with Constitutional provisions'. Attention could have been given to looking at the range of possible reform options and eliminating those which were not available because they clashed with the current constitutional framework. However, insofar as an outside observer can judge, it does not appear that any of the members of the Working Group was chosen on the basis of specialist knowledge of constitutional law. Certainly, the Options Paper does not set itself up as offering definitive guidance on the impact of the Constitution. It is stated at the outset that 'the Options Paper should not be assumed to indicate any definitive legal or constitutional position, nor did the Group seek specific legal advice on this aspect of its work.'[49] The Options Paper does offer a brief general discussion of the impact of Article 41 of the Constitution, running to a page and a half,[50] and does briefly

---

46 Options Paper note 2 above, p. 2.   47 Ibid., p. 3.   48 And it would be necessary to consider non-conjugal relationships also.   49 Options Paper, p 2.   50 Ibid., pp 23–4. Note that the Working Group stated it was confining its consideration to Art. 41 on the family. Compare text following note 37, p. 208 below, discussing the right to marry under Art. 40.3.1 and its possible

discuss constitutional issues surrounding aspects of the proposals it advances. However, it can by no means be said that the main focus of the Options Paper is to offer a constitutional analysis of the major reform options.

In the end, the Working Group appears to have dealt with the problematic nature of being asked to identify options rather than to make recommendations by effectively ignoring this limitation. The Options Paper, in fact, sets out very specific recommendations for reform – the primary sense in which 'options' are identified is that the one recommended approach involves combining a number of different types of reform (as many competing reform strategies also would).[51] Despite the inherent difficulty in its task, it does seem that it would have been possible for the Working Group to have identified a number of plausible reform strategies for consideration and to discuss the strong and weak points of each alternative package, even though, in the nature of things, not of all of these reform packages would have represented the preferred option of the Working Group itself. This approach would seem to come closest to fulfilling the mission of the Working Group, which the Group itself described as being 'to produce feasible options for the Minister to assist him in developing proposals for legislative reform.'[52] Instead, the Options Paper puts together one possible reform approach and presents it for consideration – an option rather than options. This is not to say that its discussion does not cast light on the constituent parts of possible alternative reform strategies or that the Working Group advances final positions on every issue; the fact remains, however, that the Options Paper does not attempt to assemble the various pieces of the reform jigsaw in more than one way.

This chapter does not purport to offer an in-depth consideration of all the recommendations put forward in the Options Paper. It will be useful, however, to sketch out the preferred approach of the Working Group and to comment briefly on it, before turning in the next Part to the main focus of the chapter: a consideration of the impact of the Constitution on possible civil partnership schemes.

The proposals in the options paper

A presumptive scheme for both same-sex and opposite-sex couples
The Working Group favoured the introduction of a 'presumptive' scheme which 'followed generally, but not entirely'[53] the model advanced by the LRC in its Consultation Paper.[54] According to the Working Group, '[t]he presumptive scheme is designed to protect the vulnerable dependant partner in a relationship in the absence of any formal recognition of that relationship.'[55]

impact on a civil partnership scheme.   **51** See ibid., p 34, where it is stated that the Working Group believes that 'a combination of a number of options is required to address the range of issues of concern'.   **52** Ibid., p. 3.   **53** Ibid., p. 37.   **54** Note 3 above.   **55** Options Paper, pp 37–8.

It would apply upon the termination of the relationship, including upon the death of either of the partners. The Working Group felt that the presumptive scheme should be triggered after three years of cohabitation. Where there is a child of a cohabiting relationship, the presumptive scheme would take effect immediately on the birth of a child.[56] The Working Group proposed that there should be a widespread information campaign to inform couples of the new law and the need to opt out of the scheme if they wished to avoid being governed by it. Couples would also be free to regulate their property and financial affairs by means of a contractual agreement.[57] In keeping with the overall tenor of the Options Paper, it would appear that the presumptive scheme was intended to apply to same-sex couples as much as to opposite-sex couples. This, however, is stated rather obliquely in the Options Paper. The Working Group describes itself as 'proposing' the scheme in the chapter on opposite-sex relationships.[58] By way of contrast, in the chapter on same-sex couples it is simply stated that 'the arguments for and against … [the option of] the presumptive scheme as outlined in chapter 6, for opposite sex couples, are equally valid for same-sex couples.'[59] From this, one must presumably take it that the Working Group is proposing the scheme for same-sex couples as well as for opposite-sex couples.

The Options Paper sets out specific rights and duties which would attach to the proposed presumptive scheme. The following are the main points:

(a) Property rights: Significantly, unlike the LRC's proposals, the Working Group's scheme would not allow claimants to seek a property adjustment order. The Working Group recommended, however, that '[q]ualified cohabitants should be entitled to apply to court for the right to reside in the couple's home, to the exclusion of the other partner, in exceptional circumstances'.[60] Unfortunately, the Options Paper provides no further explanation or discussion of this suggestion, which does not feature in the LRC's proposals. There may in fact be a valid case for conferring certain occupancy rights on non-owning cohabitants[61] along the lines of the jurisdiction in section 36 of the English Family Law Act 1996.[62] The English legislation limits the duration of occupation orders in favour of non-owning cohabitants to a

---

56 The Working Group stated (ibid., p. 38) that it was departing from the LRC's approach in its Consultation Paper of requiring two years of cohabitation where there is a child of the relationship.   57 See the discussion in the Options Paper, pp 36–7.   58 Ibid., p. 37.   59 Ibid., p. 49.   60 Ibid., p. 38.   61 As mentioned in Mee note 39 above, 93.   62 Note also the jurisdiction under Schedule 1 to the (English) Children Act 1989. Orders under this legislation can potentially allow a non-owning cohabitant to reside in the family home until the children reach the age of majority. For discussion of the difficulties with this jurisdiction as it currently stands, see Law Commission, *Cohabitation: the financial consequences of relationship breakdown* (Consultation Paper No. 179, May 2006), pp 81–4.

maximum of six months, with a possible renewal for one further period of up to six months.[63] Given that the Working Group's presumptive scheme does not include any provision for other forms of property adjustment order, it would seem logical to follow this aspect of the English approach (because a long-term order excluding an owner from his or her property would effectively amount to a form of property adjustment). The Working Group makes no comment on this issue nor does it propose any criteria which would guide the court's discretion in making the relevant type of order, other than using the phrase 'in exceptional circumstances', which is vague almost to the point of being meaningless. There is also no discussion of the relationship between the proposed jurisdiction and rights which might be acquired by third parties. Since it is not intended that the Family Home Protection Act 1976 would apply to those covered by the presumptive scheme, it would be possible in some cases for the defendant partner to take action prior to terminating the relationship which would render this intended safeguard nugatory, e.g. by selling or leasing the property to a third party. Overall, the fact that the relevant recommendation from the Working Group is expressed in a single sentence seriously detracts from its credibility.[64]

(b) Succession rights: Like the LRC, the Working Group favoured the creation of a discretionary jurisdiction, resembling that which currently exists for children under section 117 of the Succession Act 1965, which would allow a qualified cohabitant to apply to court on the basis that proper provision had not been made for him or her in the deceased cohabitant's will or upon intestacy.[65]

(c) Maintenance: The Court would have 'a discretionary power to award compensatory maintenance to one of the partners in exceptional circumstances where it considers it just and equitable to do so'.[66] In addition, where there is no ongoing maintenance for a custodial parent, the court would have to take account of the child-rearing costs incurred by the custodial parent when making a maintenance order under the Family Law (Maintenance of Spouses and Children) Act 1976.[67] This aspect of the Working Group's proposal follows the approach of the LRC in its Consultation Paper.[68] However, the LRC's position evolved following the consultation process and, in its Final Report, it presents a rather different proposal to the one followed by the Working Group.[69]

---

63 Family Law Act 1996, s. 36(10). 64 For some discussion of the relevant issues, see LRC Report note 4 above, pp 71–3 (concluding against the creation of this type of jurisdiction). See also Law Commission note 62 above, pp 56–8. 65 Options Paper, p 38. It was also proposed (ibid., p 39) that Order 79 of the Rules of the Superior Courts be amended to place qualified cohabitants above siblings in the list of persons entitled to extract a grant of administration. 66 Ibid., p. 39. 67 Ibid. 68 Note 3 above, chapter 5. 69 See LRC Report note 4 above,

(d) Social Welfare: No change in this area was proposed as part of the presumptive scheme.[70]

(e) Pensions: The Working Group stated that it agreed with the LRC that pension adjustment orders should not be available upon the termination of a qualified cohabitation.[71] The Working Group was not aware, it would seem, that the LRC was about to change its mind on this point in its final Report.[72] However, in any case, the Working Group had already decided not to permit applications for property adjustment orders and it would make no sense to allow applications for pension splitting orders if other forms of property adjustment order were not available.[73]

(f) Taxation: Unlike the LRC, the Working Group proposed no change to the treatment of qualified cohabitants for the purposes of capital acquisitions tax or stamp duty. Although no specific justification is offered for this stance, it appears that significance may attach to a later comment that 'a higher level of evidential proof is considered necessary to properly administer some of the provisions excluded from this proposal, but which are included in the Law Reform Commission scheme.'[74] No further elaboration of this argument is provided. This is most unfortunate, since a bald appeal to the exigencies of 'proper administration' is necessarily unconvincing. If it really would be administratively impractical to provide to unregistered cohabitants the tax reliefs proposed by the LRC, why was it not possible for the Working Group to offer even a brief explanation of the nature of the relevant difficulties?

pp 77–8; 79–81. The LRC's final proposal discards the concept of 'exceptional circumstances' and instead requires a claimant to establish 'economic dependence' as a precondition of an application for any of the various forms of ancillary relief, including maintenance. If the claimant has established economic dependence, then the claim for ancillary relief would be considered on the basis of a list of criteria which has some resemblance to those which apply in matrimonial property litigation. The LRC (ibid., p 78) adhered to another aspect of its provisional proposals, i.e. the idea of taking account of child-rearing costs incurred by the custodial parent when making an order under the Family Law (Maintenance of Spouses and Children) Act 1976.   70 Although, presumably, the intention was that the law would be changed so as to apply the so-called 'cohabitation rule' (which can defeat claims to certain classes of benefit) to same-sex as well as opposite-sex cohabitation (as was recommended by the LRC in its Report note 4 above, p 49). See Options Paper, p 49, referring to the need to ensure equal treatment under existing legislation affecting cohabitants.   71 Options Paper, p. 39.   72 See LRC Report note 4 above, pp 78–9.   73 The Working Group also suggested '[t]he amendment of public service spouses and children schemes to allow for the payment of a survivor's pension to a financially dependent partner in circumstances where there is no legal spouse and where a person nominates a cohabiting partner as a beneficiary.' See Options Paper, p 39. See also, making the same recommendation, LRC Consultation Paper note 3 above, pp 131–2; LRC Report note 4 above, p. 84.   74 Options Paper, p. 40.

(g) Other matters: The Working Group also addressed some other matters, such as those relating to health, adoption (not favouring making qualified cohabitants eligible to adopt jointly), immigration and the law of evidence.[75]

Limited civil partnership for both same-sex and opposite-sex couples
The Working Group envisaged also the introduction of a 'limited' civil registration scheme 'which extends a certain status and a limited selection of the rights and duties of marriage to cohabiting couples who choose to register their partnership'.[76] This would contrast with a 'full' civil partnership scheme which, as will be seen, would be available to same-sex couples and would carry the same consequences as marriage. The parties to a limited civil partnership would have to be 18 years of age or older and not be married or in an existing registered partnership. In terms of dissolution, the Working Group proposed that 'an immediate dissolution of the relationship would take place if both parties agree'.[77] If the parties did not agree, then the dissolution would take effect three months after one party gave notice to the other party and registered such notice.[78]

The limited civil partnership scheme would carry all the rights and duties triggered by the presumptive scheme, as well as a limited number of other consequences. Limited civil partners would be entitled to apply to court (within one year of the dissolution of the partnership) for a property adjustment order, which would only be granted in 'exceptional circumstances'. The criteria to be applied would resemble those outlined in the LRC's Consultation Paper and would focus on the (broadly defined) contributions of the parties. In fact, after considering the responses to its Consultation Paper, the LRC has since abandoned its original proposal and adopted a rather different set of criteria[79] but, once more, the Working Group does not appear to have been aware of this when publishing its paper. A further incident of limited civil partnership would be that the Family Home Protection Act 1976 would apply to the family home of registered partners. Also, limited civil partners would receive the same treatment as spouses under domestic violence legislation.

A final aspect of the Working Group's limited civil partnership was that it would confer certain taxation benefits. Civil partners would be placed in Group Threshold 1 for capital acquisitions tax and would be given the same relief as 'related persons' (i.e. 50 per cent) for stamp duty purposes. These are the same proposals which the LRC made as part of its presumptive scheme (which it later rechristened the 'redress model').[80] Since the creation

---

75 Ibid., pp 39–40.   76 Ibid., p. 41.   77 Ibid., p. 44.   78 Ibid.   79 In its Report note 4 above, pp 80–1, the LRC favoured a requirement that the applicant show 'economic dependency'. If this threshold was met, then a long (matrimonial property style) list of criteria would be considered by the court, which would make an order where it considers it just and equitable to do so.
80 LRC Consultation Paper note 3 above, pp 143–51; LRC Report note 4 above, pp 45–6.

of limited civil partnership would depend on a decision to register, rather than on a history of factual cohabitation, it might be tempting for parties to a transaction to register a limited civil partnership in order to save stamp duty, given that such a civil partnership can be dissolved immediately if the partners agree (and contractual arrangements about financial matters are also permissible). To get over this problem, the Options Paper states without further explanation that the taxation reliefs under the scheme should be 'subject to anti-avoidance and appropriate claw-back provisions.'[81]

In relation to 'appropriate claw-back provisions', it could conceivably be provided that, if the parties terminated their relationship within a specified period of taking advantage of one of the tax concessions, then some or all of the benefit would have to be repaid. This could mean, unfortunately, an unforeseen financial loss for one or both parties to a genuine intimate relationship which happens to collapse relatively soon after a relevant transaction.[82] Conversely, two non-intimate friends entering into a transaction could save money by registering a limited civil partnership and, if it unexpectedly happened that either of them wished to enter a genuine marriage or civil partnership within the claw-back period, they could immediately dissolve their bogus civil partnership and repay some or all of their gain – essentially a no-lose proposition. This suggests that anti-avoidance provisions would also be necessary but what would such provisions look like in this context? Would it be stipulated that one could not register a civil partnership with a person one did not love? The point is a serious one, since it would not be desirable to make it a pre-condition of civil partnership that the parties were actually cohabiting; given that the presumptive scheme proposed by the Working Group so closely resembles the limited civil partnership scheme, one of limited classes of couples who might be tempted to register under the latter scheme would be those in a genuine relationship who, for whatever reason, were not able to live together and would not qualify under the presumptive scheme. It is submitted that any anti-avoidance provisions would be likely to be complex to administer and potentially intrusive in their operation.

Full civil partnership for same-sex couples
The Working Group favoured the option of 'full' civil partnership for same-sex couples, regarding the introduction of marriage for such couples as being vulnerable to constitutional challenge.[83] Full civil partnership would extend

81 Options Paper, p. 43.   82 There could also be difficulties if the parties wished to implement a property settlement upon the dissolution of their civil partnership. See text to notes 94–6 below.   83 Compare *Zappone and Gilligan v. Revenue Commissioners*, unreported, High Court, 14 December 2006, where Dunne J refused to uphold a claim for the recognition of a Canadian same-sex marriage for taxation purposes in Ireland.

'the full range of rights and duties of marriage to same-sex couples who choose to register their partnership.'[84] The Working Group went on to explain that:

> The parties [to a full civil partnership] must not be married or in an existing registered partnership and must not come within the prohibited degrees of relationship. Full civil partnership must be an exclusive union between two people aged 18 years or more. The notification and other formalities before registration are the same as those for civil marriage. The partnership must be formally registered in the same way as civil marriage. All the legal provisions available on the breakdown of marriage apply to the breakdown of full civil partnership. Full civil partnership can only end on death or dissolution by a court and dissolution is subject to the same requirements as divorce.[85]

Essentially, then, the Working Group envisaged that '[f]ull civil partnership would put same-sex couples on an equal footing with opposite-sex married partners, with the notable exceptions of not ascribing a marital identity and not offering the protection the Constitution affords to marriage and family life.'[86]

A study of cohabitation/relevant legislation

In the context of its consideration of the position of opposite sex cohabiting couples, the Working Group recommended that a comprehensive study of cohabitation in Ireland be conducted with a view to informing a review of relevant legislation to see what reforms would be desirable.[87] It was argued that this review should be undertaken in tandem with the other reforms suggested in the Options Paper rather than constituting an alternative to them.[88]

Non-conjugal couples

Due to the low level of submissions in relation to non-conjugal relationships, and the absence of existing research, the Working Group found it difficult to assess the options for reform in respect of such relationships. The Working Group suggested that the comprehensive study of cohabitation in Ireland which it had previously recommended should 'include non-conjugal

---

84 Options Paper, p. 51.   85 Ibid. The Working Group stated that '[w]hile there is no constitutional impediment to a less onerous dissolution regime than divorce for full civil partnerships, the Working Group is of the view that the two institutions, i.e. marriage and full civil partnership which are equivalent in terms of the consequent rights and duties, should be subject to the same dissolution requirements'.   86 Ibid.   87 Ibid., pp 45–6.   88 Ibid., p. 46. It was also suggested (ibid.) that future family law legislation should involve a process of 'proofing' for its impact on cohabitants, where appropriate.

domestic relationships in all their diverse forms.'[89] Such a study would inform a review of legislation with a view to possible reform.[90]

Comment on the Working Group's proposed schemes

Overall, the approach of the Options Paper is considerably more conservative than that of the LRC, as is demonstrated e.g. by the fact that property adjustment orders and taxation benefits would be available under the LRC's presumptive scheme but, under the Working Group's approach, would be available only if the couple had registered a limited civil partnership. The Options Paper favours a more modest version of the presumptive scheme. This was in part because of the previously mentioned (unelaborated) concern as to the administrative workability of certain aspects of the scheme proposed by the LRC. Another reason, however, was that, unlike the LRC, the Working Group wished to link its presumptive scheme with a limited civil partnership scheme. An aim of the limited civil partnership scheme was to allow couples 'to make a public commitment, which includes signing up to a limited range of rights and responsibilities that go beyond the provisions of the presumptive scheme'.[91] As will be discussed later, the Working Group saw it as essential to the constitutional acceptability of its limited civil partnership scheme that it would be relatively limited in terms of the rights and duties it carried. This in turn meant that, since the presumptive scheme had to trigger an even lower level of rights and duties, it had to be very limited in its scope – so much so that one would strongly question the benefit of presenting it as a 'scheme' of protection rather than as a number of individual legislative reforms, since it does not amount to much more than a development in the succession law area, a specific change in relation to occupation of the home and the introduction of limited provision for maintenance. It is notable that, in England, two of these three reforms have been in place for ten years (in relation to succession[92] and occupation rights)[93] but this is not presented in that jurisdiction as amounting to anything resembling a 'presumptive' scheme for cohabitants.

In Part III of this chapter it will be argued that, as the Constitution now stands, there are serious constitutional objections to the idea of a limited civil partnership scheme. In addition, as will now be discussed, there are objections of a practical nature to the particular proposals favoured by the

---

89 Ibid., p. 58.   90 In a 28 November 2006 press release upon the publication of the Working Paper, the Tanaiste, Michael McDowell, commented that 'while noting the position arrived at by the Working Group in respect of non-conjugal relationships, the Government is of the view that the arrangements made should provide protection for people in these situations on an equal basis with other relationships of mutual dependency.' See www.justice.ie/80256E01003A02CF/vWeb/pcJUSQ6VYN2J-en.   91 Options Paper, p. 40.   92 See Law Reform (Succession) Act 1995.

Working Group. The first point is that the set of proposals made in the Options Paper would lead to an unnecessarily complex position. At present, there are essentially two options – either one is married or one is not. If the political will existed, the position could be kept equally simple, with same-sex couples simply being permitted to marry. However, given that there is to be no constitutional referendum to prepare the ground for same-sex marriage, it will be necessary to introduce a civil partnership scheme for same-sex couples. The Working Group's recommendation of such a scheme was an important one, which should be greatly welcomed. However, alongside such a full civil partnership scheme, the Options Paper wished to introduce a limited civil partnership scheme *and* a presumptive scheme. The result would be that a person could (i) be married; (ii) be a full civil partner; (iii) be a limited civil partner; (iv) be a qualified cohabitant under the presumptive scheme; or (v) be none of the above (although possibly cohabiting as a matter of fact, with consequences in areas such as social welfare law).

What is the pay-off for creating this elaborate set of legal frameworks? Upon closer consideration, the limited civil partnership scheme advanced by the Working Group is rather unappetising. In terms of state benefits accruing to a couple who register, essentially all that is on offer are two concessions in the taxation area. One of these relates to placing registered partners in Group Threshold 1 for capital acquisitions tax purposes. The impact of this is significantly reduced by a previous legislative concession which, subject to certain conditions, gives an exemption for CAT purposes in relation to gifts or inheritances of the donee's principal residence[94] (and, if it was felt that this exemption did not go far enough, it would be simple to relax the conditions by amending the relevant legislation). The other concession involves a reduction on stamp duty in relation to transfers between the civil partners. This will, of course, only be helpful if the partners wish to make a transfer of land between themselves; some couples may have reason to make such a transfer but many others never will. In fact, one obvious time when stamp duty would come into play would be if the parties were co-owners of a property and one party wished to buy out the other upon the break-up of the relationship.[95] However, there is the difficulty that the parties might no longer be civil partners by the time that they come to an agreement on a point such as this and so might not qualify for the tax concession. Furthermore, conveyances which take place shortly before the dissolution of a civil partnership might be liable to the 'clawback' provisions which were mentioned in the Options Paper.[96]

In addition to restricted positive benefits in terms of taxation, the limited civil partnership scheme would also give the parties rights against each other,

93 See Family Law Act 1996, s. 36.   94 Finance Act 2000, s. 151.   95 See Options Paper, p. 66.   96 See the discussion in the paragraph of text accompanying notes 80–2 above.

although many of these rights would already accrue if the parties lived together for long enough to trigger the presumptive scheme. In addition to the consequences triggered under the presumptive scheme, registration would open up the possibility of the parties suing each other for property compensation orders or for maintenance, their rights to make conveyances would be limited by the Family Home Protection Act 1976, and they would be treated as spouses for the purposes of domestic violence legislation. It is submitted that prospect of creating these 'hostile' rights against each other is unlikely to lead couples to enter a civil partnership, given the well-established failure of couples to contemplate the ultimate breakdown of their relationship at a time when all is going well, which is the time when they might be considering formalising their relationship in some way.

In addition to relatively anemic tax breaks and rights to sue each other, civil partnership would indeed allow the parties to make a public commit-ment to each other and obtain 'a certain status'[97] for their relationship, without having recourse to marriage. Unfortunately, the very term 'limited civil partnership' serves to suggest a second-best, or in fact a third-best, status (and conversely, the fact that parties to such a limited arrangement are termed 'civil partners' would tend to cheapen the concept of 'full' civil partnership which is being presented to same-sex couples, in lieu of marriage, as offering them long-denied public recognition for their relationships). How many men or women would get down on one knee, or perhaps merely look sheepishly in the direction of the floor, and propose limited civil partnership to their loved ones? International experience of civil partnership shows that the rate of take-up is low[98] and the variant proposed by the Working Group is pitched at such a modest level, in an attempt to avoid constitutional invalidity, that it is surely not worth the complexity which it would add to the legal position.

The Working Group was of the view that:

> Setting the presumptive scheme as the base line offering protection for vulnerable dependent partners combined with limited registered civil partnership is a pragmatic and realistic approach to offering cohabiting couples protection while providing a means for public recognition of the relationship for those who want it. Implementing either option on its own would leave a considerable gap in the level of protection offered to cohabiting couples.[99]

However, given that few couples are likely to avail themselves of such a half-hearted opt-in scheme in practice, it is submitted that it would be a mistake

97 Options Paper, p. 41.   98 As is pointed out in e.g. LRC Consultation Paper note 3 above, p. 22; Law Commission, *Cohabitation: the financial consequences of relationship breakdown*, p. 106. 99 Options Paper, p. 41.

to rely on it to fill 'a considerable gap in the level of protection for cohabiting couples'.

This Part of the chapter considers whether, in the absence of a referendum to alter the Constitution, there would be constitutional difficulties with the introduction of civil partnership into our law. It will be convenient to consider in turn the issues relating to opposite-sex couples and same-sex couples respectively.

Civil partnership for opposite-sex couples

It is submitted that, as the Constitution stands, there are serious constitutional obstacles in the way of the introduction of opposite-sex civil partnership. In analysing the matter, it is obviously necessary to bear in mind that such a scheme might take a variety of forms. Two representative variants are discussed in the Options Paper and a consideration of these will provide a useful focus for the discussion.

Full civil partnership for opposite-sex couples

This type of scheme would confer the same rights and impose the same duties as marriage, much like the civil partnership scheme introduced in the United Kingdom for same-sex couples.[1] The most obvious reason why a couple would choose this option ahead of marriage would be on the basis of an objection to the ideology of marriage, perhaps because of its traditional division of roles based on gender.[2] It seems plausible to suggest that this kind of civil partnership scheme would fall foul of Article 41.3.1 of the Constitution, in which, it will be recalled, '[t]he State pledges itself to guard with special care the institution of Marriage, on which the Family is founded, and to protect it against attack.' If the state sets up a new institution to compete with marriage – designed to cater for those who have ideological

---

1 See the Civil Partnership Act 2004.   2 It is unclear how many couples currently cohabit on the basis of an ideological objection to marriage (and there may be a tendency in academic circles to exaggerate the importance of this reason for cohabitation). There is an unfortunate lack of empirical evidence as to the reasons why people cohabit in Ireland but it seems likely that other reasons are more important, ranging from an unwillingness by one or both partners to enter any form of legal commitment at all to a simple concern with the cost of a wedding. It is, incidentally, difficult to see how ideological objections would disappear in the context of civil partnership, itself a state-sponsored institution which would operate in the context of continuing inequalities between men and women.

objections to marriage – surely this is as direct an attack on the institution of marriage as one can imagine? It appears to be conventionally accepted that the preponderance of the constitutional case law suggests that the Oireachtas may legislate to give 'marriage like' rights to cohabiting couples so long as these do not exceed in any respect those given to married couples.[3] However, in the context of the existing cases, one is considering the acceptability of legislative measures on individual matters (e.g. one aspect of the tax or social welfare codes), rather than the creation of a comprehensive package of rights which would put a comparable social institution in as favourable a position as marriage.

A key point to remember is that, although the introduction of civil partnership might be presented as a possible 'solution' to the problem of cohabitation, civil partnership would inevitably be open to all couples. Thus, as well as being chosen by that fraction of the 77,600 cohabiting couples who currently eschew marriage on ideological grounds, it would also be chosen by some of the much larger pool of couples who, in current circumstances, decide to marry. After all, the roughly 700,000 married couples in Ireland enjoy numerous privileges when compared with cohabiting couples and not all couples can afford the luxury of making material and practical sacrifices in order to indulge their ideological preferences. However, if civil partnership were available as an option to opposite sex couples, there would be no need to make any sacrifice. A couple who felt that civil partnership was ideologically preferable to marriage – or was less old-fashioned, or more trendy, or that the label simply had a more appealing ring to it – would be free to secure all the benefits of marriage without actually getting married. Therefore, it seems that there would be constitutional objections to a civil partnership scheme for opposite sex couples which resembles marriage. This is also the position taken in the Options Paper, which concluded that the introduction of this type of scheme would be unnecessary and vulnerable to constitutional challenge.[4]

Support could be found for this position in the High Court decision of *Ennis v. Butterly*,[5] where Kelly J concluded that 'agreements, the consideration for which is cohabitation, are incapable of being enforced'.[6] Kelly J felt that to allow an express cohabitation contract to be enforced would 'give it a similar status in law as [*sic*] a marriage contract' and that this would conflict with the State's obligation to guard the institution of marriage with special care.[7] In fact, Kelly J went on to argue that the failure of the legislature 'to

---

3 See e.g. LRC Consultation Paper LRC CP 32–2004 (April 2004), pp 6–8. The leading cases are *Murphy v. Attorney General* [1982] IR 241; *Muckley v. Ireland* [1985] IR 472; *Hyland v. Minister for Social Welfare* [1989] IR 624, *Greene v. Minister for Agriculture* [1990] 2 IR 17; *Mhic Mhathuna v. Ireland* [1989] IR 504 (HC); [1995] 1 IR 484 (SC); *TF v. Ireland* [1995] 1 IR 321. 4 Options Paper, p. 35.   5 [1996] I IR 426, criticized by Mee, 'Public policy for the new millennium?' (1997) 19 *DULJ* (ns) 149.   6 Ibid., 438.   7 Ibid., 438–9. The judgment in *Ennis* casts a shadow on the enforceability of contracts between cohabitants in relation to their

confer rights akin to those of married persons upon the parties to non-marital unions e.g. a right to maintenance' showed an acceptance that to do so 'would be contrary to public policy, as enunciated in the Constitution'.[8] The position of Kelly J was, in fact, an extreme one, in that it would seem to imply that a full or limited civil partnership scheme would be unconstitutional (a proposition which this author would accept) but so also would a presumptive scheme which conferred no public status on the cohabiting relationship but triggered a right to apply for maintenance, or even an isolated legislative enactment creating this right (propositions which appear to go too far, especially in relation to the last point). Thus, one of the few Irish authorities to consider the State's obligation to protect the institution of marriage takes a view which, even if moderated considerably, would still rule out the introduction of any form of civil partnership.

Limited civil partnership for opposite-sex couples

It is next necessary to consider possible civil partnership schemes which differ from marriage in terms of their practical consequences. There are many permutations. The Working Group took the view that '[t]he more comprehensive a scheme of limited civil partnership is, i.e. the closer to marriage in the rights and duties flowing from it, the more open to constitutional challenge it becomes.'[9] The Group was content that the version of limited civil partnership which it proposed 'was sufficiently different from marriage that its vulnerability to constitutional challenge is reduced.'[10]

Thus, there appear to be two lines of defence against the suggestion that a limited civil partnership scheme would infringe the Constitution. The Oireachtas Committee put forward the line that the balance of the case law indicates that it is permissible to create confer rights and privileges on unmarried couples so long as these do not exceed in any respect those associated with marriage, while the Working Group took this a step further by arguing that the more distinct from marriage the proposed scheme, the more likely that it would be constitutionally acceptable. Closer consideration, however, reveals problems with these arguments, suggesting that any limited civil partnership scheme is likely to be constitutionally dubious.

It is clear that some couples who are currently cohabiting might enter limited civil partnership on the basis that they would regard it as preferable to unmarried cohabitation and sufficiently different to the option of marriage which they would not have favoured. This seems to be what was envisaged by the Working Group, which suggests that its proposed limited civil

financial affairs, notwithstanding understandable attempts to wish away the uncertainty caused by the case (see e.g. Options Paper, pp 36–7; LRC Consultation Paper note 3 above [p.181], pp 38–42). This is another important area which would benefit if there was a modification of the constitutional definition of the family.   8 Ibid., 439.   9 Options Paper, p. 44.   10 Ibid.

partnership scheme would 'provide legal recognition and status for those cohabiting opposite-sex couples unwilling to enter into or opposed to marriage.'[11] However, the crucial point is that, in addition, a proportion of couples who would otherwise have married would find the option of limited civil partnership more attractive than marriage. Thus, some couples would choose limited civil partnership over marriage, instead of choosing it over unmarried cohabitation. It cannot be assumed that everyone who marries craves all the current rights and duties associated with marriage and could only be tempted not to marry by the creation of a competing institution which carries all the same rights and duties but which has a different name. Rather, it is reasonable to believe that people could be diverted from marriage by the creation of a competing institution which would provide 'legal recognition and status' but would not carry all of the consequences of marriage. Can it really be believed that no couples exist who would prefer an institution which, upon the breakdown of their personal relationship, would allow them to agree to an immediate termination and move on with their lives (as in the case of the Working Group's version of limited civil partnership), rather than having to live apart for four years of five in order to obtain a divorce (as in the case of marriage)? Or that there would not be couples who, in a world without civil partnership, would marry after (say) five years of life together but, if civil partnership were possible, would enter it after (say) two years and never get around to marriage?

Since it takes two people to marry, the man and the woman in the couple in question may well have divergent views as to the attractions of the extensive legal rights and duties associated with marriage. The possibility that there may be disagreement within a couple as to whether to marry or enter a civil partnership seems to further underline the constitutional difficulty with creating a civil partnership scheme for opposite-sex couples, since there is a danger that the weaker party in the relationship might be steamrollered into accepted a lesser degree of legal protection than would be provided by the constitutionally preferred option of marriage.

Another way to argue the point is to contend that creating a competing state-sponsored institution, which will prove more attractive to some couples than marriage, amounts to an inducement not to marry. The question of the significance of the creation of inducements not to marry has been considered to some extent in the case law. In *Muckley v. Ireland*,[12] the Supreme Court had to deal with an unusual legislative provision arising from the aftermath of *Murphy v. Attorney General*.[13] In the latter case, the Supreme Court had declared invalid provisions of the Income Tax Act 1967 which subjected married couples to a higher rate of taxation than a cohabiting couple. The State had responded by enacting s 21 of the Finance Act 1989 which levied

11 Ibid., p. 41.   12 [1985] IR 472.   13 [1982] IR 241.

a new tax on all married couples corresponding to the amount which would have been payable in the past if the unconstitutional provisions of the Income Tax Act 1967 had not been invalid. Thus, it was, in the words of Barrington J in the High Court, 'a thinly disguised attempt' to re-impose the unconstitutional taxation burden.[14] The State argued that the new tax created no inducement to avoid marriage, since it was entirely retrospective in nature and could not affect future decisions as to whether or not to marry. However, the Supreme Court (upholding the decision of Barrington J) rejected the view that the Supreme Court in *Murphy* 'had reached its decision *only* on the basis of the prospective inducements [not to marry]'.[15] Finlay CJ explained that 'essentially' the basis of the earlier decision had been that 'the invalid sections penalized the married state'.[16] Since the new tax similarly penalized the married state, it was also unconstitutional.

It is submitted that *Muckley* establishes only that the creation of an inducement not to marry is not a *necessary* aspect of an unconstitutional attack on marriage. The case leaves open the possibility that, given that there is more than one way to skin a constitutionally-protected institution, the creation of an inducement not to marry would be *sufficient* to violate the constitution. The issue was explored further in *Mhic Mhathuna v. Ireland*,[17] where the claimants argued *inter alia* that the existence of social welfare and taxation supports for single parents and unmarried mothers amounted to an inducement not to marry and therefore constituted an unconstitutional attack on the institution of marriage. In the High Court, Carroll J held that the impugned provisions did not, in fact, create any inducement or incentive not to marry.[18] Carroll J's decision was upheld by the Supreme Court on appeal and her stated reasons for judgment were regarded as 'correct'.[19] Thus, the Supreme Court expressed no difficulties with Carroll J's willingness to engage with the 'inducement' argument which had been advanced by the claimants. The authors of *Kelly*[20] comment that 'Carroll J did not refer to *Muckley* and consequently offered no justification for the resurrection of the inducement test'[21] which had been 'rejected by the Supreme Court in *Muckley*'.[22] It is perhaps somewhat harsh to suggest that Carroll J 'resurrected' the inducement question, when clearly she was responding to an argument by the claimant expressly based on inducement and when, as already pointed out above, the Supreme Court in *Muckley* had rejected only the argument that the existence of an inducement was invariably necessary. It is also not surprising that the Supreme Court made no specific comment on the inducement argument in *Mhic Mhathuna*, given Finlay CJ's comment that

---

14 [1985] IR 472, 482.   15 Ibid., 485 *per* Finlay CJ (emphasis supplied).   16 Ibid.   17 [1989] IR 504 (HC); [1995] 1 IR 484 (SC).   18 [1989] IR 504, 513.   19 [1995] 1 IR 484, 494–5. 20 Hogan and Whyte (eds), *J.M. Kelly: the Irish Constitution* (4th ed).   21 Ibid., p. 1836. 22 Ibid., p. 1835.

this argument had been less clearly relied upon by the claimants when the case moved to the Supreme Court.[23] It should further be noted that the authors of *Kelly* are not hostile to 'Carroll J's inducement test', stating that there is 'much to be said for [it]' in the context of the issues considered in *Mhic Mhathuna*.[24]

To sum up, it is submitted that there is a strong argument that the creation of a civil partnership scheme for opposite sex couples, which attracted a different set of rights and duties to those consequent upon marriage, would be unconstitutional as infringing Article 41.3.1. The legislation creating such a scheme would, of course, enjoy the presumption of constitutionality and, as Kenny J stated in *Murphy v. Attorney General*,[25] the onus would be on anyone seeking to challenge its constitutionality to establish 'a clear breach by the State of its pledge to guard with special care the institution of marriage and to protect it against attack'.[26] In this connection, it may be useful to make a further point relating to the existing case law in this area.

The decided cases generally involve a comparison between the position of married couples and cohabiting couples. Logically, the existence of the state of being married presupposes its opposite, the state of being unmarried. The position which our courts have reached – that there is nothing impermissible in treating both sets of couples on a par in relation to specific matters – was really unavoidable. It could hardly be contended that the law must treat married couples more favourably than cohabiting couples in absolutely every respect. The issues are different if the legislature takes it upon itself to create a new institution, conferring public recognition and status, which gives some of the same privileges as marriage but overall carries a less extensive set of legal consequences. In the nature of people's preferences, the difference between the legal consequences of the two institutions will encourage some couples to choose the rival institution over marriage. Since there was no obligation on the state to set up the rival institution in the first case, it is much harder from a constitutional point of view for the state to defend its actions than in the type of cases which have thus far arisen.

This last point is of relevance in relation the Working Group's argument that, essentially, it has pitched the rights and duties associated with its limited civil partnership scheme at a low enough level to make it sufficiently different from marriage to be constitutionally acceptable. It has been suggested already that the very fact that an institution is meaningfully distinct from marriage, because it carries a lighter range of rights and duties, could make it a more realistic competitor to marriage than a rival institution which amounted to marriage in almost everything but name. Notwithstanding this, it is reasonably plausible for the Working Group to suggest that if one tones down the level of the rights and duties low enough then the new institution

---

23 [1995] 1 IR 484, 494.   24 Note 20 [p. 205] above, p. 1836.   25 [1982] IR 241.   26 Ibid., 286–7.

would become less attractive to those who would otherwise have married (albeit, unfortunately, also to those who would otherwise have cohabited).[27] What is important, however, is that an aspect of the new institution which would subsist is that it would confer public recognition on the parties' relationship. It must be remembered that the institution of marriage has not always been clothed in warm layers of legislative regulation. Many of the incidents of marriage which we take for granted are of fairly recent origin, e.g. pension adjustment powers (1995);[28] property adjustment orders (1989);[29] family home protection (1976);[30] the spouse's legal right share in testate succession (1965); [31] eligibility as a couple to adopt (1952).[32] If one looks back in history to the institution which was entrusted to the special care of the State in the Constitution of 1937, it was more obvious that the central feature of marriage was that it provided a public validation of a relationship between two adults. A civil partnership scheme, however moderate the legislative trappings it carried, would still usurp that key function of marriage.[33] Therefore, there is a strong argument that it would be unconstitutional for the State to take it upon itself to create such an institution without consulting the people in a referendum.

Civil partnership for same-sex couples

Full civil partnership for same-sex couples
The Options Paper states that:

> Full civil partnership for same-sex couples, in contrast with opposite-sex couples, is viewed by the [Working] Group as a distinct institution separate from, and not competing with marriage. The Group believes that full civil partnership for same-sex couples does not suffer the same constitutional vulnerability as full civil partnership for opposite-sex couples.[34]

Thus, it is assumed that same-sex civil partnership does not involve a constitutionally forbidden attack on marriage. The argument seems to be that, since same-sex couples can never marry as the Constitution stands, there is no danger of their being wooed away from marriage by the creation of an alternative institution. The German Constitutional Court, as the authors of *Kelly* note, essentially accepted this argument in dealing with a broadly similar issue under German law.[35]

27 See text accompanying notes 94–9 above, which notes also that this is especially so given that the Working Group's version of limited civil partnership would be combined with a presumptive scheme which would confer many of the same limited benefits on couples without any action on their part.   28 Family Law Act 1995, ss 12–13.   29 Judicial Separation and Family Law Reform Act 1989, s. 15.   30 Family Home Protection Act 1976.   31 Succession Act 1965, ss 111–16.   32 Adoption Act 1952, s. 11 (this being the legislation which first

The counter-argument could be raised that there are some people whose sexual preferences make it possible for them to have a committed relationship with someone of either sex and that introducing a civil partnership for same-sex couples (which would carry the same benefits as marriage) would remove the incentive for such people to choose a marital relationship with someone of the opposite sex. However, it does not seem that the institution of marriage is benefited if the fiscal and other societal benefits associated with marriage induce a person to marry someone other than (and of a different gender to) the person to whom he or she would otherwise have committed himself or herself. Rather, as is evidenced by the experience of Irish society over past decades, the institution of marriage appears to be harmed by the painful breakdown of opposite sex marriages where one of the parties is homosexual and would not have entered into the marriage if society had been willing to recognize same-sex civil partnership.[36] Thus, on the whole, it seems reasonable to conclude that a court would probably find the concept of same-sex full civil partnership to be acceptable under the Constitution.[37]

In terms of the detail of a legislative scheme, constitutional issues could arise in relation to the rules surrounding the termination of a civil partnership. The Options Paper suggests that, while this is not required by the Constitution, the new institution should be subject to the same rules concerning dissolution as apply in relation to marriage and that the two institutions should be mutually exclusive, in that a person could not be both married and in a civil partnership at the same time (as is the UK approach).[38] This is a plausible approach, since same-sex couples are being offered this form of civil partnership as an alternative to marriage and it would diminish the seriousness of the institution if, for example, as in relation to the Working Group's proposed limited civil partnership scheme, either party were allowed to terminate the relationship after a short notice period.

The possible constitutional problem relates to the position of a person in a civil partnership who wishes to end that partnership and enter a constitutionally protected opposite sex marriage with someone else. This issue, although likely to arise more frequently in the context of considering civil partnership for opposite sex couples, could in principle arise in the context

---

provided for adoption in Ireland). **33** Compare *Ennis v. Butterly* [1996] I IR 426, discussed above. **34** Options Paper, p. 51. **35** See Hogan and Whyte (eds), *J.M. Kelly: The Irish Constitution* (4th ed) p. 1839. **36** I am grateful to my colleague, Dr Conor O'Mahony, for suggesting this last point to me. **37** In *Norris v. A.G.* [1984] IR 36, O'Higgins CJ commented that he 'would not think it unreasonable to conclude that an open and general increase in homosexual activity in any society must have serious consequences of a harmful nature so far as marriage is concerned. ... Homosexual conduct can be inimical to marriage and is per se harmful to it as an institution.' The conclusion in the text assumes that these views would be regarded as outmoded in Irish society today. **38** See e.g. Civil Partnership Act 2004, s. 3(1): prohibition on entering a civil partnership if either of the parties is married.

of the Working Group's proposed full civil partnership scheme for same-sex couples. If the civil partnership legislation stipulated a delay of at least four years before the civil partnership could be terminated, this could amount to an attack on the unenumerated right to marry of the person in the civil partnership.

There was limited authority on the constitutional right to marry under Article 40.3.1[39] until the matter was recently considered by Laffoy J in *O'Shea v. Ireland*.[40] The learned judge affirmed the existence of the right and held that it was infringed by the Deceased Wife's Sister's Marriage Act 1907, s 3(2)[41] which purported to prevent a woman from marrying the brother of her former husband, during the lifetime of that former husband. It was held that, where a legislative provision restricted the right to marry, it had to be justified either as being necessary in support of the constitutional protection of the family and the institution of marriage, or having regard to the requirements of the common good. The restriction on a civil partner marrying until at least four years have elapsed could not be defended as being necessary in support of marriage or the constitutionally protected family because the civil partnership scheme would not attract such constitutional protection. Therefore, the only option would be to argue that the restriction was necessary for the common good. Since the civil partnership scheme would have been introduced by the legislature following careful consideration and debate, the scheme itself could be regarded as being necessary for the public good. However, this argument could not plausibly be extended to every detail of the scheme. Therefore, there seems to be a strong argument that a restriction which would prevent a civil partner from marrying her chosen partner for at least four years is an attack on the right to marry which is not necessary in the interests of the common good. It is possible that the problem could be avoided if some lesser period for the dissolution of a civil partnership were specified in the legislation. While this would put same-sex civil partners couples in a different (and arguably more rational) position in this respect when compared to married couples, this seems to flow from the decision to impose a separate institution on such couples instead of simply allowing them to marry.

Thus, it has been suggested that, in terms of one important detail, the existing constitutional provisions on the family and the absence of constitutional protection for family arrangements other than marriage might have a distorting impact on possible civil partnership legislation for same-sex couples. In turn, of course, this again calls into question the assumption in

39 See Hogan and Whyte (eds), *J.M. Kelly: The Irish Constitution* (4th ed), pp 1468–9; see also p. 1832 discussing the right to marry as deriving from the protection of the institution of marriage in Art. 41.3.1. **40** *Irish Times*, 6 November 2006 (High Court, 17 October 2006). **41** As amended by the Deceased Brother's Widow's Marriage Act 1921.

the Oireachtas Report that there is no need to adjust the constitutional definition of the family prior to implementing legislative reform.

Limited civil partnership for same-sex couples

On the basis of the same argument made in relation to full civil partnership for same-sex couples, it would seem that there would be no constitutional objection to extending limited civil partnership to such couples. From a practical point of view, the fact that making this option available to opposite sex couples would probably be unconstitutional would lessen the attraction of implementing it for same-sex couples (alongside full civil partnership).[42]

CONCLUDING OBSERVATIONS

This chapter has considered the contributions of two documents, the Oireachtas Committee Report and the Colley Options Paper. In the final assessment, the first of these two documents has little to offer. Its only lasting impact has been to skew the reform process from the start, by imposing the conclusion (prior to any consideration of the actual issues) that a referendum to adjust the constitutional provisions on the family is unnecessary and that the way forward lies in legislation. The Options Paper, which followed on from the Oireachtas Report, was constrained to consider only options which were possible within the current constitutional framework. The Options Paper is a more useful document than the Oireachtas Committee Report, in that it actually engages with the issues. A disappointing aspect of the Options Paper, however, is that at important times a position is taken but no reasoning whatsoever is provided to back it up. To take one relatively minor example, the LRC had proposed that its presumptive scheme would apply to couples who had cohabited for three years or, if they had a child, for two years. The Working Group suggested, instead, imposing no time requirement where the couple had a child.[43] However, no reason or explanation is given for this, arguably perfectly defensible, departure from the approach of the LRC. What is the value of simply asserting the correcting of a particular approach, particularly when the approach in question is a sufficiently obvious alternative that nothing is contributed by simply identifying its existence?[44]

---

42 Admittedly, it would be possible to counter any argument based on the need to avoid discrimination against opposite-sex couples by pointing out that the reason why civil partnership schemes for same-sex couples are constitutionally acceptable is because such couples are discriminated against in being excluded from the constitutionally protected institution of marriage. 43 Options Paper, p. 38. 44 Note that the LRC in its Report considered dropping the time requirement where the couple had a child but decided against recommending this on the (again not very informative) basis that it would be 'far-reaching'. LRC 82–2006 (Dec. 2006).

That point having been made, the Options Paper is intelligently presented and makes a genuine contribution to public debate by illuminating the issues.

Having considered the relevant reform documents, the view of the present commentator is that the best way forward would be to proceed with the implementation of civil partnership for same-sex couples, with this form of partnership mirroring marriage as far as possible, consistent with the Working Group's recommendation on this issue. Of course, if one is willing to attach all the incidents of marriage to full civil partnership, then the introduction of same-sex marriage would seem to be a more honest and less begrudging approach. However, even if the political will existed in principle to take this step, a referendum would still be necessary. This may mean that the prompt introduction of full civil partnership is the most pragmatic way forward, with the ultimate possibility of a subsequent referendum to allow for same-sex marriage.

Dealing in this manner with the most obvious injustice of the current law would allow a more clear-headed appraisal of the remainder of the reform landscape. At present, the strong case for opening up marriage or its equivalent to same-sex couples tends to lend weight to other logically distinct reform options. It is, for example, interesting that the Working Group conceded in the Options Paper that it had received 'very few submissions dealing with specific concerns of cohabiting opposite-sex couples'[45] and went on to observe, again in its chapter on opposite sex cohabitants, that:

> In the absence of conclusive research on the motivation, duration and structure of conjugal cohabitation, it is difficult to identify what institutional innovations would be appropriate to the needs of cohabitants.[46]

Notwithstanding these comments, which surely point towards a cautious approach, the Working Group proceeded to recommend the immediate introduction of two specific and detailed innovations for opposite sex couples – a presumptive scheme and a limited civil partnership scheme.[47]

The Working Group also made the sensible suggestion that 'a comprehensive study of cohabitation in Ireland [be commissioned] with a view to informing a review of the relevant legislation to identify where reforms may be required'.[48] Unfortunately, it went on to argue that this idea of a study and a review of legislation was 'not put forward as an option alternative to the other options outlined in this paper but should be considered in tandem with them'.[49] It seems clearly to have been the intention of the Working Group

---

45 Ibid., p. 12.   46 Ibid., p. 13.   47 See also note 90 above (Working Group making no specific recommendations for non-conjugal relationships, due to lack of submissions and non-existence of research, but Tánaiste insistent that those in such relationships should equally be protected by reform legislation).   48 Options Paper, p. 35. See also ibid., pp 45–6.   49 Ibid., p. 46.

that their recommended major reforms would not wait for the comprehensive study of cohabitation. But why should we leap before we look? An understanding of the social phenomenon one is seeking to regulate must surely be a prerequisite of worthwhile reform.

While frequent reference is made to the increasing level of cohabitation in Ireland as a justification for legislative reform, it is vital to reflect on the nature of this cohabitation. A significant proportion may involve couples where one or both parties is still involved in a moribund marriage to a third party[50] – such couples would gain no benefit from either of the two major proposals of the Working Group and so their existence cannot help to justify such reform. Also, many cohabiting couples may be living together in an (as yet) childless relationship which either leads to marriage or terminates after a relatively small number of years. Such couples would not be covered by the presumptive scheme proposed by the Working Group unless their cohabitation lasted more than three years.[51] Furthermore, the type of injustice which might tend to arise in typical relationships may not be covered by the terms of the proposed presumptive scheme. Take the case of a female cohabitant who has a career and spends €100,000 on improving the family home, which legally belongs to her partner. Or consider a cohabitant who sells his existing house and uses the proceeds to purchase a new house in the joint names of himself and his partner (carefully ensuring that his partner gains a joint equitable as well as legal interest), not realising that the relationship will break down shortly afterwards. It is unlikely that either of these people would have any remedy under the law of equity.[52] Nothing satisfactory seems to be offered to such cohabitants by either the Working Group's presumptive scheme (which affords only the possibility of 'compensatory maintenance' or the right to live in the home to the exclusion of the other partner, when some form of property adjustment order would probably be the sensible remedy, if any, to give) or by the LRC's redress scheme (which requires as a precondition of a remedy the establishment of 'economic dependency'). The first of the guiding principles accepted by the Working Group at the outset of the Options Paper was '[t]he principle of equality [which] involves treating persons in similar situations similarly, unless differentiation is objectively justified.'[53] This principle seems to be offended if a proposed

---

50 According to data gathered during the 2002 Census, such couples represent approximately 25% of all cohabiting couples in Ireland. See Mee, 'A critique of the Law Reform Commission's proposals on the rights and duties of cohabitees' (2004) 29 *Irish Jurist* (ns) 74, 83–84; 110. It remains to be seen how the position will have changed when the data from Census 2006 becomes available.   51 Note that in its Report LRC 82–2006 (December 2006), pp 34–5, the LRC decided to allow for exceptions to the specified time periods of cohabitation 'where serious injustice would result if no right of application were granted'.   52 See generally Mee, *The property rights of cohabitees* (Oxford, 1999), chapters 2–4.   53 Options Paper, p. 3.

scheme gives a remedy to certain categories of claimant while denying a remedy to other, equally deserving, claimants.

The examples considered in the previous paragraph lead into a wider point. This whole area is a highly complex one, where part of the difficulty has been public misconceptions about the law, with people assuming that being in a 'common law marriage' confers some protection for their rights. Into this craggy terrain sweeps the lightly-shod reformer, impressing the inhabitants with high rhetoric and laying down a baffling array of new edicts, before being whisked away to battle the next social phenomenon menacing the kingdom. After this, who could blame the people if they slept soundly in their cohabiting beds? But some of them will eventually learn to their cost that none of the new laws will help them – because they are still in a long-dead marriage or because the serious loss they suffered did not involve 'economic dependency' or because the remedy they seek is not on the very limited list of remedies or because their problem was simply not anticipated because the legislation was enacted before proper research was done and subsequently the attention of the legislators was elsewhere. The Working Group did suggest a 'widespread information campaign' (albeit only in the specific context of its proposed presumptive scheme)[54] but one cannot have unrealistic expectations as to the amount of complex legal information that ordinary people will have the time or the interest to absorb.

This commentator favours a more measured approach to reform.[55] As has already been mentioned, the first step would be to put the necessary energy into the introduction of a civil partnership scheme for same-sex couples, which would carry the same rights and duties as marriage or come as close as politically possible. At the same time, it would be beneficial to initiate the comprehensive study suggested by the Working Group to provide a better understanding of the phenomenon of cohabitation in this country. If both these steps had been accomplished, it would be possible to attempt a careful assessment of the form which any further legislative and/or constitutional reform should take. It should not be assumed that our society, in its current state of development, needs a presumptive scheme or alternative institutions to marriage for opposite sex couples. It may be that in the short-term we would be better served by carefully considered reforms in areas such as succession and taxation. Interestingly, unlike the LRC's more radical proposals, the limited range of measures put forward by the Working Group actually comes close to this model. However, by labeling the proposed limited package of measures 'a presumptive model' the Working Group risks creating exaggerated public expectation as to the extent of the change

---

54 Ibid., p. 38.   55 For more extensive observations on the policy issues associated with reform, see Mee, 'Property rights and personal relationships: reflections on reform' (2004) 24 *Legal Studies* 414. See also Mee note 50 above.

envisaged and also ties itself, perhaps unnecessarily, to setting the same qualifying criteria for each distinct reform. More generally, it would be a mistake to think that there is no cost attached to enacting reforms which, whether because of constitutional problems or because society is still in the process of accepting cohabitation, are too modest to make a real difference. As well as the fact that they could lead some people to imagine that they are legally protected when they are not, there is also the difficulty that politicians will already have received the credit for tackling the difficult issues around cohabitation and it will be more difficult to get meaningful reforms enacted when the time is really ripe for this.

In the end, the reform questions are difficult but important. They require careful and detailed consideration and this chapter has attempted to make a contribution to the necessary debate.

Complicated childhood: the rights of children in committed relationships

URSULA KILKELLY

WHILE THE ADULTS INVOLVED IN committed relationships will often have made a conscious decision to enter what may be a less traditional family arrangement, the child will generally have made no such decision. Born into such arrangements, either naturally or through assisted reproduction, children will frequently have no say as to whether this is their preference or choice for a family. Where children reside with a parent who enters a second relationship, there may be a similar lack of choice although older children may of course express a view on the matter or indeed be involved in the decision-making process. Regardless of the fact that every child should enjoy equal rights regardless of their circumstances, very different approaches are taken to children's rights depending on the nature of their family and of their parents' relationship.

This contribution looks at some of the issues that arise when children are born into or become part of the committed relationships of their parents. In particular, it considers what protection children's rights enjoy under Irish law, and details the guidance available from relevant international law notably under the European Convention on Human Rights (ECHR) and the Convention on the Rights of the Child (CRC), to which Ireland is a party. It begins by looking at the definition of the family and the impact that this can have on the rights of children in it. It then considers issues of parental responsibility or guardianship, looks at the issue of contact or access and finally, addresses some questions around the child's right to identity.

DEFINITION OF FAMILY LIFE

How a family is defined can have a significant impact on the rights enjoyed by children within that unit. Yet, there is little agreement between national and international law about what constitutes a family. For example, the CRC makes it very clear that all children have the right to grow up in a safe, secure family environment but it does not define the family for this purpose. References are made throughout the Convention to parents, guardians and in some cases extended family members and this suggests a broad approach to the definition of the family. In contrast, it is well established that the family within the meaning of Article 41 of the Irish Constitution has been narrowly defined by the Irish Supreme Court as the family based on marriage.[1] That is not to say that those in non-marital families have no constitutional protection, but rather that their rights derive from Article 40.3 (the personal rights provision) rather than Article 41.[2] This undoubtedly means that such families enjoy a lesser level of protection. Despite this, and recommendations by bodies like the Constitution Review Group that the concept of the family be broadened to make it more inclusive and reflective of modern Irish society, no real change has occurred in this area for some time.[3]

The approach of the European Court of Human Rights

The concept of family life, protected by Article 8 ECHR, stands in almost complete contrast to the Irish constitutional definition.[4] Family life is a concept which has evolved steadily during the lifetime of the European Court of Human Rights to keep pace with and maintain relevance to the legal and social conditions in Convention states. In theory, the existence of family life depends on the presence, in fact, of close personal ties between the parties determined on a case-by-case basis. In practice, an increasing number of family relationships enjoy automatic protection under Article 8(1). In particular, the court has now accepted that family life exists between parents and their children in all but very exceptional cases regardless of: the parents' marital status,[5] the family's living arrangements,[6] or their apparent lack of commitment to their children.[7] With regard to other family relationships, family life may exist between children and their grandparents;[8] between siblings;[9] between an uncle and his nephew[10] and between parents and children born into second relationships.[11]

1 See *The State (Nicolaou) v. An Bord Uchtála* [1966] IR 567; *J.K. v. V.W.* [1990] 2 IR 437; *W. O'R v. E.H.* [1996] 2 IR 248.   2 See further Shatter, A., *Shatter's family law* (4th ed.) (Dublin, 1997), pp 9–10.   3 The All-Party Oireachtas Committee on the Constitution recommended no substantive change to the definition of the family in Article 41 noting that 'an amendment to extend the definition of the family would cause deep and long-lasting division in our society': All-Party Oireachtas Committee on the Constitution, *Tenth progress report: the family* (Dublin, 2005), p. 122.   4 For a broader look at ECHR issues regarding children in Irish law see Kilkelly, 'Child and family law' in Kilkelly (ed.), *ECHR and Irish law* (Bristol, 2004).   5 *Marckx v. Belgium*, no. 6833/74, Series A no. 31, (1980) 2 EHRR 330 (unmarried mother and her child); *Johnston v. Ireland*, no. 9697/92, Series A no. 12, (1987) 9 EHRR 203 (unmarried parents and their child). 6 *Berrehab v. Netherlands*, no. 10730/84, Series A no. 138, (1988) 11 EHRR 322.   7 See *C v. Belgium*, no. 21794/93, Reports 1996–III, no. 12, p. 915 and *Ahmut v. Netherlands*, no. *21702/93*, Reports 1996–VI, no. 24, p. 2017, 24 EHRR 62. See also *Söderbäck v. Sweden*, no. *24484/94*, Reports 1998–VII, no. 94. However, purely genetic relationships – such as the relationship between a sperm donor and the child born as a result – are unlikely to constitute family life. See *G v. Netherlands*, no *16944/90*, Dec. 8.2.93, 16 EHRR 38.   8 *Marckx v. Belgium* (1980) 2 EHRR 330. para. 45.   9 *Olsson v. Sweden*, no. 10465/83, Series A no 130, 11 EHRR 259. See also *Boughanemi v. France*, no. 22070/93, Reports 1996–II, no. 8, p 593, 22 EHRR 228.   10 *Boyle v. UK*, No. *16580/90* , Comm Rep, 9.2.93.   11 *Jolie & Lebrun v. Belgium*, No. *11418/85*, Dec. 14.5.86, DR

Same-sex relationships

So, family life under the ECHR is a broad concept which clearly covers the relationship between all children and their biological parents, whether in a committed relationship or not. However, the question of what protection Article 8 offers adults in same-sex relationships and, by extension, their children is far less certain. Despite the court's fairly extensive case-law on the decriminalisation of homosexuality and the age of consent, it has not yet determined whether same-sex relationships, with or without children, constitute family life. In 1992, in its decision in the *Kerkhoven* case, the Commission of Human Rights (since abolished) failed to find that a stable relationship between two women and the child born to one of them by donor insemination (DI) amounted to family life.[12]

The court has yet to consider this issue and when it does many factors are likely to influence its judgment. Increasing consensus on the right of those in same-sex partnerships to have their relationships, including with any children of the family, legally recognized is likely to be one important factor, which will reduce the margin of appreciation allowed to the state seeking to deny this protection. A factor of further influence may be the precedent set by the court in the case of *X, Y & Z v. UK*.[13] In this case, the court recognized that family life existed between a child and her social, as distinct from her biological father. In particular, it held that the relationship between a female-to-male transsexual and the child born to his female partner by DI came within the meaning of family life because their relationship was otherwise indistinguishable from that enjoyed by the traditional family.[14] Accordingly, it is highly likely that when it is eventually faced with this issue, the court will choose to extend this principle one step further and bring same-sex couples and their children within the scope of family life. Doing so would be uncontroversial insofar as it would reflect an application of Article 8 which is in line with modern social and legal conditions. It would also be consistent with the view expressed by members of the Commission and the court, many of whom come from states which have now legislated in this area, who see no reason why all forms of durable relationships between parents and their children should not be entitled to the protection of Article 8. As Professor Henry Schermers, then Dutch member of the Commission, explained:

> [p]rincipal elements of family life are mutual affection, which may exist between persons – irrespective of their sex – and between children of one or both of these persons, and the wish of such persons to found

47, p. 243.   12 *Kerkhoven, Hinke & Hinke v. the Netherlands*, No. *15666/89*, Dec. 19.5.92, unreported.   13 *X, Y & Z v. UK*, no 21830/93, Reports 1997–II no 35, p 619, 24 EHRR 143. 14 However, the court went on to find that Article 8 did not require the applicant's name to be entered onto the child's birth certificate as her father.

and/or maintain a 'family unit' by establishing a joint household, either through marriage or cohabitation.[15]

Almost a decade on from *X, Y & Z*, the increasing prevalence of non-traditional arrangements will no doubt encourage the Court to agree with Professor Schermers' view.

The ECHR and Irish law

The ECHR Act 2003 requires Irish courts to take judicial notice of the ECHR and the court's jurisprudence in relevant matters (s. 4).[16] Whether this can be achieved without some alteration of the current Irish constitutional perspective on the family is unclear; it is certainly open to the Supreme Court to consider and reject the ECHR position. However, this would, perhaps inevitably, lead to the European Court having the final say on the matter, something which the Irish judiciary may not relish. The more preferable position is that the ECHR law, persuasive as it is, should encourage a re-think of the Irish constitutional definition of the family in order to ensure that a definition more relevant and appropriate to Ireland's legal and social conditions prevails.

Further support for this view derives from the fact that the existence of family life is but the first step in the application of Article 8 and thus the difference in definition accorded to the family is not in itself sufficient to give rise to a clash between the two jurisdictions. For example, under the ECHR, anyone seeking to rely on Article 8 must first establish that his/her relationship with the child falls within the scope of family life before going on to establish that there has been an interference with his family life which is disproportionate to one of the aims set out in Article 8(2), such as protecting the rights of others. In other words, establishing the existence of family life is only the first stage in the two-stage process of proving a violation of Article 8. In this way, it may not be the difference in definition that provokes a clash between the European and the Irish courts here, but any consequences that the definition might have for the way family or child law cases are determined. These consequences may be derived from practice or from law. It is clear, for instance, that the ECHR requires equal treatment of children regardless of the marital status of their parents. At the same time, the court has recognized the legitimacy of the aim to protect the traditional family and has held that a broad variety of concrete measures may be used to implement this goal. However, where the margin of appreciation afforded to Convention States is narrow, such as where the state is acting against an

---

15 *X, Y & Z* Comm Rep, op. cit. (dissenting opinion).   16 See generally Kilkelly (ed.), *ECHR and Irish law* (Bristol, 2004).

emerging consensus in an area or where the difference in treatment is based on gender or sexual orientation, there is a burden on the state to show that it was necessary to exclude such persons, in this case those living in a same-sex or non-marital relationship, from the protection afforded to others.[17] The court has made it clear through its case law that such a distinction is exceptionally difficult to justify; that is even more the case in respect of discrimination between children given that they have no control over the circumstances of their birth. The net result, it would appear, is that as long as the effect of the Irish Constitution is to implement the principles and provisions of family law without distinction it will not be significant from which provision of the Constitution the parents' rights derive.[18] Family law must also be ECHR compliant however.

PARENTAL RESPONSIBILITY

Acquiring parental responsibility or custody of children is something married parents take for granted and many legal systems operate the presumption that the children born to a married couple are legally theirs, regardless of the biological truth. However, the issue is an important one for children born into committed relationships of same or different sex, and while the Irish legal system has some mechanisms for coping with the latter – and only when the father's name is on the birth certificate[19] – it has yet to contemplate the former.[20]

Convention on the Rights of the Child

The Convention on the Rights of the Child rightly keeps it simple in this area providing that every child has the right to know and be cared for by his or her parents (Art. 7(1)), and where the child is separated from one or both parents, he/she has the right to maintain personal relations and direct contact with them on a regular basis, except if it is contrary to the child's best interests (Art. 9(3)). The fact that the Convention does not define a parent in either social or biological terms, and more significantly, perhaps, that Article 2 outlaws discrimination against children on the basis of their parents' status or activities suggests that a broad approach is preferred here.

---

17 *Karner v. Austria*, no *40016/98* (2003), para. 41.   18 On this point the European Court has held that the question to be decided by the Court is whether the application of a particular law (as opposed to its existence) has led to an unjustified difference in the treatment contrary to Article 14. See, for example, *Elsholz v. Germany* [GC], no. 25735/94, para. 49, ECHR 2000–VIII.   19 See s. 12 Guardianship of Infants Act, 1964 as amended by the Status of Children Act, 1987.   20 For example, the Law Reform Commission's Consultation Paper on the Rights and Duties of Cohabitees gives little consideration to the rights of children in these

European Convention on Human Rights

In terms of the ECHR, the issue of parental responsibility for the children of committed relationships has arisen on more than one occasion in Strasbourg. The earliest consideration of the issue was in the *Johnston* case against Ireland[21] where the complaint concerned, *inter alia*, the inability of the child's father (who had been divorced many years before in England) to legal recognition as her guardian, along with the complaint of discrimination against her with respect to her succession rights and other fiscal matters. The applicants complained that this situation violated Article 8 (respect for family life), both alone and taken with Article 14 (non-discrimination in the enjoyment of ECHR rights). According to the court, family life existed between the three parties as their situation was otherwise indistinguishable from the family based on marriage. The court then went on to note that the child's legal position differed significantly from that of a child born within marriage, and as there were no means available to her parents to alleviate those differences, the absence of an appropriate legal regime reflecting her natural family ties amounted to a failure to respect not only her family life, but that of her parents also. The Status of Children Act, 1987 was enacted following the judgment of the court in *Johnston* providing, as a basic principle, that the relationship between a child and his/her parents would be determined irrespective of their marital status (s 3 amends the Guardianship of Infants Act, 1964). It also put in place the mechanism whereby an unmarried father can apply to become a guardian of his child (s. 12).

The principles applied by the court in *Johnston* and enacted in the Irish legislation which followed apply to cohabiting couples and their children. However, they would not appear to apply to couples in same-sex relationships or to their children despite the fact that, in Ireland at least, same-sex couples cannot avail of the one legal mechanism that will enable them to remove the inequality suffered, ie marriage or some form of registered partnership.[22] The *Kerkhoven* case challenged the application of ECHR rules to the relationship between a same-sex couple and their child born to one of the women by DI. As only the first applicant had parental responsibility over the child as her biological mother, the second applicant sought also to be granted parental responsibility to reflect the reality of their family life. This was refused on the basis that only those with legal family ties with the child could be awarded parental responsibility. In considering the application under Article 8 ECHR – that this amounted to a failure to respect the family life of all three family members – the Commission reiterated its position, without

relationships. LRC-CP 32/2004.   **21** Johnston, op. cit.   **22** This issue is also raised by Mee in his analysis of the Law Reform Commission's Consultation paper. See Mee, 'A critique of the Law Reform Commission's Consultation Paper on the Rights and Duties of Cohabitees' (2004) 29 *Irish Jurist (ns)* 74–110, pp 82–7.

offering any reasoning, that a stable relationship between two women did not fall within the scope of family life.[23] This was the case notwithstanding that there were now three people in the relationship, that they lived together as a family and both adults shared parental tasks in relation to the child. The feature distinguishing this case from *Johnston* – the couple shared the same gender, meaning that the child could be linked biologically to only one partner – clearly influenced the Commission in its decision. While it commented on what it described as 'the evolution of attitudes towards homo-sexuality', it nonetheless made it clear that it was not prepared to reflect that evolution in finding that a same-sex relationship fell within the meaning of family life under Article 8. The lack of reasoning in this case is regrettable not least because even if it had found family life to exist, it would still have been open to the Commission to determine the merits of the applicants' claim under Article 8 (2). In this regard, the most insightful part of the decision is its rejection of the applicants' claim of discrimination (Art 14 together with Article 8) where it noted that 'as regards parental authority over a child, a homosexual couple cannot be equated to a man and a woman living together'. The extent of what this means, particularly from a children's rights perspective, is unclear, although the Commission did adopt a fre-quently used technique in this case by stressing the importance of the practical, over the legal exercise of rights, ie that the legal position did not prevent the non-biological parent in this case from being involved in the child's upbringing. However expedient that reasoning, it ignores that the legal recognition of relationships is a legitimate goal in itself and one which the court has itself stressed in the *Marckx* and *Johnston* cases. Failure to determine the issue fully on its merits also leaves important issues around succession rights unresolved.

X Y & Z v. UK, decided by the court in 1996, shared some of the features of the earlier *Kerkhoven* decision. The court's initial conclusion in this case was to find that family life existed between a mother, her partner (a female to male transsexual) and their child born by DI. Although this was undoubtedly a positive conclusion, it did not determine the outcome of the central complaint which was that the father's inability to have his name entered onto the child's birth certificate constituted a failure to respect their family life. In this respect, the court reiterated its case law that where a family tie with a child exists, the state must act in a manner calculated to enable that tie to be developed and legal safeguards must be established that render possible, from the moment of birth, the child's integration in his family. However, it went on to note that this principle had hitherto only been applied in cases where there was a biological link between parent and child. The present case, it said, raised different issues about which there was much

23 No. *15666/89 Kerkhoven, Hinke & Hinke v. the Netherlands*, Dec 19.5.92, unreported.

uncertainty and a general lack of consensus in Europe. These included state practice in relation to the parental rights of transsexuals, as well as the broader issue of how the social relationship between a child conceived by assisted reproduction using donor gametes and the person who performs the role of father should be reflected in law. Despite existing advice from the Committee on the Rights of the Child in favour of the child's right to identity, it also noted that there was uncertainty in respect of whether the interests of a child conceived in such a way are best served by preserving the anonymity of the donor of the sperm or whether the child should have the right to know the donor's identity. This uncertainty all gave the UK a wide margin of appreciation as to how it observed Article 8 rights and so, unconvinced by the legal and practical consequences which flowed from the lack of recognition, the Court rejected the applicants' complaint.

While the court could be said to be correct that a lack of consensus has dominated the issues thrown up by *X, Y & Z*, there is also little doubt that this has not prevented states from granting legal recognition to the relationship between parents in more traditional family arrangements and a child born by DI. Indeed, where those parties are married, there exists in many legal systems a presumption of paternity, whose effect is to register the child's social father on the child's birth certificate without any thought whatsoever for the child's right to identity.[24] A number of points fall to be made about *X, Y & Z* in this context. First, the case was undeniably about the right of a transsexual to have his name recorded on his child's birth certificate – it did not seriously consider the challenges of DI in this context, the issue of donor anonymity or the rights of the child to identity, to inheritance or to grow up in a secure family environment. In making the assumption – contrary to its judgments in *Marckx* and *Johnston* – that it was possible for the applicants to simply surmount the practical legal difficulties and the awkward social moments that arise as a result of their situation – the court made it very clear that it was not giving serious consideration to what was at stake for all of the parties, including the child. In giving weight to the fact that the applicant was not prevented from 'acting as the child's father in the social sense', could give her his surname, or apply for a joint residence order, the court stressed its preference for the importance of social over legal ties. However, it did at least admit that it was 'impossible to predict the extent to which the absence of a legal connection between X (the father) and Z (the child) will affect the latter's development', going on to find that in the light of the uncertainty with regard to how the interests of children in Z's position can best be protected, it was not going to adopt or impose any single viewpoint.

It thereby, fortunately, left open the possibility of a reconsideration of the issue into the future. In some ways, this reconsideration has already

---

24 See further below.

happened. The *Goodwin* case decided in 2002 reversed much of the court's earlier case law on the rights of transsexuals under Article 8 (finding that the applicant had a right to a birth certificate which reflected her assigned gender) and under Article 12, finding that she had a right to marry.[25] The emerging international consensus in this area was the overwhelmingly dominant factor in this case but the court also stressed the impact on the applicant's life of the inaccurate birth certificate and the lack of justification for this harsh treatment. While *X, Y & Z* had a different focus, the court nonetheless attached weight in that case to the fact that the birth certificate was not in common use for administrative or identification purposes[26] suggesting clearly that the fundamental basis for its overall conclusion in that case has now changed radically.

CONTACT BETWEEN PARENTS AND THEIR CHILDREN

It is firmly established in the case law of Article 8 of the ECHR, as well as under the CRC, that both parents and children enjoy a mutual right of contact as part of respect for family life. This contact can be restricted, however, in line with the need to protect the child's best interests and what is proportionate to achieve that protection, while also supporting the child's right to know his/her parents. This is a well established approach in child law systems, which regard the best interests of the child as paramount in these circumstances. Under s. 3 of the Guardianship of Infants Act 1964, for example, the welfare of the child is to be the first and paramount consideration in any judicial proceedings regarding the custody or guardianship.[27] A guardian who does not enjoy custody can apply to the court for access to the child under s. 11 of the same Act.[28] Again, decisions as to access or contact must be determined by what is in the best interests of the child, a concept which can be problematic in application as a case against Portugal before the European Court of Human Rights illustrates.

The fact that cohabiting couples and their children enjoy family life within the meaning of Article 8 means that there is no difference in Strasbourg law between their situation and that of a married couple regarding the right of mutual contact even where the parties do not all live together. But, what about the situation of a child's right to contact with a parent and his/her new same-sex partner? This arose in the case of *Salgueiro Da Silva Mouta v. Portugal* where a father who had separated from his wife and entered a same-sex relationship sought to challenge the Portuguese courts' denial of his custody and contact rights with respect to his daughter

---

25 *Goodwin v. UK*, no. 28957/95 (2002) 35 EHRR 18.   26 Ibid., para 49.   27 See also s. 11.
28 See generally, Shatter, *Family law*, pp 531–94.

on the grounds of his sexual orientation.[29] While the original court had awarded him custody because it deemed him the fitter of the two parents to look after the child, the Lisbon Court of Appeal had been persuaded by the mother's concerns about her child living with her father and his male partner. Despite the protests of the Portuguese government before the European Court that the custody decision was based on what was in the best interests of the child, the court concluded from the domestic judgment that indeed the father's sexual orientation *had* been the decisive factor. In particular, it noted the following passage from that judgment:

> It is not our task here to determine whether homosexuality is or is not an illness or whether it is a sexual orientation towards persons of the same sex. In both cases it is an abnormality and children should not grow up in the shadow of abnormal situations.[30]

The court also concluded that the child should, instead, live in a traditional Portuguese family thereby proving to the European Court that the father's sexual orientation had been decisive in the final decision. That conclusion was supported, the European Court said, by the fact that the Court of Appeal, when ruling on the applicant's right to contact, warned him 'not to adopt conduct which might make the child realise that her father was living with another man in conditions resembling those of man and wife'.[31] The European Court concluded therefore that the difference in treatment suffered by the applicant was unjustified and disproportionate to any aim it sought to achieve.

Da Silva Mouta is a strong statement that discrimination on the grounds of sexual orientation will not be tolerated and, even where children are concerned, will require serious and weighty justification to be Convention compliant. This position of clarity has been muddled by the Court in cases involving legal recognition of family ties (*X, Y & Z*), as explained above, and on eligibility to adopt (see below) although the one feature to distinguish these cases from the Portuguese case is the absence of a biological link. In such cases, the way family life is defined is both influential while at the same time appears to be a typically nebulous Convention concept.

ADOPTION

Eligibility to adopt

It is widely recognized that, when the child's first chance at a family has failed, then it is vital to get the second chance right. This consideration over-

29 *Salgueiro da Silva Mouta v. Portugal*, no. 33290/96 (2001) 31 EHRR 1055.   30 Ibid., para 34.   31 Ibid., para 35.

whelmingly justifies the use of eligibility or suitability criteria for those seeking to become adoptive parents and it is universally accepted also that the child's rights and interests must be paramount in this process. While the choice of those criteria will fall largely within the state's margin of appreciation, the principle of non-discrimination under Article 14 ECHR allows the state to differentiate between adoptive parents only where the difference in treatment is based on objective and reasonable grounds.

It would appear, therefore, that an adoption system may exclude as ineligible persons who do not meet reasonable and objective criteria. This suggests that only criteria relevant to an individual's suitability to adopt or parent a child may be used to exclude them from the adoption process. On this basis, it is submitted, the state would not be able to use grounds such as sexual orientation, age, or marital status to exclude some-one from eligibility. Or, so it seemed before the court's ruling in *Fretté v. France*[32] where it was found to be compatible with the Convention to exclude the single, male applicant from the eligibility process on the grounds of his sexual orientation. This was notwithstanding his clear suitability as an adoptive parent, and the fact that the eligibility process was only the first of two steps to adopting a child under French law. This decision flies in the face of the best interests principle (he was deemed eligible to adopt and was otherwise considered highly suitable) as well as the European Court's otherwise intolerant approach of discrimination on the grounds of sexual orientation. It is of further concern that the decision fails to make clear whether a blanket exclusion of such categories from the eligibility process would be ECHR compliant or whether a case-by-case analysis of their suitability is nonetheless required. The principle of proportionality would appear to favour the latter approach, although the absence of a European wide consensus on this issue would widen the margin of appreciation giving states greater discretion in this area.

The position of the birth father

The position of birth parents in the adoption process is another contentious issue in this context. In *Keegan v. Ireland* in 1996, the Court held that placing a child for adoption without first informing or seeking the consent of the birth father was an infringement of both his right to respect for his family life under Article 8 and his right to a fair trial under Article 6 of the Convention. At the very least, therefore, birth fathers must, in most circumstances, be consulted where their child is placed by the mother for adoption. It is unclear, however, whether they should consequently enjoy a preferential right to adopt their child, where the mother is unwilling or unable to do so,

32 *Fretté v. France*, no. 10828/97, [2003] 2 FLR 9.

although such an approach is clearly in line with respect for the child's right to know and be raised by his/her parents under Article 9 of the CRC.

Parents in new relationships

Adults in committed relationships who look after the children of one of them often seek to have that relationship legally recognized for reasons of certainty, to reflect the permanent nature of their union and so that their social relationship enjoys legal recognition. In many states, including Ireland, the only available means to achieve this recognition is through adoption, although this does not apply to same-sex relationships. This question has arisen on several occasions in Strasbourg, where the court appears more tolerant of those using adoption to seek such certainty or permanency for the child – such as where the mother's new partner applies to adopt the child thereby overruling any objection by the birth father – than for the purpose of alternative care where all legal ties with the child's birth family may be extinguished. Whatever its purpose, there is growing concern that adoption is a draconian measure, one of last resort, whose use is not always appropriate in such circumstances. At the heart of this challenge is the child's right to identity and the importance to every human being of knowing their background, their heritage, and their medical, social and family history.[33] There is a growing acknowledgement of the need to find an alternative way of achieving this certainty without compromising or placing at risk the child's right to identity.[34]

Under Irish law, eligibility criteria for both domestic and international adoption are set out in section 10(2) of the Adoption Act 1992 and they are limited to a relative of the child, a married couple, living together, a widow or widower or 'where it is considered desirable', a single person. As Mee and Ronayne point out, '[t]here is no facility for couples, other than married couples, to adopt a child'[35] and thus those in all forms of committed relationships are excluded as a blanket category from eligibility criteria. Moreover, as they also note, 'it is not possible for a partner in a same-sex relationship to apply to adopt the natural child of his/her partner as a single person'[36]. This excludes the use of adoption to regularize or formalize the relationship between the adults in a committed relationship and the child born to one of them.[37] As the Equality Authority highlights, the Irish legal

---

33 See for example, Dillon, 'Making legal regimes for intercountry adoption reflect human rights principles: transforming the United Nations Convention on the Rights of the Child with the Hague Convention on Intercountry Adoption' 21 (2) *Boston University International Law Journal* (Fall 2003) 179.   34 It was in this context that the concept of special guardianship was proposed in the recent consultation process on Irish adoption law: Department of Health and Children, *Adoption legislation: 2003 consultation and proposals for change* (Dublin, 2005), p 74–5.
35 Mee and Ronayne, *Report on partnership rights of same sex couples* (Dublin, 2000), p 6.
36 Ibid.   37 The position of guardianship is also excluded. As Mee and Ronayne note, 'the

situation has important practical considerations for children: 'the absence of adoption rights or guardianship rights means that a child has no automatic right to continue in a relationship with their second parent should their biological or legal parent become incapable of caring for them through death or serious illness'.[38]

Although the Law Reform Commission chose not to express a view on the eligibility issue in its report on the rights of cohabitees,[39] it was given some consideration during the Department of Health and Children's consultation on Ireland's adoption laws. The consultation process did not produce consensus as to who should be eligible to adopt, although there was general agreement that any decision made regarding the adoption of a child must be predicated on the best interests of the child being paramount.[40] According to the Equality Authority, 'rights relating to parenting, fostering and adoption should operate on an equal basis for same-sex couples, individuals, married and non-married heterosexual couples and should be based on the core principles of attaching rights to children and responsibilities to parents and carers'.[41] While the Adoption Consultation recognized the need to focus on the interests of the child in setting eligibility criteria rather than any perceived rights of the adult to adopt, it identified key questions to be asked in deciding who should be eligible to adopt as 'what is in the best interests of the child; what are the wishes of the child; what are the wishes of the natural parents; is there a pre-existing relationship between the child and the adopter; what are the implications for the child of his or her parent's partner not having guardianship rights; and what type of society is the child being adopted into'.[42] Despite these questions arguably favouring a system which might be flexible to cope with all manner of adoptive situations, it is perhaps surprising that the report concluded that 'the presupposition that stranger adopters should be a married couple should remain'.[43] This was mainly due to the fact that 'providing eligibility rights to cohabiting couples is fraught with difficulty in Ireland in the absence of any formal cohabitation agreement system which would also address the situation of children should the couple break up'.[44]

issue of guardianship may arise where one of the partners, who has guardianship rights in a child from a previous relationship, wishes the other partner to have guardianship rights in regard to that child ... Under current legislation, there is no facility for such an arrangement. Ibid., p. 7.   **38** Equality Authority, *Implementing equality for lesbians, gays and bisexuals* (Dublin, 2002) p. 24.   **39** LRC CP 32–2004. Law Reform Commission, *Consultation paper on the rights and duties of cohabitees*, pp 157–8.   **40** Department of Health and Children *Adoption legislation: 2003 consultation and proposals for change* (Dublin, 2005), p. 14.   **41** Equality Authority, *Implementing equality for lesbians, gays and bisexuals*, p. 30.   **42** Department of Health and Children *Adoption legislation: 2003 consultation and proposals for change*, p. 27.   **43** Ibid., p. 28. Similarly, it was not considered appropriate that arrangements for special guardianship – to allow foster- and step-parents to have their relationship with the child legally recognized – extend to cohabiting couples. Ibid., p. 76.   **44** Ibid., p. 27.

ASSISTED HUMAN REPRODUCTION (AHR)

Access to AHR by those in committed relationships

In Ireland, family adoption accounts for nearly 70 per cent of all adoption orders made meaning that adoption is a significantly reduced option for those who want a family, but are unable to conceive naturally, for whatever reason. Assisted human reproduction has become the preferred choice of many, and the only option for others in this situation, although it still operates in a legislative vacuum in Ireland.[45]

Unlike some clinics in the UK, most Irish fertility clinics currently limit access to their service to married couples or heterosexual couples who have cohabited for over three years. This raises a clear question of equal access to services by those in shorter relationships, in same-sex relationships and single parents, and there may well be a case to answer under the Equal Status Acts, 2000–2004. This was the view of the Commission on Assisted Human Reproduction which recommended in 2005 that AHR services be available 'without discrimination on the grounds of gender, marital status or sexual orientation'. In this regard, the Commission recommended that any relevant legislation on the provision of AHR services should reflect the general principles of the Equal Status Acts 2000-4 with the normal qualifications relating to eligibility criteria such as age.[46]

It is not clear how the best interests principle – which the Commission refers to in the context of 'any children that may be born' – is to operate here. Although it clearly requires consideration to be given to the likely medical, psychological and emotional needs of such children, it is also possible that, despite the non-discriminatory intentions of the above recommendation, it might be used in practice to exclude certain people or couples, such as those in same-sex relationships, from accessing AHR services either on a blanket or on a case-by-case basis.[47] Admittedly, this is not an area without difficulty, although it is submitted that a rights-based approach on a case-by-case basis might prove more effective in securing respect for the rights of any children born by AHR procedures.[48]

45 See further Madden, 'Recent developments in assisted human reproduction: legal and ethical issues' (2001) 7(2) *Medico-Legal Journal of Ireland* 53. More generally see Madden, *Medicine, ethics and the law* (Dublin, 2002). See the *Report of the Commission on Assisted Human Reproduction* (Dublin, 2005).   46 *Report of the Commission on Assisted Human Reproduction*, ibid., p. 34.   47 This is despite the fact that research shows that children born to lesbian couples compare well with other assisted conception children in terms of emotional, behavioural and gender development. See HFEA, 'Tomorrow's Children: A consultation on guidance to licensed fertility clinics on taking into account the welfare of children to be born of assisted conception treatment' (London: HFEA, 2005) p. 6.   48 Some have made the case for either non- or less state-regulation or involvement here. See *Human reproductive technologies and the law*, House of Commons Select Committee on Science and Technology, Session

Those seeking to rely on international law here should remember that neither the ECHR nor the CRC recognizes the right *to* a child. While the European Court in *Keegan* did recognize that the Convention offered protection to potential family life, this was in the context of an existing child, with whom the applicant had a proven biological link. A more likely argument could be made under Article 12, perhaps, which guarantees the right to marry and found a family. While up until the *Goodwin* decision in 2002, the Court had asserted that this was one right, which could not be broken down into its constituent parts, the judgment in that case clearly acknowledged what we all know to be true, ie that the right to marry is not or at least should not be confined to those that can have children.[49] The question remains, however, whether that also works the other way around, ie whether unmarried people who cannot conceive naturally have a right under Article 12 to assisted reproduction services. Some answers may be found in the European Court's case law on eligibility to adopt as already outlined.

AHR and the child's right to identity

Assisted human reproduction has traditionally been shrouded in secrecy with an undeniably adult focus. Concern has focused on protecting the anonymity of the donor, in order to ensure a constant supply of gametes, the belief being that if the donor were identified, the supply would dry up. The medical profession has concentrated on the patient, the prospective parent, and the donor who enables the treatment to take place with insufficient attention being given to the child despite the fact that they are the product of the process and the only indicator of its success. While Ireland has failed to legislate in this area, in many jurisdictions the policy of anonymity and secrecy once compounded by the legislative approach is dissipating in favour of the child's right to identity.

Practice abroad

Early attempts to regulate the area took a paternalistic approach. In England and Wales in 1984, the Warnock Committee recommended that parents be open about the means of conception. Yet although the Warnock Report emphasized the need for children to have knowledge of their medical history, it did not recognize the right of children born by donation to know the identity of their genetic parents.[50] Accordingly, the Human Fertilisation and Embryology Act 1990 adopted subsequently provides that regardless of the use of sperm or egg donation, the couple which undertakes IVF is named on

2004–2005, Fifth Report, HC 7–1 (2005) and McClean, 'De-regulating assisted reproduction: some reflections' 7 *Medical Law International* (2006) 233–47.   **49** Goodwin, op. cit., para. 98. **50** *Report of the Committee of Inquiry into Human Fertilisation and Embryology* Cmnd. 9314, 1984.

the child's birth certificate as the child's mother and father.[51] Moreover, the State conspires in the secrecy of the arrangement by issuing birth certificates in the name of the social parents with no notification on the register of the genetic parents or even the manner of conception. (While new birth certificates are issued for adopted children the original is always maintained, yet the birth records of children by donation are genetically inaccurate from the start.)

In contrast, Sweden introduced legislation in 1984 to allow offspring to have access to the identity of their donors[52] and in New Zealand, the same result has been achieved without legislation, and no donors have been recruited there in the last fifteen years who are not prepared to be identified to the offspring in the future. One of the critical changes that occurred there was that the clinicians moved from a position where they felt that secrecy and anonymity were important to a position in which they began to think about the needs and interests of the families.[53]

Australia too has revised its earlier position of anonymity in favour of recognizing the child's right to identity. While the Infertility (Medical Procedures) Act 1984, adopted in the state of Victoria, had been the first Australian state to give donor conceived children the right to obtain non-identifying information about their genetic heritage,[54] the more recent Infertility Treatment Act 1995, which came into effect in 1998, makes provision for the use of identified donors (s. 18). In particular, it provides for access by children born by donor conception to identifying information when they reach 18 years. This is clearly a significant improvement in the effectiveness of the right of the donor child to access information about his/her origins.[55] On the level of principle, the Act also takes the important step of incorporating into the legislation the requirement that the interests of the child born as a result of the procedure are paramount (s. 5). Three other guiding principles, in descending order of importance are: the preservation of human life; consideration of the interest of the family and that infertile couples be assisted in fulfilling their desire to have children.

Change came about more recently in England and Wales where the situation was changed in 2005. While previously, non-identifying information (eg physical characteristics, ethnic group, marital status, and whether the donor has other children) was collected by the Register maintained by the

---

51 Section 29. This is in direct contrast to the situation in *X, Y & Z* highlighted above.   52 This, incidentally, had no long term effect on the number of donors who presented. See Mclean and Mclean, 'Keeping secrets in assisted reproduction – the tension between donor anonymity and the need of the child for information' [1996] *CFLQ* 243.   53 For further information see the extensive assisted human reproduction bibliographical database compiled by Professor Ken Daniels of the University of Canterbury, Christchurch, New Zealand, with thanks to my colleague, Dr Deirdre Madden, for this information.   54 See further Roberts, 'A right to right to know for children by donation – any assistance from down under?' 12(4) *CFLQ* (2000) 371.   55 Roberts, op. cit.

Human Fertilisation and Embryology Authority and made available to donor conceived children on reaching 18 years, under new regulations effective since 1 April 2005 the donor's identity (eg name and address) is also entered onto the Register meaning that unless the donor agrees otherwise, the first information will be made available to donor conceived children in 2023.[56]

The Irish position

In the absence of Irish legislation dealing with Assisted Human Reproduction, the child's right to identity is defined only by the Constitution and its case-law relating to anonymity in adoption. In this context, existing case-law does not favour a general right of access to information. In the 1998 case of *O'T v. B*, the Supreme Court recognized that the child has an unenumerated constitutional right to know the identity of his/her mother.[57] However, this right, which flows from the natural and special relationship existing between a mother and her child, is not absolute and must be balanced against the natural mother's constitutional rights to privacy and anonymity. On the facts of the case, the Court held that the mother's right to privacy outweighed that of the child, given what was at stake for her. Interestingly, this case concerned an informal adoption arrangement rather than a full adoption although the Supreme Court referred to legal adoption. In particular, Barron J noted that 'secrecy has always been a paramount consideration in adoption law' and went on to consider that while 'the public attitude to absolute secrecy has been weakened' there does not appear to have been any cases where 'communication has taken place against the wishes of the mother'.[58]

In 2005, the Commission on Assisted Human Reproduction recommended that the process of obtaining the consent of donors should include the information that their identity be kept on record and a resulting child 'may be given access to that record on request'. Accordingly, it recommended that any child born with the use of donor gametes or embryos should 'on maturity be able to identify the donors involved'.[59] The language used here (e.g. 'may be given access') suggests a certain conditionality, in addition to the child reaching the age of majority before access to the information can be sought. It is significant that this recommendation is not underpinned by a clear rights-basis; nor is it accompanied by a clear statement of the importance to children of receiving information about their identity and origins or the extent to which this is in children's best interests. Its view that parents

---

56 A review of the Human Fertilisation and Embryology Act 1990 is underway in Great Britain. For a review of some developments see McClean, 'De-regulating assisted reproduction: some reflections' 7 *Medical Law International* (2006) 233–47. 57 *O'T v. B* [1998] 2 IR 321. A remarkably similar decision was handed down by the European Court of Human Rights in Strasbourg in *Odievre v. France* in 2003. See further below. 58 Ibid., at pp 380–1. 59 *Report of the Commission on Assisted Human Reproduction*, p. 46.

should be encouraged to tell children of the circumstances of their conception but that to enforce this would be impracticable appears unduly
defeatist. It ignores the role that education can play in raising awareness
among parents and donors alike about the child's right to identity. There is
also a clear argument that in the application of the best interests of the child
weight should be attached to this factor – in the form of assessing the
parents' attitude to disclosing this information to any child born – in all
circumstances. The Commission's weak position in this important area
stands in remarkable contrast with its view on the donor's perspective where,
for example, it recognizes that 'it is important for psychological and emotional reasons' for donors to know whether children have resulted from their
donation.[60] In this way, the Commission's report reflects a position out of
line with other jurisdictions and with the similar, although clearly not
identical position of adoption.

International developments and the recent proposals for Irish law are
welcome insofar as they highlight a momentum in favour of full recognition
of the child's right to identity in AHR procedures in line with obligations
under the Convention on the Rights of the Child. However, the picture is
still not complete due to the fact that a child will only ask questions about
his/her origins when prompted to do so. In this regard, the position of
children born to same-sex parents is obviously very different from those born
to a heterosexual couple as the former will be confronted with the dilemma
of their origins without much prompting. In the latter case, however, the
exercise of the child's right to know his/her parents will be almost entirely
dependent on his/her parents first telling him about the nature of his/her
conception. So, without first being told you have been born with the use of
donor gametes, how will you ever know to ask who that donor was? It is not
yet clear whether the amendment to the HEA Act will incorporate such a
duty on parents or if it does, how it might be enforced. Would making access
to AHR services dependent on an agreement to tell the child be too
draconian a step, even where the donor him or herself has agreed to give such
consent? Surely if the right of the child to know his/her origins is to be
practical and effective in the words of the European Court of Human Rights,
something along these lines must be considered. Isn't this required by a truly
child focused approach to AHR?

Even if the law goes so far as to make access to the service conditional on
a more open approach, what about the loopholes that exist? The relatively
exclusive access to assisted human reproduction services in the UK and Ireland
encourages the use of DIY approaches.[61] Enter ManNotIncluded.com, more

60 Ibid, p. 47.   61 See Almack, 'Seeking sperm: accounts of lesbian couples' reproductive
decision-making and understandings of the needs of the child' 20 *International Journal of Law,
Policy and the Family* (2006) 1–22.

recently known as Fertility4Life.com, described on its website as 'the world's only confidential and anonymous sperm donation service'. According to the website, this is 'a non-discriminatory, confidential and totally anonymous sperm donation service available to any woman wishing to conceive, regardless of sexual orientation or marital status' although age restrictions apply. Because insemination takes place 'in the comfort of your own home', and sells fresh sperm (involving no storage) it falls outside the scope of the HFE legislation, which regulates only the activities of UK clinics providing IVF, donor insemination or the storage of eggs, sperm or embryos. So, what has happened to this service since the new regulations come into force there in 2005? The answer is nothing, and this is in fact explicitly stated on the website which also affirms that after health and safety, donor anonymity is the essence of and paramount to the service. Thus, while non-identifying information (eg age, height, weight, hair and eye colour, sexual preference, status, ethnicity, country of origin, current city of residence) about donors is provided, the fact that the sperm is fresh rather than stored means that the service continues to fall outside HFEA regulation. A couple or individual wishing to pursue DI treatment who do not want the complication of having to tell their child the truth of his/her conception may simply logon to the internet based service, no questions asked. It is vital that this loop-hole is closed in future Irish legislation dealing with the area.

Apart from the issue of anonymity, the sale of sperm in one jurisdiction and its purchase and successful use in another raises issues that make even international adoption look uncomplicated. To return to the CRC's definition of identity, in this scenario, the element of unknown or incomplete understanding of one's nationality is added to the complicated question mark over family relations or origins. But what about using the sperm in those jurisdictions which have no statutory provision protecting the child's right to identity or even the AHR process? This is not an unfamiliar dilemma in Ireland where infertility clinics use donor sperm imported mostly from England and from Sweden. What are the implications of the UK regulation in this jurisdiction therefore? Will the sperm come with its identity attached, allowing this information either to be stored by the clinic or passed onto the couple being treated? Or will it remain on the Register in the clinic in England from which it was delivered. Either way, access to information clarifying details of the donor's personal identity and nationality will remain contentious with the child possibly left in the dark in this complicated situation in which he/she has a central role.

One might be tempted to respond that the answers to these questions are far too difficult and complex to tackle. Those who are sceptical of the usefulness of the rights based approach might ask whether it is not for the parents to decide what and when to tell their children about the circumstances of their conception. Or, they might acknowledge, as the current

HFEA Code of Practice does, that a 'potential need' for donor information exists but question whether there is a corresponding right to that information.[62] Difficult as these questions are, the answer is nonetheless relatively straightforward. Supported by considerable research and the development of best practice across the world, the strong consensus emerging is that it is without a doubt not only in children's interests to know the full details of their history (and indeed that of their family) but that an overwhelming number of them request, want and need that information. Moreover, responses to the UK's consultation in this area in 2003 shows some interesting results.[63] While, as might be expected, a high number of those born as a result of assisted human reproduction favoured a more open process, a significant number of those who had received treatment using donor gametes or embryos and the donors themselves also favoured providing access to both identifying and non-identifying information. For those children who are not interested in receiving identifying information about the sperm or egg donor who contributed to their make-up, there is clearly no obligation on them to do so. It is vital, however, in any understanding of human rights and the rights of children in particular, that they are actively given that choice.

Identity in adoption

The Irish constitutional position in relation to adoption has been outlined above. Although it recognizes the child's right to know the identity of his/her mother, this is a right that must be balanced against the mother's constitutional right to privacy.[64] Moreover, the recent consultation process stopped short of giving adopted children a right to their adoption records. While it recognized clearly the need of adoption children to have identifying information, it recommended that this information be passed on to the child's adoptive parents rather than to the child him/herself.[65] With respect to adults wishing to have information about their backgrounds, it recommended that mechanisms be put in place to balance the adopted person's right to information about his/her origins and background while also preserving the constitutional right of the natural parent to anonymity and privacy.[66]

The position in England and Wales, set out in the Adoption and Children Act 2002, is somewhat different. Section 60 provides that an adopted person has the right to information relating to the adoption record once they reach 18 years. However, in practice, few adopted children have to wait until they reach adulthood as it is now well established policy for adoption agencies to

---

62 HFEA, *Code of Practice*, 6th ed. (London, 2003), p. 31. 63 See www.hfea.gov.uk. 64 *O'T v. B*, op. cit. See also Shatter, *Shatter's family law*, op. cit., pp 505–9. 65 Department of Health and Children, *Adoption legislation: 2003 consultation and proposals for change*, pp 64–5.

obtain from couples selected as adoptive parents a commitment to tell their adopted children about the circumstances of their adoption. This is clearly recognized best practice and there would appear to be much that Ireland can learn from the UK in this respect.

Identity under ECHR law

What guidance, then, from the ECHR? There is no express protection for the right to identity in Article 8 or any other Convention provision, although this has not prevented the Court from considering such issues in this context and demonstrating its awareness of the importance of the child's right to identity. In *Gaskin v. UK*, it first recognized expressly the importance for everyone of being able to establish details of their identity as human beings.[67] Gaskin had spent his childhood in care and he sought to challenge the refusal of social services to give him access to the confidential records held on him, something which he alleged violated his Article 8 rights. Weighing up whether this was the case, the court acknowledged on the one hand, the importance of receiving information 'necessary to know and understand ... childhood and early development' and also that persons who have spent the majority of their lives in care have a 'vital interest, protected by the Convention, in receiving that information'.[68] On the other hand, however, the court recognized the contribution which the policy of confidentiality makes to the overall effectiveness of the child care system. It concluded, therefore, that it was not the confidential nature of social services records that violated Article 8, but the lack of independent procedures for determining the merits of individual applications for access to such information.[69]

The court thus stopped short, in *Gaskin*, of finding a general right of access to information about family ties or personal background and found instead that compliance with respect for private life requires the state to put in place an independent system which adjudicates on disputes regarding access to confidential data. Systems of blanket anonymity which operate in the area of adoption law or the law governing artificial reproduction, therefore, will only be Convention compliant where requests for information vital to a person's private life can be determined by an independent procedure.[70]

The Court continued its recognition of the importance to a child of information identifying his or her parents in *Mikulic v. Croatia* in 2002.[71] The five year old applicant and her mother instituted civil proceedings to establish paternity and when the alleged father failed to attend for DNA

66 Ibid., pp 87–94. **67** *Gaskin v. UK*, no. 10454/83, Series A no. 160, 12 EHRR 36. **68** Ibid., para. 49. **69** Se also *MG v. UK*, Admissibility Decision of 3 July 2001. **70** On deficiencies in Irish adoption law see McIntyre, 'Adoption law: the case for reform' (2001) *1 IJFL* 6. See also Kilkelly, 'The reform of Irish adoption law: compliance with international obligations' *IJFL* (2004). **71** No. 53176/99, 7 Feb 2002, unreported.

testing on several occasions, the domestic court gave judgment that this corroborated the mother's testimony that he was the child's father. The applicant argued before the European Court that her right to respect for her private and family life had been violated because the domestic courts had been inefficient in deciding her paternity claim thereby leaving her uncertain as to her personal identity. The Court agreed unanimously and in doing so, it noted that the procedure available to establish paternity, whereby there were no procedural measures to compel the alleged father to comply with the court's order, did not strike a fair balance between the right of the child to have her uncertainty as to her personal identity eliminated without unnecessary delay and that of her supposed father not to undergo a DNA test. Again, the clear message is that the ECHR requires the availability of a mechanism which can weigh up fairly the merits of both the child's and the parent's claims in this area. While proportionality is the device to be used in striking a fair balance, there is more than a suggestion that, from the outset, the scales are tipped in favour of the child whose fundamental right to identity is at stake.

Yet, this position appeared to be ignored when the Court considered the specific issue of access to birth information following adoption in *Odievre v. France* in 2003.[72] The applicant submitted that her inability to trace her birth mother, who had abandoned her at birth and expressly requested that information about the birth remain confidential, violated her rights under Article 8. Rejecting her complaint, the Grand Chamber held that the French legislation, which entitled adopted children to certain non-identifying information about their birth parents but prohibited contact where birth parents withheld consent, struck a proportionate balance between the competing interests given the wide margin of appreciation enjoyed by the State in this complex and sensitive area. There was, accordingly, no violation of Article 8.

This decision can be criticized for a number of reasons. First, the main basis for the Court's conclusion was the wide margin of appreciation which it afforded to France in this area notwithstanding that the concept of anonymous births, which is at the heart of the judgment, is relatively rare throughout Europe. In fact, as the Court noted, a far greater number of states actually *require* the names of both mother and father to be registered at birth and so the exceptional nature of the French approach should not have entitled the State to such wide discretion in this area. In addition, legislation passed in France in 2002 has put in place a national authority with the power to determine requests from adopted children and their birth parents for identifying information and to assist those seeking to trace birth relatives. This legislation, the court acknowledged, may well entitle the applicant to contact her birth mother and thus the practical value and relevance of the *Odievre* judgment is questionable.

---

72 No. 42326/98, 13 Feb 2003, unreported.

It is perhaps more significant that the court's judgment was supported by a slim majority of ten votes to seven and that four of the majority wrote separate opinions. Moreover, the view of the minority – that the court had failed to give proper consideration to whether France had reached an appropriate balance between the parties in the light of the clearly established importance of birth information to adopted children – is clearly a more accurate reflection of international law and best practice on the issue of secrecy in adoption. Rather than acknowledging, as the majority did, that contacting birth parents is a risky process for all parties, the minority view, more correctly it is submitted, recognizes the suffering that lack of information about family origins can cause. It thereby coincides more readily with other standards in international law, including both the Hague Convention on Intercountry Adoption and the Convention on the Rights of the Child, both of which attach importance to the right to birth information. The narrow context of the circumstances prevalent in *Odievre* and the apparent flaws in that judgment clearly undermine its value. In any event, the judgment itself does nothing to diminish the well established precedents of *Gaskin* and *Mikulic*, which are entirely consistent with the court's emphasis on providing mechanisms within which a fair balance between competing rights may be independently determined. It is to these judgments that attention should turn, therefore, on the issue of birth information and contact.

Both *Mikulic* and *Gaskin* recognize the importance to children of accessing information about their identity, their origins and the identity of their birth parents. Neither judgment suggested that the applicants were entitled to this information as a matter of absolute right, but rather interpreted the duty of the State as one to put in place an independent authority whose function it is to determine the merits of the applicants' claims to such information. In order to be compatible with the Convention, therefore, the function of this mechanism is to achieve an appropriate balance between the rights of the individuals concerned (children, birth parents and adoptive parents) and the public interest in maintaining the integrity of a confidential system of information in whom the public and the parties can have confidence. The principle of proportionality is the standard to be used when deciding whether ex post facto a child should have access to information relating to their birth and identity.

CONCLUSION

What this paper makes clear is that while attention has to date focussed on the adult perspective on committed relationships and the framework that suits the Irish legal system and social context, there is a lot of work to be done in giving careful consideration to the multitude of many challenging children's rights issues that are also at stake. Issues of identity are particularly problematic here and currently, Irish law and proposals for law reform do not appear to be fully compliant with Ireland's international obligations and best practice. At the same time, the question arises as to what level of protection the child's right to identity receives even in those jurisdictions which pass on identity information to adopted or donor conceived children insofar as the vindication of the child's right to identity appears only to take place once childhood is over.

Despite the difficult and sensitive nature of the issues addressed here, accepting well established international principles and best practice is a good place to start when tackling them – the principle of non-discrimination, best interests of the child and the child's rights to a safe, secure family environment, the right to know his/her parents and the right to enjoy social and economic rights including maintenance and succession – these are provisions of the Convention on the Rights of the Child which Ireland, through ratification, has committed itself to implement. It is also important to remember that like many things in this world, these situations are not of children's making. As an absolute minimum, they should not be made to suffer the consequences.

Committed non-marital couples and the Irish Constitution

EOIN CAROLAN

CONFORMING IN ITS CIVIL and political protections to the classical tenets of liberal democratic thought, the Irish Constitution, in its stated societal vision, draws instead on the very different teachings of Catholic social policy. This oft-identified philosophical faultline has led the courts to interpret the text in a politically liberal but socially conservative manner. Adopting a highly traditional conception of society, the Constitution proclaims the married nuclear family as the foundational unit of civil society, requiring the State, *inter alia*, to respect parental authority in matters of moral, religious and social education, and to defend the institution of marriage 'with special care'.[1] Expressly envisaging the married family as a privileged institution of social and moral significance, it is scarcely surprising that the courts, in their interpretation of the Constitution, have found little support for alternative formulations of the family. Conjugal cohabitees, extended family units and same-sex couples can invoke, in the courts' view, only those rights to which they are residually entitled as individuals.[2] The family-type units which they form, falling outside the document's designated paradigm, receive no constitutional recognition.

CHANGING SOCIAL CIRCUMSTANCES

Across the common law world however, such enduring social orthodoxies are under pressure. Declining support for the traditional understanding of marriage; the increasing separation of sexual relationships from their historically central procreative purpose; the growing social acceptance of the legitimacy of homosexual couples; and the proliferation of non-traditional family forms all pose significant challenges for the narrow, conventional conception of the family found in Articles 41 and 42. The Constitution's

---

* I would like to thank Roderic O'Gorman and Dr Ailbhe O'Neill for their helpful suggestions, and Gillian McNally for her comments on, and assistance with, the writing of this article. Any errors are obviously my own.   1 Article 41.3.1.   2 *State (Nicolaou) v. An Bord Uchtála* [1966] IR 567.

continued insistence on the married family as the basic unit of Irish society rings increasingly hollow in an environment when one in three births now occur outside marriage.[3] The shifting nature of society has placed these articles 'under … strain'.[4] Inspired by what appears to be an increasingly anachronistic understanding of society, there is a clear risk that Articles 41 and 42 may come to be regarded as an embarrassing irrelevance; at best naively aspirational; at worst a hopelessly outdated impediment to reform. There is an obvious difficulty with a situation whereby constitutional provisions which purport to protect the basic institutional structures of our society fail to reflect the realities of everyday life – or, even more problematically – in fact inhibit attempts to regulate contemporary realities. The Constitution Review Group, for example, has urged that these articles be updated in order to accommodate current social trends. In the absence of such a constitutional amendment however, it will likely fall to the courts to address the problems posed by the changing social conceptions of the family.

This topic is clearly a question of enormous social significance and, as such, ought to be debated in primarily political and social terms. Legislators and policymakers ought to play the leading role in any attempt to redefine the basic constituent elements of our society. However, the experience in many common law countries has been that it is the courts who often find themselves asked to form a putative vanguard for such reforms. This is not a new development. For many years the courts in Ireland and elsewhere have already had to confront the difficulties caused by legislative inactivity on the issue of unmarried cohabiting couples, seeking to provide some level of fiscal protection to those individuals unjustly exposed to economic hardship upon the break-up of the relationship.[5] Yet in recent years the courts in Canada,[6] South Africa[7] and elsewhere[8] have also been asked to adjudicate on the more controversial question of the social and legal status of same-sex unions. In several jurisdictions, the courts have extended the common law definition of marriage to include such couples, thereby effecting a very significant change in the social policies of those states. In each case, the decision to recast the traditional concept of marriage in more expansive terms rested on what the court construed as the constitutional impermissibility of denying individual's

---

3 Central Statistics Office, *Vital Statistics: Fourth Quarter and Yearly Summary 2004* (Dublin, 2005).   4 Hogan & Whyte (eds), *Kelly's The Irish Constitution* (Dublin, 2003), at 1829.   5 See, for example, *L. v. L.* [1992] 2 IR 77.   6 *EGALE Canada Inc. v. Canada* (2003) 225 DLR (4th) 472; 2003 BCCA 251: *Halpern v. Canada* (2003) 225 DLR (4th) 529; 65 O.R. (3d) 161 (C.A.); *Hendricks v. Quebec Procureur Général* [2002] RJQ 2506; *Barbeau v. British Columbia* (2003) 225 DLR (4th) 472 (BCCA); *Dunbar & Edge v. Yukon* 2004 YKSC 54.   7 *Fourie v. Minsiter for Home Affairs* 2005 (3) BCLR 241 (SCA).   8 See, for example, *Goodridge v. Department of Public Health* 440 Mass 309 (2003); 798 NE 2nd 941, and *Standhart v. Superior Court of Arizona* 206 Ariz. 276; 77 P.3d 451(2003).

'access to an institution that all agree is vital to society, ... central to social life and human relationships ... [and] central to our self-definition as humans'.[9] Such an exclusionary approach was held to infringe the constitutional rights of the affected individual citizens. Thus it was the courts, through their interpretation of their respective constitutional texts, that ultimately took responsibility for amending and updating the normative understanding of marriage, the family and society. With the *Zapone* litigation due for hearing before the High Court in the upcoming months, the Irish courts may too find themselves forced to address these important social issues.

In her extensive consideration of the changing concept of marriage, Bailey noted that:

> The western legal culture pattern of legal reform that has taken place [in these areas] has included: a) the introduction of no-fault divorce; b) legal equality of husband and wife in relation to marital and parental rights and obligations; c) decriminalization of homosexuality; d) prohibition of discrimination on the basis of sex or sexual orientation; e) recognition of heterosexual cohabiting couples for 'negative' reasons, e.g., a live-in partner might disqualify a party from government benefits; f) a reduction in 'family' benefits and increase in 'individual' benefits; g) recognition of heterosexual cohabiting couples for 'positive' reasons, e.g., for some government or employee benefits; h) extension of some government or employee benefits and some marital or 'parental' rights and obligations to same-sex couples; i) introduction of registered partnerships for same-sex couples or for both same-sex and opposite-sex couples; j) move towards same-sex marriage.[10]

On this basis, it seems likely that the debate in Ireland at this point will concentrate chiefly on the provision of some form of legal recognition of committed relationships. In the absence of legislative action in this area (and the recent LRC report[11] suggests that some government legislation could be forthcoming in the near future), those campaigning for reform are likely to turn their attention to the courts, arguing, in particular, that the constitutional entitlements of the citizen warrant some form of legal recognition. However, as a primarily conservative social text, the Irish Constitution – unlike its Canadian and South African equivalents – may represent a significantly less useful vehicle for social reform. In fact, in the document's firm commitment to the protection of marriage as a constitutional norm, it

---

9 2005 (3) BCLR 241 (SCA), at para. 14.   10 Bailey, *Marriage and marriage-like relationships* (Law Commission of Canada, Ottawa, 2000), available at <http://www.lcc.gc.ca/research_project/00_relationships-en.asp> (last visited July 28, 2005).   11 The LRC report is considered in detail by John Mee elsewhere in this volume.

could constitute a significant obstacle to such reforms. The Article 41.3.1 obligation on the State could preclude the establishment of any alternative social institution which might be construed as a threat to the conventional concept of the married family. In addition to the more internationally typical debate over the constitution's capacity to act as the engine of social reform, this article will therefore address the possible negative implications of the Irish constitutional text on any proposed legislative action. Section II of the article will consider this issue. Section I will first, however, examine the extent (if any) to which the Constitution might require the adoption of significant reforms.

THE CONSTITUTION AS A SOURCE OF COMMITTED RELATIONSHIP RIGHTS

The equality guarantee

Irish equality jurisprudence
Marriage, at common law, has been historically defined by reference to the long-standing *Hyde* test – that 'marriage, as understood in Christendom, [is] the voluntary union for life of one man and one woman, to the exclusion of all others'.[12] That this exclusionary conception of marriage applied in Ireland was confirmed by Costello J's description of the institution as 'the voluntary and permanent union of one man and one woman to the exclusion of all others for life'.[13] As the sole domestic judicial authority on this question, is to be assumed that this represents the current Irish constitutional orthodoxy.

This conventional characterization of marriage evidently deprives homo-sexuals of access to this important social institution, thereby constituting a clear case of unequal treatment. The Canadian and South African cases on this issue have therefore centred chiefly (and successfully) on the equality guarantees in each state. The courts in each jurisdiction regarded the traditional *Hyde* test as an unjustifiable infringement of 'the values which underlie an open and democratic society based on freedom and equality'.[14] In Irish terms, the *prima facie* objectionability of such an exclusionary approach is, arguably, only exacerbated by marriage's elevated Article 41.3 status. If marriage is indeed, as our Constitution ordains, a normatively superior method of social arrangement, the *Hyde* definition automatically denies some citizens the opportunity to arrange their affairs in the

---

12 *Hyde v. Hyde & Woodmansee* (1866) 1 P. & D. 130, at 133.   13 *B. v. R.* [1996] 3 IR 549, at 554.   14 Mosikatsana, 'The definitional exclusion of gays and lesbians from family status' (1996) 12 *SAJHR* 549 566, cited with approval in *Fourie & Bonthuys v. Minister for Home Affairs*, at para. 16.

constitutionally-celebrated manner because of their sexual orientation. The impact of so narrowly-drawn a definition on these individuals is considerable. '[D]enied access to a central social institution ... gays and lesbians are effectively excluded from full membership of society.'[15]

Article 40.1 however, as the Irish courts have repeatedly affirmed, is not a guarantee of absolute equality. On the contrary, it insists only that 'we treat equals equally and unequals unequally'.[16] Furthermore, Article 40.1 expressly provides for the possibility of disparate treatment where such discrimination is based on 'differences of capacity, moral and physical, and of social function'. Thus textually constrained, the article's impact has been further affected by the tentative way in which it has been traditionally interpreted by the courts. 'Sidelined by ... restrictive judicial interpretation',[17] the article's constitutional utility was severely hampered by the courts' insistence that it covered only 'the essentials of the concept of human personality',[18] thereby exempting a wide range of inequalities from constitutional challenge.

The effective abandonment in recent times of the restrictions imposed by the human personality and invidious discrimination doctrines has, to a certain extent, freed Article 40.1 from the fetters of its underdeveloped past. It remains, however, a constitutional guarantee of comparatively limited value. The most recent Supreme Court cases have tended to favour the adoption of a rationality-type standard of review, according to which 'equality-derogating classifications are legitimate where they effect a legitimate legislative purpose'.[19] Where the discrimination arises from an essential human attribute – such as sexual orientation – it has been argued that the burden of proof rests on the State.[20] Although the adoption of this standard of review does represent a significant advance on the traditional Irish approach to this issue, it lags far behind the higher strict scrutiny standards applied in other jurisdictions to cases of asserted inequality – especially those based on inherent personal characteristics such as orientation.[21]

More pertinently, the text of Article 40.1 makes clear that considerations of moral capacity and social function can constitute a legitimate legislative purpose in this context. Involving, as this debate does, questions of social utility and moral belief, these textual qualifications on the equality guarantee are likely to loom large in any judicial examination of this issue.

15 Thomas J, dissenting, in *Quilter v. A.G.* [1998] 1 NZLR 523.   16 *de Burca v. A.G.* [1976] IR 38, at 68.   17 Hogan & Whyte, op. cit., at 1324–5.   18 *Quinn's Supermarket v. A.G.* [1972] IR 1, at 31.   19 Doyle, *Constitutional equality law* (Dublin, 2004), at 110.   20 *See* Hogan & Whyte, op. cit., at 1356–60.   21 The US courts, for example, have, since *United States v. Carolene Products Co.* 304 US 144 (1938) applied a 'strict scrutiny' standard to discriminatory legislation based on such 'suspect characteristics' (*Regents of the University of California v. Bakke* 438 US 265 (1978)).

The moral capacity of same-sex couples

Turning first to the question of moral capacity, the decision of the Supreme Court in *Norris v. A.G.*[22] provides a clear, if controversial, authority for the proposition that homosexual couples are in some way morally inferior to their heterosexual counterparts. O'Higgins CJ, in the leading majority judgment, regarded this as a self-evident truth, remarking that 'homosexual conduct is, of course, morally wrong, and has been so regarded by mankind through the centuries'.[23] These *dicta* would plainly support the argument that the exclusion of homosexuals from the common law definition of marriage is justified on the basis of their differing moral capacity. The Chief Justice noticeably failed to articulate the rationale or reasons underpinning his position, relying instead on its apparent intuitive appeal. The invocation by O'Higgins CJ of such ostensibly self-evident moral values appears suspiciously similar to the reliance by the judge on his own personal beliefs. Is this an example of judicial subjectivity masquerading as objective self-evidence?[24]

On the one hand, O'Higgins CJ's judgment does appear to proceed from his own strong personal views. On the other hand, however, it has to be accepted that the Irish Constitution's clear affirmation of a Christian moral code offers some support for his position. Costello J, for example, derived the Irish constitutional understanding of marriage from the 'Christian notion of a partnership based on an irrevocable personal consent'.[25] Christian morality has traditionally regarded homosexual practices as in some way morally inferior to the heterosexual paradigm. Even today, when the Catholic Church speaks of the necessity to treat its homosexual members with 'respect, compassion and sensitivity', it continues to regard any legal recognition of same-sex couples as inevitably tending to 'obscure certain basic moral values'.[26]

Nonetheless, the Christian consensus on the moral inferiority of same-sex relationships is beginning to break down. Although the recognition of such relationships remains a highly divisive issue, some Christian churches have moved to acknowledge the moral worth and value of committed same-sex couples.[27] Any analysis of the moral capacity of such couples is clearly a

---

22 [1984] IR 36. 23 [1984] IR 36, at 64. 24 This echoes the unsatisfactory way in which this concept was used by the Supreme Court in *State (Nicoloau) v. An Bord Uchtala* [1966] IR 567 where Walsh J, overlooking the obviously concerned character of the applicant, held that, in his view, unmarried fathers lack moral capacity. Walsh J based this view not on any statistics but on his own self-evident view, at 641, that 'it is rare for a natural father to take any interest in his offspring'. 25 [1985] IR 532, at 536. 26 Extracts taken from the speech of Archbishop Sean Brady on 'Supporting Marriage and the Family', delivered at the Irish Bishops' Conference on Supporting Marriage and Family Life, May 3, 2004. *See* <http://www.catholiccommunications.ie/marriageandfamily2004/archbishopseanbrady.html> (last visited June 22, 2005). 27 The Unitarian Universalist Church, Quaker faith, and United Church of Christ already allow same-sex marriage ceremonies to occur in their churches while the Methodist Church in Britain offers same-sex blessings. The decision by the Diocese of Westminster in British Columbia to

more complicated undertaking than it may have been at the time of the *Norris* case. It is likely that a court seeking to rely today on any asserted differences of moral capacity would have to expound a more sophisticated explanation of the basis of its decision.

On a more abstract level, such a court could also have to establish sufficient justification for their ability to involve itself in, what is increasingly regarded as a matter of purely private interest. The general entitlement of the State to define and determine moral standards is no longer unquestioned. The reference in Article 40.1 to differences of moral capacity dates from an era when State intervention in the normative regulation of family structures was a common feature of contemporary legal systems. The prohibition of judicial divorce was an example of the tendency of governments to inhibit the development of alternative forms of the family, thereby indirectly ensuring the primacy of the preferred marital model. Over time, however 'prescriptive laws regulating family structure [became] increasingly perceived as ineffective and illegitimate', leading to the removal of such restrictions in most jurisdictions – thereby 'marking the withdrawal of the state from normative interventions into family life'.[28] The removal of the long-standing constitutional ban on divorce could be construed as the belated beginning of a similar trend in Irish law and society. The continuing emergence of alternative family structures would corroborate this claim. It is thus questionable whether the State or courts should continue to attempt to unilaterally dictate the dominant moral norms and values of Irish society.

Obviously, the constitutional reference to moral capacity remains. However, a contemporary court could prove reluctant to invoke it in litigation on this, or any other, issue. In the absence of a clear moral consensus, curial considerations of moral standards can lead to the institution of personal beliefs as constitutional norms. Such a development would be manifestly undesirable. Furthermore, a court may wish to take account of changing social attitudes, in particular the growing resistance to the notion that the State is entitled to dictate what constitutes a central moral value.

The social function of marriage

While a general acceptance of the capacity of the State to invoke moral values in support of its conduct may no longer exist, there remains a societal

---

allow such marriage ceremonies has polarized the Anglican congregation. See, for example, Harmon, 'Anglicanism at the crossroads', *The Guardian*, 19 February 2005, and Bates, 'Vengeance in the air as churches face expulsion', *The Guardian*, 22 June 2005. Although the Catholic Church officially opposes homosexual conduct, it should also be noted that McWilliam J accepted in *Norris v. A.G.* the existence of 'responsible Christian theologians who question the interpretation of the scriptures which condemn homosexual acts outright' [1984] IR 36, at 42. This is obviously only indirectly relevant to the issue of same-sex marriage but does illustrate the point that Christian, even Catholic, theology does not present a monolithic front.   28 Bailey, op. cit.

acknowledgment of the ability of the government to consider the social status and utility of a class of citizens in its legislative enactments. An analysis of the 'social function' of marriage and of same-sex couples is therefore relevant to any examination of Article 40.1 in this context.

The social utility of the institution of marriage is widely accepted but rarely defined. Marriage is perceived, both in law and at large, as a socially valuable form of familial arrangement but this approving societal consensus often conceals a surprising lack of agreement as to the objectives which it purports to achieve. Bailey lists the objectives of marriage as follows:

   a) Procreation.
   b) Provision of a stable and nurturing environment for children.
   c) Provision of a social support system.
   d) Social stability and cohesion.

It is immediately obvious that these objectives incline in different directions with regard to the legal status of same-sex couples. The extension of the definition of marriage to include same-sex couples would encourage social stability and cohesion (sub-heading d), as well as providing a recognized social support system, thereby enhancing the level of social protection available to vulnerable individuals (sub-heading c). The depiction of marriage as a primarily procreative institution, on the other hand, would tend to favour the continued restriction of the definition to opposite-sex couples who are inherently capable of 'natural' procreation.[29] It is thus necessary to examine the Irish courts' understanding of the purposes of marriage before undertaking any analysis of the social function of homosexual couples.

Although the Irish courts have never expressly considered this question, the majority of the caselaw tends to connect the Constitution's protection of marriage with its procreative purpose. Budd J in *McGee* defended the citizen's right to marry in stridently child-centred terms, characterising it as the 'important personal right [of the individual] ... to determine in marriage his attitude and resolve his mode of life concerning the procreation of children'.[30] This emphasis on the couple's reproductive capacity was echoed by Costello J in his description of the 'procreation and education of children' as an 'especially ordained' element of the constitutional concept of marriage[31]. Kenny J, similarly, upheld the State's assertion in *Murphy* that married couples served a differing social function by reference to 'the vital roles under the Constitution of married couples as parents, or potential parents'.[32]

---

29 The capacity of such couples to provide a stable and nurturing environment is a matter of much sociological debate and is outside the scope of this article.   30 *McGee v. The Attorney General* [1974] IR 284, at 322.   31 [1985] IR 532, at 536.   32 [1982] IR 241, at 284.

That is not to say however that the Constitution envisages the married family in purely reproductive terms. The attempt by the Attorney General to confine the protection of Articles 41 and 42 to couples with children was rejected by Costello J in *Murray v. Ireland*. The judge felt that the constitutional definition of the family, although restricted to married couples, could not be further confined to those to whom children had already been born:

> A married couple without children can properly be described as a 'unit group' of society such as is referred to in Article 41 and the life-long relationship to which each married person is committed is certainly a 'moral institution'. The words used in the article to describe the 'Family' are therefore apt to describe both a married couple with children and a married couple without children.[33]

This broader definition of the constitutional concept of marriage, in its emphasis on notions of lifelong commitment and social cohesion, does not appear to *prima facie* exclude same-sex couples. Evidently, Costello J's comments were not directed at this issue. However, the objectives which he describes as underlying the constitutionally privileged position of marriage would appear to apply equally to claims for the legal recognition of homosexual unions. Such couples are perfectly capable of forming a stable, lifelong association which, like a childless married union, serves the socially valuable objectives of societal cohesion and individual protection. If the courts were to interpret marriage in light of these objectives, it would be much more difficult for the State to claim legitimate legislative justification for the existing inequalities, even when relying on asserted differences of social function.

It is clear therefore that the court's choice of interpretation of the purpose of marriage is crucial to any assessment of the alleged justification for the current inequality of access to the institution of marriage between heterosexual and homosexual couples. The North American jurisprudence on this topic confirms the pivotal importance of this question of purposive interpretation. Whereas the Supreme Court in *Egan v. Canada*[34] viewed marriage in primarily procreative terms, the Ontario Court of Appeal in *Halpern* concentrated instead on the symbolism of this type of public commitment. This divergence of initial emphasis underpins the differing conclusions to which the two courts came.

La Forest J, for the majority in *Egan*, maintained that:

---

33 [1985] IR 532, at 537.   34 (1995) 124 DLR (4th) 609.

> [marriage's] ultimate *raison d'être* transcends [religious and philo-
> sophical traditions] and is firmly anchored in the biological and social
> realities that heterosexual couples have the unique ability to procreate,
> that most children are the product of these relationships, and that they
> are generally cared for and nurtured by those who live in that
> relationship.[35]

The majority felt that it was perfectly acceptable for the legislature to
discriminate between heterosexual and homosexual couples.

The *Halpern* court instead favoured an understanding of marriage
premised, not on its social role, but on its importance to the individual
citizen.

> Marriage is, without dispute, one of the most significant forms of
> personal relationships ... Through the institution of marriage, individ-
> uals can publicly express their love and commitment to each other.
> Through this institution, society publicly recognizes expressions of
> love and commitment between individuals, granting them respect and
> legitimacy as a couple. This public recognition and sanction of marital
> relationships reflects society's approbation of the personal hopes,
> desires and aspirations that underlie loving, committed conjugal
> relationships.[36]

The decision of the Massachusetts Supreme Court in *Goodridge*[37] again
illustrates the decisive influence of this initial definitional step. Marshall CJ,
for the majority, emphasized the importance of community recognition of
marriage, insisting that:

> extending civil marriage to same-sex couples reinforces the importance
> of marriage to individuals and communities. That same-sex couples are
> willing to embrace marriage's solemn obligations of exclusivity, mutual
> support, and commitment to one another is a testament to the enduring
> place of marriage in our laws and in the human spirit.[38]

On the other hand, Cordy J, for the three-judge minority, presented marriage
as 'the important legal and normative link between heterosexual intercourse
and procreation on the one hand and family responsibilities on the other',
and therefore went on to hold that the exclusion of same-sex couples from
the legal conception of marriage was a rational and permissible means of
furthering a legitimate state objective.

---

35 (1995) 124 DLR (4th) 609, at 625.   **36** (2003) 225 DLR (4th) 529, at 538.   **37** *Goodridge v.
Department of Public Health* 440 Mass 309 (2003).   **38** 440 Mass 309 (2003), at 337.

As long as marriage is limited to opposite sex couples who can at least theoretically procreate, society is able to communicate a consistent message to its citizens that marriage is a (normatively) necessary part of their procreative endeavour ... If society proceeds similarly to recognize marriages between same-sex couples who cannot procreate, it could be perceived as an abandonment of this claim, and might result in the mistaken view that civil marriage has little to do with pro-creation: just as the potential of procreation would not be necessary for a marriage to be valid, marriage would not be necessary for optimal procreation and child rearing to occur.[39]

In a very real sense therefore, the court's interpretation of the purposes of marriage can conclusively determine the outcome of a challenge to the exclusion of same-sex couples from the institution.

Which understanding of marriage is an Irish court likely to adopt? The *Halpern* approach, rooted as it is in a concern chiefly for the needs and entitlements of the individual citizen, is, perhaps, less obviously attuned to the philosophical or social outlook of a constitutional text which expressly and sonorously proclaims the societal benefits of the institution of marriage. This is especially so in the context of an Article 40.1 challenge, where the focus of the analysis is on the asserted social function of the institution and, accordingly, of those claiming access to it. The existing domestic authorities, taken together with the textual juxtaposition of the marriage guarantee with the constitutional provisions relating to the education and upbringing of children, would appear to regard marriage as a predominantly procreative concept. Given the bare rationality threshold employed by the Irish courts in this area, it is probable that an Irish court would therefore, in reliance on their different procreative capacity, uphold the exclusion of same-sex couples from the institution of marriage as a legitimate legal position in light of their differing social function.

Right to privacy

Another right often invoked in the context of conjugal debates is the constitutional entitlement of the individual to respect for his or her sexual privacy. Nonetheless, the obviously negative implications of this 'right to be let alone', as McCarthy J described it in *Norris*,[40] deprive it of any utility in this area. In strictly Hohfeldian terms, the right to privacy is, more correctly, a legal immunity which removes the ability of the State to regulate the matter in question. It thus imposes a legal disability on the State rather than the sort of positive duty to act more typically associated with constitutional rights. It

---

39 440 Mass 309 (2003), at 391.   40 [1984] IR 36, at 101, quoting Brandeis J with approval.

is therefore clearly irrelevant to any claim that the Constitution obliges the State to provide any form of legal recognition for committed non-marital relationships.

Dignity and autonomy – is there a right to recognition?

The importance of marriage to the individual
An alternative ground of challenge to the existing constitutional conception of marriage could arise under the Article 40.3.1 personal rights guarantee. Various personal values – in particular the autonomy and dignity of the individual – have been considered in the context of this debate. The *Halpern* and *Fourie* courts both regarded the *Hyde* definition of marriage as an unconstitutional affront to the dignity of the homosexual citizen.

Dignity, in Irish constitutional terms, is, however, something of an underdeveloped ideal. Denham J in *In re Ward of Court (No. 2)*[41] expressly acknowledged it as an actual right, inherent in the individual, rather than as a significant social value. Nonetheless, she failed to further define this newly-recognized *right* to dignity, and it has not been successfully invoked in any subsequent case. Taking account of these considerations, it would not appear prudent to base a constitutional challenge on this ground.

However, the dignity of the individual – to which the Preamble refers – remains a constitutionally-significant value, and one which could more usefully be relied upon as an aspect of an asserted right to marry. Affirmed in *Murray* as an aspect of Article 40.3., this right to marry might be more precisely termed, in the context of the present debate, the right of the individual to the legal recognition and protection of his or her marriage-like relationship.

The South African Supreme Court of Appeal outlined this argument at some length:

> At issue is access to an institution that all agree is vital to society and central to social life and human relationships. More than this, marriage and the capacity to get married remain central to our self-definition as humans ... The capacity to choose to get married enhances the liberty, the autonomy and the dignity of a couple committed for life to each other. It offers them the option of entering an honourable and profound estate that is adorned with legal and social recognition, rewarded with many privileges and secured by many automatic obligations. It offers a social and legal shrine for love and for commitment and for a future shared with another human being to the exclusion of all others.

41 [1996] 2 IR 79.

The current common law definition of marriage deprives committed same-sex couples of this choice. In this our common law denies gays and lesbians who wish to solemnize their union a host of benefits, protections and duties ... More deeply, the exclusionary definition of marriage injures gays and lesbians because it implies a judgment on them. It suggests not only that their relationships and commitments and loving bonds are inferior, but that they themselves can never be fully part of the community of moral equals that the Constitution promises to create for all.[42]

Unlike equality-based arguments, which founder on the Irish Constitution's express acknowledgment of the social benefits peculiar to the traditional conception of marriage, this type of argument turns this characterisation of marriage as a central social good to its advantage by presenting access to this socially-significant institution as an essential aspect of human personhood. The denial of such access, therefore, is argued to represent an illegitimate restriction on the individual's civic and constitutional entitlements.

This applies whether the Article is interpreted as an acknowledgment of the individual or public interest in the encouragement of marriage. If the court adopts an individualistic perspective, these entitlements are argued to derive from the freedom, dignity and autonomy of the individual citizen, who, it is asserted, ought to be able to secure social and legal recognition of his choice of committed relationship. If the court instead interprets the Article 41.3.1. guarantee in terms of its beneficial impact on society, it is more difficult to identify the utility involved in refusing to recognize relationships capable of securing what the Constitution dictates are socially valuable objectives. Thus, it becomes much more difficult to contend that the common good or social interest precludes any recognition of these relationships.

This argument again necessitates an examination of the social purposes of the institution of marriage, outlined above. The focus of this analysis does, however, differ significantly. The question, in terms of Article 40.1., concerned only the capacity of the State to distinguish between homosexual and heterosexual couples. Equality claims aspire only to a parity of treatment, rather than to any substantive individual entitlement.[43] The identification of a rational basis for such discrimination exhausts an equality analysis.[44]

---

42 2005 (3) BCLR 241 (SCA), at paras. 14–16.   43 In the unlikely event that the courts held equality to require a bare parity of benefits, the obvious argument would arise that this is an example of the 'separate but equal' reasoning rejected as impermissible by the US Supreme Court in *Brown v. Board of Education* (1954) 347 US 483. Again, this issue would be complicated in Ireland by Article 40. 1.'s references to 'moral capacity' and 'social function', which could be argued to permit such a situation to pass constitutional muster.   44 At least in Ireland. Cf. US caselaw at fn. 21.

The argument for a right to some degree of legal recognition and protection for an individual's committed relationship is, on the contrary, a claim to a positive entitlement, which flows from important constitutional values. Unlike with Article 40.1., it is insufficient for the State to establish a rational reason for favouring married heterosexual couples. Rather, assuming the courts were to find that this right was protected under the Constitution, the State would then have to explain and justify its failure to provide this inherent and essential aspect of individual personhood.

The construction of marriage in primarily procreative terms does not, therefore, conclude the analysis of this issue. Rather, the court is required to consider the asserted social benefits of marriage (or of a marriage-like status) in order to assess the constitutional veracity of the denial of that access to these legal and social advantages which is claimed to constitute personal right under Article 40.3.

The right to marry, as has already been noted, was accepted in *Murray* as falling within Article 40.3. Costello J's understanding of the concept was clearly tied to traditional notions of a heterosexual, procreative partnership – as he later confirmed in *B. v. R.* He did, however, also accept the legitimacy of the childless married couple as a family, or 'unit group' of special constitutional significance. It is clear, therefore, that he did not regard the potential for procreation as the sole justification for the special constitutional status of marriage. Rather, he spoke approvingly of the lifelong nature of the commitment entered into by a married but childless couple, as well as of their status as a 'unit group' of society.

Yet, it could plausibly be argued that a same-sex union, or cohabiting heterosexual couple are equally capable of being described in such terms. Allowing such couples to legitimize their relationships in the eyes of the law would achieve the same objectives of social cohesion, familial stability and the establishment of a social network for the protection of the vulnerable which marriage is claimed to support. The Irish courts have already accepted the economic protection of individual members of the married family as a legitimate objective of the common good.[45] Why then should this protection be denied to individual members of committed, long-term relationships?

Intertwined with this issue of the social justification for a lack of legal recognition of alternative committed relationships is the increasingly

---

45 *In the matter of Article 26 of the Constitution and in the matter of The Matrimonial Home Bill, 1993* [1994] 1 IR 305. Finlay CJ, speaking for the Court, said 'The Court accepts that the provisions of this Bill are directed to encourage the joint ownership of matrimonial homes and that such an objective is clearly an important element of the common good conducive to the stability of marriage and the general protection of the institution of the family' going on to add that 'joint ownership in family homes [is] conducive to the dignity, reassurance and independence of each of the spouses and to the partnership concept of marriage which is fundamental to it', at 325–6.

contentious question of what constitutes 'natural' procreation. The assumption that an emphasis on the procreative aspect of marriage or family life automatically excludes homosexual couples proceeds from a presumption that they are incapable of natural reproduction. Technological advances, coupled with the increasing numbers of infertile heterosexual couples, have, however, called into question traditional conceptions of procreative capacity. As the Ontario Court of Appeal pointed out '[w]hile it is true that, due to biological realities only opposite-sex couples can 'naturally' procreate, same-sex couples can choose to have children by other means, such as adoption, surrogacy and donor insemination'.[46] With increasing numbers of heterosexual couples having to avail of such 'unnatural' methods of procreation, is it appropriate for the courts to treat the single, traditional method of reproduction as somehow socially superior? What justifies such a notion of procreative pre-eminence? And if it is not appropriate, does that not undermine the claim that same-sex unions, in their lack of reproductive capacity, lack the entitlement to some degree of legal recognition?

Qualifications to a constitutional right of recognition

Although this is undoubtedly the strongest constitutional argument available to advocates of Irish reform, its potential utility is constrained by a number of considerations. The first is that an Irish court may feel that the dignity, autonomy and related personal interests invoked could be vindicated by the provision of some lesser form of legal recognition. A statutory regime in which couples would be able to publicly establish their status as a committed relationship, as well as obtain some form of reciprocal economic security, might be regarded by the court as satisfying the essential personal entitlements outlined above. The special position of marriage, taken in conjunction with the received constitutional view of the concept as a union of man and woman, would, in all likelihood, encourage the court to adopt this position. Such a decision would probably proceed from a view of this issue as a primarily legislative concern. On such an interpretation, the prioritisation of certain family structures would be upheld as a matter within the Oireachtas' margin of appreciation on social affairs.

Obviously, the establishment of some form of legal partnership regime would represent a considerable advance for those committed couples whose relationships remain currently unrecognized. It is arguable, however, that the selection by the State of one form of family unit as a sort of social paradigm implicitly offends the societal validity of all other relationships in the way in which it indirectly envisages them as normatively inferior models. This dignity-based argument found favour with the Ontario Court of Appeal.

46 (2003) 225 DLR (4th) 529, at 558.

Concluding that the exclusion of same-sex couples from the common law definition of marriage – even where they were able to avail of equivalent statutory benefits – constituted a breach of such couples' rights, the Court located this illegitimacy in the manner in which such a two-tier legal approach:

> reflects the stereotypical application of presumed group or personal characteristics, or ... otherwise has the effect of perpetuating or promoting the view that the individual is less capable or worthy of recognition or value as a human being or as a member of Canadian society, equally deserving of concern, respect, and consideration.[47]

A focus on solely statutory benefits overlooks the fact that, for individuals, married status provides advantages which 'are frequently materially valuable but also confers [others] which are relatively intangible, [a]mongst them ... community recognition, status and support'.[48] For the courts to insist only on the legal and economic recognition of committed couples would neglect the importance to the individual of this symbolic status. On balance however, the relative immaturity of the Irish courts' conception of dignity, coupled with the Constitution's expressly-permissive approach to the prioritisation of marriage,[49] makes the success of such an argument unlikely. Article 40.3. may advance the status of committed relationships to a certain extent – but it is unlikely to secure the access to the institution of marriage for such couples upon which some advocates of reform insist.

The second point to bear in mind is that the focus of these allegations of constitutional invalidity is the exclusion of the affected couple from the legal definition of marriage. Cohabiting heterosexual couples are thus unable to challenge the state's lack of legal recognition of their relationship on this ground. The symbolic public status and security of economic and emotional partnership which they seek is at all times available to them through the institution of marriage. There is no absolute state denial of legal recognition. Any automatic extension of the statutory benefits of marriage to such cohabiting couples would, in fact, appear to infringe the very values of dignity and autonomy already at issue. If the state is to be constitutionally obliged, out of concern for these values, to provide legal recognition for the couple's choice of relationship, it is equally required to facilitate those who wish to enter into a committed relationship without acquiring any form of

---

47 (2003) 225 DLR (4th) 529, at 550, quoting Iacobucci J. in *Law v. Canada (Minister for Employment and Immigration)* (1999) 170 DLR (4th) 1; [1999] 1 S.C.R. 497, at 529.   48 New Zealand Human Rights Commission, *The problem of inequality* (2000), available at <http://www.hrc.co.nz/index.php?p=13681&id=13688> (last visited July 26, 2005).   49 The question of whether Article 41.3.1 is, in fact, a constitutional imperative requiring the active promotion of the institution of marriage shall be canvassed below.

public, statutory or constitutional status.[50] The state at present arguably respects the inherent dignity of such cohabiting arrangements by allowing them to freely determine whether they remain outside or opt into the available legal framework for the recognition and acknowledgment of committed relationships. The asserted unconstitutional denial of such acknowledgment evidently only applies to those couples – most notably same-sex relationships – automatically excluded from the state's designated social norm.

Social reform and judicial competence

Of course, the crucial element in any consideration of this issue will be the court's own opinion of their ability to effect what, it must be remembered, would be a significant societal reform. It is telling that those courts in Canada and South Africa which decided to unilaterally extend the definition of marriage regarded themselves as constitutionally-entitled – in fact obliged – to develop and reform traditional social norms. The *Halpern* court expressly adopted what it termed the doctrine of progressive constitutional interpretation. This notion of the constitutional text as a 'living tree capable of growth and expansion within its natural limits' required the Court to amend existing legal rules in order 'to meet new social, political and historical realities often unimagined by its framers'.[51]

The *Fourie* court, meanwhile, delivered its decision in an even more reform-friendly context, relying heavily on the South African Constitution's express direction that it 'must promote the spirit, purport and objects of the Bill of Rights'[52] by 'apply[ing], or if necessary develop[ing], the common law to the extent that [it] does not give effect to th[e Bill of Rights]'.[53] This understanding of the courts as an engine of social change depicts the judiciary as exercising an 'educative function',[54] according to which they are entitled to amend and update legal provisions so that they more accurately echo what the court regards as appropriate social values. Cameron JA was quite clear that the decision in *Fourie* did not reflect the beliefs or opinions of a significant section of South African society. Nevertheless, he felt the Constitution obliged the court to exercise a 'simultaneously creative and declaratory function'[55] under which it ought to give life to the values of the constitutional text by positively reforming the offending legal rules.

---

50 This argument also applies to those homosexual couples who do not wish to avail of what they see as the heterosexually-based concept of marriage. See the discussion of some of the different views of marriage found in the gay community in Clayton, 'Legal recognition of same-sex relationships: where to from here?' (1996) 3 (3) *Murdoch University Electronic Journal of Law*. **51** (2003) 225 DLR (4th) 529, at 546, *per* Lord Sankey in *Edwards v. A.G. Canada* [1930] AC 124, at 136; *per* Dickson J. in *Hunter v. Southam Inc.* [1984] 2 SCR 145, at 155. **52** Section 39 (2). **53** Section 8 (3). **54** Nicholson, 'The changing concept of family: The significance of recognition and protection' (1996) 3(3) *Murdoch University Electronic Journal of Law*, at para. 4. **55** 2005 (3) BCLR 241 (SCA), at para. 23.

The Irish courts, however, have never adopted a progressive canon of constitutional interpretation. The recent jurisprudence of the Supreme Court in fact demonstrates a markedly deferential acceptance of the legislature's pre-eminence in matters of social policy. The decisions in *Sinnott*[56] and *T.D.*[57] indicate an inherent unwillingness on the part of the present Supreme Court to involve itself in questions of *prima facie* legislative competence, even where expressly-guaranteed constitutional rights are at issue. This comparatively conservative outlook could lead the court to regard the legal recognition of same-sex couples as an issue of exclusively legislative concern. The *prima facie* opinion of the majority judges in *T.D.* derived from clearly held a *priorii* conceptions of the courts' limited jurisdiction. It is difficult to confidently predict what might be the Supreme Court's intuitive understanding of the extent of its powers on this issue. Nevertheless, that this matter might require the court to inaugurate an enormously significant and controversial social change may persuade it to adopt a restricted view of its ability to effect such a reform.[58] That the leading Irish political parties have begun to express their approval for such a step may – from the point of view of political pragmatism – further confirm the court in its conservatism.[59] Instinctively reluctant to engage in questions of what it sees as primarily legislative concern, the prospect of an impending statutory solution might convince the current Supreme Court to abjure its involvement in this issue.

THE CONSTITUTION AS A RESTRICTION ON THE RECOGNITION OF COMMITTED RELATIONSHIPS

The obligation to guard marriage with 'special care'

The innate conservatism of the current Supreme Court, combined with the clearly Catholic ethos of *Bunreacht na hÉireann*, makes it much more likely that the Constitution will impact on this matter in a negative way. The increasingly favourable political climate, alluded to above, suggests that a government will soon make some sort of statutory provision for the recognition of committed relationships.[60] If this is to occur, it is probable that

---

56 *Sinnott v. Minister for Education* [2001] 2 IR 505.   **57** *TD v. Minister for Education* [2001] 4 IR 259.   **58** This attitude is evident in the minority decision of Farlam JA in *Fourie*, of the Massachusetts Supreme Court in *Goodridge*, of the British Columbia Court of Appeal in *Egale*, and of the Divisional Court in *Halpern* (215 DLR (4th) 223 (2002)) to find the existing common law definition of marriage to be unconstitutional, but to suspend the effect of their decision for a period of time, so as to allow the legislature to exercise their primary entitlement to rule on this matter.   **59** The Minister for Justice, Michael McDowell, recently announced his intention to legislate for the legal recognition of opposite-sex couples, describing it as a 'question of how rather than if'. See Fitzgerald, 'McDowell to introduce legislation on same-sex couples', *Irish Times*, 29 July 2005.   **60** An alternative approach would be for the Oireachtas to statutorily redefine the legal meaning of the term marriage. However, there is an

the courts will be called upon to consider whether this type of partnership regime infringes any aspect of the constitutional text – specifically the Article 41.3.1 obligation to guard the institution of marriage with special care. Does this article seek to protect married couples from penal or unfavourable treatment? Or is it a constitutional imperative which obliges the State to actively promote the institution of marriage as the primary mechanism of conjugal commitment? Evidently, the analysis of Article 41.3.1 adopted by the courts will have considerable consequences for the constitutional legitimacy of any statutory partnership scheme.

The case law on this article offers varying views of the extent of the obligation it imposes on the State. Henchy J in *Nicoloau* expressed the opinion that Article 41.3.1 precluded any attempt on the part of the State to treat unmarried and married couples in an equivalent manner. He felt that:

> If the solemn guarantees and rights which the Article gives to the family were held to be extended to units of people founded on extra-marital unions, such interpretation would be quite inconsistent with the letter and the spirit of the Article ... [T]o award equal constitutional protection to the family founded on marriage and the 'family' founded on an extra-marital union would in effect be a disregard of the pledge which the State gives in Article 41, s. 3, sub-s. 1 to guard with special care the institution of marriage.[61]

Similarly, Kelly J in the High Court case of *Ennis v. Butterly* insisted that 'non-marital cohabitation ... cannot have the same constitutional status as marriage'.[62] These comments clearly relate only to the enhanced constitutional status of the married couple. That non-marital relationships are denied access to the special rights bestowed on the married family by Articles 41 and 42 does not, of itself, preclude some lesser degree of legal recognition of their commitment.

Kelly J went on to assert, in the context of his consideration of the lack of legislative action on this issue, that 'it would be contrary to public policy, as enunciated in the Constitution, to confer legal rights on persons in non-marital unions akin to those who are married'.[63] Although these comments are *obiter* expressions of personal opinion, they do clearly represent an understanding of Article 41.3.1 as a constitutional imperative to promote and prioritize the institution of marriage. Once again, however, Kelly J does not

obvious argument that this would subvert the intention of the framers of the Constitution, as well as the primacy of the people in the amendment of constitutionally-designated social norms. This approach will not be considered in the context of this piece as it is politically improbable, and, more importantly, raises separate issues of interpretative norms, legislative power and judicial deference which ought to be treated in a fuller manner elsewhere.
61 [1966] IR 567, at 622.   62 [1996] 1 IR 426, at 438.   63 Ibid., at 439.

exclude the possibility of some form of legal recognition. Rather, he proffers the opinion that any such statutory rights must be clearly inferior to those to which married couples are entitled. Kelly J's judgment appears to rule out the possibility of a system of statutory equivalence.

On the other hand, other decisions of the Supreme Court do not seem to share this apparent insistence on maintaining marriage in a legally privileged position. The decisions in *Murphy* and *Muckley* seemed instead to envisage the article solely as a guarantee that married couples would not be penalized as a result of their status. This implied that parity of treatment between married and unmarried couples would be constitutionally permissible. In fact, Finlay CJ expressly rejected the suggestion in *Muckley* that Article 41.3.1 obliged the State to ensure that it did not effectively induce couples to remain in a non-marital relationship.

> It was submitted on behalf of the defendants that the decision of this Court … [in *Murphy*] was based on the acceptance by the Court of a submission … that these sections constituted an inducement to men and women to live together without entering into a contract of marriage, or, if married, to separate to avoid the increased burden of taxation … This is to misunderstand the essential basis of the decision of the Court in *Murphy's Case* … Essentially the decision is to the effect that the invalid sections *penalized* the married state.[64]

The primacy of this 'penalty' test was, however, undermined by the decision of Carroll J. in *Mhic Mhathúna*[65] when she, without reference to the earlier authorities, appeared to resurrect the language of inducements. Although Carroll J rejected the applicant's challenge, she considered the impact of the impugned sections of the social welfare code in terms of the possibility that they would encourage a woman to bear a child out of marriage so as to obtain the unmarried mother's allowance. On the facts, she found that the comparatively greater monetary value of this allowance reflected the difficulties involved in raising a child alone and did not constitute an impermissible inducement not to marry.

Consequences of the courts' approach

The caselaw thus fails to provide a clear impression of the parameters of the Article 41.3.1 guarantee. The Supreme Court authorities favour a restricted understanding of the State's obligation to guard marriage with special care, insisting only that married couples not be disadvantaged as a result of their union. This interpretation of the Article, with its limited requirement of a

---

64 [1985] IR 472, at 484. Emphasis added.   65 [1989] IR 504.

parity of esteem, would evidently pose few problems for a statutory partnership regime. The *Murphy* and *Muckley* line of authority therefore appears to allow the State to institute such a scheme, provided that the legal, social or economic benefits it proffers do not exceed those available to married couples.

The alternative understanding of Article 41.3.1 as an acknowledgment of the State's obligation to secure the position of marriage as the preferred model of conjugal commitment evidently poses greater problems for any purported statutory reform. The inducement test affirms the special status of marriage in constitutional terms. However, Carroll J's decision in *Mhic Mhathúna* should not be interpreted as a denial of the entitlement of the State to legislate for alternative forms of family arrangement. Rather this decision appears to posit an understanding of Article 41.3.1 according to which the State is not obliged to consistently prioritize, and therefore favour, the married family in all its enactments. On the contrary, it can extend significant benefits to non-married families in particular instances where such preferential treatment is justified, provided that the overall effect of such actions is not to establish a more attractive model of family life. The inducement test does not inhibit the ability of the Oireachtas to support such family units. What it does do, however, is to impose limits on the extent of such support.

These limits may vary as regards the recognition of same-sex and opposite-sex cohabiting couples. The Irish courts have repeatedly recognized the reality that homosexuality is a congenital and irreversible aspect of the human personality of some citizens.[66] The extension of benefits equivalent to those available to married couples to such individuals could not in any way be regarded as an inducement to them not to marry, given their automatic exclusion from the existing understanding of the institution of marriage.

It is feasible however that the courts could interpret the extension of such benefits to cohabiting heterosexual couples as an impermissible inducement to such couples not to marry. This would clearly depend on the details of any legislative proposals. If, however, the courts construed the advantages of such a partnership scheme as approximating to those to which married couples are currently entitled, they could regard that as an attack upon the institution of marriage. This would tally, for example, with Kelly J's *Butterly* insistence that cohabiting couples could not be given the same legal rights as married families. Even Carroll J's less stringent inducement test could be regarded as requiring cohabiting couples to be treated in a less favourable manner. Equivalence, it could be argued, could constitute an inducement not to marry. This would be especially so were the benefits of marriage to be extended to cohabiting couples without also imposing the duties and

66 See, for example, *Norris v. A.G.* [1984] IR 36, and *U.C. v. J.C.* [1991] 2 IR 330.

responsibilities associated with marriage upon them. A failure, for example, to require such couples to satisfy the constitutional criteria for divorce when wishing to dissolve their partnership could be regarded as an inducement to heterosexual couples not to enter into what would then be the comparatively more restrictive marital relationship.[67] It remains to be seen whether the courts would regard an equality of treatment as an attack upon the institution of marriage. It is clear however that the adoption of the inducement test would restrict the ability of the Oireachtas to legislate for those cohabiting heterosexual couples whom the Constitution insists ought to be encouraged to marry.

Perhaps the most problematic consequence of any endorsement by the courts of the inducement test would be the position of bisexuals, or of those individuals described in *Norris* as 'homosexually orientated'.[68] While it is obvious that the existence of a statutory regime for the recognition of same-sex relationships cannot possibly constitute an inducement for 'exclusive' homosexuals not to marry, the same cannot be said of those individuals who are capable of entering into a married heterosexual relationship. The Irish courts have already recognized sexuality as a fluid concept rather than as a simple binary choice. Keane J. in *U.C. v. J.C.*[69] accepted that an individual's orientation occupies a position on a spectrum between hetero- and homosexuality. The implications for this issue are obvious. If the courts are to accept the reality that many individuals are neither exclusively hetero- nor homosexual but hetero- or homosexually inclined, the adoption of an inducement test in the context of Article 41.3.1. logically requires that same-sex partnerships be confined to those who are exclusively homosexual.

From a practical point of view, this is obviously hugely problematic. The idea that the State is obliged to assess the extent of an individual's homosexuality before allowing him or her to enter into a civil partnership is ridiculous in the extreme. Furthermore, the extent to which individuals are likely to allow the law to determine what is a deeply personal choice of partner is doubtful. The Chief Justice of the Australian Family Court was highly critical of this type of analysis, commenting that:

> One of the most politically potent but patently false ideas is that the recognition of lesbian and gay men's relationships will somehow encourage those who would otherwise be heterosexual to opt instead for a same-sex relationship ... [I]t strikes me as absurd to imagine that the achievement of limited legal protections would induce someone to reorient their sexuality. It seems to me that politicians take themselves

---

67 It could obviously be equally argued that some couples might regard this restriction as a beneficial guarantee of security. A court would obviously have to assess the reality of any asserted inducement on this, or any other basis.   68 [1984] IR 36, at 62.   69 [1991] 2 IR 330.

far too seriously if they really believe that any legislation they pass will have any effect, one way or the other, upon this issue.[70]

Nonetheless, this notion is not without constitutional precedent in Ireland. In fact, the minority judgements in *Norris*, turned precisely on this point. Henchy and McCarthy JJ found the criminalisation of homosexual conduct unconstitutional on the basis of its application to the 'exclusively' homosexual. Henchy J felt that:

> the essence of the unconstitutionality claimed lies not in the prohibition, as a crime, of homosexual acts between consenting adult males but primarily in making that prohibition apply without qualification to consenting adult males who are exclusively and obligatorily homosexual ... The true and justifiable gravamen of the complaint against the sections under review is that they are in constitutional error for overreach or overbreadth. They lack necessary discrimination and precision as to when and how they are to apply.[71]

The obvious implication, as both Henchy and McCarthy JJ confirmed was that the State was entitled (in fact, obliged in their view) to distinguish between the exclusively homosexual and homosexually-inclined citizen in its criminalisation of the acts impugned.

An adoption of the inducement test therefore risks placing the courts in an extremely invidious position. On the one hand, they can adhere to the outdated and inaccurate notion of sexual orientation as a rigidly demarcated dichotomy. On the other hand, they can continue to recognize the essential fluidity of human sexuality, thereby logically obliging the State to engage in an invasive, demeaning and hugely impractical process of screening same-sex partnerships to ensure that individuals who are capable of forming committed heterosexual couples have not been induced to avoid the constitutionally-celebrated model of conjugal relationships. The inherently insoluble nature of this dilemma should, of itself, convince the courts to favour the *Murphy–Muckley* line of Supreme Court authority which the doctrine of precedent also enjoins them to adopt.

Conclusion

It is difficult to predict with any degree of confidence the interpretation of the Constitution likely to be adopted by our superior courts. Although the judiciary have, at times, been called upon to consider and construe our constitutional notions of marriage, family and commitment, they have never

---

70 Nicholson, loc. cit., at para. 9.   71 [1984] IR 36, at 78–9.

had to directly address the question as to whether the provisions of *Bunreacht na hÉireann* demand, or, in the alternative, preclude the legal recognition of such non-marital relationships. The case law, however, can be argued to support a number of speculative conclusions.

The first is that the Constitution, in contrast to the experience of several other common law states, is more likely to obstruct than to assist any process of reform. The equality and dignity guarantees which applicants have successfully invoked elsewhere offer comparatively limited protection to prospective Irish claimants. Already encumbered by the weakness of the relevant constitutional rights, arguments in favour of reform are further hampered by the procreative conception of marriage commonly adopted by the Irish courts. This could encourage the courts to exclude same-sex couples from any attempt to derive a dignity-based individual entitlement to legal recognition from the asserted social utility of such status. Furthermore, the current Supreme Court's tendency to defer to the Oireachtas on issues it sees as of a primarily legislative character is likely to deter it from inaugurating social reforms of such significance.

On a purely political calculation, such instinctive deference is likely to be strengthened by the prospect of imminent legislative action. With the major political parties increasingly committed to the legal recognition of committed relationships, the Constitution seems more likely to be invoked in the context of a challenge to such a regime on the basis of Article 41.3.1.[72] In this context, it has been argued above that the courts should adopt the *Murphy–Muckley* 'penalty' test in their assessment of whether a partnership regime undermines the State's pledge the guard the institution of marriage with special care. This approach would avoid the practical problems logically demanded by the alternative 'inducement' test in the area of same-sex couples. It would also, if the Oireachtas so desired, increase the likelihood of an opposite-sex partnership regime passing constitutional muster.

In the long-term, the reform of the social provisions of the Constitution would avoid many of the problems posed by the increasing disparity between the document's stated social vision, and the everyday reality of today's Ireland. Whether the State should continue to regulate the social norms of our society by denoting one form of family relationship as socially, or morally, superior is a question for another occasion. However, the existing constitutional affirmation of marriage as the paradigm social structure should not preclude some recognition of committed relationships. This is especially so for those same-sex couples denied the possibility of any legal acknowledgment of their relationship. The clearly Christian ethos of

---

72 The importance of ensuring that such relationships have a secure legal foundation and cannot be retrospectively invalidated could encourage the President to refer any Bill on this matter to the Supreme Court under Article 26.

Bunreacht na hÉireann makes it unlikely that this reform will be effected by our courts but it should not prove an insurmountable impediment to the legislative enactment of this pressing social reform.

POSTSCRIPT

Since this article was written, a number of significant developments have occurred – most notably the bringing into force of the Civil Registration Act 2004[73] in December 2005, and the delivery, a year later, of the decision of the High Court in *Zappone v. Revenue Commissioners*.[74]

Dunne J's judgment in *Zappone* clarified, to some extent, the constitutional position of committed non-marital couples in Ireland. Consideration was given to many of the issues examined in this piece. Extensive evidence was, for example, adduced of scientific and sociological studies which had been conducted into the possible impact on children of being raised in a same-sex household. In essence, however, Dunne J's decision turned on a relatively net question of constitutional interpretation. It is important, therefore, that the precedential implications of the judgment not be overestimated. By virtue of the constrained nature of the claim before her, several significant matters were (quite properly) not addressed by the court. The decision offers useful guidance as to the way in which the courts *might* approach such issues, but it certainly does not resolve all of the complex questions arising in this area.

The main body of this article drew attention to the fact that the decisions of the Canadian and South African courts which legitimized same-sex relationships were premised, in part, on notions of progressive constitutional interpretation. A key issue in the Irish case was therefore whether the Constitution ought to be interpreted in a progressive or historical matter. Counsel for the plaintiffs therefore sought to portray the State's case as 'an appeal solely and exclusively to history' which aimed to fossilise the meaning of marriage by reference to the norms of 1937.

Dunne J accepted – as the Supreme Court so forcefully opined in *A*[75] – the dynamic and evolutionary nature of constitutional concepts. Unlike the courts in *Halpern* and *Fourie*, however, she envisaged the courts acting in a responsive, rather than an activist or educative way. The changing nature of the Constitution was to be determined, in her view, by reference to 'prevailing ideas and concepts'.[76] Judicial interpretation of the Constitution ought not to lead society but to follow it. The 2004 Act, the lack of a social

---

73 S. 2 (2) (e) of the Act provides that 'there is an impediment to a marriage if … both parties are of the same sex'. It was brought into force by the Civil Registration Act 2004 (Commencement) Order 2005 (SI 764 of 2005).   74 High Court, Dunne J, 14 December 2006.   75 *A. v. The Governor of Arbour Hill Prison* [2006] IESC 45.   76 Citing Walsh J in *McGee v. A.G.* [1978] IR 284, at 319.

consensus in favour of reform, and the limited international support for same-sex marriage all indicated, in her view, that the prevailing under-standing of marriage was still one based on an opposite-sex union.

This confirmed the suggestion outlined above that the Irish courts were unlikely to follow the example of their Canadian and South African coun-terparts in the absence of an equivalent constitutional mandate for reform-oriented interpretation. Marriage in Ireland continues to be strictly conceived in traditional Article 41 terms. Any difference of treatment between married and committed non-marital couples is therefore constitu-tionally justified. As Section I speculated, the claim for a positive entitlement to same-sex marriage is not supported by the text of the Irish Constitution – or (in terms of Dunne J's decision) crucially, by contemporary society's prevailing interpretation of its terms.

Of course, the decision in *Zappone* does not directly deal with the question considered earlier – whether the Constitution might in fact preclude the statutory extension of marriage rights to same-sex couples. There was, for example, no discussion of the appropriateness or otherwise of the penalty or inducement tests which have been alternatively canvassed in the caselaw. To draw even the most tentative inferences from the judgment about the courts' possible approach to this issue may therefore seem unduly speculative. With such hesitancy in mind, however, some aspects of Dunne J's decision will be noted in passing.

The State interestingly did not attempt to define marriage in terms of the procreative potential of the marital union. This had, of course, been the basis on which the Supreme Court of Canada had denied the possibility of same-sex marriage in *Egan*. The High Court did, however, expend a considerable amount of time and energy on examining the potential welfare implications for children of growing up in a same-sex household. Dunne J's judgment thus indicates that, even where the strict matter of the procreative act is discounted, the Irish Constitution continues to conceive of marriage as a child-oriented institution.

This is significant because of the fact that – as the main body of the article has noted – marriage is more likely to be extended to encompass same-sex unions where it is envisaged in individualistic rather than child-focused terms. It is more difficult to rationally deny committed couples access to the institution where it is presented, not as a framework for bearing or rearing children, but as a 'a social and legal shrine for love'[77]. The emphasis *Zappone* attaches to the position of children could therefore be argued to incline in favour of the view that the Constitution's protection of marriage inevitably excludes its extension to same-sex couples.

---

77 2005 (3) BCLR 241 (SCA), at para. 14.

This suggestion is further strengthened by the High Court's expressed unwillingness to accept as unarguable that 'children of same sex couples or raised by same sex couples are no worse off from an emotional or any other relevant perspective than the children of or raised by heterosexual couples'. Dunne J instead found that:

> [T]here is simply not enough evidence from the research done to date that could allow firm conclusions to be drawn as to the consequences of same sex marriage, particularly in the area of the welfare of children.

It is important to note that the judge emphasized that no adverse effects had been demonstrated by the studies surveyed. It remains the case, however, that same-sex unions have been judicially accepted as inherently suspect[78] in child welfare terms. When taken together with the courts' adoption of a child-centred conception of marriage, there is clearly a case to be made that Article 41 may prevent the introduction of same-sex marriages.

Allowing for these indications to the contrary, it is, however, submitted that the better view may be that the decision does not construe the Constitution as an obstacle to the statutory recognition of committed same-sex couples. Dunne J, for example, expressed the hope that legislative reform would soon occur on this issue. That she did so without any reference to prospective Article 41 difficulties may offer some encouragement to the view there may not be constitutional infirmities in such a course of action.

More concretely, her interpretation of the constitutional conception of marriage is one which logically accepts that an alternative meaning may be adopted in the future. By tying the interpretation of the text to prevailing social ideas, Dunne J implicitly accepts that the Christian conception of marriage which animated the Constitution's drafters is not fixed for all time. Necessarily provisional in nature, it cannot constitute an inflexible obstacle to sub-constitutional reforms.

In fact, it was telling that the court looked to a range of extra-constitutional sources as a guide to the meaning of Article 41. This seems to suggest a situation in which social practice (including, critically, recent statutes) informs the constitutional conception of marriage, rather than the other way round. With its meaning apparently rooted in contemporary social mores, the Constitution's references to marriage cannot logically be taken to prohibit any particular social changes in advance.

Furthermore, the fact that Dunne J relied so heavily on the Civil Registration Act 2004 as indicative of the nature of the existing social

---

78 It should be noted that this notion of same-sex couples as a suspect class did not reflect any inherent scepticism or hostility on the part of Dunne J. Rather, the court adopted the neutral view of taking no position until further evidence was available.

consensus suggests a pre-eminent role for the Oireachtas in determining the social (and thus constitutional) appropriateness of any future amendments to the meaning of marriage. The Court in *Zappone* used statute rather than its own experience as evidence of the prevailing social view. Were this approach to be replicated in the future, it would logically suggest that any statutory reform in favour of civil partnership or same-sex marriage should thereby be taken to signify a changing social consensus on this issue. It certainly implies that a court should exercise considerable restraint in preferring its own perception of society's norms to that evinced in a statutory enactment.

Dunne J thus does not seem to envisage Article 41 as a fixed restriction on these reforms. She instead appears to posit the existence of a more complex and dynamic relationship in which statute in some way informs the meaning of the constitutional text. The *Zappone* decision therefore not only accepts the possibility of future changes to the constitutional meaning of marriage, but also suggests that such changes should be inferred (at least in part) from any statutory reforms. It is difficult to see how the courts' adoption of such a provisional and statute-sensitive definition of marriage could sensibly support the claim that Article 41 absolutely precludes any attempts by the Oireachtas to confer legal recognition on same-sex couples. On balance, therefore, *Zappone* appears to imply that the Constitution may not represent an insurmountable impediment to Oireachtas action in this area.

Committed relationships and the law: the impact of the European Convention on Human Rights

EIMEAR BROWN*

THE EUROPEAN CONVENTION ON HUMAN RIGHTS ACT 2003 (hereinafter the ECHR Act) has finally given the Convention some measure of domestic effect in this jurisdiction, a full half a century after Ireland ratified the ground-breaking treaty and gave her citizens the right to take individual petitions before the Court of Human Rights. The debate as to how great the impact of this legislation will be has been heated, with commentators divided between those who argue that the impact of the incorporation[1] of the Convention into Irish law will be negligible,[2] and those who contend that it has the potential to develop our fundamental rights jurisprudence.[3] The ECHR Act only came into force on 31 December 2003, and at this stage the only certainty is that the Act allows litigants to rely directly upon the Convention before the Irish courts in a manner that was previously precluded.

---

* Elements of this chapter are drawn from the author's PhD thesis on the incorporation of the ECHR into Irish law.   1 The word 'incorporation' is used here out of expediency – the one point of congruence for all those interested by the coming into force of the European Convention on Human Rights Act, 2003, is that the legislation, like its UK equivalent, actually stops short of real incorporation and merely 'gives further effect' to the Convention in domestic law. On this point, see, *inter alia*, the judgment of the Supreme Court in *Dublin City Council v. Jeanette Fennell and Ors* [2005] 2 ILRM 288 (Kearns J; Denham, McGuinness, Fennelly, McCracken JJ concurring).   2 Some have argued that the Act will make little difference to the Irish litigant, on the ground that the rights set out in the Convention are already given expression in the Constitution (see, e.g. Michael McDowell, TD, Minster for Justice, Equality and Law Reform, 'The European Convention on Human Rights Act, 2003: What the act will mean', Speech to the Law Society and Human Rights Commission Conference on New Human Rights Legislation, 18 October 2003), and that the Irish courts were not entirely ignorant of the Convention case law prior to the coming into force of the Act (see, e.g. Ronan Keane, 'Issues for the judiciary in the application of the ECHR Act, 2003', Speech to the Law Society and Human Rights Commission Conference on New Human Rights Legislation, 18 October 2003).   3 See, generally, Ursula Kilkelly (ed.), *ECHR and Irish law* (Bristol, 2004), and Nial Fennelly, 'Introduction to the European Convention on Human Rights Act 2003', Speech to the Law Society Conference on the European Convention on Human Rights Act, 2003: 'A Practitioner's Guide to Effective Remedies', 29 January 2003.

The relevance of the ECHR Act to a discussion of the legal status of committed relationships in Ireland lies in the fact that the Court of Human Rights arguably takes a more progressive and liberal view of a number of the issues affecting committed relationships than the does the Irish Constitution. That is not to say that the European Convention mandates such radical measures as the legalisation of marriage between homosexuals; or that the state will be obliged to accord *de facto* and married couples the same protection;[4] but it does, however, apply a much broader definition of family life than the Irish courts have been used to doing. Furthermore, the views of the Court of Human Rights on issues such as gender reassignment and discrimination based on sexual orientation also have an impact on how Strasbourg views more unorthodox committed relationships.[5] The question posed in this chapter is whether the coming into force of the ECHR Act will threaten the more conservative constitutional position in relation to committed relationships. To that end, it will be necessary to briefly explain how the 2003 Act itself operates, before examining the ways in which the European Convention has, and could, require certain reform of Irish law.

THE IMPACT OF EUROPEAN CONVENTION ON HUMAN RIGHTS ACT 2003

Firstly, it should be noted that Ireland's failure to grant the ECHR domestic force until 2003 in no way amounted to a breach of that Convention. The ECHR is an international treaty, ratified by states ('High Contracting Parties') who have undertaken to uphold the minimum standards of fundamental rights enumerated therein, and to allow their citizens to make an application to the European Court of Human Rights (the ECtHR) when they feel that the state has failed to do so.[6] The Convention was, in Drzemczewski's words, 'binding on the State but not within the State'.[7] Thus, although the Irish courts could not directly apply the provisions of the Convention,[8] they

---

4 This point has been made in a recent Report commissioned by the Irish Human Rights Commission; *see* Judy Walsh and Fergus Ryan in *The rights of* de facto *couples* (Irish Human Rights Commission, March 2006), at 52.   5 The term 'unorthodox' is used here to refer to heterosexual or homosexual couples, with or without children, cohabiting outside marriage. For statistics on Irish households, see *Census 2002, Volume 3, Household Composition and Family Status* (Dublin, 2004), analysed by Judy Walsh and Fergus Ryan, op. cit., at 2ff.   6 The right to make individual applications to the Court of Human Rights is a key part of the Convention's enforcement mechanism, but was originally optional, in that States could ratify the treaty without agreeing to this right; Ireland and Sweden were the first states to accept the right of individual petition to the Court. On the early years of the Convention mechanism, see, *inter alia*, Andrew Z. Drzemczewski, *European Human Rights Convention in domestic law* (Oxford, 1983).   7 Ibid., at 172.   8 The leading case on this was *In re Ó Laighleis* [1960] IR 93, in which the Supreme Court refused to apply the ECHR on the ground that the Oireachtas had

did occasionally use the ECHR and the case law of its court in interpreting Irish law.[9]

The ECHR Act was intended to 'give further effect' to the Convention in Irish law, making it possible to rely upon its terms in the domestic courts in a manner that was hitherto impossible. Briefly, the ECHR Act follows the model used by the UK in the Human Rights Act of 1998.[10] It is an interpretation act; section 2 of the ECHR Act obliges judges, when 'interpreting and applying any statutory provision or rule of law' to do so in a manner consistent with the state's obligations under the Convention provisions 'in so far as is possible'. It appears that this interpretive obligation applies to both statute and common law.[11] Like their colleagues in the UK, Irish judges may not twist the words of a law beyond their natural meaning – where it is *not* possible to interpret Irish law in a manner consonant with the ECHR, the remedy lies in a declaration of incompatibility (*infra*). It is certainly arguable that, if the Irish courts choose to seize the opportunity, this section could have far-reaching implications for Irish law and practice.

The Irish courts must also 'take judicial notice' not only of the provisions of the ECHR, but of the decisions of the European Court of Human Rights, the Committee of Ministers, and the (now defunct) European Commission of Human Rights. The phrase 'judicial notice' appears to be new to Irish legislation, and is not defined in the statute. It would appear from this wording that Irish judges are not bound by the decisions of these international bodies – an unsurprising state of affairs, since the reverse would be a serious circumscription of the judicial independence of our courts. However, it would not be wholly unreasonable to assume that this provision will lead to more frequent reference to the case law of the Court of Human Rights, and may increase the degree to which the obligations on the State are informed by Strasbourg.

Section 3 obliges every organ of the state to perform its functions in a manner compatible with the ECHR; where state organs fail in this duty with the result that loss is incurred, the injured party may institute an action in damages – the 'teeth' of the section.[12] Admittedly, it is a condition precedent

not yet seen fit to make it part of Irish law (at 125). **9** See Ronan Keane, 'Issues for the judiciary in the Application of the ECHR Act, 2003'. **10** For this reason, Donncha O'Connell has described it as the 'Delia Smith' method of giving domestic effect to the Convention, in the sense that it had been prepared earlier; see Donncha O'Connell, 'The ECHR Act 2003: a critical perspective' from *ECHR and Irish law* (Bristol, 2004), 1, at 2. It could just as easily have been called the 'Blue Peter' model, for precisely the same reason. **11** See e.g. Michael McDowell, TD, Minster for Justice, Equality and Law Reform, loc. cit., at 3; and Mr Justice Nial Fennelly, loc. cit., at 3. **12** Mr Justice Nial Fennelly, loc. cit., at 12. It should be noted that this section is more limited in scope than its equivalent in the UK legislation, in that it specifically excludes the courts themselves – perhaps in an attempt to limit judicial activism: see James MacGuill, 'Implications for criminal law', Speech to the Law Society Conference on the European Convention on Human Rights Act, 2003: 'A Practitioner's Guide to Effective

to the exercise of this statutory right of action that no other remedy in damages be available – so it is possible that the courts could take the view that, where a person could institute proceedings in tort, or for breach of constitutional rights, they could be excluded from the ambit of the section. Quantum will be limited by the usual rules covering the jurisdiction of the High and Circuit Courts in tort, depending on where the plaintiff had chosen to institute proceedings.[13] The introduction of this section is salutary, in that our courts are generally much more generous in assessing compensation for torts than is the Court of Human Rights.[14] A disadvantage of the section is its extremely short time limit for taking proceedings: less than one year from the contravention of Convention rights by the state organ can have passed by the institution of proceedings.[15] Another problematic feature is that section 3 provides for only one type of remedy: there is no jurisdiction in the courts to grant other types of orders, even though it is not difficult to envisage situations where it may be more appropriate to grant injunctions restraining persistent and ongoing breaches of Convention rights.[16]

Under section 5, application may be made for a 'declaration of incompatibility' in the High Court[17] when no other remedy is appropriate and where the court is unable to read the statutory provision or rule of law as being compatible with the state's obligations under the Convention.[18] Unlike a finding of unconstitutionality, this declaration does not result in the offending provision being struck down; rather, its validity and continued operation are entirely unaffected.[19] It is up to the government to propose that the provision or rule of law be repealed, an unsatisfactory situation which could theoretically lead to the same piece of legislation being declared to be incompatible several times as the result of several different legal actions. The only real consequence of a declaration of incompatibility is that the Taoiseach is obliged to lay a copy of the court order before both Houses within 21 days of the decision on which each House has sat.[20] Irish commentators have described the consequences of obtaining a declaration as 'dilute in the extreme,'[21] while the Human Rights Commission has been highly critical of

---

Remedies', 29 January 2003, 52, at 77.   13 Section 3(3).   14 For example, in Application No. 29177/95 *Finucane v. United Kingdom* (2003) 37 EHRR 29, the widow of murdered Belfast solicitor Patrick Finucane succeeded in persuading the Strasbourg Court that the UK authorities had breached her husband's Article 2 right to life; the court accepted that there had been a failure to adequately investigate the crime. However, even in that case, the successful applicant received only one third of the amount she had claimed *in costs and expenses* – Mrs Finucane had sought almost £94,000stg, but received only £30,000 (Euro 43,000).   15 Section 3(5)(a).   16 There have been calls to expand the range of remedies available under section 3: see, e.g. Donncha O'Connell, 'The ECHR Act 2003: a critical perspective' 1, at 8, and Gerard Hogan, 'Incorporation of the ECHR: some issues of methodology and process' from *ECHR and Irish law* (Bristol, 2004), 13, at 33.   17 Only the High Court and the Supreme Court may grant declarations of incompatibility.   18 Section 5(1).   19 Section 5(2)(a) of the Bill. 20 Section 5(3).   21 MacGuill, at 78.

the absence of any practical effect of a declaration for a successful litigant, who is ultimately left without an effective remedy.[22]

It is important to realise that the actions for damages for a breach of Convention rights that seeking a declaration of incompatibility are distinct and separate procedures. As we have seen, section 3 actions for damages can be brought in either the Circuit Court or the High Court; applications for declarations of incompatibility can only be made in the High Court (and, on appeal, in the Supreme Court). Where a declaration of incompatibility is the most appropriate course, the person whose Convention rights have been infringed *is* permitted to apply to the Attorney General for compensation for any injury, loss or damage suffered;[23] however, it is at the government's *discretion* to decide whether any *ex gratia* payment will be made.[24] There is no entitlement to financial recompense, no matter what the nature of the loss sustained as a result of the breach – not even where the breach amounts to quantifiable financial loss resulting from a breach of the property rights guarantee contained in Article 1 of the First Protocol. Furthermore, as many commentators have emphasized, the legislation makes specific reference to the awards made by the ECtHR pursuant to Article 41 – awards which are typically very low.[25]

Some difficulties exist in relation to the temporal application of the Act. The Supreme Court has categorically stated that the Act is not retrospective: see *Dublin City Council v. Jeannette Fennell and Others*,[26] in which the defendant unsuccessfully argued that the interpretative obligation under section 2 of the ECHR act should apply to proceedings whose genesis occurred before that act came into force.[27] By the time *Fennell* was heard, the High Court had already reached a similar conclusion in relation to section 3 in *Lelimo v. Minister for Justice*,[28] in which the applicant in judicial review proceedings sought leave to amend her submissions to include grounds based on Articles 2[29] and 3[30] of the Convention. Laffoy J refused the application, not least because the applicant had already been refused permission to include those grounds at her original application for leave,[31] and a judge of

---

22 Human Rights Commission, 'Submission to the Joint Oireachtas Committee on Justice, Equality, Defence and Women's Rights', at 4. Donncha O'Connell is also sceptical as to whether the declaration of incompatibility can ever be viewed as an effective domestic remedy, as required by Article 13 ECHR; loc. cit., at 5.   23 Section 5(4)(b).   24 Section 5(4)(c). 25 Ursula Kilkelly, 'Introduction' from *ECHR and Irish Law* (Bristol, 2004), at lvii.   26 [2005] 2 ILRM 288 (Kearns J; Denham, McGuinness, Fennelly, McCracken JJ concurring).   27 The applicant had been ejected from her Council-owned dwelling by the District Court prior to the coming into force of the ECHR Act; the ejectment proceedings were set down by section 62 of the Housing Act, 1966 (as amended). Her appeal was to be heard by the Circuit Court *after* the 2003 Act had come into force, and when she sought to rely on section 2 Linnane J stated a case to the Supreme Court.   28 [2004] 2 IR 178.   29 Article 2 ECHR protects the right to life. 30 Article 3 ECHR contains an absolute prohibition on torture, degrading and inhuman treatment.   31 Admittedly, the application for leave to apply for judicial review was heard prior

the High Court did not have jurisdiction to overrule an earlier order of the same court.[32] However, the learned judge took the view that the applicant could not rely on the ECHR in any case, since she was challenging a deportation order made before that Act came into force, and the obligations placed on the State by section 3 of the ECHR Act (to act in a way compatible with its Convention obligations) was not retrospective. By contrast, the possibility of obtaining a declaration that a law is incompatible with the Convention (under section 5) does, on the words of the section, appear to apply to laws that were in force prior to the coming into force of the ECHR Act.

Nevertheless, the ECHR Act does have the potential to influence both the manner in which Irish laws are interpreted and, via the declaration of incompatibility, future law reform in this jurisdiction. A note of caution before we examine the substantive case law of the Convention: the ECHR Act naturally does not give the Convention higher status than the Constitution, and where there is a disparity between the terms of the Constitution and the Convention jurisprudence the Constitution retains its higher status in the hierarchy of norms.

THE CONSTITUTION AND IRISH FAMILY LAW: A SYNOPSIS

Constitutional attitudes to committed relationships are discussed in great detail elsewhere in this book, but it is necessary to briefly mention the main constitutional trends in order to highlight the differences between our most fundamental law, as read by the Irish courts, and the European Convention on Human Rights as interpreted by Strasbourg. It is well settled that the Irish Constitution jealously guards the status of the family. Under the Constitution, 'the Family' is recognized as 'the natural primary and fundamental unit group of Society, and as a moral institution possessing inalienable and impresecriptible rights, antecedent and superior to all positive law'.[33] However, the only family units which are viewed as the focus of this impressive legal recognition are those based on marriage,[34] a position that had been repeatedly affirmed by the Irish courts.[35] It has been suggested that the Constitution thus requires the state to ensure that families based on marriage receive treatment that is at least as equally favourable as that received by the non-marital family, and even authorizes the state to discriminate in favour of the marital family.[36] Nor

to the coming into force of the ECHR Act, so O'Sullivan J had no option but to refuse leave on ECHR grounds at that stage.   **32** On this point, see, e.g. *LR v. Minister for Justice* [2002] 1 IR 260, at 267.   **33** Article 41.1.1 of the Constitution.   **34** Article 41.3.1 states: 'The State pledges itself to guard with special care the institution of Marriage, on which the Family is founded and to protect it against attack.'   **35** See, e.g. *The State (Nicolaou) v. An Bord Uchtála* [1966] IR 567.   **36** Gerard Hogan and Gerry Whyte (eds), *J.M. Kelly, The Irish Constitution* (third ed. Dublin, 1994).

do those considering law reform envisage any alteration in the privileged constitutional position of the marital family.[37]

That is not to say that members of non-marital families have absolutely no constitutional rights arising out of their relationship; however, these rights are not based on Articles 41 and 42 of the Constitution, and largely exclude the father. For example, the courts accept that unmarried mothers have rights in relation to their children, but these rights arise out of Article 40.3, and are not expressed in such strident terms as those under Articles 41 and 42: see, for example, *The State (Nicolaou) v. An Bord Uchtála*[38] and *G v. An Bord Uchtála*,[39] in which the Supreme Court confirmed that unmarried mothers and their children were not families in the sense of Article 41.

The constitutional position of unmarried fathers is still more tenuous, as its exemplified by the judgment of the Supreme Court in *Nicolaou*. At the time of that judgment, fathers of non-marital children had effectively no rights whatsoever in relation to their offspring. That position has been attenuated somewhat by the passage of legislation granting them *some* rights (and, to some extent, this may be linked to certain judgments of the Court of Human Rights – see below); a prime example of this was the reform of the Guardianship of Infants Act to allow unmarried fathers to apply to the District Court to be appointed as joint guardians of their children (married mothers and fathers automatically have this right, as do unmarried mothers).

Interestingly, while the practice of granting the marital family favoured treatment does not appear to breach the Constitution, neither does it necessarily amount to a breach of the Convention either: the Court of Human Rights has recognized that differential treatment may be justified in the interests of protecting the traditional family structure: see, e.g., *Saucedo Gomez v. Spain*,[40] in which the ECtHR held that Spanish law, which did not provide for maintenance in the case of the break-up of *de facto* relationships, was not in breach of the Convention. This would appear to accord with the favoured position marriage and the marital family have been accorded both under the Constitution and as a matter of Irish socio-religious culture, and also means that the current absence of any provision for maintenance in respect of an unmarried partner (as opposed to a spouse) does not run contrary to Ireland's Convention obligations.

But although the Court of Human Rights accepts that it can be legitimate for the state to favour the marital family, when it comes to protecting the institution of marriage the Irish courts are in a league of their own. They have struck down tax and social welfare provisions which would have the effect of favouring unmarried families: see *Murphy v. Attorney General*[41] and

---

37 For example, a majority of the All-Party Oireachtas Committee on the Constitution (2006), *Tenth progress report* (Stationery Office), at 122, discussed by Ryan and Walsh at 5ff.   **38** [1966] IR 567. **39** [1980] IR 32. **40** Application No. 37784/97, *Saucedo Gomez v. Spain* 26 January 1999; discussed by Walsh and Ryan at 54. **41** [1982] IR 241.

Hyland v. Minister for Social Welfare[42] respectively.[43] There have even been indications that to accord the *de facto* family equal treatment could amount to an attack on the special position accorded marriage by the Constitution.[44]

On its face, this constitutionally sanctioned discrimination against the non-marital family appears somewhat anachronistic. As Walsh and Ryan note, *some* Irish statutes have attempted to extend equal rights to non-marital couples in certain situations: thus, barring and safety orders can be sought in cases of domestic violence;[45] an action for wrongful death can be maintained where a partner has been killed.[46] However, even these provisions raise a number of problems, not least the fact that 'the meaning of the term [family] can vary quite significantly depending on the context',[47] with significant variations in the length of time the couple must cohabit before they can maintain an action under the different Acts.[48] Furthermore, those provisions which do appear to accord *de facto* couples similar rights to married couples appear to be confined to heterosexuals.[49]

THE CONVENTION AND IRISH FAMILY LAW

The Convention had some role in the reform of Irish family law prior to the coming into force of the ECHR Act, via the medium of judgments of the Court of Human Rights. Once again, it should be noted that the Court of Human Rights has no power to order law reform in a Contracting State; all it can do is rule that the current law is breaching Convention rights. However, such a judgment undoubtedly places pressure on the State to remedy the problem.

The relevant cases are well known and do not require detailed exposition here. Briefly, the case of *Airey v. Ireland*[50] led to the extension of civil legal aid to family matters, a major development whose impact has been all the greater since the enactment of the Family Law (Divorce) Act 1996. In *Johnston v. Ireland*,[51] the Court of Human Rights accepted that Article 8 applied to a heterosexual couple and their child who lived together outside

---

42 [1989] IR 624.   **43** Discussed by Walsh and Ryan at 81.   **44** See *Ennis v. Butterly* [1996] 1 IR 426; *per* Kelly J at 438. *See also* Walsh and Ryan, ibid.   **45** Section 3 of the Domestic Violence Act 1996.   **46** Section 1 of the Civil Liability (Amendment) Act 1996.   **47** At 84. **48** The requisite period varies from six months to three years; under the Domestic Violence Act, the time can be cumulative (i.e. six months out of the nine immediately preceding the application for a barring order, or six out of the previous twelve in the case of a safety order – no reason for the distinction is given), or continuous (three years minimum in the caser of the Civil Liability Amendment Act). This inconsistency is criticized by Walsh and Ryan at 84. **49** Walsh and Ryan, at 86.   **50** (1979–1980) 2 EHRR 305. The applicant alleged that her Article 6 right of access to the courts had been violated by the total absence of legal aid in relation to family law applications.   **51** (1987) 9 EHRR 203.

marriage; the Court of Human Rights also took a dim view of the discrimi-natory position of their illegitimate child under Irish law at the time.[52] However, the court stopped short of requiring Ireland to introduce divorce, which would have allowed the couple of marry (as one of them was still legally married to another). *Keegan v. Ireland*[53] led to some reform of Irish adoption law after the ECtHR held that the adoption of the applicant's non-marital child in the face of his opposition amounted to a breach of his Article 8 right to family life.[54]

Now that the Irish courts are under a statutory duty to 'take judicial notice' of the judgments of the Court of Human Rights, the potential for legal challenges to our existing laws has increased, particularly given the less favourable position of the heterosexual *de facto* family, and the absence of any real consideration of its homosexual equivalent. Three Convention Articles are particularly important in this context: Articles 8, 12 and 14. Article 8 ECHR protects a number of rights:

1. Everyone has the right to respect for is private and family life, his home and correspondence.
2. There shall be no interference by a public authority with the exercise of this right except such as in accordance with the law and is necessary in a democratic society in the interests of national security, public safety or the economic well-being of the country, for the prevention of disorder or crime, for the protection of health or morals, or for the protection of the rights and freedoms of others.

Article 12 ECHR is also relevant from the perspective of family law:

Men and women of marriageable age have the right to marry and to found a family, according to the national laws governing the exercise of this right.

Finally, Article 14 ECHR is important in that it prohibits any discrimination in the vindication of the other Convention rights by the State:

---

52 Illegitimate children had a less favourable position in Irish law in a number of ways, not least in that they had no rights in respect of their fathers' property under the Succession Acts or on intestacy. Most distinctions were resolved by the Status of Children Act 1987.   53 (1994) 18 EHRR 263.   54 The current position is that unmarried fathers can oppose the adoption of their children in certain circumstances; however, there is still no automatic right of veto, nor is there any guarantee that the father will be awarded custody even where he successfully prevents the adoption going ahead. The position as regards the adoption of marital children is completely different, with adoption being difficult even where it is demonstrably in the child's best interests.

> The enjoyment of the rights and freedoms set forth in this Convention
> shall be secured without discrimination on any ground such as sex,
> race, colour, language, political or other opinion, national or social origin,
> association with a national minority, property, birth or other status.[55]

Article 14 is frequently used in conjunction with other Convention Articles
to bolster claims that the applicant has received less favourable treatment on
one of the prohibited grounds (prime examples include the challenges to laws
discriminating between ages of consent on the grounds of sexuality). In
many of the cases discussed below, the applicant relied upon Article 8 and/or
Article 12 in addition to Article 14. However, Article 14 does not guarantee
success: the state can escape an adverse judgment if they can show that the
distinction pursues a legitimate aim and if the means used are proportionate
to that aim.[56]

A caveat must be entered at this juncture: although it is certainly true that
the Court of Human Rights takes a broader and less marriage-centred view
of family life than the Irish Constitution, the doctrine of the margin of
appreciation has the potential to mitigate against more radical judgments by
the Strasbourg Court. The margin of appreciation is the leeway accorded to
Contracting States in situations where the Court feels that the national
authorities are better placed to assess the cultural and moral traditions of
their society, and can be a reason for the ECtHR's refusal to intervene in
sensitive cases, even where the court itself may prefer a different approach
from that taken by the state.[57]

Article 8 ECHR

In relation to Article 8, the ECtHR has come to take a dim view of discrimination based on gender, illegitimacy, or sexual orientation.[58] The most
obvious example is the manner in which the Court of Human Rights has
effectively championed the decriminalisation of consensual homosexual
activity in a number of Contracting Parties, Ireland included: see, *inter alia*,
Norris v. Ireland;[59] and *Dudgeon v. United Kingdom.*[60] These cases were based
on a different aspect of Article 8, i.e. the right to private life.

---

55 The original Convention contained no free-standing anti-discrimination provision; the
Council of Europe has sought to remedy this with the Adoption of Protocol 12, which Ireland
has not yet ratified.   **56** On this point, *see* Walsh and Ryan, op. cit., at 46.   **57** Prime examples
of the margin of appreciation's operation include *Otto Preminger Institut v. Austria* (1995) 19
EHRR 34, in which the Court of Human Rights held that there had been no violation of Article
10 ECHR (the free expression guarantee) in circumstances where the state had confiscated a
satirical film on the basis that it might offend the local Roman Catholic population. The margin
of appreciation appears to be particularly broad in cases involving moral issues and the attendant
sensitivities, and thus necessarily has some application in relation to family law.   **58** Walsh and
Ryan, op. cit., at 47.   **59** (1988) 13 EHRR 186.   **60** (1981) 4 EHRR; homosexual acts between

The Court of Human Rights has also moved to condemn other forms of discrimination based on sexual orientation.[61] The Court has little difficulty in accepting the need for an age of consent in respect of sexual activity in the interests of protecting vulnerable younger members of society – but it does, now, require equality in relation to such provisions as between heterosexuals and homosexuals:[62] see, e.g., *BB v. United Kingdom*,[63] where the Court of Human Rights held that the UK was in breach of Article 14, in conjunction with Article 8, in circumstances where the age of consent for heterosexuals in England was 16 years, but was 18 years (reduced from 21 by the Criminal Justice and Public Order Act 1994) in respect of male homosexuals.[64] The Court has given similar judgments in analogous cases,[65] demonstrating the ever-evolving nature of the Convention jurisprudence: even during the 1990s, the European Commission on Human Rights rejected applications based on laws that differentiated between the age of consent for male homosexuals and the rest of the populace: see *Zukrigl v. Austria*,[66] for example. The age of consent cases also serve to demonstrate the weight the ECtHR's judgments carry in the eyes of the Member States: both Austria and the UK equalized the age of consent following decisions against them by the court. Strasbourg's apparent 'moral authority' is clearly a force to be reckoned with; something Ireland should bear in mind should the Court of Human Rights ever decide that our failure to legally recognize same-sex partnerships violates one or more of the Convention's provisions. In a more immediate sense, the Oireachtas should be cognisant that the amendments to the age of consent currently being mooted should take account of Strasbourg's antipathy for discrimination based on both sexuality and gender.[67]

consenting male adults had been decriminalized in most of the UK; however, they remained on the statute book in N. Ireland, leading Mr Dudgeon to apply to the court following interference with his private life by police.   **61** An obvious example includes the court's criticism of prohibitions on homosexuals serving in the armed forces (see, *inter alia*, Application Nos. 33985/96 and 33986/96, *Smith and Grady v. United Kingdom*, Judgment of the Court of Human Rights of 27 September 1999).   **62** Where states have chosen to legislate for different ages of consent, they have generally distinguished between homosexual men and the rest of the population, rather than making a straightforward distinction between heterosexuals and homosexuals in general.   **63** Application No. 53760, Judgment of 10 February 2004.   **64** BB, who had had sex with a 16-year-old boy, was not actually convicted of an offence; however, he was not informed that the Crown Prosecution Service would not be proceeding until after he had undergone a medical examination, his home had been searched by police, and he had appeared before the Magistrate's Court; the Court of Human Rights held these interferences to be sufficient to justify a finding that the State had violated BB's rights. **65** See, *inter alia*, Application Nos. 118084/02 and 15306/02 *HG and GB v. Austria*, 2 September 2005; Application Nos. 69756/01 and 6306/02 *Woditschka and Wifling v. Austria*, 21 January 2005; and Application No. 5263/03, *Wolfmeyer v. Austria*, 12 October 2005. **66** Application No. 17279/90, *Zukrigl v. Austria*, Decision of the European Commission of Human Rights of 13 May 1992.   **67** The Minister for Justice suggests setting the age of consent at 17 for both girls and boys; however, he has suggested that, where two people aged

Nevertheless, the fact that bans on homosexual activity *per se* amount to a breach of the right to privacy does not mean that all consensual sexual activity of whatever kind is permissible, even where it takes place in private. Where the sexual activity in question involves causing bodily harm to another, the court has had little difficulty in upholding domestic laws precluding and punishing such behaviour. The most famous case in point is, of course, *Laskey, Jaggard and Brown v. United Kingdom*,[68] in which the applicants were members of a group of homosexual men who took part in consensual sadomasochistic activities. They were convicted of various offences under the Offences against the Person Act, 1861. The Court of Human Rights found that there had been no violation of Article 8 by the state authorities: the state was entitled to use the criminal law to regulate activities which caused physical harm, whether they involved sex or not. Given the 'significant' risk of injury inherent in the applicants' activities, the state could not be seen to have overreacted.[69] It is submitted that, in this case, the sexual orientation of the applicants was of tangential relevance at best: the Strasbourg authorities are likely to take exactly the same view where heterosexuals engage in sadomasochistic sexual behaviour.[70]

As regards the Article 8 guarantee of respect for family life, it is clear that the Court of Human Rights will not allow states to rely on the margin of appreciation in order to adopt too narrow a definition of that concept. Relying on Article 8, the Court of Human Rights has held that Article 8 can apply to heterosexual couples cohabiting together (see *Johnston, above*) and an unmarried mother and her child.[71] As is clear from *Keegan* (*above*), family life can also exist between unmarried fathers and their children – a concept that Irish law has been slow to acknowledge and which still receives much less domestic legal protection than any other type of parent-child relationship. As Walsh and Ryan note, however, even the Court of Human Rights accepts

under 17 but over 15 have intercourse, the boy commits an offence but the girl does not. The rationale behind this proposed distinction is to avoid stigma attaching to teenage unmarried mothers; it remains to be seen whether that reasoning would constitute an adequate basis for the discrimination against young men in the eyes of the Court of Human Rights. **68** (1997) 24 EHRR 39. **69** Paragraph 45. **70** This very issue was raised before the Commission in Application No. 22170/93, *V, W, Y and Z v. United Kingdom*, Decision of the European Commission of Human Rights of 18 January 1995. In that application, the first applicant was a homosexual man and founder of a group for gays interested in sadomasochistic activities; the second and third applicants were heterosexuals with a predilection for sadomasochistic activities; the fourth applicant was a lesbian with similar interests. The application was held to be manifestly unfounded as the Commission took the view that the applicants lacked the necessary standing to make the application; none had been so much as threatened with prosecution. **71** *Marckx v. Belgium* (1979–1980) 2 EHRR 330. The case involved a Belgian unmarried mother who was technically obliged by national law to adopt her own child in order to secure her succession and other rights. The Court of Human Rights had little difficulty in finding that this situation breached the applicant's Article 8 right to family life.

that fathers of non-marital children do not automatically have rights in relation to those children under Article 8: generally, successful applicants have been able to show that they cohabited with the child (as in *Keegan* and *Kroon v. Netherlands*),[72] although more recent decisions appear to attenuate this requirement depending on the circumstances of the individual case.[73] The ECtHR's approach is practical and fact-centred; if the applicants can establish a factual scenario that, in the view of the court, amounts to *de facto* family life, then they will be entitled to protection under Article 8.

As regards the right to family life of cohabiting homosexual couples, Strasbourg has been much slower to recognize that such relationships amounted to family life in the same manner as an equivalent heterosexual couple. The court has yet to explicitly accept that gay couples can rely on the family life guarantee of Article 8, a conclusion which reflects the lack of consensus on this point among the Contracting States (although there is a growing trend towards granting legal recognition of homosexual relationships). It has been suggested that the judgment in *Karner v. Austria*[74] may herald a change in this regard.[75] In that case, the applicant was a gay man whose partner died. The deceased and the applicant had been living together for five years, and the former had named the latter as his heir. On the death, the landlord sought to terminate the tenancy, in circumstances where the applicant's right to the tenancy would have been protected had he been in a heterosexual relationship. A majority of the Court of Human Rights held that this difference in treatment amounted to a breach of Article 14 in conjunction with Article 8; a result Walsh and Ryan argue may indicate that the margin of appreciation is narrowing as regards sexuality-based distinctions where there was no objective justification.[76] However, as they acknowledge, Mr Karner based his application on the Article 8 right to respect for his home, not on the right to family life,[77] and it would be stretching the point to argue that the case is authority for suggesting that homosexuals can rely on Article 8 to establish that they are a family within the meaning of the Convention.

In a narrower sense, *Karner* highlights a potential lacuna in Irish law: under the Residential Tenancies Act 2004, heterosexual couples have the right to succeed to a tenancy on the death of the partner with whom they have been cohabiting.[78] This is so whether the parties were married or not, a situation which takes account of the *de facto* family in a manner of which the Court of Human Rights would surely approve. However, it does not appear that this right extends to homosexual couples.[79]

---

72 (1994) 9 EHRR 263.   73 See *Soderback v. Sweden* [1999] 1 FLR 250. This point is discussed by Walsh and Ryan, op. cit., at 49.   74 [2003] 2 FLR 623.   75 Walsh and Ryan, op. cit., at 50. 76 Ibid.   77 Ibid.   78 Section 39.   79 See Walsh and Ryan, at 86.

Article 12 ECHR

As we have seen, Article 12 ECHR protects the right of 'men and women' to marry. There are a number of points to note in relation to Article 12. Firstly, the Court of Human Rights has interpreted the Article to mean that the Convention guarantees the right of men and women to marry one another – not the right of men or women generally to marry whomever they choose, whatever their gender (Walsh and Ryan argue that the latter interpretation is not impossible on the face of the Article, but it is submitted that, whatever the merits of such a suggestion, it would certainly be departing from the intention of the drafters).[80] Furthermore, even in the case of heterosexual couples, Article 12 does not connote an absolute right to marry whatever the circumstances. In *Johnston v. Ireland* (discussed *above*) there was no obligation on Ireland to introduce divorce so that the applicant could end one marriage and begin another. Nor, it is submitted, is there any obligation on the State to allow polygamy where the social, religious and historical character of the state militate against it. While the question of 'gay' marriage has become extremely topical of late, there has certainly been no decision to date condemning a state for refusing to legalize marriage between homosexuals (nor even requiring the adoption of measures along the lines of those taken by the UK to allow Civil Partnerships).[81] However, it is not beyond the bounds of possibility that the ECtHR's attitude may change, particularly in light of a growing consensus among some Council of Europe Member States[82] that gay partnerships and/or marriage should be facilitated.

By contrast, the court has adopted a more radical approach to the Article 12 rights of post-operative transsexuals – in sharp contrast to its earlier case law, which did not even recognize a right to alter a birth certificate to reflect the new gender. In *Rees v. United Kingdom*,[83] the applicant, a female to male transsexual, argued that Article 8 ECHR placed a positive obligation on the state to alter his birth certificate so that it gave his gender as male rather than female, in the manner allowed by some other Contracting Parties to the Convention. The Court of Human Rights noted that the UK had taken steps to facilitate the applicant's new identity: his operations and treatment had been carried out by the National Health Service, and the law permitted him to change his name relatively easily. The court also noted that, in the UK, the

---

80 At 56 of the Report the authors point out that '[Article 12] does not explicitly state that men and women may only marry *each other*.' However, it is submitted that that is exactly how the provision has been interpreted.   81 The Civil Partnership Act 2004. Under this Act, relationships between homosexuals may be officially registered, granting them an enhanced legal status which may only be terminated on the dissolution or annulment of the civil partnership, or on the death of one of the parties thereto. Even more radical steps have been taken in other jurisdictions, where homosexuals may undertake civil marriage in the same manner as heterosexuals.   82 States which accord such relationships varying degrees of protection include the UK, France and Spain.   83 (1987) 9 EHRR 56.

usual forms of identification were passports and driving licences; in the case of transsexuals, these documents could reflect the person's new gender (in the applicant's case, Mr Rees rather than Ms Rees).[84] The situations in which production of a birth certificate would be required were relatively limited.[85] The court concluded that there was no breach of Article 8; the UK had 'endeavoured to meet the applicant's demands to the fullest extent that the system allowed',[86] and the ECtHR would not force the state to go further.[87] This judgment was followed in *Sheffield and Horsham v. United Kingdom*.[88] (In this context, the judgments involving the United Kingdom are of some relevance to Ireland, since the same observations about the production of identification and the limited uses to which birth certificates are put also apply here.)[89]

The consequence of the Rees decision, and the similar ruling in *Cossey v. United Kingdom*,[90] was that transsexuals were precluded from marrying in their new gender, since their birth certificates still reflected the gender of their birth. Bizarrely, this situation arguably allowed same-sex marriage – provided that one spouse had undergone gender reassignment – in that a male-to-female transsexual could presumably still marry a woman. The importance of information to be entered on official documents such as birth certificates was again highlighted in *X, Y and Z v. United Kingdom*.[91] In that case, X was a female to male transsexual; Y was his female partner, and Z was the child conceived by Y through artificial insemination by donor. X's complaint was that he had not been allowed to be registered as the child's father (nor could he, as a female to male transsexual, marry a woman). Under English law the usual position is that where children are conceived by artificial insemination by an unmarried woman, her male partner will be treated as the father of the child, rather than the donor.[92] The court rejected the applicants' argument that Article 8 placed a positive obligation on the state to allow X to be registered as the child's father. The ECtHR noted a number of factors which militated against such a conclusion: the applicants were in a similar position to many other families where for some reason the

---

84 Para. 20 of the judgment of the Court of Human Rights.   85 Para. 25.   86 Para. 42.
87 The Court of Human Rights reached an identical conclusion in the case of *Cossey v. United Kingdom* (1991) 13 EHRR 622.   88 Application No. 22985/93; 23390/94 *Sheffield and Horsham v. United Kingdom* 30 July 1998.   89 However, this is not the case in other jurisdictions: in Application No. 57/1990/248/319, *B v. France* 24 January 1992, the court accepted that the applicant's Article 8 rights had been infringed by France's refusal to alter her birth certificate and official identity documents from male to female, to facilitate her marriage to a man. The court accepted that there were notable differences between the law on civil status in France and England: most notably, the English birth certificate resembled a document of historic record, whereas the French version was intended to be updated throughout its owner's life (paragraph 52); nor was there any French law preventing a note being made on the certificate updating the document to reflect the applicant's assigned gender (para. 55).
90 (1991) 13 EHRR 622.   91 (1997) 24 EHRR 143.   92 See paragraph 22 of the judgment.

person performing the role of father was not registered as such;[93] the child's birth certificate would not be commonly used for administrative purposes in the UK;[94] the absence of X's name on the child's birth certificate in no way prevented him from acting as her father 'in the social sense';[95] furthermore, he and Y could apply for a joint residence order in respect of the child, which could grant them full parental responsibility for her.[96] Finally, given the 'complex scientific, legal, moral and social issues' raised by transsexuality, not to mention the absence of a Europe-wide consensus on the issue, the fact that the UK did not allow for 'special legal recognition' of X and Z's relationship did not amount to a breach of their right to family life under Article 8.

However, once again the passage of time was to lead to a revolution in the ECtHR's attitude; in *Goodwin v. United Kingdom*[97] the court was to reverse its earlier position. In that case, the applicant, like Rees and Cossey, complained of the fact that the gender on her birth certificate could not be altered; alteration was only permitted where the genital sex of a child had been wrongly identified or where there had been a factual error.[98] Furthermore, English law, like Article 12 of the Convention, defined marriage as a union between a man and a woman; section 11(b) of the Matrimonial Causes Act 1973 rendered void any marriage where this was not so, and according to case law a marriage between a transsexual and another person might also be avoided on the basis that the transsexual was incapable of properly consummating the marriage.[99]

Rather than following its previous jurisprudence, the ECtHR noted that, as a mechanism for human rights protection, it had an obligation to take into account changing conditions in the UK and in other Contracting States, and 'to maintain a dynamic and evolutive approach'.[1] Noting that birth certificates may be altered in the cases of adoption and legitimisation, the Court felt that making a further exception in favour of transsexuals (of whom it estimated that there were only 2,000–5,000 in the UK), would not seriously undermine the system.[2] Most significantly from the perspective of this chapter, the Court also held that the refusal of the right to marry constituted a breach of the applicant's Article 12 rights. In a remarkable passage, the majority of the Court state:

> It is true that the first sentence [of Article 12] refers to the right of a man and a woman to marry. The Court is not persuaded that at the date of this case it can still be assumed that these terms must refer to a

---

93 Para. 49.   94 Para. 49.   95 Para. 50.   96 Para. 50.   97 *Goodwin v. United Kingdom* (2002) 35 EHRR 18. For a discussion of the *Goodwin* case, see, *inter alia*, Fergus Ryan, 'Marriage at the boundaries of gender: the "transsexual dilemma" resolved?' [2004] *Irish Journal of Family Law* 1.   98 Para. 25.   99 *Corbett v. Corbett* [1971] Probate Reports 83, discussed at paragraphs 21 and 22 of the judgment of the Court of Human Rights.   1 Para. 74.   2 Para. 87.

determination of gender by purely biological criteria ... There have been major social changes in the institution of marriage since the adoption of the Convention as well as dramatic changes brought about by the fields of medicine and science in the field of transsexuality ... In that regard it finds that it is artificial to assert that post-operative trans-sexuals have not been deprived of the right to marry as, according to law, they remain able to marry a person of their former opposite sex.[3]

Somewhat surprisingly, the court did not feel that this was a matter that should be left entirely within the margin of appreciation of the respondent state, and held that the total ban on transsexuals marrying a person of their new opposite sex was unjustified.[4] This conclusion was all the more startling considering the court's acceptance of the fact that there was no real consensus on the marriage issue among the Member States of the Council of Europe; even civil rights group Liberty had pointed out that more countries allow transsexuals to marry in their assigned gender than provide for legal recognition of that new gender.[5]

The *Goodwin* case has the potential to fundamentally challenge Irish law, which is currently similar to that of the UK at the time of the challenge. In the *Foy v. An t-Ard Claraitheoir and Others*,[6] a post-operative transsexual sought to have her birth certificate altered to reflect her new gender. The High Court found against her, but the Supreme Court, on appeal, ruled that the intervening *Goodwin* judgment warranted a re-hearing of the *Foy* case by the High Court.[7] That case has yet to be heard, but it is at least arguable that, should the current position be found to be in breach of the Convention, it would require a constitutional amendment to extend the right to marry in their acquired gender to transsexuals.

CONCLUSION

It is clear that the European Convention on Human Rights, and the jurisprudence of its Court, are in many ways more progressive and, it is submitted, more practical than our constitutional guarantees. This is evidenced by the fact-based test the ECtHR applies when deciding if a family relationship based on Article 8 exists, its progressive approach to the rights of unmarried fathers (as well as the rights of their children) and the court's consistent refusal to accept discrimination where it is not based on adequate justification (as in the case of gender or sexual orientation). In these times, few of Strasbourg's judgments seem particularly radical – with the possible

3 Paras. 100–1.   4 Para. 103.   5 Para. 103.   6 [2002] IEHC 116.   7 See *Irish Times*, 7 November 2005.

exception of the *Goodwin* case which, it is submitted, has the potential to fundamentally challenge our definition of marriage under Irish law if it is applied by the High Court in the upcoming *Foy* re-hearing. Nonetheless, there are many areas in which Irish law and that of the Convention concur: both recognize the special status of marriage, which is currently confined to heterosexual couples; unmarried fathers do not have automatic or absolute rights in relation to their children under either system; discrimination against non-marital families is permissible where it can be justified. The main distinction between the two systems appears to lie in Strasbourg's willingness to evolve, to interpret the Convention in line with the ever-changing mores of European society, and to recognize if not equal rights, then at least a diminution in the distinctions that should be drawn between people on the grounds of marital status, gender or sexual orientation. Further developments by the ECtHR cannot be ruled out; as the case law shows, over time the court is wont to revise its views quite substantially. Thus far, the Irish courts have not chosen to interpret the Constitution along similar lines; an unsurprising fact given the trenchant language in which that document describes the family 'based on marriage'. However, if Ireland is to keep abreast of her Convention obligations, it appears that some change is inevitable.

Index

Bib. # ~~346. 41705~~
50x144

346.4170
CoM

Ollscoil na hÉireann, Gaillimh

3 1111 40186 8607